Artificial Intelligence in Second Language
Learning

SECOND LANGUAGE ACQUISITION
Series Editor: Professor David Singleton, *Trinity College, Dublin, Ireland*

This new series will bring together titles dealing with a variety of aspects of language acquisition and processing in situations where a language or languages other than the native language is involved. Second language will thus be interpreted in its broadest possible sense. The volumes included in the series will all in their different ways offer, on the one hand, exposition and discussion of empirical findings and, on the other, some degree of theoretical reflection. In this latter connection, no particular theoretical stance will be privileged in the series; nor will any relevant perspective – sociolinguistic, psycholinguistic, neurolinguistic, etc. – be deemed out of place. The intended readership of the series will be final-year undergraduates working on second language acquisition projects, postgraduate students involved in second language acquisition research, and researchers and teachers in general whose interests include a second language acquisition component.

Other Books in the Series
Portraits of the L2 User
  Vivian Cook (ed.)
Learning to Request in a Second Language: A Study of Child Interlanguage Pragmatics
  Machiko Achiba
Effects of Second Language on the First
  Vivian Cook (ed.)
Age and the Acquisition of English as a Foreign Language
  María del Pilar García Mayo and Maria Luisa García Lecumberri (eds)
Fossilization in Adult Second Language Acquisition
  ZhaoHong Han
Silence in Second Language Learning: A Psychoanalytic Reading
  Colette A. Granger
Age, Accent and Experience in Second Language Acquisition
  Alene Moyer
Studying Speaking to Inform Second Language Learning
  Diana Boxer and Andrew D. Cohen (eds)
Language Acquisition: The Age Factor (2nd edition)
  David Singleton and Lisa Ryan
Focus on French as a Foreign Language: Multidisciplinary Approaches
  Jean-Marc Dewaele (ed.)
Second Language Writing Systems
  Vivian Cook and Benedetta Bassetti (eds)
Third Language Learners: Pragmatic Production and Awareness
  Maria Pilar Safont Jordà

For more details of these or any other of our publications, please contact:
Multilingual Matters, Frankfurt Lodge, Clevedon Hall,
Victoria Road, Clevedon, BS21 7HH, England
http://www.multilingual-matters.com

SECOND LANGUAGE ACQUISITION 13
Series Editor: David Singleton, *Trinity College, Dublin, Ireland*

Artificial Intelligence in Second Language Learning
Raising Error Awareness

Marina Dodigovic

MULTILINGUAL MATTERS LTD
Clevedon • Buffalo • Toronto

Library of Congress Cataloging in Publication Data
Dodigovic, Marina
Artificial Intelligence in Second Language Learning: Raising Error Awareness
Marina Dodigovic.
Second Language Acquisition: 13
Includes bibliographical references and index.
1. Language and languages–Computer-assisted instruction. 2. Second language
acquisition. 3. Language and languages–Study and teaching–Error analysis.
4. English language–Computer-assisted instruction for foreign speakers.
I. Title. II. Second Language Acquisition (Clevedon, England): 13.
P53.28.D638 2005
408'.00285–dc22   2005014805

British Library Cataloguing in Publication Data
A catalogue entry for this book is available from the British Library.

ISBN 1-85359-830-5 /EAN 978-1-85359-830-2 (hbk)
ISBN 1-85359-829-1 /EAN 978-1-85359-829-6 (pbk)

Multilingual Matters Ltd
UK: Frankfurt Lodge, Clevedon Hall, Victoria Road, Clevedon BS21 7HH.
USA: UTP, 2250 Military Road, Tonawanda, NY 14150, USA.
Canada: UTP, 5201 Dufferin Street, North York, Ontario M3H 5T8, Canada.

Typeset by Archetype-IT Ltd (http://www.archetype-it.com).
Printed and bound in Great Britain by the Cromwell Press Ltd.

407
DOD

Contents

Acknowledgements

Much as writing may be a cognitive process developing in the mind of an individual, research is, and always will be, a social process, one in which an individual is inspired by the ideas of others and receives help at every step of the way. Consequently, the publication of this book would not have been possible without the help of a number of individuals, groups and organisations, all of whom I would like to acknowledge as far as possible in this way.

First and foremost, I would like to thank Macquarie University for the research and development grants, which covered important parts of the research leading to this and other publications. Similarly, I am grateful to Zayed University for a research grant, a part of which supported the investigation described in Chapter 6. I am also much indebted to Piphawin Suphawat, who conducted one of the studies described here as my postgraduate student. I also thank my former colleagues for instances of theoretical input. Aliy Fowler of the University of Kent, on the other hand, very capably translated my program into SICSTUS PROLOG, and added a lot of her own thought to it as well as to the user interface in PERL, which altogether relies on her superb programming skills. Without her, the Intelligent Tutor described in this book would have never appeared on the Web.

Apart from the above, I have received help in many other ways. Thus, my friend Min Yong single handedly organised the shipment of my private library, much needed for the literature review, while the librarians at Zayed University, Remia Philip, Ramza Al Soury and Rajen Munoo, went out of their way to enable easy access to hard-to-get books. Friends and colleagues, David Palfreyman, Frank Borchardt, Abdellatif Sellami and Lynnette Crane, read chapters of this book and provided useful and thought-provoking comments. I should not forget the students who participated in numerous studies described here, who inspired and supported the author. Thanks also to my mother and all who encouraged me to persevere with this endeavour.

One organisation, however, made a huge difference; it enabled the quantum leap from local research to global communication. This organisation is my publisher, Multilingual Matters, whom I must thank for having faith in me and deciding to support this effort. In particular I am grateful to my contact person, Marjukka Grover, who has been a delight to work with. My thanks are of course due to the series editor David Singleton and the confidential referees, whose comments have been most helpful. I am also indebted to CALICO, CALL and Language Awareness Journals for showing interest in and publishing articles on aspects of this research at various stages of completion. Finally, I would also like to acknowledge the value of the Language Awareness organisation, which provided an exciting forum for the exchange of ideas and their dissemination to a broader public. Thanks indeed to everyone who assisted in any way while this book was in the making and perhaps kindly overlooked some of the author's less praiseworthy idiosyncrasies.

Introduction

Second language learners all over the world seem doomed to making errors, which clearly label them as non-native speakers of English, Chinese, Arabic, French, German, Indonesian or indeed any other language they are trying to acquire in addition to their mother tongue. The idiosyncrasies of their expression are sometimes met with patience and understanding by the native speakers of that language, while at other times, the patience and understanding seem to wane. An anecdotal example is my attempt to master some Polish while I was visiting a good friend in that country. At one time, my hostess wanted me to pronounce a particularly difficult word and I gave it my very best try. After having delivered what I thought was a reasonable instance of pronunciation at that stage, her whole family burst into laughter over my word stress. Moreover, this became a subject of teasing all through my visit, which even though well meant did cause me some frustration. Needless to say, my Polish is still at the beginner level.

Van Lier (1996) agrees that sometimes intolerance of non-native-like speech prevails and native speakers put the onus back on the non-native speaker to bring their expression in line with the standard. This can lead to frustration on both sides, especially if the non-native speaker cannot bring forth the expected correct language. How that can affect the non-native speaker's motivation is quite clear from my encounter with the Polish language. Yet, many language learners worldwide expose themselves willingly to such risks. They do so by temporarily or permanently moving to another country, often with the purpose of completing their tertiary education there. While in some technical degree programs the mastery of language perhaps plays second fiddle, and the effects of being a non-native speaker are minimised, in the humanities and social sciences language is the crucial factor influencing academic success, often to the disadvantage of the non-native speaker.

Just how devastating the criticism of one's second language could be is exemplified by the stories of many students I have encountered over the years in my English teaching career. Two such examples stand out. The first one is of a Japanese girl who kept sobbing for hours because the feedback to her essay said that some of her sentences could not be understood by the lecturer. Another example is of a student from a different Asian country

1

who having passed a certain English proficiency test decided that his English was good enough and took any attempt on the part of the teachers to improve it very personally. I am not sure what had happened to the first student – I just remember my very strong sense of concern for her. The second student, however, dropped out of at least four universities, his anger and frustration spiralling. I was concerned about him, too.

I was also deeply concerned about my apparent inability to do more for either of those students. I assume that most language teachers would have had similar moments of self-doubt, moments in which they wished that by magic they could have removed the often stigmatising idiosyncrasies of their students' language. My way of dealing with the issue was to resort to the magic of our time – artificial intelligence. I thought that having a computer, which unlike some of their lecturers understood their erroneous language and offered remedy in a socially non-threatening way, would help. Thus I devoted a lot of my energy to developing what is considered to be a specimen of Intelligent Computer Assisted Language Learning (ICALL).

The concept of 'artificial intelligence' or AI is what sets certain software apart from computer programs in general. Thus, the majority of programs we use nowadays for data processing, i.e. spreadsheets, calculators, database applications, are not considered to be artificially intelligent. The reason for this is that these programs are most of the time equipped with a finite number of alternative paths or procedures. Thus, given the data, we can easily predict which route the program will follow. Artificial intelligence, on the other hand, can deal with new problems, once it has learnt the general principle. For example, in order to process a student's erroneous sentence, a non-intelligent program would have to have the exact same erroneous form hard-wired into its system. For the same kind of error, committed in a different sentence, using different vocabulary, this program would again have to have the exact wording pre-stored in its memory. However, an intelligent program would only have to have a rule the student uses for such erroneous production. The program could theoretically recognise the same type of error in any context and with any vocabulary. For this very reason artificial intelligence could possibly become the student's and the teacher's best ally in dealing with second language errors.

This book examines the conditions under which ICALL could be truly useful to second language learners. Its purpose is also to demonstrate the learnability of a second language by focusing on some interlanguage problems and their proposed remediation. The interlanguages researched and described here are Chinese and Indonesian with English as the target language. Some reference is also made to Arabic, but only in comparison with Chinese and Indonesian. The remediation device proposed is an artificially intelligent computer program designed to raise the learners' general language awareness, in particular the error awareness. This is therefore a cross-disciplinary volume bringing together instances of research in second language acquisition (SLA), language awareness, computer assisted language learning and natural language processing. It is written for language teachers, students in applied linguistics and language engineering as well as for applied linguists in general. While trying to bring the SLA terminology and approaches closer to a wide range of audiences (Chapter 1), it also makes an attempt to clarify the issues in ICALL to an equally wide array of language specialists (Chapter 4). By doing so, the book aims to become a mediator between what are sometimes regarded as two different groups of audiences – language teachers and applied linguists on the one hand and ICALL specialists on the other.

Thus the aim of this book is to cater to a wide range of audiences associated with the field of CALL. Because of the cross-disciplinary nature of our field of study, it is, as experts admit, very difficult to assess the prior knowledge of the potential readership. For this very reason, this book assumes very little and can therefore be seen as at times overly theoretical. This is not to say that the assumption is made that every individual reader would bring along very little knowledge. To the contrary, it is assumed that the reader will often be an expert in one or more of the feeder disciplines of CALL. Such readers often bring along a deep theoretical curiosity concerning the disciplines that are not a part of their portfolio. It is also expected that the title might attract a novice or even an expert in foreign or second language teaching, but not necessarily in the area of CALL. Such a reader may be encouraged by the book's easy and informative approach to the use of AI in language teaching. On the other hand, it is likely that a computational linguist without much background in language pedagogy might become interested in the application of AI in language teaching and learning. In this case, the book will provide the necessary information regarding the language learning theories and their impact on CALL. Naturally, this is a strategy based on much compromise and may be asking for some patience of each individual reader. However, I am convinced that everyone interested in this topic will find at least something in this book that provides answers or stimulates the mind. It is the bringing together of all the nuts and bolts of CALL, viewed from varying perspectives, in a language understood by every reader, that this book has set out to accomplish. A brief overview follows.

The pivotal issues in this book are language, second language learning and the learner. Linguistic theories differ greatly in their views of language (Graddol, 1994), which in turn affect language learning theories. In Graddol's (1994) terminology there are three historical models of language description: the structuralist, the sociolinguistic and the post-modern. In my view, the structuralist model revolves around an idealised code called language that belongs to no person in particular, but is available to all.

While the sociolinguistic model shifts the focus from the code to the code user and his or her social identity, the post-modern view abandons the construct of a consistent self and puts forward the contextualised discourse as the locus of language. Accordingly, three types of language learning theories are distinguished by their understanding of the locus and ownership of language. So the nativist theories converge with the structural linguistic views through their focus on the common and impersonal linguistic code, in a way relieving the individual of the responsibility for language learning. The cognitivist learning theories, akin to sociolinguistic theories, put the onus for language learning and its ownership on the individual, while the interactionist theories, which correspond to post-modern linguistic theories, make the social group responsible for an individual's language learning.

In addition to having completely different views on the nature and the locus of language, language learning theories also seem to be designed for different types of learners (Oxford, 1995). While the cognitive language learning theories may have an analytical (Willing, 1989) learner in mind, the interactionist language learning theories seem to be geared toward a communicative learner (Willing, 1989). Nativist theories do not seem to have a learner in mind at all, as according to Chomsky (1965) or Krashen (1987) language is something that takes care of itself. These and similar issues will be discussed in more detail throughout the book, in particular though in Chapter 1.

Technology, as will be shown in Chapters 3 and 4 of this volume, can conform to any linguistic or language learning theory. Thus it is regarded as theory neutral (Levy, 1998; Warschauer, 1999; Murray, 2000). Any approach facilitated by a particular computer program is merely a reflection of its author's view of language learning and his or her particular slant on linguistic theory. This gives rise to thinking that CALL should be more generously used for theory testing (Chapelle *et al.*, 1996), as we shall see in Chapter 2. However, while the theory may or may not include the learner specifics, the practice most certainly should pay attention to the characteristics of the potential learners (Hubbard, 1996; Levy, 1997b). Therefore, Chapter 5 examines the intended learner of the Intelligent Tutor of Academic English on the Web, the development and the evaluation of which is systematically followed in the same and the following chapters respectively.

As pointed out in the title of this book, artificial intelligence merely provides a perspective, a technological opportunity to try out less commonly practised CALL approaches, such as natural communication, i.e. interaction between man and machine that resembles that between humans. It also has the potential to parse the learner-free style output and assess its accuracy. If such a device were to be available to the learner for limitless practice and feedback, this could mean an effective attack on learner errors, regarding which there is much resignation in SLA circles. Some nativists even believe that certain errors may be beyond any student's learnability grasp (Yip, 1995). This belief is based on the notion that learners learn from positive evidence or what can be found in the language they encounter (input). If negative evidence, or any kind of feedback following the error, is taken as a solid basis for learning, then software that uses artificial intelligence to provide learners with feedback regarding their errors can be seen as extremely useful. Describing the development of such a program as well as discussing a number of relevant issues pertaining to it is the subject of this book. In the following each chapter will be briefly outlined.

Chapter 1 of the volume addresses the question: 'Can another language be learnt?' This chapter discusses SLA theories, especially the current interlanguage theories (Yip, 1995; Selinker, 1997) and their implications for the learnability of a second or a foreign language. The concept of interlanguage (i.e. 'between languages') is derived from the notion that when acquiring a new language the learners create systems in which the information gaps concerning the target language are bridged by either relying on the rules of the native language or by overgeneralising/over-simplifying from the target language rules the learner already knows. Thus interlanguage as a rule incorporates linguistic errors in a systematic way. These errors tend to become fossilised at a certain level from which the learners do not seem to make any progress. More recent language learning research (N. Ellis, 2002) has shown that raising language awareness can significantly contribute to language learning. Thus error awareness and timely correction seems to matter, firstly in preventing the errors from being fossilised, and secondly in helping with the de-fossilisation of the already fossilised errors. It is therefore deemed that an artificially intelligent error correction aid would be absolutely conducive to error eradication or de-fossilisation and therefore to language learning. While this chapter may be of more interest to the readers without much background in second language acquisition theories, even SLA experts may wish to skim through it to find out what the theoretical underpinnings of the Intelligent Tutor are.

Chapter 2 is entitled 'Where does research end and CALL development begin?' and discusses the role of research in CALL development projects. It is difficult to imagine a good CALL (Computer Assisted Language Learning) development project which would be completely detached from research. From close observation, it follows that two software development phases stand out in terms of research opportunities: needs analysis and evaluation (McDonough & McDonough, 1997). Accordingly, this chapter makes a distinction between pre-developmental and post-developmental research, attempting to demonstrate that the literature on CALL related research often neglects the former. However, the chapter also argues that it is difficult to draw a clear line between research and non-research in CALL, as its development is cyclic and prone to re-examination. This chapter may be of interest to all readers, regardless of their professional backgrounds, in particular though to CALL practitioners.

The question asked in Chapter 3 is: 'Why the Web?'. This is an attempt to justify the choice of the first technology selected for the dissemination of the Intelligent Tutor, the software whose development is described later in this volume. This chapter views the intelligent language tutor as an innovation. Thus it looks into the theoretical underpinnings for the diffusion and acceptance of innovation in general (Rogers, 1983). It then argues that due to its similarity with a large library of materials, a concept that the user already knows, and therefore compatibility with the accepted social values (Geoghegan, 1998) the Intelligent Tutor is more likely to be accepted if offered on the Web than in any other mode. In addition, it seems to conform to the two dominant learning theories, cognitivism and social learning theory (Levy, 1998). Again, this chapter may interest readers of widely diverse backgrounds.

The fourth chapter juxtaposes the pros and cons to the question: 'Can computers correct language errors?'. It examines the current state of the art in the area of artificial intelligence and natural language processing. It is argued that most parsers or programs designed to analyse utterances made in a natural language would ignore an error one way or another (Dodigovic, 2002). The so-called rule-based parser (Smith, 1991) would not have a rule by which to recognise an erroneous utterance, whereas a probabilistic parser based on language statistics (Jurafsky & Martin, 2000) may not be able to recognise the error for what it is or offer pedagogically sound feedback. It is proposed that a pedagogical parser used for error correction should be trained on learner interlanguage (James, 1998). This would provide it with the ability to capture student produced errors and provide comment in an appropriate way. The above conclusion is hence the basis for the development work described next. This chapter may be particularly informative to the readers with a background in CALL without previous training in AI. It can also be useful to AI specialists not previously trained in language teaching, but no particular readership should feel excluded.

In Chapter 5 we learn how to develop an artificially intelligent language tutor. The premise for this is the notion that individual learner differences can be very well accommodated by an intelligent writing tutor program. Such a program takes into account the personality related learning style and typical errors made by the learner in a foreign or second language learning environment. As a result, each learner can utilise the strategies most helpful to her in the process of language acquisition. Accordingly, this chapter describes three studies conducted in the lead-up to the program development: the first one in learner styles, the second one in the target language of instruction, and the third one in the student interlanguage

(Dodigovic, 2002). As the target language in this context happens to be academic English, a semiotic based theoretical framework leading to the linguistic description of this register is also presented. The chapter concludes with the implementation of the research data in the programming language called SICSTUS PROLOG and some examples of use. While the trained language teacher is the primary intended audience for this chapter, anyone else with an interest in CALL should be able to gain something from it, not the least an impression of what it takes to design CALL programs for language learners. To some this chapter may appear overly theoretical. However, the theory is there to demonstrate clearly what an intelligent program must 'know' and indeed 'knows' in order to address learner specific needs. This being a declarative, knowledge based and not merely a procedural program, the outworking of its knowledge base, as well as the underlying knowledge itself, should be a matter important enough to communicate to the reader.

The final chapter poses the question: 'How does it work?'. It describes the functioning of the artificially intelligent language tutor and evaluates it in several different ways, using both learners and fellow teachers for that purpose. It points out which aspects are most useful to particular learner types. Finally it presents a simple effectiveness study with suggestions for future development. All readers should be able to find something of interest in this chapter.

Despite the obstacles faced in the phases of needs analysis, development and evaluation, this book is cautiously optimistic about the future of artificial intelligence in language learning, in particular when it comes to combating learner errors, whether fossilised or not. It also welcomes the opportunity that ICALL provides for students like the two described at the beginning of the chapter, the opportunity to receive correction in the privacy of their own study, without having to risk public loss of face. The question asked here is: can such a program be effective? Chapter 6 will hopefully demonstrate so. However, what seems like simple efficiency in terms of learning outcomes may prove to be much, much more. It may prove to be an instrument of empowerment, putting language learners once and for all in control of their own learning as well as the resulting educational success.

Chapter 1

Can Another Language Be Learnt?

Background

Occasionally one hears that so-and-so speaks five or seven languages fluently, which seems like a truly remarkable achievement, except for the fact that the speaker as a rule fails to deliver any accurate measure of so-and-so's proficiency in any of those languages. Those who have struggled with another language to little or no avail would most certainly greet such an unqualified statement with a sound dose of scepticism, as they might hold the belief that another language cannot be really mastered to perfection. Is it then possible to learn and use a language other than one's mother tongue with a native like proficiency? If so, at what age would one be most likely to achieve this? Moreover, would that mastery extend to every aspect of the target language, including lexicon and grammar; all language skills including speaking, listening, reading, writing; features such as idiomatic expressions and language based humour; and the command of functional varieties of that language like sociolects or registers? Given the above questions, second language learnability appears to be somewhat of an undefined term, which we will seek to clarify in the following review of literature. In the interim, the stance taken here is that speakers of languages other than English can achieve error free use of written academic English, regardless of their age, especially if provided with a learning aid that accommodates their specific learning needs.

The situation that has produced the above assertion is the following. Imagine a university in an English speaking country, e.g. Australia, Canada, New Zealand, UK or US, which enrols considerably large numbers of students for whom English is a second language. Prior to enrolment, these students would have had to demonstrate some sort of acceptable standard of English, be it through one of the international proficiency tests, such as IELTS 6.5 or TOEFL 550/580, the institution's own internal test or an equivalent language proficiency score. Based on those scores, the institution's assumption is frequently that this population of students is sufficiently equipped to attend to the content delivered in the classes (Severino, 2001). Under the increasing pressure of two factors, this assumption has however begun to weaken, the factors being the varying academic success of this group of students and the increasing body of research in second language acquisition. Consequently, a number of universities are now offering additional language assistance to non-native speakers (NNS) of English, be it English for Academic Purposes (EAP) programs, Writing/Language Across the Curriculum (WAC/LAC), writing centres, study skills or similar (Johns, 1997).

The specific multi-national, predominantly South-East Asian, student population discussed in this book was enrolled in an Australian university and came from a variety of disciplines and modes of study. They had access to a battery of EAP programs, consisting of two credit courses in academic writing, an array of non-credit courses on varying topics of interest, only one of which – and that poorly attended – was devoted to grammar, in addition to individual consultations available at the time of their choice. Careful monitoring of the effect of all of the above measures yielded encouraging results in terms of overall achievement. The students generally seemed to have acquired more efficient reading skills and more successful approaches to writing, leading to an overall better academic performance as demonstrated by improved grades in their content-related subjects. However, one thing remained – language errors, which sometimes obscured the meaning and distracted from the message (Eskenazi, 1999) even in a well structured and most carefully researched assignment. Even though a local survey (Simmons & Thurstun, 1995) had established that the lecturers valued content much more than the linguistic form, the grades they awarded painted a slightly different picture. It is arguable that non-native-like and therefore unexpected linguistic structures would make the comprehension of the message (and therefore content) more difficult. Hence, the lecturers might have in reality been struggling with the meaning affected by form. Be that as it may, language errors became identified as a problem and their eradication a desired outcome.

The students themselves are either overseas students or recent migrants, mostly very self-conscious and uncertain when it comes to the issue of language errors. Most are struggling with a new culture and a new academic tradition, in which the participants such as students and teachers have new and different social roles (Scollon & Scollon, 1995). Not only is the teaching process new and different (Ballard & Clanchy, 1984), but the finances are not always certain or sufficient. Financial crises in their countries of origin as well as civil unrests are a constant source of concern. Nevertheless, most are determined to succeed.

In order to give the reader a better feel for this student population, I would like to introduce two particular representatives: Eric and Jean. The names are of course aliases designed to protect the real identity of the two students, although both actually used different English aliases. These students are very different from the two mentioned in the Introduction to this volume, in the sense that their coping with a second language environment seemed to be much better. Moreover, they were the students most likely to accept extra help and benefit from it. At the beginning of this study Eric was a 19-year-old undergraduate student of Economics and Finance from Indonesia. His spoken English was fluent; however, in his writing, which was well structured, he often confused parts of speech, omitted the copula and confused finite and non-finite forms. He seemed confident and friendly, but corrections made by a female teacher seemed to be a sensitive issue. He was facing a personal crisis as his funding was interrupted through civil unrests in his country. The university provided him with an interim scholarship, which made him feel somewhat uncomfortable. He was also concerned for the safety of his parents back home. Jean was 23 and came from mainland China. She was a graduate in music, very disciplined and determined. However, communicating with her on-campus supervisor was a challenge. As language was not the main area of her expertise, writing presented a major challenge. Verb inflection and transitivity were the grammar areas in which she willingly sought improvement. Funding was not an issue for Jean and she was satisfied that both her parents were safe and sound. Both of these students were keen on improving their English in anticipation of perceived advantages they might gain with the eradication of language errors. Eric's and Jean's profiles will hopefully come to mind when the phrase 'our EAP students' is mentioned in the course of this book.

Thus the small number of academics in charge of the EAP programs at the university where our EAP students were enrolled faced the daunting challenge of understanding and successfully combating the linguistic errors of a rather large and diversified student population. Besides gaining a thorough understanding of theoretical explanations for the persistence of such errors and their rather diametrally opposite prognoses of success, potentially successful remediation strategies had to be identified and a vehicle for their implementation selected. As the latter required nothing short of a miracle, artificial intelligence was isolated as the only concept that might work. Several chapters of this book grapple with the issue of learner errors in writing and finding ways of their remediation, while one of them is specifically dedicated to the use of artificial intelligence for this purpose. For now, however, we will return to the more general matters addressed in this volume.

Terminology

So far we have mentioned terms such as 'mother tongue', 'another language' and 'second language' to distinguish between different relationships one can assume toward languages one has had exposure to. It is now time to establish a uniform nomenclature, the one that is generally accepted in the relevant literature (Larsen-Freeman & Long, 1991; Cook,

1993; Ellis, 1997), namely the distinction between the first language (L1) and the second language (L2). The first language can be equated with the mother tongue, native language or simply the language one has acquired first. A second language is any language other than L1 a learner is seeking to acquire, even though this might in reality be their fourth or fifth language (Larsen-Freeman & Long, 1991). However, the distinction between L1 and L2 becomes problematic in the case of simultaneous bilingualism which, according to Larsen-Freeman & Long (1991: 7), means mastery of two first languages. Sometimes, distinction is made according to the setting in which L2 is learnt. Thus we speak of a foreign language if it is learnt outside the country or countries where it is spoken as the first language, and of a second language if the acquisition takes place in an environment where the target language features as the first language (Oxford, 1990; Mitchell & Myles, 1998; Grabe & Kaplan, 1996). For instance a Korean student learning English at a school in Korea would be learning a foreign language, whereas the same student learning English in Australia would be learning it as a second language. It could also be assumed that the learning purposes would be different in these two cases: the purpose of the former would most probably be to enhance the general education of the student, whereas the latter would be to communicate and function successfully in another society. We will follow the now established tradition of the discipline and subsume both instances under L2, since even though learning purposes and therefore the teaching context may be different (Grabe & Kaplan, 1996), the learning processes are perceived as identical (Mitchell & Myles, 1998).

The discipline referred to in the previous paragraph is the study of second language acquisition (SLA). Nunan (1992: 232) defines SLA as 'the process through which individuals develop skills in a second or foreign language in tutored or untutored environments'. This definition circumvents the distinction between 'learning' and 'acquisition', which is how the term will be used throughout the book. It is however worth mentioning that the distinction, if not in terminology at least in principle, does have an almost 80 year long history. Thus Palmer (1926, cited in Cook, 1993: 63) proposes a distinction between two different capacities for language learning: 'spontaneous' and 'studious'. Krashen (1987), probably the best known proponent of this distinction, postulates an acquisition/learning hypothesis, which presumes that acquisition is a spontaneous process, similar to the one that children engage in when learning their first language. Learning (Krashen, 1987), on the other hand, is considered to be a conscious process, used exclusively for monitoring the output. Of the two, only the former is really essential, leading to acquired knowledge, deemed to be productive in L2 use (Krashen, 1987). In this book learning and acquisition will be used interchangeably.

Theory

The use of terminology discussed in the previous section was sparked off by a debate not only concerning the nature of the language learning process, but also of the product, the knowledge of language itself. Nowadays, we can choose from an array of theories, some of which include a more comprehensive theory of language. What is meant by theory is a constructed framework intended to explain and predict the real life phenomena (Larsen-Freeman & Long, 1991). Having a theory allows the researcher to ask research questions and postulate hypotheses before the commencement of research (Ellis, 1997; Nunan, 1992; McDonough & McDonough, 1997; Gregg, 2001). This is an approach opposite to data-driven research (McDonough & McDonough, 1997), which collects data first and looks for emerging patterns to ask questions about. Theory is however valued for its contribution of systematicity that it can provide research and practise with (Ellis, 1997; Grabe & Kaplan, 1996; Gregg, 2001).

Cook (1993: 246) subdivides SLA theoretical approaches into two main groups: (1) those that assume that language is acquired and represented by the human mind in a way which is unique to it, and (2) those that believe that language is no exception to the way people acquire and store knowledge in general. The first group is mainly under the influence of Chomsky's Universal Grammar, whereas the second group is recruited from a number of different psychological, psycholinguistic and sociolinguistic camps. Larsen-Freeman and Long (1991) subdivide all SLA theories into nativist, environmentalist and interactionist. The nativist theories are those claiming that the ability to learn a language is innate, specific to language and different to any other mental ability. Thus these are identical with Cook's (1993) first group. Environmentalists believe that nurture, rather than nature is key to learning, whereas interactionists acknowledge the role of both nature and nurture, the innate and environmental factors. Oxford (1995) talks about novice-to-expert, constructivist and individual difference paradigms. While the first paradigm is one of progress from the stage of being a novice to the stage of being an expert, the second paradigm is associated with constructivism in psychology and will be discussed in more detail later. The individual difference theory suggests that learners learn in different ways and therefore no single methodology will serve all learners equally well.

While SLA overviews, such as that of Mitchell and Myles (1998), observe the theoretical paradigms in light of their relationship to language in general, the human mind, L1 and L2, individual differences and the learning context, it seems that different theories are not simply different statements about the same phenomena, but more often than not differing statements regarding different phenomena (Oxford, 1995). Thus, while UG linguistics is more interested in the explanation of language itself, the cognitivist theories are primarily interested in the internal processes of the mind that enable learning, whereas the sociolinguistic perspective looks at language in its social use. We will therefore have to view the theories in light of the specific answers they provide to our very specific question: Can adult learners of English from various linguistic backgrounds eradicate grammatical errors in their L2 academic writing? The specific variables we are interested in are the learner's age, the writing skills and the development of grammar. The development of grammar entails the identification of common errors and their intended decrease in frequency and number as a result of an intervention.

In order to answer the above question, it might be purposeful to look at the general issues at hand in any language learning situation. The process of learning has to do with the language learnt, the learner herself and the context, whether social or not (Levy, 1997b). The underlying notion in most SLA theories, be they linguistic, psychological, psycholinguistic, sociolinguistic or sociological, is a particular understanding of the ownership of language. Thus, Chomskyan linguistics places the ownership of language outside the human being, either as an individual or a society. Language is rather seen as 'a separate entity because it has an independent existence unrelated to human production or use' (Grabe & Kaplan, 1996: 176). Even though this linguistic approach claims that the language acquisition device (LAD), a special and uniquely human partition of the mind responsible for language learning, is inborn or genetic, it is not clear how it came into being. LAD seems given, a premise that is not only in accord with idealist philosophy, but which also suggests a creationist view of the human mind. The very word 'genetic', used to describe it, comes from the term *genesis*, which in its meaning includes the act of creation (Petkovic, 1984), rather than referring to a long process of evolution. A radically different view of language, supported by cognitivists, who see no difference between language learning and other problem-solving processes in the mind, is that language is owned by the individual in the form of neural pathways established through that individual's unique mental activity, which only reflect a complex linguistic environment surrounding the individual (N. Ellis, 2001). The third view of language is that of social interactionists, functional linguists and sociolinguists (Long, 1996; Halliday, 1999; Givon, 1979) who believe that language is the property of a community, as its meaning – its *raison d'être* – is developed and negotiated in social interaction.

Determining whether the locus of language ownership is an individual consciousness, the society or the genes, seems crucial to answering our initial question: Can our adult NNS university students learn how to improve their erroneous academic English? Thus, if the view is that language is not subject to the will and consciousness of an individual or a group, but rather to the predetermined coding of the genes, then this potentially leads to a negative answer to our question, e.g. in case the genes are not programmed for SLA in adulthood. The answer is likely to be negative since our NNS students are still making errors despite the fact that their consciousness as well as the respective social group, i.e. the university, may be focused on the goal of their language learning progress. On the other hand, if the view is that language is owned by the individual, then this becomes an empowering impetus for the learner to persevere, as she can expect to be successful. Responsibility for the outcome is however entirely her own. Finally, if the view is that the language is owned by a social group, then learning will only be possible in social interaction, thus making the group responsible for the success of the individual. Let us now examine to what extent the research conducted on each of the three premises conforms to the hypotheses we have just expressed.

Universal Grammar (UG) and language learning

Let us first examine the success prognosis given to the adult L2 learner from the UG perspective of genes as language owners. As an explanation of language acquisition, which is not its primary purpose, Chomsky (1965) as the founder of UG claims that each child is equipped with a highly specialised language acquisition device (LAD) that does not serve any other cognitive purposes but language acquisition alone. This device in a later version becomes equated with the universal grammar. UG consists of principles which are universal to all human languages, e.g. that each phrase has a head, and the parameters that differ from language to language, e.g. the position of the head in a phrase. The way LAD works is by setting the language specific parameters when a certain language structure in L1 is encountered, presumably in early childhood (Manning, 1991). The main argument in favour of such a device is the apparently insufficient input a child receives in its language development phase. Thus, so the argument goes, as the child cannot learn the language by imitating its environment, it has to have an innate ability that eventually results in a very creative use of language, enabling the child to produce a number of sentences they have never heard before. With age, this ability to set the parameters decays, which does not raise much hope for adult learners of L2, including our EAP students.

Indeed, research influenced by UG has yielded four different hypotheses about second language learning (Mitchell & Myles, 1998; Doughty & Williams, 1998b) and only one of them seems really optimistic. This one postulates that when learning an L2, the learner has access to the same UG features (principles and parameters) responsible for their learning L1. The other three hypotheses range from total dismissal of UG availability over partial UG availability for L2 learning to indirect availability of UG via L1. The prognosis for any L2 learning outcomes without direct access to UG must be grim coming from this group of linguists, as we must remember that they do believe that LAD, sometimes equated with UG, is solely responsible for language acquisition.

The first UG-based SLA hypothesis, the one that allows for the availability of UG to adult learners, comes from Flynn (1996) and is the most recent development. The second one, involving total denial, was based on the observation of immigrants to the USA, who only seemed to attain native-like proficiency in English if they arrived not later than the age of seven (Mitchell & Myles, 1998). Partial access hypothesis is based on the observation of partial success of L2 learners, while the indirect access hypothesis is associated with the notion of critical period, during which only at a young age does an L2 learner have a window of opportunity to access UG and be successful (Mitchell & Myles, 1998). Thereafter, L2 can only be accessed indirectly through L1 and native-like competence can therefore not be attained. According to UG theorists, indeed, adult learners do not seem to have fair chances of L2 acquisition, perhaps because, as we noticed, within the framework of this theory language is not viewed as being fully owned by the individual or social consciousness. Even though this theory does not promise much hope for our adult NNS students, it is, according to Gregg (2001), the only SLA theory based on a linguistic theoretical framework, which has its own merits.

It is in the context of nativism and UG that Stephen Krashen's (1987) take on SLA is sometimes accounted for (see e.g. Cook, 1993 and Larsen-Freeman & Long, 1991). On the surface, it would seem that Krashen (1987) would have something in common with UG, since he evokes LAD as the aspect of mind responsible for language acquisition in general, but he does not explain its internal workings. Krashen's (1987) general theory is based on five premises called 'hypotheses', even though Larsen-Freeman and Long (1991) rightly point out that they cannot really be considered hypotheses in the technical sense of the term, being neither falsifiable nor verifiable. The five 'hypotheses' are thus Acquisition-Learning Hypothesis, the Monitor Hypothesis, the Natural Order Hypothesis, the Input Hypothesis and the Affective Filter Hypothesis. We shall briefly outline each one in turn.

Krashen (1987) distinguishes between 'acquisition', which is a subconscious process and really responsible for building up the linguistic ability, and 'learning', which is conscious and contributes to knowledge about language. This knowledge about language assumes the role of a monitor, which is used to alter and edit already subconsciously initiated utterances. Whatever one does to learn a language, the rules of that language are always acquired in the same order. Krashen (1987) argues that humans acquire languages in one way only and that is by comprehending input, hence exposure to comprehensible input (i+1, which is deemed to be slightly above the learner's current ability) is the only action leading to L2 acquisition. The acquisition from comprehensible input can however only proceed when the learner has lowered her affective filter enough to allow acquisition.

Not only has Krashen's (1987) model departed from UG, but it has also been heavily criticised in its own right, mainly for its fault as a theory which cannot be either falsified or verified. While earlier SLA theories come from the background of linguistics or psychology (Cook, 1993) and Krashen's is the first and the most comprehensive of SLA theories arising directly from the SLA milieu (Larsen-Freeman & Long, 1991), it does not seem to answer our question very well and is not specific about the age of the learner or the context related to academic writing. Our learners would have every predisposition to acquire the correct grammatical forms, as they are exposed to a lot of input, which the EAP programs try to make comprehensible and EAP teachers are really taking every step imaginable to help them build down their anxieties and lower their affective filters. However, spontaneous acquisition somehow fails to materialise.

What seems to be causing problems to the UG theory when it tries to account for SLA is the construct of competence. Competence and performance as used here go back to Chomsky (1965), who defines 'competence' as speaker's knowledge and 'performance' as the use of language in concrete situations. Competence as a mental reality is hardly accessible directly and its proponents would not allow it to be assessed through performance. Thus competence is mostly assessed via grammaticality judgement tests (Ellis, 1997), in which the learner has to decide whether an utterance is grammatically correct or not. Considering the fact that language acquisition is notably a process, and even UG proponents agree with that, it does not seem very purposeful to assess competence, which seems to be a static rather than a dynamic construct (Cook, 1993). Furthermore, this theory is unable to inform us about the writing proficiency of our students, nor does it look at the language in its function to serve an academic audience within the dynamic of intertextual exchange. With all due respect for its explanatory power regarding the form of language, UG does not seem a likely candidate to answer our initial question in a satisfactory way. Thus we turn to the next candidate – the view that language is owned by the individual, which is largely influenced by two different models in psychology: behaviourism and cognitivism.

Behaviourist view of language learning

Perhaps the earliest among the psychological approaches was Skinner's (1957) behaviourist view of language as a mere form of behaviour, namely verbal behaviour (Larsen-Freeman & Long, 1991: 10). In behaviourist view (Bloomfield, 1933; Skinner, 1957; Thorndike, 1932) human beings are seen as being exposed to a number of external stimuli, to which they have a chance to respond. Successful responses to stimuli cause reinforcement, which then through repetition leads to the formation of habits, e.g. to greet when meeting people or to deliver an appropriate response in other situations. Thus language learning means the formation of verbal habits and is not radically different from any other kind of learning.

According to the tenets of behaviourism, learning a first language is a simple process (Skinner, 1957), implying the formation of a set of new habits. However, learning a second language posits a considerable problem, based on the fact that verbal habits have already been well established in L1 and would therefore have to be replaced by new ones. One could therefore expect that the old L1 habits would interfere with new L2 habits, thus making this process more difficult than learning L1.

The proposed way to learn L2 in a behaviourist setup is twofold: (1) involving a lot of drill and practice to form new habits, and (2) focusing on the areas that are different in L1 and L2 and therefore deemed difficult. The former led to practices promoting overlearning and the prevention of errors, which if committed might get reinforced and therefore established as a habit very difficult to eradicate (James, 1998: 241). The latter gave rise to contrastive analysis (CA), or a rigorous step-by-step comparison between L1 and L2 (Cook, 1993: 10–11), which has two distinct purposes. The first purpose of CA is to establish which elements of L1 and L2 are similar enough to be *transferred* from L1 to L2. The second purpose is to pinpoint those elements of L2 that are radically different from their L1 equivalents and are therefore expected to be difficult. Behaviourism in SLA is closely associated with structural linguistics (James, 1998: 4). As both attracted strong criticism from the new developments in psychology as well as in linguistics (Mitchell & Myles, 1998), most of the strong claims of this approach have been abandoned. Thus, as CA has not proved very successful in predicting areas of difficulty and the potential for learner errors (James: 1998: 4), which can be considered its strong claim (Larsen-Freeman & Long, 1991: 57), it is still being used in its weak claim. The latter is restricted to explaining learner errors in terms of L1 transfer.

Behaviourist is a positivist view of reality (Bigge & Shermis, 1999), implying its tireless optimism, its strong belief in progress and the success of appropriate strategies. Its heavy reliance on the body of language production and the documentation of errors brings it closer to our needs than UG could ever come. If we didn't have more recent theories available to us for the purpose of answering our initial question, we would be encouraged after having queried behaviourism, because it would tell us that all we had to do was identify the difficulties, avoid error traps and overlearn the correct forms. Finding out, on the other hand, that this recipe does not really work would be very frustrating. Thus we turn to some of the more recent cognitivist theories.

Cognitivist approach to language learning

While Chomskyan linguistics is interested in the rather abstract and static notion of competence (Chomsky, 1965), which almost seems detached from the learner and her cognitive efforts, the cognitivist approach is all about performance and cognitive processing of complex input the learner receives in the course of learning. As cognitive processes alone are deemed to be responsible for the attainment of knowledge, the learner's mind is seen as an active constructor and therefore the owner of knowledge. The memory and its active manipulation is seen as pivotal to the learning processes (N. Ellis, 2001; Doughty, 2001; MacWhinney, 2001; Chamot & O'Malley, 1990), which is why most cognitive theories distinguish between different types of memory. Most of these theories do not distinguish between the knowledge of language and any other knowledge, although some may allow that physiologically, some parts of the brain specialise to carry segments of linguistic information, which is what happens over a long period of time. While nativists (Krashen, 1987) believe that language can be acquired without paying attention to it, cognitive theories see paying attention (Schmidt, 2001) and noticing (Doughty, 2001; Swain, 1998; Long & Robinson, 1998) as the key to learning. Let us review four of those theories which seem to have been productive in SLA.

Cook (1993) and Mitchell and Myles (1998) single out Anderson's Adaptive Control of Thought (ACT) model, McLaughlin's information processing model, MacWhinney's competition model and connectionism. What these theories have in common is a semantic notion of language learning. Thus, learning a language would mean discovering the relationship between a familiar semantic structure and an unknown linguistic structure. In order for this newly discovered connection to take hold, the learner needs to receive feedback. Further, all of the above models seem to distinguish between the areas of the mind that are more active and the ones that are less so. Learning is seen as initialising and maintaining activity in the mind. A final common feature of this psychologically oriented tradition is that language learning is based on very simple mental processes applied generally in problem solving (N. Ellis, 2001).

Anderson's ACT model relies on the belief that the human mind is a unitary construction, thus implying that the language faculty is really the whole cognitive system (Cook, 1993: 262). According to this theory (Anderson, 1983; Chamot & O'Malley, 1994) there are two types of knowledge: declarative and procedural. While declarative knowledge consists of facts, i.e. the 'what', the procedural knowledge covers the 'how'. The core concept of procedural knowledge is the production system based on production rules, which resemble the modern computational algorithms in that they include a number of 'IF goal . . . THEN subgoal' statements (Anderson, 1983). When learning something new, the mind moves from the declarative stage via the knowledge compilation stage, at which associations are formed between the 'what' and the 'how', to the tuning stage, where productions are fine-tuned. Thus, second language learning specifically, like any other learning, implies starting from deliberate efforts to learn the facts, which are then compiled in order to become procedural, and subsequently fine-tuned to become automatic and native-like (Anderson, 1983; Cook, 1993: 249).

Anderson (1983) has been criticised for maintaining that all knowledge starts as declarative. However, his model has had a huge impact on another SLA theory, as adopted by Chamot and O'Malley (1994, 1990) in their Cognitive Academic Language Learning Approach (CALLA). Thus they assert that in addition to being taught content, learners should also be helped with the skills of using their mind more efficiently. In this respect they distinguish three types of learning strategies that the learners can also be encouraged to develop: metacognitive, cognitive and social/affective. Metacognitive strategies include planning for learning, monitoring and self-evaluation; cognitive strategies include manipulating the material to be learnt, while social and affective strategies involve interacting with another person to assist learning. According to the authors, these strategies can be learnt and transferred to another task and are particularly helpful in the task of mastering academic language. Academic language here means language in the content area of an academic discipline or a school subject. Both the concept of academic language and that of learning strategies seem promising in terms of our own learners' needs and will be explored in the following chapters.

McLaughlin's information processing model (McLaughlin *et al.*, 1983) bears a great resemblance to Anderson's ACT model, although its terminology is different (Cook, 1993: 253). This model sees a human being as essentially an information processing entity. In the effort to process information, such a processor is restricted by the amount of attention devoted to a task and the quality of the processing itself. Thus some processes are *automatic*, while others are *controlled*. An automatic process, which has been established by practice, is quick and requires little attention, whereas a controlled process is exactly the opposite. Learning starts with a controlled process and gradually builds up through practice to an automatic stage. While this may seem somewhat reminiscent of the behaviourist habit formation, its essential difference is in the initial controlled phase, where the control comes from the learner and not from the external circumstances. This theme will be picked up again later in this chapter. The implications of McLaughlin's information processing model for L2 translate into the improved performance speed with increased exposure to L2.

A spin-off from McLaughlin's model (McLauglin *et al.*, 1983) is the approach taken by Hulstijn and Hulstijn (1983 cited in Cook, 1993: 254) in an experiment in which they distinguish between two types of control the learners can assume over the process. These are referred to as *implicit* and *explicit* knowledge. The former is intuitive in the sense that it is not accessible for verbalisation, whereas the latter is conscious and can be easily verbalised. Ellis (1997: 111) exemplifies this distinction in the following way: when native speakers tacitly know a large number of grammatical rules, but cannot verbalise them, they are relying on their implicit knowledge. The conscious verbalisation of grammar rules on the other hand indicates that explicit knowledge is at work. Whereas Ellis (1997: 112) allows for both kinds of knowledge (implicit and explicit) to become subject to either type of processing (controlled or automatic), his model does not seem to allow for any overlaps between the implicit and explicit knowledge.

The third cognitive approach in Cook's (1993) taxonomy of cognitive approaches to SLA is MacWhinney's Competition Model. This model views language learning in general as a constructive process relying on data sampling, within which three major entities play the key role: the input, the context and the brain (MacWhinney, 2001). In relation to input processing, a language learner relies on certain linguistic cues to identify the linguistic functions of the words in a sentence. Within one language several sentence elements may compete for the same function, e.g. that of the subject. Thus in English, one can rely on the definite article, the nominative case, the initial position in the sentence and the agreement with the verb to identify the subject and eliminate other competing elements. In the case of an L2 learner, linguistic cues from L1 and L2 will compete with each other. Thus German learners of English may choose to rely on the German language requirement that the subject be animate rather than on the English word order cue to identify the subject (MacWhinney, 2001). The basic claim of the Competition Model is that learning a new language is a system of function-form mappings which is driven by cue reliability. How reliable a cue is depends on the likelihood of its association with a certain function, which is more or less statistical.

The other two key players in the Competition Model, the brain and the context, place this approach in close relationship with connectionism, although it was originally developed to complement Anderson's model (Cook, 1993: 257). Connectionism explains the complexity of language and its acquisition by very simple neural association processes, sometimes called bootstrapping (N. Ellis, 2001). The learning occurs through repetitive processes of data sampling, building links between form and meaning based on frequency and strengthening neural paths thus leading to automaticity. Therefore the right amount of practice in a stimulating environment can compensate even for the lack of brain plasticity that adult L2 learners encounter.

Because of its extensive reliance on repetition and automaticity, connectionism has been compared with neo-behaviourism (Larsen-Freemen & Long, 1991), a label that does not seem altogether fair because much more than behaviourism ever has, connectionism is looking for a scientific explanation of the learning processes while attempting to build links with neurology and neurobiology. It thus manages to explain rule-like behaviour as behaviour that is not necessarily rule-governed, but has come to be developed through a series of neural associations, which is why this theory was previously known as associationist (N. Ellis, 2001). In laboratory environment computerised neural networks have been successfully applied to simulate language learning processes by association, resulting in some stunning similarity between machine and human learning.

This theory, in particular one of its representatives, N. Ellis (2001), sees language processing as text chunking and chunk memorisation. Rather than using isolated words and rules to form new utterances, one uses pre-stored, pre-packaged chunks, including collocations, phrases and even sentences (N. Ellis, 2001; Schmidt, 2001). The older the person, the longer and more complex the chunks of text she can commit to memory, but so much more the chances that they will not always grammatically agree with each other in use (Cochran *et al.*, 1999). This theory has a great explanatory power for the behaviour of our EAP students. It is also very much focused on language use and is more than willing to analyse production data in the form of language corpora, which seems like a sensible approach when investigating typical errors. Connectionism also inspires hope that the learners can be successful in mastering a second language, quite regardless of their age, especially if they develop an autosupport system (Mac-Whinney, 2001) by using their neural circuits within carefully recruited social contexts (e.g. listening to radio, TV, movies, tapes, rehearsing, practising and studying grammar). The effect of this system will counter even the loss of neural plasticity associated with age, especially if the initial success triggers the emission of stimulating chemicals into their system and so leads to even more success (MacWhinney, 2001).

Thus cognitivist theories seem to have a lot of potential for providing us with hope that we can successfully combat the recurring grammatical errors of our adult university student population. Rather than stopping at this satisfactory answer, let us explore one more broad category of SLA theories that view language as the property of a social group and hold the group therefore to some extent responsible for the individual's learning which has to occur through interaction. What makes this category so broad is the fact that it includes sociological, sociolinguistic, functional linguistic and instructional views, which we will briefly review in the following.

Functionalist, interactionist, sociocultural and sociolinguistic theories of language learning

The rise of functional approach in linguistics was based on the increased recognition of communicative purpose, of the language user's need to communicate, which was in stark contrast with the exclusive focus on studying the linguistic form, as observed in UG. To the functionalist the need to communicate precedes the desire to be accurate. Thus the functionalists strive to look for evidence of the same principle in SLA. The theoretical background was provided by Givon (1979) in the form of distinction between 'pragmatic' and 'syntactic' modes of expression. The former gives preference to the message and meaning and is characteristic of informal and learner speech, whereas the latter pays more attention to form and regularly occurs in a more formal setting. Thus, a study by Dittmar (1984) explores the consistency and integrity in the learner's interlanguage in the expressions of temporality, which in informal contexts do not follow the usual morphological patterns of target language. While this approach has potential for our study because of its regard for the textual organisation of the learner's discourse and the insight it might provide into the internal workings of the interlanguage itself, the previous research in this area has mostly focused on early stages of L2 learning, which is not so relevant to our purpose. We will also have to look elsewhere for models of the investigation of the interaction context that might have contributed to the learner's output.

Input and interaction are seen as crucial to language learning by another group of theorists. While we have already mentioned Krashen (1987), who pointed out the role of input, we have not yet introduced the relevant views on the role of interaction. Let us do that now. Interactionists' attention has been focused on caretaker speech or child directed speech (CDS), which was seen as a rich source of language acquisition by the facilitation of attention management, promotion of positive affect, improving intelligibility, the facilitation of segmentation, the provision of feedback and correct models, reduction of processing load, encouragement of conversational participation and explicit teaching of social routines. A counterpart of the CDS phenomenon in the world of SLA is foreigner talk discourse (FTD), which as Long was convinced (Mitchell & Myles, 1998: 127) had a direct bearing on what the L2 learners produced and how. Thus he formulated an Interaction Hypothesis (Long, 1996), which sees certain native speaker strategies in communication with non-native speakers as conducive to L2 learning. These strategies are repetitions, confirmation checks, comprehension checks and clarification requests. Empirical studies have also linked interaction as the negotiation of meaning with comprehension and learning (Pica *et al.*, 1987), although not all of them have been conclusive (Gass & Varonis, 1994). The legacy of the interactionist approach is pointing out the value of positive and negative evidence a learner gains from the input, while simultaneously bringing attention, consciousness raising and focus on form to the forefront. This approach seems positively useful in the treatment of our problem and will be relied upon to devise one of the remedial strategies.

The next theoretical model is the one based on Vygotsky's sociocultural theory (Vygotsky, 1997; Lantolf & Appel, 1994). Vygotsky's view of learning is largely that of social interaction, first social, then individual (Vygotsky, 1997: 5). Thus, in this psychological theory based on the perception of all social phenomena as semiotic systems, creating meaning between minds has the precedence and with it the understanding of language, which as one of the semiotic systems in human culture is owned not by the individual, but by the society. Learning according to this theory happens through regulation of one's activity, initially through external regulation and subsequently through self-regulation. Through a process of supportive dialogue, also known as Bruner's (Bigge & Shermis, 1999) scaffolding, the learner's attention is directed to the key features of the environment, thus inducing the shift from inter-mental to intra-mental activity. Learning takes place in the Zone of Proximal Development (ZPD), i.e. a domain where the learner is not yet capable of independent functioning, but can accomplish tasks with the help of scaffolding, which elicits interest in the task and makes sure that that interest continues, simplifies the task, draws attention to its critical elements, controls the frustration and demonstrates the target version. Thus each act of scaffolding illustrates microgenesis in which ontogenesis becomes the repetition of phylogenesis. In language learning, the central role is occupied by private speech, social activity and scaffolding. As SLA research within the domain of this theory is as expected qualitative and ethnographic, the correlation between these three activities and learning is not quite clear. It is however an option to consider when trying to help our EAP students.

The last in the row of different approaches based on the view that language is a social rather than an individual phenomenon is a diverse group of sociolinguistic perspectives. One of their few similarities is that they understand language learning as primarily social rather than an individual activity. Another similarity is the fact that they rarely do extensive linguistic analysis of L2 learner's output. Similarly they mostly view the learner's identity as changing and adjusting to the new roles it assumes within a social group. The phenomena they are interested in are the ethnography of L2 communication, variation in second language use, pidginisation and acculturation and second language socialisation. Studies in the ethnography of communication focus on the social use of language which reflects the power relations in L2 communication, change in cultural expectation, speakers' identity and self-esteem paired with affect and emotion in L2 use. Learner variability in L2 use tries to account for simultaneous existence of correct and incorrect forms in the learner's output in both a qualitative and quantitative way. Some of the identified causes of variation are the linguistic context, the psychological processing, the social context and the language function. Schumann's (1987) pidginisation and acculturation theory sees similarities between the learner's fossilised stages of interlanguage, an autonomous linguistic system of an L2 learner, and pidgins, artificially contrived languages used for communication where no other common language exists. Even though L2 interlanguages have demonstrated greater variability and tendency to change, this may be a useful metaphor (Lakoff

& Johnson, 1981) when examining the fossilised errors in our EAP population. Furthermore, understanding the power relations within the academic
discourse community (Benesch, 2001) into which our students are being
initialised seems one of the keys to success, and so do their cultural expectations and the sense of face and identity. We will examine some theories
more closely in our discussion of the productivity of SLA theories when it
comes to academic writing.

One common aspect of SLA theories needs to be mentioned before the
close of this section, namely their underlying overt or covert understanding
of language. While the early UG theory views language as structure, i.e.
pure form (Graddol, 1994), more recent interests of SLA have turned to the
view of language as vocabulary (Nation, 1990; Singleton, 1999; Lewis,
2003). This may well have happened under the influence of systemic functional linguistics, which does not draw a clear distinction between lexicon
and grammar and the lexical functional linguistics, which, as we will see in
Chapter 4, attributes a lot of purely formal characteristics to lexicon. Even
the Chomskyan approach has recently accepted the lexicon as the locus of
linguistic form (Singleton, 1999: 18). In an attempt to classify SLA theories
in respect of their preference for either grammar or lexicon, we could say
that the nativists experience language as form mainly, cognitivists pay
attention to semantics and hence to vocabulary, while the interactionists
look at larger units, i.e. utterances within their social context. Lexicon
versus grammar will really become a significant issue in Chapter 5, in
which we make an attempt to describe the EAP students' interlanguage.

Whether driven by the above theories of language or by data, SLA
research has focused on segments rather than on systems, thus not being
quite conclusive in terms of language instruction needs. As correctly
pointed out by Mitchell and Myles (1998), this has given rise to peaceful
coexistence of, rather than competition among, the various theoretical perspectives. Ellis (1997) on the other hand highlights a seeming lack of
relevance of the body of SLA theory and research for the classroom
practice. The EAP students in our study face the same problem: they do
seem to be held up at a plateau of language acquisition, which puts them at
a social disadvantage. The practitioners looking to theory and research to
guide their remedial instruction of these students may get confused or dis-
appointed, as there are no clear unanimous directions for a case like that.
This is especially true when it comes to the link between the SLA research
and academic writing. In the following we shall briefly review the most
recent accounts of that particular language skill.

L2 writing theories and research

William Grabe (2001) laments the lack of a comprehensive theory of L2
writing and lists a number of desiderata for such a theory. It would be able
to explain how writing is carried out, what constitutes good writing and

why, what circumstances contribute to good writing for certain students and how to help students develop writing skills under varying circumstances. With the aid of such a theory one would understand the success and failure of individuals and programs in educational systems. One would inevitably design better curricula, respond better to the needs of students and assess their ability in a more responsible manner. In order to construct a theory of L2 writing, Grabe (2001) points out, one would need to rely on a number of supporting theories, including a theory of language, a theory of knowledge, a theory of writing processes, a theory of motivation and affective variables, a theory of social context influences and a theory of learning. In essence, many SLA theories have tried to accommodate such a tiered structure, as we have seen in the previous section, with more or less success.

L1 writing has traditionally been subject to a number of theories, from those of literary criticism and genre to discourse analysis (Swales, 1990), functional approach (Halliday, 1999) and sociolinguistic approach (Scollon & Scollon, 1995). L2 writing however developed mainly from the background of English for Specific Purposes (ESP), contrastive rhetoric, functional language use and English for Academic Purposes (EAP) (Grabe, 2001: 43; Johns, 1997). Sometimes it has focused on L1 influences and error analysis, while sociolinguistic approaches have examined the power relations within the new discourse community into which the L2 learner needs to be apprenticed. Grabe (2001) points out that an L2 writer differs from an L1 writer in a number of aspects, from merely linguistic ones to those of cultural awareness. Leki and Carson (1997) list the following points of difference for the L2 writers: epistemological issues including cultural socialisation and belief systems, functions of writing, writing topics, knowledge storage where L1 based knowledge creates complexities for L2 writers, writing from reading, audience awareness, textual issues, plagiarism, experimenting with L2 and the social issue of students' right to their own language. However, until quite recently, L2 research on writing has not looked at those issues comprehensively, but has been closely dependent on L1 research (Grabe & Kaplan, 1996; Johns, 1997). According to Grabe and Kaplan (1996), however, three areas of L2 research have so far allowed an independent path to the understanding of L2 writing, these being contrastive rhetoric, English for Specific Purposes (ESP), and writing assessment. We will discuss these in more detail after having tried to understand the models of writing adopted by L1 research.

Still on the lookout for a comprehensive theory of writing, Grabe (2001) realises that models of writing are available, even though they are descriptive, often offering *post hoc* explanations rather than reliable predictions. Theory of writing, much like the theory of language and the general SLA theory, varies according to the basic underlying belief regarding the ownership of language. As discussed in the previous section, we have come to the conclusion that there are three major ways of understanding the ownership of language: impersonal, individual and social. The first view, mostly associated with generative grammar and UG principles, is that language does not strictly belong to any of the participants of social discourses. Moreover, language cannot be studied by observing its use, thus making both the society and the individual's expressive needs external to the phenomenon of language. The abstract native speaker competence, gained in an inexplicable process of parameter settings, becomes the seat of language.

The system, or the langue, has thus become reified in the depths of the possibly universally alike native speaker minds. The word has become flesh and has paved the way for an idolatrous approach to the native speaker as the sole and mysterious source of language competence (James, 1998; Cook, 1993; Phillipson, 1992). In SLA this leads to a series of what Phillipson (1992) calls fallacies, the most important ones being the monolingual fallacy and the native speaker fallacy. The first one is based on the tenet that English should be taught monolingually, while the other is based on the tenet that it should be taught by native speakers, both derived from the Commonwealth Conference on the Teaching of English as a Second Language, held at Makerere, Uganda in 1961(Makerere, 1961). The attitude to monolingual fallacy is echoed by Cook (1993), who is similarly opposed to the monolingual treatment of L2 learning, an activity that is supposed to lead to bilingualism. Cook (1993) equally criticises the belief that human beings are innately monolingual and that therefore each L2 learner has to be viewed as an unsuccessful monolingual in a second language. In accord with Phillipson's (1992) view of the native speaker fallacy, Carl James (1998) exposes 'nativespeakerism' a tendency to look up to the native speaker in the L2 instruction process as the source of knowledge and therefore power.

Give or take both cognitive and social implications of the monolingual fallacy (Phillipson, 1992) arising from some interpretations of UG, the fact is that UG approach focuses on the sentence level in writing, where its main objective becomes counting T-units (defined as a main clause and all the dependent clauses) per text or sentence, the number of words per T-unit, the number of clauses per T-unit as well as the number of words per clause. These measures, including the number of clauses per T-unit, the average length of T-unit and type-token ratio, are sometimes used in L2 writing assessment as a measure of fluency in writing (Polio, 2001). On the other hand, Larsen-Freeman and Long (1991) report the introduction of the average number of words per T-unit and the number of error-free T-units into the assessment of L2 accuracy. Other researchers report counting errors for accuracy assessment purposes, with or without classification (Polio, 2001). Even though counting and classifying errors will not be our main focus, we will use it as a valid approach to understanding our EAP students' writing at one level. We will however not stop at that level, but will try to understand as many aspects of it as possible.

In addition to T-unit counting, the sentence level approach also focuses on certain other features such as the nominal complexity, the use of passives, relative clauses and similar (Halliday, 1999). These are useful indicators that can help us paint a picture of what successful writers do, or at least what their final drafts look like. We will explore this option as one of the components in the process of finding out what targets our EAP students are supposed to achieve. We will also use another off-shoot of this approach, specifically related to L2 writing, and that is error analysis.

Examining the learner's output in terms of errors enforces the view of an L2 learner as a defective L2 speaker and therefore, as Cook (1993: 244) puts it, as 'failing or inefficient in some way compared to L1 children'. Cook (1993) holds the UG approach responsible for this view, as it seems to assume that it is normal to know one language rather than two or more. Our EAP learners, including Eric and Jean, indeed suffer from the same perception of themselves as being less competent learners than native speakers due to the faults of their L2. While one has to agree with Severino (2001) and provide advocacy for such students toward the academic community at large, one also empathises with them and wishes to get to the core of the problem, identifying the causes of persistent errors and finding a remedy that would successfully reintegrate them into the world of academia.

The next view of the ownership of language is associated with psychological cognitivism, implying that language is a collection of mental processes and therefore the property of an individual. In the study of writing, a cognitive approach has resulted in two prominent models of writing as a process. Writing in this tradition is viewed in a radically different light from any of the preceding approaches. While literary criticism, the UG approach or even the functional linguistic, text linguistic or discourse analysis are mainly concerned with the text as a product, the cognitive approaches focus on the process of writing. In this tradition we can single out two models: Flower and Hayes (1980) and Bereiter and Scardamalia (1987). Let us examine them briefly.

The Flower and Hayes (1980) model is based on the notion of composing, which 'involves the combining of structural sentence units into a more-or-less unique, cohesive and coherent larger structure' (Grabe & Kaplan, 1996: 4). The model includes three assertions: (1) that composing processes are interactive and possibly simultaneous, (2) that composing is directed by goals, and (3) that expert writers compose differently to novice writers. Thus, this model is based on the novice-to-expert view of the learning process (Oxford, 1995). It might be worth while pointing out that their early model was based on Artificial Intelligence (AI) processing models (Grabe & Kaplan, 1996). In its most common form of representation, the Flower and Hayes (1980) model divides the composing process into three major components: the composing processor, the task environment and the writer's long-term memory. Within the composing processor, three operational processes are responsible for the generation of written text: planning, translating and reviewing. The planning process comprises three major components: generating ideas, organising information and setting goals. All composing processes are managed by an executive control called monitor. This model was obtained based on protocol analysis, sometimes called think-aloud protocol (McDonough & McDonough, 1997), a research approach used in cognitive psychology to examine goal-oriented behaviour, which raised the issue of its validity and applicability to all writing situations (Grabe & Kaplan, 1996: 93). However, this model has raised the understanding of recursion in writing, and this is something that we need to consider in our study as well.

The Bereiter and Scardamalia (1987) model assumes that expert writers use a process different from that employed by novice writers. While the latter use simple knowledge-telling, the skilled writers engage in a knowledge transforming process. This conclusion was based on the observation that less skilled writers focus on content and less on planning or composing. They are not guided by the main ideas and seem incapable of reorganising the content in the revision process. Thus, based on their content and discourse knowledge, it is their primary goal to tell what they know. In order to accomplish this task, they locate the topic, identify the genre, retrieve content from the memory and write. In the knowledge-transformation model, knowledge-telling becomes just one of the processes involved in writing. Writing starts from problem analysis and goal setting toward knowledge-telling. However, in-between Flower and Hayes (1980) locate two other entities: the content problem space and the rhetorical problem space, between which there is a constant communication. Thus a solution of a content related problem may lead to the creation of a new problem in the rhetorical space area, and vice versa.

Much as the two cognitive models of writing, the one by Flower and Hayes (1980) and the other by Bereiter and Scardamalia (1987), illuminate the mental processes writers engage in, they have often been criticised for their lack of consideration of context, purpose, audience and the influence of the discourse community. We shall now turn to the views of both language and writing as a social practice, and therefore controlled or 'owned' by a group rather than the individual. In particular, research on writing in specialised and academic contexts (Grabe & Kaplan, 1996: 174) has yielded a number of quite unexpected insights into the nature of social function of writing. Thus the research suggests that much science writing is not neutral and objective as expected, but rather highly rhetorical and value laden (Cooper, 1989; Johns, 1997; Pera, 1999), designed to persuade a social group of scientists to accept their ideas and proposals. Within this group, knowledge is socially constructed, and owned, by the established discourse community (Swales, 1990). Therefore, in order to be recognised as a legitimate part of that discourse community, the writer has to recognise her audience, establish intertextuality of ideas and be persuasive without appearing to be so.

Functional linguistics (Halliday, 1986, 1999) has introduced the need to communicate as the main impetus for writing and has thus built on the ideas of social semiotic, which sees language as one of the systems within a culture responsible for creating and communicating meaning. Thus, apart from an ideational or denotative function, language has a textual function, which in writing becomes responsible for textual cohesion (Halliday & Hassan, 1986) and an interpersonal function which houses the writer's awareness of the audience and all attempts to meet the reader's needs as well as to enable the writer to express her individuality. Within this tradition, genre studies came to reflect a concern for the requirements of particular audiences and discourse communities.

The definition of discourse community has not been unproblematic. We shall review two prominent attempts at defining this term, firstly the one by Swales (1990: 23–7) and secondly the one by Cooper (1989). According to Swales (1990) a discourse community must have enough members who share common public goals and provide a forum for discussion, including the provision of feedback and information. This community also develops genres as norms as well as genre expectations. Cooper (1989) sees discourse communities as the authorities in respect of knowledge, values and power. An individual seeking entry into the discourse community needs to be apprenticed into it. If however the novice comes from a background that is different from that sanctioned by the discourse community, then the community will withhold power from that individual. Thus, a discourse community is seen as both facilitating and restraining in terms of its impact on the individual. As our EAP students come from different ethnic backgrounds and potentially bring into writing their own systems of values and rhetorical practices, they may well be perceived as outsiders who have to adopt the goals, values and practices of the discourse community they wish to be initiated into or else face the prospect of being ignored or excluded. Thus, this perspective is of vital interest and we will pursue it when formulating the theoretical framework for a remedial, perhaps even a redemptive action.

While discourse analysis has made us aware of the social context of the discourse our EAP students are expected to produce, by recognising the importance of context and prior text, contrastive rhetoric can help us understand the EAP students' writing in terms of explaining how written texts operate in the larger context of their original culture (Grabe & Kaplan, 1996: 179). This relatively new discipline is primarily interested in the distinctive features of writing as opposed to spoken discourse. In addition it seeks to understand what constitutes various genres in different languages.

While research in contrastive rhetoric has yielded a number of valuable genre descriptions for languages such as English, German, Spanish, Chinese, Japanese, Korean, Vietnamese, Arabic, Hindi, Portuguese and Thai, it has failed to systematically compare similar text genres across cultures and the writing of the same subject in L1 and L2. Moreover, with EAP students, the focus of the early research has been on the deviation of their writing from the English norm, rather than on the influence of L1 discourse. Finally, contrastive rhetoric has, especially in its beginnings, focused on the product, rather than the process of writing and has failed to produce a universal theoretical model. Nonetheless, it has to be taken into account when deciding how to assist our group of EAP students toward a qualitative shift in their writing.

Building on the strength of their precursors and the model of communicative competence (Chapelle *et al.*, 1993), Grabe & Kaplan (1996) propose a model of the communicative theory of writing. This model is designed to answer the most common relevant questions about writing (Cooper, 1979, cited in Grabe & Kaplan, 1996: 203): 'Who writes what to whom, for what purpose, why, when, where and how?' The answer is provided in the taxonomy of academic writing skills, knowledge bases and processes, which will be discussed in more detail in Chapter 5. At this stage suffice it to say that what is needed are educational settings, writing tasks and educational source texts, topics for academic writing, the writer's goals and intentions, the knowledge of language, discourse, sociolinguistics, audience, the world, writing process and its strategies. The Grabe and Kaplan (1996) model specifies communicative language use as comprising context for use and the user's verbal memory. The context includes situation, comprising participants, setting, task, text and topic, while the performance accounts for the textual output, which results from the processes taking place in the verbal working memory. The same memory also has access to the knowledge of the world, language competence and internal goal setting. Metacognitive processing connects these components and results in the internal processing output, which is assessed against the internal goals and if satisfactory becomes the textual output.

Grabe and Kaplan (1996) acknowledge the limitations of this model, as it does not account for the processes of revision, nor for the varying goals, the social construction of writing and the difference between L1 and L2 writers. Despite its limitations, this is a very relevant model which covers a whole range of issues that come up in writing.

Before we wrap up the theoretical approaches to SLA and L2 learning, we need to review the results of L2 writing research so far. L2 writing research has so far addressed the text as a product, writing as a process, the context of writing, the writing instruction and the writing curriculum design, all of which may have a relevant bearing on our study. Thus some recent sociocognitive studies (Berkenkotter & Huckin, 1995; Cazden &

Gray, 1992 cited in Grabe & Kaplan, 1996: 238) point out the need for models of writing in L2 and raising the students' awareness of all textual levels, including the linguistic, the rhetorical and the communicative. Raimes (1991) suggests that L2 students should not be viewed as L1 writers, especially not as the lower level L1 writers, while Campbell (1990) finds that L2 writers tend to be more bound to the source readings than L1 writers. Other writing process research has established that L2 proficiency does not necessarily have an impact on L2 composing skills, which might be positively transferred from L1. Research in functional approaches to genre development has highlighted the need for raising the students' awareness of genre structure (Johns, 1997; Swales, 1990; Derewianka, 1990; Christie, 1992 cited in Grabe & Kaplan, 1996). Similarly, an awareness of audience concerns seems to improve the writing efforts (Bonk, 1990 cited in Grabe & Kaplan, 1996). From Vygotskyan perspective, writing development requires apprenticeship, practice and expert guidance (Vygotsky, 1997). Finally, the investigation of instructional techniques has shown that explicit training in metacognitive strategies, techniques from planning, drafting and revising and maximising on feedback on writing are very helpful to the L2 writer. When planning the course of action to take with our EAP students, we will review both theory and research to determine what links have already been established and what specifically we need to find out about our student population and their needs.

EAP Student Characteristics

The time has come to list explicitly what we believe to know about our EAP students, including Eric and Jean, from theory and research. They are a population of adults, between 19 and roughly 60 years of age, learning English in an ESL (English as a second language) setting, i.e. in a country where L2 is the main means of communication. Thus classroom exposure to English is not their only source of L2 learning. They are surrounded by native speakers and target language media, in fact they have to perform a number of mundane tasks by using English. Moreover, they have without exception passed one or more of the international English language tests such as IELTS or TOEFL at a more advanced level. So, academics and university administrations dealing with those students tend to believe, as Severino (2001) points out, that the English learning process has somehow wound down to a close and no further language difficulties should be expected. If the difficulties persist, then somehow the students experiencing them must be at fault.

Grabe and Kaplan (1996: 250) list a number of issues and situations that place international students at a social and structural disadvantage, actively inhibiting learning. The first challenge is insufficient exposure to the full range of host country cultural experience, especially if coming from a country that has strained political relations with the host country. In the latter case stereotyping both ways might prevent successful communication. In addition, the academic requirements at the host university might be very much at odds with the academic culture of their own country, and the power held by the academics and written academic sources in their original cultures may make it very difficult for the students to express an honest opinion or to openly disagree with a theory. Finally, they may experience frustration over not being able to formulate complex ideas in L2 which they would be able to express adequately in their L1.

Ballard and Clanchy (1984) argue that the overseas students bring a set of different cultural variables to their host country. The differences can be seen not only in their literacy style as discussed previously under the topic of contrastive rhetoric, but also in attitudes to knowledge and learning styles. Ballard and Clanchy (1984) differentiate between two basic attitudes to knowledge: conserving and extending. A conserving attitude to knowledge implies that there is a common and unchanging pool of knowledge, about which there is a unanimous consensus. Consequently, every member of academic community knows all facts, thus making all learned people universalists. In this tradition form and content are inseparable and hence equally preserved, making unintroduced and unexplained quotation welcome as everyone is supposed to be able to recognise it. Thus the quoted text is not seen as individual intellectual property, but rather as the common property of an educated discourse community. An extending attitude to knowledge on the other hand implies that there is a common pool of knowledge which is changed and questioned, with possibly only a limited consensus about certain facts. Here members of the academic community do not share all facts equally, but different persons know different facts thus leading to specialisation. When citing sources, only content is preserved to some extent and quotation is tolerated in small amounts, which requires careful referencing. Due to a high degree of specialisation, quotation requires extra explanation since not everyone is supposed to recognise unmarked quotations. Unreferenced quotation is unlawful use of somebody else's words or ideas since the quoted text is seen as individual intellectual property.

Ballard and Clanchy (1984) explain the rote learning habits and the plagiarism perceived as frequent in the overseas student approach by their apparent conserving attitude to knowledge. It could be argued that plagiarism is not necessarily caused by a particular attitude to knowledge, but often by the lack of in-depth understanding of the written sources and the lack of confidence in their own L2 abilities. The distinction between the conserving and extending attitude to knowledge is further seen by Ballard and Clanchy (1984) as leading to a three-way distinction between learning approaches: the reproductive (based on memorisation), analytical (based on critical thinking) and speculative (involving a deliberate search for new knowledge). Thus, the reproductive style, often resulting in rote learning, seems most frequently associated with students from certain cultures (Bedell & Oxford, 1996) and is seen as a weakness (Ballard & Clanchy, 1984), at least from an Anglo-Saxon-centric point of view (Palfreyman, 2003). Interestingly, cognitive theories of L2 learning would see rote memorisation as one of the key components in language learning (Hulstijn, 2001; Ellis, 1997). How is it then that our EAP students, who are supposed to be proficient practitioners of rote learning, do not use such a powerful tool where it helps most, in L2 learning? An array of variables may be responsible for this, ranging from different learning strategies, motivation, beliefs about language acquisition, cognitive style and attitude toward L2. These will therefore have to become subject to our investigation, described in a later chapter. Another explanation also comes to mind, namely that perhaps international students do not practise as much of rote learning as assumed, since according to Bedell and Oxford (1996: 60), 'culture should not be seen as a strait jacket, binding students to a particular set of learning strategies'. The latter is also confirmed by Willing (1988), who discovered that there was little correlation between cultural background and learning style in adult migrant population in Australia.

What we believe to know about the variables from the previous paragraph is stated in Grabe and Kaplan (1996: 251) in the form of a taxonomy of approaches, skills and strategies necessary for success in L2 writing. Thus, the learners are supposed to bring in a positive approach, comprising some empathy for L2, belief in their own success, an open attitude to the new academic environment and being willing to engage in a number of learning practices. In SLA theory these are sometimes subsumed under social identity and sometimes under motivation. Secondly, they need appropriate skills and a set of workable learning strategies (Oxford, 1990). In the following we shall briefly address the theoretical and research based take on each of these phenomena.

In order to be positively disposed toward the task of language learning, the learner needs to be grounded in her social identity, self-esteem and beyond the reach of face-threatening events. The term face is sometimes identified with self-esteem and other times with the image one projects outward (Asdjodi, 2001). Borrowed from social psychology, the concept of social identity denotes the self-concept grounded in the individual's membership of a social group, including the emotional implications of this membership and a dynamic of change (Mitchell & Myles, 1998: 168). The research of Nelson and Murphy (1991, cited in Leki, 2001: 22) suggests that cross-culturally novel classroom practices, such as peer-response to writing within small groups, can negatively impact on the individual's sense of social identity. From the list of cross-cultural disadvantages cited in Grabe and Kaplan (1996) which affect international students, it can be seen that the social identity of our EAP students may already be shaken.

Thus pointing out errors may present a potentially face-threatening situation resulting in the students becoming trapped in a social identity based on the erroneous usage of their second language. Therefore the electronic tutor designed to help this group of students eradicate language errors in L2 writing must be as little face-threatening as possible.

The previous paragraph has examined learners as social beings. As Grabe and Kaplan (1996) point out, the learners bring into L2 learning other individual differences, which are in the SLA theory classified as affective and cognitive factors (Mitchell & Myles, 1998). Affective factors include language attitudes, motivation, language anxiety and personality traits. Research on language attitudes, mainly articulated as attitudes toward native speakers of L2, has largely been conducted within the context of motivation and the two concepts have not always been viewed in separation (Larsen-Freeman & Long, 1991: 175). Early SLA borrowed Bruner's cognitive-interactionist view of motivation as being 'extrinsic' and 'intrinsic' (Bigge & Shermis, 1999). Bruner sees learning as a goal-directed activity, capable of generating the feeling of success or failure, which are inherent to the task at hand and are responsible for intrinsic motivation. Reward and punishment on the other hand come from the outside and are therefore extrinsic. According to Gardner and Lambert (1972), language learning motivation can be either instrumental, which means that the learner is motivated to learn for utilitarian purposes, e.g. to pass exams, or integrative, with the purpose of becoming an integral part of L2 society. It was believed that integrative motivation is much stronger than instrumental. In a sociocultural setting described above, some of our EAP students may have instrumental motivation, thus being at a further disadvantage. The revised model of motivation by Tremblay and Gardner (1995) suggests however that models of motivation and learning can be improved by motivational behaviours, including effort, persistence and attention. In addition, a strong link between motivation and learning strategies has been found (Schmidt, 2001: 9), which suggests that we should carefully examine the learning strategies of our EAP students. A later chapter indeed is partly devoted to such a study.

Language anxiety is a learner characteristic examined by Gardner and MacIntyre (1993). The effects of anxiety are not always the same. Thus anxiety can sometimes be facilitating and other times debilitating, so that the relationship between anxiety and performance cannot be viewed as simple or linear. Sawyer and Ranta (2001) indicate that a ubiquitous phenomenon such as anxiety can hardly be classified as a personality trait. Our EAP learners will be no exception to anxiety and its possibly debilitating consequences. For this reason the learning aid we develop must among other things be instrumental to reducing anxiety levels.

Personality traits are known in personality research as risk-taking on the one hand and social style, sociability and introversion/extroversion on the other hand (Sawyer & Ranta, 2001). Risk-taking behaviours in language learning (Beebe, 1983) are considered to be willingness to guess, appear foolish in order to communicate and willingness to create novel utterances with the existing knowledge. Like anxiety, risk-taking behaviours may be facilitating or detrimental. In a study of university students, Ely (1986) found that risk-taking behaviours were a positive predictor of oral correctness in classroom participation. Cultural stereotypes of our EAP students would probably depict them as not exceedingly willing to take risks (Bedell & Oxford, 1996), even though this could be hardly said of someone who leaves the familiarity of one's own country to study in a foreign environment, often at great financial risk to self and family. Nevertheless, cultures may restrict risk-taking behaviour to certain areas, for instance personal endeavour, and completely inhibit it in others, for instance academic discourse. For this reason, we may have to provide extra opportunities for supervised individual language practice, without the need to compete with fellow students for those opportunities and break the politeness rules of one's own culture. Other personality traits, i.e. social style, sociability and introversion/extroversion, have been studied as overlapping. While according to Larsen-Freeman & Long (1991) the folk wisdom has it that extroverts are better language learners, research studies have been inconclusive. As Sawyer and Ranta, (2001) point out, questionnaire studies have not yielded positive results, whereas field studies have.

SLA literature sometimes lists inhibition vs. ego permeability, empathy, sensitivity to rejection as personality traits and tolerance of ambiguity (Larsen-Freeman & Long, 1991). The studies of the ego permeability and general empathy on language learning have been inconclusive so far, and so have those of sensitivity to rejection, which was investigated in its own right, even though seen as the reverse of risk-taking. Unlike the first three variables, tolerance of ambiguity has reportedly significant correlations with language learning (Naiman, 1978 cited in Larsen-Freeman & Long, 1991; Chapelle & Roberts, 1986). This characteristic is experienced when linguistic signals are encountered which are not fully understood. Learners with low ambiguity tolerance get very frustrated if they do not understand everything, whereas those with higher tolerance levels tend to perform better. In our approach, which is intended to explain every detail, even the students with low ambiguity tolerance threshold will be able to benefit from instruction. In fact, the electronic tutor will be well adjusted to that type of learner.

This sums up our discussion of affective factors and personality traits. The most potent factors in the learning process will however be the cognitive factors: intelligence, language aptitude and learning styles and strategies. According to Mitchell and Myles (1998) there is clear evidence that intelligence is one of the factors which positively affect language learning, at least in classroom settings. The concept of intelligence itself is however less straightforward than one may assume. Gardner (1983) in his multiple intelligences theory suggests that what has been perceived as intelligence so far and measured in terms of IQ, has really been one aspect of intelligence, namely the verbal one. In fact, early intelligence tests included the so-called 'linguality test' (Davidson, 2003). It does not surprise then that Neufeld (1978 cited in Larsen-Freeman & Long, 1991: 170) claims that intelligence is responsible for language skills, thus excluding a special faculty called language aptitude. This latter faculty has nevertheless been examined in two different ways. The first one is Carrol and Sapon's (1959 cited in Sawyer & Ranta, 2001) language aptitude, which includes phonetic ability, grammatical sensitivity, rote learning ability and inductive language learning ability. In contrast, Pimsleur's model of language aptitude (Larsen-Freeman & Long, 1991) includes verbal intelligence, motivation and auditory ability. Despite the differences, both models are good at predicting language learning success. In our project, the subjects are university students, who would have scored high in the IQ test at some stage of their education, which is a unifying factor in the study.

Cognitive psychology introduces the idea of cognitive style into the theory of learning. According to Larsen-Freeman and Long (1991: 193) one of the cognitive styles most frequently exploited in SLA literature is that of field independence/dependence. Field independence is the ability to isolate an element from the context and vice versa (Ehrman, 1998). Most of available evidence offers support for a relationship between field independence and L2 learning success. Another cognitive style is known as category width (Larsen-Freeman & Long, 1991: 194) and includes tendency to categorise broadly (put many items in a category, i.e. overgeneralise) or narrowly (put few items in a category, i.e. produce more rules than necessary). Naiman *et al.* (1978 cited in Larsen-Freeman & Long, 1991: 195) hypothesised that the best language learners would not generalise too much or too little. Another type of cognitive style categorisation is that between reflectivity and impulsivity. An impulsive person would tend to make a quick guess faced with uncertainty, while a reflective person would take a lot of time. In SLA research (Larsen-Freeman & Long 1991: 196) reflectivity is often associated with L2 learning success. One would expect that impulsive persons perform better in terms of fluency, while the reflective ones achieve better accuracy. The distinction between the aural and visual styles refers to the person's preferred mode of presentation. Research reports that learners taught through their preferred modality learn better. The final dichotomy of cognitive styles is that between analytic and gestalt. The latter are data gatherers, more successful with fluency, whereas the former are rule-formers, more successful at accuracy. Cognitive style is something that we should know about in relation to our EAP students, as it will help us design a more successful learning aid.

Learning strategies according to Mitchell and Myles (1998) are special ways of learning that distinguish successful learners from the less success-ful ones. Learning strategies theory agrees that there are two different types of such actions: those that permit learning and those that actually contrib-ute to learning (Rubin, 1981). The former are called metacognitive strategies by Chamot and O'Malley (1994) or macro-tactics by Seliger (1984), while the latter are respectively called cognitive strategies and micro-tactics. Chamot and O'Malley (1994) believe that metacognitive strategies are better developed at higher levels of L2 proficiency. Thus, one would expect that our EAP students would be able to capitalise on their developed metacognitve strategies, which are briefly outlined at the beginning of this chapter and will be discussed in more detail later. Oxford's (1990) model of learning strategies matches the model of commu-nicative competence mentioned afore (Chapelle *et al.*, 1993) and is also based on the distinction between direct and indirect strategies. The former are cognitive, compensation and memory strategies, while the latter comprise metacognitive, affective and social strategies. We will examine all these models in more detail in a later chapter.

A few other factors that can influence language learning are memory, awareness, will, language disability, interest, gender, birth order and prior experience (Larsen-Freeman & Long, 1991). Cognitive psychology has more recently come to connect memory with the chunking process leading to 'the development of associative connections in long-term storage [which] is the process that underlies the attainment of automaticity and fluency in language' (N. Ellis, 2001: 38). Chunking becomes more efficient with practice, thus increasing the language ability. Our tutor should therefore give the EAP students in this study, including Eric and Jean, ample opportunities for practice.

The next factor is awareness, a concept which has in SLA developed toward two distinct terms. One is Consciousness Raising (CR) or explana-tion and the other is Language Awareness (LA) or explication (James, 1998: 260). According to James (1998) the former means helping learners to notice what they do not know, while the latter means providing explicit insight into something that the learners already know implicitly. Both are deemed helpful and we shall make every effort to raise both the consciousness and awareness of EAP students to linguistic form. In order for the above processes to be successful, an act of volition is required (Leontiev, 1981). Success in L2 might also be negatively correlated with materialistic interests (Henning, 1983 cited in Larsen-Freeman & Long, 1991: 204). As language disability students do not study EAP with mainstream students in this study, this issue will not be discussed here.

Regarding the rest of the factors, research has found some differences between male and female language learners, but on the whole it would be difficult to generalise about the possible advantages of either gender. For example, Farhady (1982) found that his female subjects did better on listening comprehension tests, while Eisenstein (1982) found that females performed better on dialect discrimination task. Gass and Varonis (1986) found that men dominated the conversations and interrupted more often than did women. In addition to gender, birth order also seems to play a role, although this needs more investigation. It was found though that good imitators, which is supposed to be one of the features of good language learners, were either first born or only children (Larsen-Freeman & Long, 1991: 205). Finally, prior experience seems to be a bonus in L2 learning. Thus language skills seem to be transferable from the first or a foreign language to the target language (Larsen-Freeman & Long, 1991: 205).

Interlanguage and Learnability

This book discusses an application of natural language processing (NLP), to a specific second language learning situation for the purpose of raising the learners' error awareness and thus potentially improving the learning outcomes. Although NLP is an interdisciplinary area which *per se* seems to defy simple definition, Clive Matthews (1998) has successfully and succinctly defined this technological advance as 'the capacity of the computer to "understand" natural language' (Matthews, 1998: 3). This capacity seemed to be the answer to the learning needs of a number of overseas students, including Eric and Jean, studying at a university where English is spoken as a first language. Their particular problem was that they appeared to have reached a plateau in the acquisition of English as a second language (L2) and were finding it difficult to make further progress. This problem had become most blatantly obvious in their academic writing, an activity upon which the academic success hinges in the Anglo-Saxon tradition, where their non-standard use of grammar and expression would often obscure the meaning, thus severely limiting their chances of success. The NLP approach was deemed capable of providing this group of students with automatic analysis of their typed English sentences supplying them also with meaningful feedback concerning the grammatical correctness of their output.

However, although the concept of NLP as such was readily available along with the matching technological platform, an appropriate computer program based on this technology had yet to be devised. For the reasons discussed below, the most fruitful approach seemed to be a study of typical errors made by this student population. The knowledge of how these students produce target language (TL) could then be 'taught' to the NLP based tutor in addition to the knowledge of standard academic English, as observed in a wide variety of acclaimed academic publications. Equipped also with appropriate feedback strategies, the program-tutor would consequently have the capacity firstly to separate the correct surface structures from the incorrect ones, and secondly draw the users' attention to the errors that are most common among the target group. Note, however, that most NLP devices, otherwise called parsers, either ignore erroneous input or manage to process it, but do not necessarily provide pedagogically sound correction. Thus, although able to identify most incorrect input as such, the parser described here is supposed to be able to give meaningful feedback to and correction of a limited set of syntactic errors. Needless to say, the entire effort is based on the belief that L2 is both learnable and teachable, regardless of the learner's age. In addition to the theoretical underpinnings for this notion cited above, we will here elaborate on a few more crucial concepts.

The focal point of this study is the concept of interlanguage or IL, defined by Cook (1993: 17) as a linguistic system developed by an L2 learner which does not conform to either L1 (the first language of the learner) or L2 (the learner's second language) rules. Nemser (1971) first captured the phenomenon using the term 'approximative system'. The term *interlanguage* itself was first introduced by Larry Selinker (1972), who claims that IL depends on five central processes: (1) language transfer, (2) overgeneralisation of L2 rules, (3) transfer of training, (4) strategies of L2 learning, and (5) communication strategies. Thus Selinker postulates both an independent grammar and a psychological process leading to IL creation (Cook, 1993: 19). The research of the processes is largely indirect in nature and is not the subject of this book. The grammar, on the other hand, as captured at a particular stage of IL development, is a viable subject of empirical linguistic research and is used here to find out about the particular linguistic challenges of the target population.

The criticism that has often been levelled at the observational data research in SLA is that it bases its conclusions regarding competence on mere analysis of performance (Cook, 1993: 49). Competence and performance as used here go back to Chomsky (1965), who defines 'competence' as speaker's knowledge and 'performance' as the use of language in concrete situations. Competence as a mental reality is hardly accessible directly and can be only assessed indirectly through performance. From the perspective of instructed L2 acquisition, Ellis (1997: 101) advocates 'proficiency' as the centrepiece of SLA theory. Proficiency according to Widdowson (1983 cited in Ellis, 1997: 101) is the 'capacity to produce and understand utterances by using the resources of grammar in association with features of context to make meaning'. However, no matter what capacity is addressed by theory, empirical research will still have to be restricted to analysing language production data, a process that is sometimes referred to as performance analysis (PA) (James, 1998: 18), which is the case in this study.

Another concept relied upon here is that of error analysis (EA). Error analysis approaches L2 learning in terms of detailed analysis of the learner's output (Cook, 1993: 20). Corder (1967) views errors as evidence of L2 learners testing out their hypotheses about the target language.

According to James (1998: 5) the paradigm of EA involves objective description of learners' IL and is therefore a methodology dealing with data (Cook 1993: 22). Data elicitation in this study falls between the two categories postulated by James (1998: 19) as 'broad trawl' error elicitation and 'targeted elicitation'. The former means gaining the first impression of the learner's limitations, whereas the latter targets the specific areas in which errors are anticipated. Thus anecdotal evidence suggests that the high stake errors, those that put the student at risk of failing university courses, are often syntactic in nature and regularly occur in academic writing. Based on those criteria, targeted elicitation (James, 1998: 20) could proceed within an observational framework to take samples of writing of the most at-risk students, those enrolled in a remedial writing course, English for Academic Purposes (EAP) I.

Given the evidence of errors committed by the target population, the purpose of the parser depicted in this study is either to prevent or undo fossilisation. This is defined by Selinker (1972) as 'the long term persistence of plateaus of non-target-like structures in the interlanguage (IL) of non-native speakers'. Selinker (1972) believes that any of the above mentioned five processes of IL could 'force fossilizable material upon surface IL utterances'. According to Selinker and Lakshmanan (1993), fossilisation can be partially explained by the multiple effects principle (MEP). In brief, this principle applies when two or more SLA factors work together to prevent the learner from internalising the correct linguistic item, thus having a more permanent effect on the retention of incorrect forms.

The task of countering the forces of pending or existing fossilisation becomes even more daunting when one considers the fact that SLA theory has not always provided support for error correction as a means of explicit L2 instruction (James, 1998). For example, the Universal Grammar (UG) proponents in SLA do not seem to believe that L2 is fully learnable by adults, which is attributed to the lack of access to UG principles in this population (Cook, 1993: 211). Not even explicit instruction or awareness raising are deemed helpful (Selinker & Lakshmanan, 1993). Children, on the other hand, are claimed to have access to UG in the process of L2 learning, which seems to explain why they are able to avoid fossilisation. Hope for adult learners, however, comes from other SLA sources. A theoretical one is the Teachability Hypothesis (Pienemann, 1989), which postulates that an L2 structure can be learnt from instruction when the learner's interlanguage is at a point of development where this structure is naturally acquired. Empirical studies (Pavesi, 1986; Harley, 1993) corroborate the value of explicit instruction and error correction. The latter is seen as a means of bringing about de-fossilisation. In addition, a study by Ehri, Gibbs and Underwood (1988 cited in James, 1998: 242) as well as that by Spada and Lightbown (1993) underlines the value of regular, contextualised and immediate correction, which prevents errors from being fossilised. Indeed, adult L2 students seem intuitively to feel that correction is exactly what they need (Willing, 1988). Thus the parser in this study has immediate, regular and contextualised error correction as one of its main goals.

Error correction referred to in this text has a twofold purpose. One is Consciousness Raising (CR) or explanation and the other is Language Awareness (LA) or explication (James, 1998: 260). According to James (1998) the former means helping learners to notice what they do not know, while the latter means providing explicit insight into something that learners already know implicitly. In this study, CR occurs when the parser encounters one of the typical errors it is familiar with. By offering an array of reactions, the parser tries to decide whether this is a slip, an odd mistake or a systemic error (James, 1998). A slip is expected to result in self-correction, a mistake calls for feedback, in this case a clue to the required structure, and error calls for full correction of the erroneous structure. Each instance of self-correction, whether preceded by a clue or not is followed by explication or the parse tree that reveals the details of grammatical structure for that particular sentence. Thus the learner is made aware of what he or she may already know implicitly.

The user interface that enables access to the parser is designed as a dialogue in which the computer generated questions to be answered by the user are designed if not to induce the error itself, so at least to induce an attempt at producing the potentially problematic structure. Two studies by Tomasello and Herron (1988, 1989 cited in Ellis, 1997) present some empirical evidence in favour of inducing errors and offering overt feedback. If correction is understood as explicit instruction (James, 1998), this constitutes proof that instructed L2 learning can be effective. Moreover, James (1998) argues that error correction as a curative way of instruction is more effective than preventive instruction based on error avoidance. Considering the integration of all the above methods and principles, the tutor described here seems to have considerable potential for supporting L2 learning.

The evidence briefly listed above as well as a multitude of other empirical studies that for the reasons of space constraints shall remain unmentioned here clearly testify to the fact that a second language can be learnt by adults and that pursuing this goal is therefore worth every effort. One of the reasons why this is not always recognised lies in what Cook (1993) calls the 'monolingual prejudice'. The phrase denotes the tacit expectation that L2 learners will add another L1 to their repertoire, which Cook (1993) juxtaposes with his own term – multi-competence. The latter covers all stages of L2 acquisition. Thus according to Cook (1993) the aim in SLA should not be producing a monolingual in two different languages, but a competence that is radically different, i.e. the multi-competence. This approach avoids the pitfalls of setting the unattainable standards for L2 learners and so does the approach taken in this study by recognising that the path to L2 knowledge is strewn with errors.

Agenda for Needs Analysis

Let us now recapitulate what we know about our students and their language learning abilities. We know that, regardless of their age and circumstances, they are able to improve in English as their second language, provided they are motivated, have the right attitude toward English and its native speakers, are in a culturally acceptable and non-threatening setting and are instructed in a way that meets their learning needs as well as their cognitive, affective and other personality traits. Raising their awareness and consciousness of linguistic form should be one of the main objectives of the electronic tutor, paired with the goal of utilising and sometimes challenging their learning strategies while providing plenty of input as well as opportunities for practice and feedback.

What we do not know about our EAP students boils down to a number of variables. Even though we may for instance know a person's language proficiency expressed in terms of IELTS or TOEFL scores, we may be well and truly unable to outline their actual interlanguage. For this reason, we need to pinpoint the characteristics of their IL, both in terms of omissions (i.e. those areas that are missing in their production) and typical errors. Next we have to find out what the target performance should be, at all levels, linguistic, textual and contextual. We also need to profile their beliefs about L2 learning, their motivation, cognitive styles and learning strategies. As they will be using a computerised tutor, we also need to know about their familiarity with the medium computer, their attitude toward it, and their beliefs about computer assisted language learning (CALL).

Collated, all this information will assist us in designing the right tutor for our specific target audience. In order to design this tutor we need to obtain a set of design specifications which will be based on what we already know about our student population as well as on the information that we are yet to obtain. The latter pertains to the entire array of individual and group variables such as the linguistic, cognitive, affective, sociocultural and other personality factors. We will collect this information by using a range of data collection techniques, including questionnaire surveys and document analysis based on a number of linguistic approaches. The theoretical background that we have already researched in this chapter along with the results of our own research will constitute the first critical step in the complex and non-linear process of instructional software development. Thus, instructional software development, being a learner centred activity, will undergo all the necessary stages known from best practice (Hemard & Cushion, 1999) including needs analysis, specification drafting, design, development and evaluation. The latter is subdivided into formative and summative evaluation, with the formative evaluation running parallel to the development process and summative evaluation following the development phase (Levy, 1997b).

The importance of needs analysis within the realm of software engineering coincides with the increased attention paid to needs analysis in second language teaching (Munby, 1981; Willing, 1988; Reid, 2001; Doughty & Long, 2003). Drawing on the findings of SLA research, Chapelle (1998) recommends that the following should inform the design of hypermedia learning environments: (1) making salient the linguistic features of L2, (2) offering modification of linguistic input based on learner needs, (3) providing opportunities for the learner to produce comprehensible output, (4) enabling learners to identify their errors, (5) providing means for learners to correct their output, (6) supporting interaction between user and computer, and (7) enabling the user to accomplish a communicative task. These are of course specific to the communicative learning theory.

An intelligent tutor containing a parser, the device of natural language processing (NLP) would account for meeting the first six of the seven requirements outlined by Chapelle. It would make salient linguistic features of L2 by much more sophisticated means than originally suggested by Chapelle (1998). While Chapelle (1998) proposes that this be achieved through colour or highlighting alternatively, our parser would return a parse tree for any L2 sentence, using metalanguage, which is not necessarily a part of the communicative approach (Lightbown, 1998). In addition, a concordancing tool enabling searches on salient linguistic features would help the students clearly identify the paradigms on a number of language samples. The intelligent tutor would enable not only help and hints, but also access to lessons specifically designed to help with the item dealt with as well as accessories such as dictionaries, glossaries, encyclopedias, thesauri, quizzes and relevant current pages anywhere on the Web. The learners will be able to produce comprehensible output by typing it in on the parser prompt. The parser would in turn analyse it and identify their error precisely with various options for the correction. This procedure would be well supported by clear interaction strategies between the learner and the interface. Finally, even though the communication with the parser would be similar to that with other humans, thus classifying as what is called 'natural communication' (Marsic *et al.*, 2000), the learner would have instant access to email, electronic bulletin boards and chat relays. In addition, the teacher could provide more comprehensive feedback by using a semi-automatic marking tool for longer written output.

As discussed above, the parser would not be the only module used in the intelligent tutor, nor would natural language processing be the only technology applied. To the contrary, the software is meant to include a whole range of interactive tools and hypermedia add-ons, all to be used within a curricular structure that had worked in focus-on-form instruction for Harley (1998). The ideal platform for such a comprehensive coverage is the Web. For this reason, the entire set-up was going to be Web-browser readable and placed on a Web server. This would not only enable the flexi-bility for the learner to use it in her own space and time without having to provide for platform transferability and portability herself, but would also allow quick and easy access to useful current Web pages designed elsewhere. However, the integration of locally run material stored on other media would still be available and easily integrated.

Thus, the learner would be able to access in the first place the informa-tion about a relevant topic. Secondly, the user could utilise various on-line tools, i.e. dictionaries, glossaries, concordances, etc. to make both the input and output comprehensible. Lastly, the software would contain particu-larly interactive elements. In the order of interactivity they are tutorials paced at the student's progress rate, quizzes, and of course the parser module. Therefore, the computer would play a dual role in the process of learning: of a tutor and a tool. Levy (1999) calls this a hybrid system, whereas Bradin Siskin (2004) prefers the term blended learning. According to Levy (1997a: 210), the role of the computer as a tutor is central to the process, whereas its role as a tool is supplementary. While the tutor evaluates student output, the tool does not (Levy, 1999). According to Higgins (1988) the computer would have the role of both the tutor and the pedagogue or the teacher who directs the learning process and the one who is directed by the student's interests respectively. The former is similar to Levy's (1997b) notion of tutor in that it follows its own structured syllabus, while the pedagogue, just like the ancient Greek slave teacher after whom it is named, answers the student-generated questions. While to some the clear line between tutor and tool appears to be more and more blurred (Bradin Siskin, 2004), others discriminate against the tutor and in favour of the tool (Wolff, 1999). It is, however, not clear that either of these extremes even contemplate artificial intelligence as an option. We will describe the entire system Academic English on the Web as a hybrid system or a blended environment with the Intelligent Tutor as its tutor component capable of correcting some learner errors.

Based on what we know therefore about both our students and the criteria for successful instructional hypermedia design, the following software layout emerges: (1) hypertext course notes, (2) interactive tasks, (3) grammar and vocabulary tests, (4) essay marking aid, and (5) a corpus explorer (Dodigovic, 1998).

(1) The hypertext course notes are mainly text with hypertext links between the lecture notes, essay readings and a number of external resources, including CD-ROM multimedia dictionaries, concord-

ancing software, pronunciation aids or simply external Web sites, email, bulletin boards and chat relays.

(2) The interactive tasks are closely related to concepts explained in the notes, thus providing individualised feedback within a learner centred approach. This module contains a considerable innovation in an EAP learning package: an intelligent parser based interface capable of analysing student sentences for grammatical correctness. If desired, the learner can also use this interface in a more structured way, allowing it to ask her questions about the essay topic that will reveal one of the possible organisational patterns for the essay on the topic. Some tasks will require human–human communication through email, bulletin boards and chat relays.

(3) Grammar and vocabulary tests are automatic assessment tools designed to free up the lecturer for more creative tasks, like research or a more individualised approach to teaching.

(4) Essay marking aid provides the means for delivering feedback in a more efficient way. Based on research of individual and group variables, student errors are classified into several distinctive groups. Providing comment on them is possible by choosing an appropriate sentence from the database on the click of a button.

(5) The corpus explorer enables the user to search for examples of use of a particular word in a body of academic writing. The user has a choice of various commercially available or research based corpora.

All modules are interconnected via hypertext links and can be used for tutorial or non-tutorial learning. Our theorising has thus led us to a very practical step – outlining the specification framework for a tutor from which we expect to contribute to much L2 learning. This is the Intelligent Tutor, a device that can identify and correct some of the most persistent learner errors. The device is, however, used in a rich on-line learning context, connected to the curriculum, as outlined in the five points above.

We have so far reviewed the SLA literature in light of our hypothesis that the EAP students studying in an English speaking university program in an English speaking country will be able to learn certain grammar features of the target language that are either likely to or have already erroneously fossilised in their interlanguage. Cognitive and interactionist theories along with research findings give us hope that it is not too late for our adult students, including Eric and Jean, to expect an improvement in their L2. In an effort to assist them toward that goal, we will design an artificially intelligent tutor embedded in a hypermedia Web based environment, which is related to their curriculum. In order to achieve a perfect fit between the learner needs and the facilities of the tutor, we have examined what we already know from research and theory that is generally applicable to our student population. Chapter 5 will set out to describe the research concerning the unknown individual cognitive, affective and other variables pertaining to the target student population. Subsequently the results will be presented in the light of a number of relevant theories and how they facilitated software development will be explained. Before, however, proceeding to describe the research activities, this volume will discuss the use of the Web and artificial intelligence in an EAP setting. First and foremost though, the next chapter will examine the current views of the role of research in CALL development projects within their epistemological context.

Chapter 2

Where Does Research End and CALL Development Begin?

Research Opportunities: Developmental and Evaluative

In a systematic approach to identifying the ESL (English as a second language) learning needs of a group of NNS students at an English speaking university, the computer was identified as a possibly ideal medium of remedial instruction as well as a potentially promising learning aid. The discipline that is pertinent to this endeavour is nowadays widely recognised as that of Computer Assisted Language Learning (CALL). One of its most prominent theorists, Mike Levy (1997b: 1), defines CALL as 'the search for and study of applications of the computer in language teaching and learning'. He associates its development with the development of the medium of computer. However, Levy (1997b) as well as Chapelle (2001) recognise the interdisciplinary nature of CALL and the input a range of other disciplines have had on its development. Both of these authors acknowledge the fact that research has a place in CALL, especially in CALL development projects (Levy, 1997a, 1997b, 1999; Chapelle, 2001; Chapelle *et al.*, 1996; Chapelle, 1997). In our own CALL development project research plays a very important part, in a way that is perhaps different from the role it has in the majority of published CALL studies. While in this study research is used for the purposes of needs analysis and formative as well as summative evaluation (or the equivalent as will be seen in Chapter 6), in other projects it is mostly used for the purposes of summative evaluation or SLA theory testing (see Levy, 1999). Formative evaluation is conducted during the development, whereas the summative evaluation is conducted on completion of a software development project (Boyle 1997, cited in Levy, 1997b: 98). The difference in research approaches prompts us to examine carefully the contexts and the purposes of research in CALL development projects in general.

It is difficult to imagine a good CALL development project which would be completely detached from research. Much like applied linguistics (Ellis, 1997) to which it is closely related, this area requires a multidisciplinary approach to software design and implementation, drawing all the time on the leading edge research in disciplines such as linguistics, sociolinguistics, phonology, language acquisition, psychology, learning theory, instruction methodology and software engineering. Bringing these disciplines together poses new research questions to be answered in the course of development activities. Very often CALL programs are intended to address a particular learning problem, which requires a scientific explanation in the first place, or they need to be based on a teaching method which can only be confirmed and justified upon implementation. Whatever the CALL development project, research often seems to be an important part of it (Levy, 1997b); yet, it was not until the late 1990s that the apparent lack of documented research in this area (Cameron, 1997; Brett, 1998) had begun to close. Recent years have seen a cline in the number of contributions addressing the issue of research in CALL, each trying in its own way to determine the purpose and the directions for CALL related research. Shedding light on this difference in views might be conducive to understanding the role of research underlying this particular project.

Approaches to CALL related research seem generally to fall into one of the following two categories: (1) development oriented, and (2) effect oriented. These roughly correspond to two stages in instructional development that lend themselves to research, i.e. needs analysis and evaluation (McDonough & McDonough, 1997). The former comes from a traditionally CALL focused milieu and is concerned among other things with producing better, more relevant CALL programs. The latter, though also a concern of CALL software developers, in its exclusive form seems to be advocated primarily by SLA circles and is mainly concerned with the effect of CALL materials on learners. Development oriented research is listed as a viable option in Levy (1999: 100): ' . . . investigating learner differences in specific CALL contexts using a variety of data collection devices . . . using research to inform and develop a taxonomy of tasks for tool-based uses of the computer . . . ' The Joint Policy Statement of three CALL organisations, EUROCALL, CALICO and IALL underlines a similar view: 'Crucially, of course, CALL research also includes developmental and prototypal computing' (Davies, 2001: 26). To sum up, developmental research would include all systematic investigative activities preceding and accompanying the design phase in the cycle of CALL software development, e.g. learner interlanguage or target register profiling, surveying cognitive, affective, social and other learner related variables, investigating a particular instructional method or systematically collecting performance data on a particular computational technique as well as testing out design elements during the development phase. Effect oriented research on the other hand is best exemplified in Chapelle *et al.* (1996). The research options for CALL listed in this paper are restricted to examining the effects of CALL software on learners, be it in terms of psychometric, interactionist, ethnographic or discourse analysis tradition (Chapelle *et al.*, 1996), which are discussed in the following paragraph. Thus, effect oriented research has no claim over the design accompanying activities in the cycle of software development. It observes the consequences that the application of a CALL program or a general software tool may have.

The term 'effect' as used here might cause some confusion, given that Chapelle *et al.* (1996: 33) use it in a more restricted sense when referring to the psychometric tradition in CALL research. This is the early approach seeking to evaluate the effectiveness of electronic tutors and to some extent justify the then high costs associated with developing software (Dodigovic, 1995). However, Chapelle *et al.* (1996: 33) use this term in a more specific sense i.e. 'the effects of CALL on learning outcomes', which often translates into cognitive or affective outcomes. Let us now explain the SLA specific research methods as advocated for CALL applications by Chapelle *et al.* (1996). Psychometric research is primarily interested in how much the students have learnt using a piece of software or what their attitude towards it was, which places it in the tradition of confirmatory empirical enquiry (Ellis, 1997). According to Ellis (1997), confirmatory research is interventionist in nature by seeking to establish whether the object of investigation is viable in some respect. By contrast, the interpretive tradition is merely seeking to understand the object of its investigation (Ellis, 1997) and can be seen as a broad term to describe the rest of SLA research strategies identified by Chapelle *et al.* (1996). These strategies are interaction analysis, discourse analysis and ethnographic research. Interaction analysis documents specific teacher and learner behaviours in the classroom, in an attempt to interpret them. The object of interest in discourse analysis oriented research are types of discourse functions generated during the interaction of students with the computer, with each other and with the teacher. Finally, ethnographic research in CALL is concerned with a holistic approach to the CALL classroom, while its main concern is whether CALL can create an empowering learning environment. This type of research examines everything within the given context and seeks to establish relations between all its components. What all of the above approaches have in common, except for being qualitative or interpretive (McDonough & McDonough, 1997), is an ex-post-facto chronology, i.e. the research takes place after the software has been developed and introduced in a learning situation. Thus, what remains to observe are its *effects* rather than its causes.

Garry Motteram (1999) is sceptical in regard to the proposal that CALL research be exclusively aligned with SLA objectives (Chapelle *et al.*, 1996). He, just like Ellis (1997) and McDonough and McDonough (1997), is also concerned to see the language teaching process more firmly integrated into classroom research paradigm, thus making the teacher central to the process, rather than having the teacher as an external consumer of research. Having the teacher involved would not only have positive outcomes for the teaching process but would make research meaningfully connected to the classroom practice. The kind of research referred to here is called action research (Ellis, 1997; McDonough & McDonough, 1997) and will be revisited shortly in this section. Motteram (1999: 206) also proposes that the research paradigm adopted for the purpose of CALL be qualitative, which according to the author ideally matches the classroom practice, where the variables cannot always be controlled. In an effort to see CALL aligned much more broadly with an array of disciplines practising qualitative research, he suggests to adopt the four types of qualitative research methodology: case study, ethnography, phenomenology and grounded theory. While case study refers to an attempt to understand a single case in-depth, ethnography seeks to understand the relationship between behaviour and culture. Phenomenology on the other hand seeks to describe the experience from the participants' point of view, whereas a grounded theory links the participants' perspectives to general social science theories. Thus, Motteram (1999) views CALL as an integral part of social sciences, a perspective, which however valid, leaves out the vital link to the technology and its design. Thus, as a non-developer, he also seems to adopt an effect oriented approach.

While the research methods described above can yield valuable data, Nunan (1992: 11–12) cautions against inappropriate assertions that might occasionally arise from studies using some of these or in fact any other research methods. In particular, individual case studies cannot be expected to yield widely generalisable results, while ethnographies may not compare well enough to allow for any generalisations (Nunan, 1992; McDonough & McDonough, 1997). The assumption here is that at some level, research in general, although not necessarily every study, should be able to lead to some generalisations about certain objects of interest if it is to be relevant to the community at large. It is however often argued that by triangulation and compilation of a large body of data on a single problem, action research, which often resorts to interpretive of qualitative methods, can lend itself to generalisation (Ellis, 1997; McDonough & McDonough, 1997).

Mike Levy (1999) on the other hand recognises the importance of theory testing and therefore post-developmental, effect oriented research. However, he also stresses the significance of the learning context and the characteristics of the learner, including the ways they interact with a particular software design. All of these are presented as valid points of departure for CALL research and all have a role in developmental research. His concern is therefore to create enough specificity in research design and thus avoid overgeneralisation. He does not see a need to restrict research methods to any particular type. Levy's position here and elsewhere (1997a; 1997b) is that of a CALL software developer with a deep intellectual interest in understanding his subject and placing it within a broader framework of human thought.

The research questions anticipated for CALL in the near future suggest that there are a variety of perspectives and research approaches. Phil Hubbard (2003) has for example collected a number of worthwhile research questions articulated by a considerable number of CALL practitioners around the globe and organised them around the emerging theme patterns. Thus, research needs are seen in the areas of software or CALL activity design, computational modelling of teacher and learner expertise, content and learner engagement, corpus-informed learning, development models, evaluation, human–computer interface, multimedia tools and physical environment issues. Many, if not all of these issues are developmental issues and thus indicate that the research focus in CALL is shifting from the purely effect oriented to one that is concerned with developmental matters as well. A recent study by Levy (2000) also indicates a smaller number of CALL research publications devoted to evaluation issues.

The fundamental difference between the two approaches to research in CALL, developmental and effect oriented, has been categorised elsewhere (Weiss, 1997 cited in Ellis, 1997) as the difference between a *decision-driven model* and *knowledge-driven model* of research. Whereas the decision-driven model is aimed at informing a particular decision, e.g. which approach to take in instructional software design, the knowledge-driven model aims to advance a knowledge base of a discipline. While the former may have a practitioner in view as the target audience, the latter is devised for other academics, thus being perhaps less accessible to the teacher-practitioner.

We stipulated before that as regards CALL, these two research models, knowledge-driven and data-driven, are being mainly supported from within two different camps – those of SLA theorists and those of CALL developers and practitioners respectively. Not surprisingly, SLA has often been criticised for its knowledge-driven approach to research and the ensuing lack of applicability to the teaching practice (Larsen-Freeman & Long, 1991; Nunan, 1992; Ellis, 1997; Motteram, 1999). On the other hand, the technology-driven model in decision making about software development has been depicted as one of the notorious practices of CALL leading to poor quality software (Levy, 1997b). Thus disciplines seem to drift apart in both their beliefs and practices. This trend toward the separation of disciplines, which is sometimes referred to as separatism, is explained by Cook and Seidlhofer (1995: 1) in terms of being an easy option for any discipline. Cook and Seidlhofer (1995: 1) differentiate between inter-disciplinary separatism 'which ignores other areas of enquiry' and 'intra-disciplinary separatism which creates manageable sub-disciplines'. Accordingly, the support for data-driven research from the CALL developer camp coincides with interdisciplinary separatism, being an attempt to hedge out CALL toward all other disciplines, including SLA. On the other hand, the support for knowledge-driven research comes from the position of intradisciplinary separatism, reflected in the fact that CALL is perceived as a subdiscipline of SLA.

Cook and Seidlhofer (1995: 2) point out that certain objects of enquiry, if not perhaps all of them, do not necessarily lend themselves to isolationism and highlight language as the epitome of such an object. If language alone in its complexity and relatedness to all human issues defies compartmentalisation, then how much more should CALL resist being boxed into the square outlined for it by SLA theorists or indeed any other group. As early as 1992 an emerging self-awareness of the then young discipline of CALL suggested a projected image of itself as that of being interdisciplinary. Following an international CALICO conference in Maastricht, titled 'Bridges', the 1993 volume of the CALICO Journal brings out the interdisciplinary perspective of CALL as a positive virtue. In fact SLA itself is often depicted as interdisciplinary by its theorists (Cook, 1993; Larsen-Freeman & Long, 1991; Ellis, 1997) and prone to multiple perspectives. Therefore it surprises that precisely the SLA theory would want to confine CALL to a territory much smaller than it already occupies. While SLA deals with a range of issues including language as both construct and a social and pragmatic reality, the learner as a complex social being, an individual and a marvellous living organism as well as with the learning processes, the area of CALL encompasses all these and much, much more. CALL has its one foot firmly on the IT ground, including issues such as hardware platforms, software engineering, ergonomic principles, electronic communications and access and equity issues. These things do not simply add on to a string of independent variables, but produce a new quality, which can benefit from a multiplicity of ever changing angels and perspectives. Thus, SLA research definitely has a common ground with CALL, but there are inevitably areas in which each produces its own unique values and insights, none of which should be discarded for the sake of the other.

> What this pattern of thought suggests is an unusual ability to engage two ways of seeing simultaneously, to hold a contradiction, not to surrender to the easier intellectual option of seeing different perspectives as exclusive alternatives and then professing allegiance to only one. (Cook & Seidlhofer, 1995: 12)

Following the above observations about Widdowson made by Cook and Seidlhofer (1995), this book subscribes to both views of CALL specific research, development oriented or decision driven as well as effect oriented or knowledge driven. In fact, while trying to integrate practical and technical knowledge in its attempt at understanding a particular learning challenge to a particular population of students and providing a suitable answer, it promotes an *interactive model* of research (Ellis, 1997), which includes the practitioner as well as the researcher and does not always follow the straight path from research to decision making or vice versa.

Thus described, it fits perfectly into the framework of *action research*, by bridging the gap between researcher and teacher (Ellis, 1997; McDonough & McDonough, 1997) and answers the needs of learner centred CALL software development (Hemard & Cushion, 1999), whose primary focus is on the learners and their learning needs, rather than on testing a particular SLA theory on an unspecified learner. That said, testing an SLA theory is seen as a perfectly legitimate goal for CALL research, so long as it does not neglect the specificity of the learner (Oxford, 1995) and the given learning environment (McDonough & McDonough, 1997). The better part of the book is dedicated to depicting a series of research projects from the development oriented category. In contrast with the SLA theorists' view of CALL related research, this book takes the view that research can and sometimes legitimately needs to either precede the development of CALL programs or accompany it at various stages, especially if one is interested in designing a program that is informed by the knowledge of a particular student population, their learning habits, their interlanguage or a particular register of the target language to be taught. Nonetheless, research should also follow the application of the thus developed CALL software. Therefore, the life cycle of a software program can be said to have completed a full cycle – from research, via development back to research. Hence the approach to research in CALL should not necessarily be viewed as a linear one, which is discussed in more detail in the following section.

Research vs. Development in CALL

Why is research not uniformly seen and recognised as a constituent part in CALL development projects? These are the questions asked by Dodigovic (1998) and Davies (2001). The reasons can be sought both within the area of CALL and outside it. Within CALL, the most common obstacles seem to be either political or technological in nature. These can however only be understood when the context outside CALL is given proper consideration. A possible answer outside CALL can be found in sciences, which tend to keep development apart from research, claiming that development is a mere application of research results (Valter, 1988). Similar view can be found in the Macquarie Dictionary (1996), which defines the term *research and development* as 'that part of industry concerned with scientific research and the technological development of the results'. Maybe it is this very distinction that seems to bipolarise the CALL developers themselves. Mike Levy (1997b) finds that the area of CALL development is divided between those who make a particular theory their point of departure (formalists), and those who make discoveries by writing programs (proceduralists). The former appear to think that completed research is a prerequisite for successful development, whereas the latter seem to allow for the integration of research into the development process.

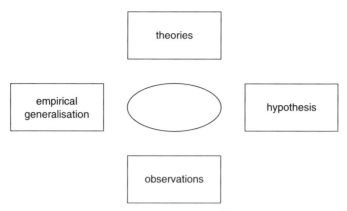

Figure 2.1 Circular model of scholarly enquiry[1]

In his extremely thoughtful essay on theory driven CALL, Mike Levy (1997b) acknowledges the fact that revision of the original theory is a recurrent factor when development is undertaken in a multidisciplinary area such as CALL. This means that knowledge gained in the course of development feeds back into the theory, thus altering and improving it. Therefore, the research process is far from completed when a theory is selected to serve as a basis for a CALL development project. This insight coincides with a contemporary circular approach to scientific method (Lewins, 1990), which presents research activity as a circle where a theory is followed by a hypothesis resulting in observation, which in turn leads to empirical generalisation having an effect on the theory itself. According to this model, theory is not the only valid starting point for research activities; research can legitimately start at any of the four stages in the cycle.

Figure 2.1 breaks away from the previously held linear approach to research (Lewins, 1990), which starts out with a theory or a hypothesis, continues with collection and classification of data, and concludes with generalisations. Although maybe perplexing for some scholars, the circular view of the scientific method seems to gain acceptance in the academia (Lewins, 1990; Levy 1997a, Little, 1998 cited in Motteram, 1999). The concept of action research (Nunan, 1992; Ellis, 1997; McDonough & McDonough, 1997; Motteram, 1999) itself in fact coincides with the changed notion of research paradigm. Yet, the very acceptance of the circular research model poses again the crucial question: Why is CALL development unlikely to be treated as a research activity, despite the fact that it can change and refine theories and provide systematic inquiry into the subject in order to gain new knowledge? The only plausible answer to this question seems to be the difference between the academia as an institution (Dodigovic, 1993) and the approach to scientific method as a theory or belief held by a number of academics. Theories and beliefs are the first to change; there is less inertia in this area than there is in the institution. This is however only likely to happen when the new beliefs can mobilise and exploit the already existing conceptual schemata (Rogers, 1983). The institution itself can only change to accommodate a new model when that model has been comfortably accepted by the majority of its members (Petkovic, 1984). The academia, as an institution, still greatly relies on the linear method, so it may take some time for it to adapt to the changes dictated by the new insights in epistemology.

The above discussion is based on the views of the Russian school of semiotic (Petkovic 1984), according to which culture is seen as a finite set of conventions, having a *centre* (the standard, high culture or canonical forms), a *periphery* (substandard or subculture) and a border (to divide culture from non-culture or a culture from another culture). The changes in a culture, either coming from within (*evolution*) or without (*genesis*) always occur at the periphery, so that every innovation at first has the stigma of being a substandard form. The academia as an institution is a culture in its own right, and therefore a new perception of the scientific method, as being circular rather than linear, has still a somewhat peripheral position. However, culture is seen as dynamic, which means that substandard forms, if supported, are likely to move from the periphery towards the centre, and eventually become the standard themselves, which will probably be the case with the circular view of the scientific method at a certain point in time. If and when this happens, it will be due to the fact that the notion itself is compatible with the current beliefs and practices of the accepting population (Rogers, 1983). In fact, the emergence of action research testifies to the compatibility of circular research schema with the practitioners' belief that research should not be external to the teaching practice, as is the case with the linear research model. However, the resilience of knowledge-driven research model in disciplines such as SLA indicates that the time for a more general acceptance of the circular research model is yet to come. Until then, there will be a constant need, as there always is within a culture, to bridge the gap between the no longer adequate standard and the growing substandard form.

Further to this discussion, Davies (2001) identifies the following obstacles to a wider acceptance of CALL related research: (1) concerns about its validity, (2) institutional politics favouring 'pure' research, and (3) limited availability of designated funding for this area. These are largely due to the linear view of research and can be seen as reasons outside CALL. Indeed, the traditional linear model influences the whole infrastructure of CALL development funding, frequently requiring that the development funds be provided by trusts different from research agencies. In turn, research funding bodies may fail to see the value of CALL research other than a contribution to the scholarship of teaching, which is sometimes grounds enough to refuse funding. In addition, academics seeking funding for their CALL development projects which incorporate some explicitly formulated research are likely to be refused funding on the grounds of their proposal being research and not development oriented. Few academics have the time and energy to submit two separate applications – one for research, one for development. They are more likely to apply for funding from one source, in order to minimise not only the administrative effort invested in the application, but also the risk of obtaining none or only one of the grants where two are really necessary to succeed. Finally, even where funding is granted, it can easily discontinue, leaving costly unfinished projects stranded (Holland, 1995).

Thus, economic rationalism seems to be another barrier that keeps CALL development officially apart from research. Anecdotal evidence relates that European LINGUA agency specialised in funding language learning development programs was at the beginning overly concerned to exclude research from CALL development applications, the reason being the fear that research activities would lead to research papers rather than to practical software solutions. Apart from the development rationalisation occurring in the academia, the CALL development conducted in commercial institutions must be facing a similar, if not even more restrictive set of regulations. These indicate a production floor view of research as being predominantly knowledge driven and therefore irrelevant to decision making process. Cook and Seidlhofer (1995: 1) call this line of thinking the divorce of theory from practice, which to them is also a form of separatism.

Finally, there is a major reason within CALL itself that prevents research from being considered in development projects. As pointed out by Levy (1997b), some of the CALL development projects are mainly technology driven. They do not pay enough attention to linguistic or methodological implications of the program, but appear to be spurred by what the computer can or cannot do. Even though there may be a lot of potential for research in such projects, the developers seem not to take notice of it, so the development project fails to deliver new theoretical insights. This situation can be explained by the fact that, from the semiotic point of view (Petkovic, 1984), CALL itself is still a substandard or peripheral discipline, sometimes seen as one big experiment (Chapelle, 1997), so that it does not necessarily conform to the canonical procedure of the establishment. In other words, CALL fashioned in this way embraces interdisciplinary separatism (Cook & Seidlhofer, 1995) by upholding the belief that theory has nothing to do with practice.

The divorce of theory from practice is even supported by the academia. At some universities, research grants tend to be valued more than development grants in terms of career management, to the extent that junior academics often refrain from applying for development grants in order to be free for what is considered to be pure research. In the academia, CALL is obviously perceived as practice only. In support of this assertion, Davies (2001: 21) relates that even engaging in CALL activities often confronts the CALL researchers with an uncomfortable choice to either migrate to an IT department, where their efforts receive more recognition, or simply give up their CALL ambitions, both of which inflict a considerable loss on language departments. In this way, the study of language is forcefully separated from what is not perceived as language. 'The discipline becomes a federation of academic principalities with a common defence policy and tough immigration laws' (Cook & Seidlhofer, 1995: 2).

Thus, it takes some courage to embark on a CALL development project, considering the ramifications of a wise career choice. Being able to prove that there is room for research in CALL development seems to be a crucial step towards the emancipation of CALL as a discipline. Indeed, there are some noteworthy recent efforts to ascertain that CALL never runs out of research questions (Hubbard, 2003). After all, the academia is supposed to be dynamic and open to change (Petkovic, 1984), by the very virtue of being a culture of its own. A possible step towards that change may be to identify the research components in every intended CALL development project, to organise research projects around them, with or without separate funding and, most importantly, to present the results of these research projects in separate research publications (McDonough & McDonough, 1997). Such a strategy is not only likely to provide an answer in case of a personal career dilemma, but it is also likely to yield valuable contributions towards CALL as a research area, strengthening its position in the academic world, and with it the significance of every individual CALL researcher. Moreover, as pointed out by the proponents of action research (Ellis, 1997; McDonough & McDonough, 1997), a large body of action research on the same subject can contribute to a better understanding of the problem. In fact, as these lines are being written, prominent CALL conference organisers and publication editors seem to devote more and more time and space to research, which is quite likely to advance CALL as a discipline in general.

As discussed above, there are two strong reasons for failing to categorise CALL development activities as contributing to research, housed either inside or outside the discipline. The most compelling of these seems to be the linear approach to research, which comes from without CALL and is still strongly incorporated in the academic institution. This principle strictly differentiates between research and development in terms of funding, thus frequently placing the development outside the scope of research funding. The principle is also closely associated with a one-sided view of the research process as being mainly knowledge driven rather than decision driven. The second main reason comes from the discipline itself in the form of technology driven development. All of the above represent some form of separatism and could prevent a variety of research models in CALL from being planned and carried out.

CALL Research in its Context

In the previous sections we introduced a number of dichotomies related to CALL research, such as research/development, analysis/evaluation, theory/practice, CALL/SLA, development oriented/effect oriented, decision driven/knowledge driven, data driven/theory driven, linear/ circular. They were meant to help us examine the research issues in CALL from every angle and perspective, rather than stifling our view by the adoption of rigid categorisation. It is hoped that the complexity of this subject has been brought out without excessive theorising.

Very much like language teaching, to which it is closely associated, CALL exists, functions and develops in a complex social context, in which the often competing groups and subcultures seek to affirm and implement their ideas, ideologies and practices. It does therefore reflect the social, pragmatic and intellectual dynamic of society at large and the language teaching profession in particular. Thus CALL research does not stand in a socially unbiased vacuum, but reflects values, beliefs and theories coming from politically very different angles (McDonough & McDonough, 1997; Johns, 1997). Consequently we need to re-examine the ideals of logical posi- tivism and rationalism, which view research as a path to the objective and universally coherent truth leading to the linear progress of the society (Bigge & Shermis, 1999). In the light of post-modernism, the world is seen as 'decentered, destabilised, fragmented, indeterminate, incongruent, highlighted by difference, and open to question (*problematisation*) and challenge (*contestation*) because there is no ascertainable truth but rather just truth claims about reality' (Santos, 2001: 174). Therefore language loses its humanist categorisation as an unbiased medium and breaks apart into the discourses of social groups or disciplines. Thus discourse becomes a way to organise knowledge, meaning and identity, lending itself ideally to analysis or deconstruction, which will expose its particular ideology. As an interdisciplinary field, CALL has become a battlefield of 'feeder' discipline discourses. In the following we shall examine some of our own CALL ter- minology and its connections to the various discourses it originates from and then we will try to understand the implications of these connections. This does not mean that the book espouses the extreme belief of the critical theory, whose practice is being borrowed here, that human relations, including CALL, 'are nothing but political' (Santos, 2001: 181). It merely tries to comprehend the motivation of much of the CALL theory and practice in its synchronic and diachronic setting.

Claire Kramsch (1995) points out that due to its multidisciplinary nature, applied linguistics has become a repository of elements borrowed from various discourses. Here we will follow her example and compile a list of such loan terms while trying to explain how and why they are being used in the discussion of a particular CALL research and development project. The terms *interlanguage* and *learner needs* come from SLA theory, in particular from a 'democratic discourse that values learner autonomy . . . [and distrusts] any manipulation of a learner's interlanguage by social or political forces' (Kramsch, 1995: 50). *Communicative language learning* also comes from SLA, but it perceives learning as interaction. The terms *input* and *output* were originally borrowed from electrical engineering for the purpose of bringing applied linguistics more in line with prestigious upcoming fields of knowledge. Loans such as *language awareness, consciousness raising, saliency* come from psychology, sociology or education and fit with the notions of learning and teaching. The acronym *CALL*, along with the notions of *tutorial* and *non-tutorial, tutor or tool*, are a recent coinage developed within the framework of computer-assisted learning in general, which also reflect behaviourist and non-behaviourist approaches to CALL. The notion of *learning strategy* comes from cognitive psychology and psycholinguistics, while *objectives, outcomes* and *evaluation* are borrowed from the discourse of organisational management, the jargon of business and industry, 'to show efficiency, rentability and utility' (Kramsch, 1995: 47). *Natural communication, parsing and natural language processing* are taken from artificial intelligence and computational linguistics, which along with the name of the discipline itself are all based on the metaphoric use of human features when describing computers (Lakoff & Johnson, 1981). Finally, such vocabulary as *software specification, software engineering* and *user interface* all come from information science, the prestigious upcoming discipline of our era.

So far we have identified elements of a number of discourses in our own text, thus decomposing it and exposing its various sources. The sources however vary not only according to the discipline the expression was borrowed from, but also as to how they were going to be used and for what purpose. Prabhu (2001) distinguishes four different components, and we would say levels of meaning, to teaching theory and practice, which can be very well appropriated to CALL. These are the ideational, operational, ideological and managerial component. The ideational level encompasses knowledge of language and learning and teaching processes. In CALL it also includes knowledge of educational computing and natural language processing. The operational component includes practical experience as related to knowledge, while the ideological component involves the pursuit of an ideal. We have seen in the preceding paragraph that CALL has borrowed ideals from its feeder disciplines, which may be responsible for the variety of interests and pursuits within the discipline. Finally, the managerial component refers to decision making and planning in the teaching process, both at the individual teacher's and the institutional level.

In the case of our project, this component will include decisions regarding the choice of technology, areas for research, the structuring of the projects, the budgeting, the choice of the funding body or bodies to apply to for grants and the management of projects as units of financial accountability.

Thus this and other chapters of this book will reflect not only the ideational idiom borrowed from the disciplines related to CALL, but also the operational language of teacher intuition or the ideological discourse of social, institutional and commercial goals and finally the managerial jargon of project structuring and management. It follows that knowledge will only cover a part of our discourse. We can explain this by using Brumfit's (2001: 31) argument that post-modernism has greatly changed the attitude to knowledge encouraging disbelief in its privileged state of objectivity. As suggested by Kramsch (1995: 49) this also means that the book speaks to the position of a mediator between the communities of CALL and SLA specialists on the one hand and novices, the language learners and the academia as an institution on the other.

Identification of Research Components in a CALL Project

The importance of early planning

The identification of research components within a CALL development project should ideally start as early as the phase of needs analysis and planning. This is usually proposed by the supporters of the linear method (Manning, 1991), and even though not always feasible, it does have certain advantages, e.g. one can produce a neat time-line of activities, much appreciated by the funding bodies as an instrument that can be used for accountability purposes. This way, it becomes possible to point out the research potential of the project at an early stage and take appropriate steps to organise both the research and the development in an optimal way. The shortcoming of such an approach, of course, is that some questions for further research will not be identifiable until an advanced stage of the project. The institutional structure, however, being based on the expectation of linear scientific method, affects the choices available in research planning, having a strong preference for early identification.

Since instiutionalised research is also viewed in terms of being financially justifiable, individual projects are often seen as enterprises, which may or may not meet their intended objectives. The objectives in this case are often hypotheses to prove. Late identification of such hypotheses is then more likely to be seen as an unfortunate side-effect, rather than as a success of the project.

There are numerous opportunities for good research when developing a CALL package. Scholars conducting such development may, however, not be aware of the implications early research planning can have for the entire project, or cluster. For the purpose of this text, let cluster mean a major development project with all the research projects emerging from it. The institution is likely to support and gratify work on problems anticipated in advance. Yet, despite all the careful planning, by virtue of the very nature of the scientific method (Lewins, 1990), the unpredictable can happen. Even the most exciting discovery which requires that some further action be taken, will most probably, if not anticipated in advance, be regarded as a failure in financial planning. As a result, a new project would have to be drafted around that discovery, which then may yield results conflicting with those of the previous project from which it originally emerged. Consequences to consider here lie in the possibility that refuting the results of the previous research conducted by the same person could then be seen as a proof of cost-ineffectiveness of that previous research and therefore reason to refuse further funding. As suggested in literature:

> ... governments and other purse holders are unlikely to place their confidence in disciplines and individuals that they perceive as always changing identity, always courting change and confusion, always coming up with new theories only immediately to reveal their weaknesses. (Cook & Seidlhofer, 1995: 2)

Thus, ramifications are many and getting actively involved in CALL research seems a daunting task. However, it is not an impossible task. The solutions offered here will be based on the author's own experience in articulating her research needs within the context of CALL development. The following section will tie our discussion back to the CALL development project geared toward our particular population of EAP students. It will also present its context and introduce the disciplines relevant to the project as a whole.

Example cluster: Teaching Academic English on the Web

This section will provide more detail on research planning while also providing an example of what can be considered an early identification of research needs within a CALL development project. The project all the references are made to within this section is called *Teaching Academic English on the Web*. In particular one of its modules, the artificially intelligent Tutor interface, is in the focus of this book. The product as a whole was to enable the EAP program (English for Academic Purposes) at an Australian university to be extended in a flexible way to improve learning outcomes.

What we believed to know from theory and previous research about our EAP students, such as Eric and Jean, was that they were capable of L2 learning regardless of their age and circumstances if they were motivated, had an appropriate attitude toward English and its native speakers, were in a culturally acceptable and non-threatening setting and learning in a way that meets their individual needs and matches their cognitive and affective characteristics as well as other personality traits. One of the main objectives of the instructional aid was to raise their awareness and consciousness of linguistic form as well as to utilise and sometimes influence their learning strategies while providing ample input and opportunities for output generation and feedback.

The subject to be taught, or rather the unit to be supported, was English for Academic Purposes, providing a range of linguistic and study skill services for up to 500 national and international students across all schools at the university every year. This project was to cover three credit courses offered by the Unit: English for Academic Purposes I (EAP100), English for Academic Purposes II (EAP101) and EAP200, as well as a number of non-credit workshops. The workshops were at the time offered to all NESB (non-English speaking background) students, the topics ranging from Vocabulary of Academic English, Academic Speaking and Discussion Skills to Postgraduate Writing. Being optional non-credit courses, the workshops did not require students to do any homework, nor were the tutors encouraged to hand out and mark written assignments. Making an interactive EAP learning package available to these students was to greatly improve the quality of their learning, giving them much more feedback and individual guidance than ever before. It was also expected to enhance the learning in the three credit courses in both distance and on-campus modes as well as to support the lecturers, who were mostly too busy to give effective feedback to each and every student-produced piece of writing. Most of all, it was expected to contribute to the eradication and de-fossilisation of some of the most common linguistic errors committed by the target population.

In particular, the purpose of its module – called the Intelligent Tutor – was to serve as an interactive learning environment in which students would be able to experiment with topic related writing. The concept of a learning environment is borrowed from Breen (1979 cited in Levy, 1997b: 11) and denotes *process* materials, with the help of which students can practise communicative skills, as opposed to content materials, which contain data and information. Based on the SLA literature review presented in the first chapter of this book, it was deemed that the electronic writing assistance offered to students could be twofold. Firstly, users would be asked specific leading questions, designed as scaffolding to help them come to terms with text structure and organisation and secondly, their attempted answers in form of written sentences would be parsed for grammatical correctness or otherwise for the presence of typical error patterns. Informative feedback would be given in each case to foster both language awareness and consciousness raising (James, 1998). The idea of constructing scaffolding by posing well sequenced generic questions designed to aid and, if necessary, induce the processes of planning for writing is found in other interactive learning environments such as DIWE (Daedalus Interactive Writing Environment). The Intelligent Tutor takes this strategy a step further in that it asks specific topic and reading related questions. However, while DIWE uses an interpersonal communicative strategy and involves a number of users simultaneously, the Intelligent Tutor relies on the human–computer interaction known in the computer world as natural communication (Marsic *et al.*, 2000). Natural communication with computers uses the modalities comfortable for the human: sound, sight and touch. When it comes to linguistic communication, the technologies used are natural language processing, voice recognition and speech synthesis. The IT uses only the first one, natural language processing, which makes it a powerful communicator in writing. This way the students could experiment with sentence structures in a safe environment, without the risk of losing face, otherwise always present when approaching teachers or colleagues for feedback or help.

Program objectives were: to make the course available to award and non-award students in both on-campus and distance mode; to facilitate flexible, student centred, self-paced learning; to introduce truly innovative ways of language exploration and self-assessment; and to capitalise on the fascination the majority of students find in computers, as suggested by research (Dodigovic, 1995, 1998). In addition, this project was to provide organised hypertext links to other Internet resources, thus utilising the enormous potential of the Web (Borchardt, 1998a) as pure content and a library of up-to-date authentic language texts.

Specific outcomes proposed were a high level of flexibility and individualisation in learning, a substantial improvement in the quality of course delivery and finally outreach to both national and international communities with the potential to adapt to the learning strategies which work most efficiently with individual students (Oxford, 1990). The students would be free to work with the package in their own space and time, exploring those aspects of particular personal interest by choosing the most efficient strategy, and receiving highly individualised feedback.

The teaching methods implemented were to be *tutorial* and *non-tutorial* (Higgins, 1988). The *tutorial* method involves the provision of explicit guidance, as if the student were working under the close supervision of a tutor. *Non-tutorial* refers to the exploratory mode of learning where the students are free to browse through the materials at their own pace as well as in the order of their preference or undertake an activity which requires a synthetic command of the target language (Higgins, 1988). In addition, the system accommodates provisions for different learning strategies (Bull, 1997). This means that students would be given a choice of learning techniques and the system would help them find out which one works best for them (Liou, 1997).

The aim of the overall program was to give the three EAP courses a Web supported, flexible learning structure. The main modules of the Web package are (1) hypertext course notes, (2) interactive tasks, (3) grammar and vocabulary tests, (4) essay marking aid, and (5) a corpus explorer. All modules are interconnected via hypertext links and can be used for tutorial or exploratory learning.

Thus, the package epitomises the entire breadth and depth of CALL in its most interdisciplinary form, utilising a wide range of media and approaches. While the lecture notes merely inform, the hyperlinks between them encourage students to adopt a new and different non-linear reading style, which comes as part and parcel of the modern electronic literacies (Warschauer, 1999). Similarly, interactive links to glossaries, dictionaries and other reference materials encourage the use of computer as a tool (Levy, 1997a: 210) for both effective reading and writing. The corpus explorer introduces the entire concordancing area borrowed from the research methods in corpus linguistics (Jones, 1994 cited in Levy 1997a; Stubbs, 1995; Holmes, 1999). Interactive tasks cater to both learning and instruction, whereas tests reflect the most recent offshoot of CALL, namely Computer Assisted Language Testing or CALT. The essay marking aid is a variation of Markin32 (Burston, 1998), a tool used by the teacher to insert standardised comments while marking a piece of writing. Whereas the idea of making tools available to either teachers or learners reflects an effort to make repetitive tasks such as looking up words or typing in similar comments easier and the performers of those tasks more productive (Matthews, 1998), the idea of offering an artificially intelligent agent able to judge the grammaticality of a student's sentence is radically different. Not only does it tap into the archetypal dream of repeating a creation act believed to be divine prerogative, but it also invites the involvement of natural language processing, held by some to be a branch of artificial intelligence (Jager, 2001).

Thus the innovative aspect of this project is the intelligent sentence parser, a part of the Intelligent Tutor, which evaluates the grammar of student sentences and provides quick feedback and correction to facilitate active learning, based on its knowledge of typical errors. Although parsers have been developed at a number of research institutes, their full potential in education has not been exploited on a wider scale. In fact, astonishingly few language teaching programs make use of parsers, mainly because there is traditionally a wide gap between research in natural language processing and courseware development. One of the few exceptions is the University of Exeter (Pollard & Yazdani 1993; O'Brien, 1993), joined by Holland's (1995) team in USA, who contributed pioneering efforts to the integration of natural language processing (NLP) into CALL. Normally, the parsers developed for research purposes can either only handle correct use of language or if they are robust they can accept erroneous input, usually without much ado or useful corrective feedback. In order to be able to deal appropriately with incorrect language produced by students, they must have a component dealing with the erroneous grammar, based on the model of the student's hypotheses about grammar rules (O'Brien, 1995). Such grammars are best developed by analysing a corpus representative of a particular user type (James, 1998). Thus, the bulk of pre-developmental research was going to be devoted to conducting error analysis on the representative sample of users.

Evaluation and monitoring was to be conducted in several steps. Formative evaluation was planned as a series of user and peer testing sessions throughout the prototyping and full-scale development phases. The summative evaluation or its substitute (see Chapter 6 of this volume) was conducted on a small scale, including user testing and free-style feedback along with some effectiveness tests. The comments of other CALL specialists have also been collected. All phases are described in full detail in the subsequent chapters.

This paragraph will briefly summarise how this CALL package was conceptualised (Levy, 1997a) in terms of the point of departure, language learning and teaching philosophy, role of computer, role of the teacher, hardware and software, and the development process. The points of departure in this undertaking are combined: top-down (Levy, 1997a: 2), in that we start out from language theories and curriculum design, and bottom-up, in that we address a particular problem on the operational level (Prabhu, 2001) of the teaching process. Our approach to language learning and teaching is from a multi-theoretical perspective with a clear understanding that teaching does not equal learning. The role of the computer is going to fulfil the requirements of both tutor and a tool, combined with the features of both content and process supporting materials. The teacher is going to be both the author and the contributor to the project, while envisioning the project, collecting the necessary data through a number of research projects and where necessary also doing some actual coding. Considering that the Internet was selected as the platform, the hardware standardisation became less relevant, whereas its intelligent module lent itself ideally to the use of SICSTUS PROLOG, the Internet version of one of the most powerful AI languages with PERL used for the development of user interface. The development process includes the literature review, linguistic research, design, development and evaluation. Thus this particular instance of CALL software development is among other things also research-based (Kemmis, 1977 cited in Levy, 1997a), in that it starts at the level of knowledge (Prabhu, 2001), which is conceptually higher than the operational level, i.e. the level of teacher intuition.

Research components in the EAP cluster

While the above decisions were based on what was known about our learners from theory and previous research, this section is devoted to those areas that we identified as targets for research. As pointed out in Chapter 1, it seemed important to identify the characteristics of the EAP student interlanguage, both in terms of what the students avoided in their production (omissions) and typical errors. Secondly, it appeared crucial to provide a detailed description of the target discourse in L2 at all levels, linguistic, textual and contextual. Thirdly, the students' beliefs about L2 learning, their motivation, cognitive styles and learning strategies were chosen as a subject of careful investigation. Finally, there was an urgent need to find out about the students' familiarity with the medium computer, their attitude toward it, and their beliefs about CALL.

The above project description has clearly identified three development stages as having a great research potential, these being the general developmental needs analysis, the intelligent sentence parser design and the evaluation phases. These loosely match the identification of learner characteristics and familiarity with the medium computer, the learner interlanguage and target idiom investigation and finally the evaluative use of the software, which should be related to learning. The first two categories, however, have a lot in common. CALL program development in general requires careful user and content analysis (Decoo & Colpaert, 1999a). Translated into the requirements for an intelligent tutoring system (ITS), research had to define the features of the three modules of classical ITS, these being the expert, the student and the teacher modules (Schulze, 2001). While the expert represents the knowledge of language, the student and the teacher modules house the knowledge about how teachers teach and how learners learn. In this case, the student model had to be appended by our understanding of typical errors made by the target student population (Dodigovic, 2002). This will be explained though in much more detail in subsequent chapters. Thus, research clearly had to focus on firstly, the linguistic content as required to meet the standards of academic writing, secondly, the learners and their real as well as perceived needs, and thirdly, the teaching strategies. Whereas the first two seemed best chronologically placed before and during the development, the third, while requiring its own needs analysis, had in its evaluative phase yet to be investigated upon the completion of development.

Table 2.1 demonstrates the amount of time identified as needed for each project stage as well as the envisaged sequence of events. The areas requiring the most extensive research are in upper case. It is clear from the table that the NLP based student model design and summative evaluation together account for approximately one-half of the total time to be spent on the project. It was only fair to organise each of these two activities around a separate research project. Such organisation guarantees scientific validity of the content on the one hand, and the procedural validity of the evaluation process on the other, and is designed to meet the criteria of the linear research method favouring academia.

In other projects, research components may be identifiable at different stages. For example, the needs analysis can require a complex survey or the

Table 2.1 Timeline

	Year 1						Year 2					
	Jan–Feb	Mar–Apr	May–Jun	Jul–Aug	Sep–Oct	Nov–Dec	Jan–Feb	Mar–Apr	May–Jun	Jul–Aug	Sep–Oct	Nov–Dec
NEEDS ANALYSIS		■	■									
Beginning			■									
Prototyping				■	■				■			
Style Guidelines					■							
Implementation						■						
USER TESTING					■				■	■		■
PEER TESTING						■	■				■	
Revision							■	■				
Full Style Manual												
Imaging						■				■		
Student model des.				■	■				■			
Full-Scale Devel.						■	■	■	■	■		
EVALUATION							■	■	■	■		
End												■

teaching strategy applied may need a strengthened theoretical or empirical foundation. In any case, elements suited for research will always be the ones that require a scientific answer to a new or specific question.

Research methodology

As we have seen from the discussion at the beginning of this chapter, one of the central epistemological questions of both CALL and SLA is whether either of them needs its own indigenous research methodology rather than a general pool of scientific research methods. We quoted Chapelle *et al.* (1996) who accept Chaudron's (1988 cited in Nunan, 1992: 3) special plea on behalf of applied linguistics along with his argument that the traditional general scientific distinction between qualitative and quantitative research is no longer relevant to SLA. In an attempt to go beyond this dichotomy, Chaudron (1988, cited in Nunan, 1992: 3) argues that there are four research traditions in applied linguistics: the psychometric tradition, interaction analysis, discourse analysis and ethnography. Whether or not it is justified to accept uncritically this taxonomy and want to impose it on CALL, which we agreed only partly overlaps with SLA (let alone applied linguistics), can be an issue for a long-lasting debate. Suffice it to say that sometimes the quantitative/qualitative distinction in research methodology is rejected as too naive or crude (Nunan, 1992).

One other alternative research model in addition to the one described certainly deserves a mention. It is van Lier's (1990, cited in Nunan, 1992: 5) model of research in applied linguistics, which can be analysed in terms of two parameters: intervention and selectivity. Intervention means the degree to which the process is being intervened with in order to be observed, while selectivity refers to the degree to which the phenomena for observation are specified. Nunan (1992), however, seriously challenges the denial of relevance to the quantitative/qualitative dichotomy, mostly by observing its overt and covert application to a large number of studies. Larsen-Freeman and Long (1991) uphold the dichotomy, but as the opposite ends of a continuum. Thus the interdisciplinary separatism exerted by applied linguists against a uniform categorisation of research methods forces us to look closely at the issues at hand in our CALL development project and select a model which will bring together the feeder disciplines and procedures rather than separating them.

Since we have committed to conducting research as a part of a CALL development project, it is only fair to examine models of software engineering and see if there are any similarities between our research phases and modules in the software engineering process. Software engineering means using the knowledge of computers and computing to solve problems by developing quality software (Pfleeger, 1998; Sommerville, 2001). While computer science feeds theories, computer functions and practices to software engineering, the client or the intended user, sometimes called the stakeholder, contributes her own detailed knowledge of the problem. Together developers and users work out what the needs are for the new system. This phase is known as requirement/needs analysis/assessment or definition. It is followed by system design, a phase which converts the analysis data into a system-level description of what the system will do (from a user perspective). The design document is handed over to programmers, who develop a program design document, which contains the specifics on how to implement the system in computer code. Once the program is written (implementation phase), the testing at various levels can commence, which if successful leads to system delivery and subsequent maintenance.

The above sequence of steps is often presented in a cascaded linear succession, called the waterfall model. In reality, Pfleeger (1998: 50) claims that the software development process is circular, much like Lewins' (1990) model of research presented earlier in this chapter, one phase feeding the other in a cycle. The needs analysis phase, which has a great research potential for our project, is conducted by means that very much resemble general research methodology and instruments. Thus, data elicitation techniques in needs analysis phase include questionnaire surveys, focus groups, interviews, document analysis and observation (Reeves, 1994). This is a range of instruments often used in applied linguistics as well: so in this study we are not really forced to choose one of the two philosophies – software engineering or the applied linguistic one. The two can happily coexist within this book, while we can even remain within one discourse that is fairly universal and acceptable to researchers in many disciplines.

Our needs analysis had to establish three things: (1) the profile of written academic English our students should aspire to, (2) the profile of our students' academic writing, and (3) the learning styles and habits of our student population including their attitude to the medium computer. The first two phases will use corpus linguistic approach to text analysis. From the point of view of software engineering, this procedure can be described as document analysis. For the third one we will use a questionnaire survey.

Corpus linguistics is sometimes viewed as both a theory and a methodology (Tognini- Bonelli, 2001: 1). The term corpus commonly 'refers to an electronic text' (Holmes, 1999: 241). Corpus linguistics is a methodology in that it applies certain principles, but it also defines its own set of rules before application, which gives it the status of a theory. It is concerned with an empirical approach to language use within the framework of a contextual and functional theory of meaning. Being data driven, this empirical approach to linguistic research lends itself ideally to the inductive method. Inductivism has been depicted as naive considering the fact that any single disconfirming instance can at any time falsify a categorical assertion arising from an inductive approach (Popper, 1972 cited in Nunan, 1992). Looking at certain data rather than some other also means conscious selection and therefore some sort of hypothesising or deduction. Be that as it may, having a corpus of authentic language data gives us the opportunity either to postulate very specific hypotheses or follow hunches in our data analysis and obtain corpus evidence. As a method, corpus linguistics allows for a quantitative approach, whereby the frequency of occurrence of a certain linguistic phenomenon in the corpus correlates with its frequency of use. In our study we will use both general purpose corpora and specific purpose corpora. By specific purpose corpora we mean those that will enable us to profile a certain register, i.e. professional writing in academic English, and a learner corpus of academic writing that will enable us to analyse learner errors. We will be able to read these compilations of representative text chunks in a vertical, pattern forming fashion which is insightful in a systemic way. Not only will we be able to engage in lexical analyses, but by using annotated corpora, we will be able to conduct sophisticated grammatical studies of the investigated registers (Holmes, 1999). A full discussion of these and related issues follows in Chapter 5 of this book.

In our approach to the investigation of learning styles, strategies and attitudes we will apply concepts developed particularly for use in an SLA context. This means that we will rely on Willing's (1989) taxonomy of learning styles, Oxford's (1990) learning strategies and the body of CALL literature to define attitudes to CALL. This part of the study was fully and independently designed by Piphawin Suphawat, who was at the time a graduate student at the author's institution. By basing our concepts on theory and published research we are accepting constructs that have some currency and therefore are likely to give our study some degree of construct validity. By surveying a segment of the target population in a standardised way we are hoping to achieve some degree of reliability. The validity (Nunan, 1992) will ensure that the results really point to variables under investigation, while the reliability (Nunan, 1992) will ensure that the study can be replicated and similar results obtained.

What we have described so far are fairly standard and mostly universal elements of the research procedure in very general terms, which is really encouraging for a study that has an interdisciplinary claim. Thus, avoiding interdisciplinary as well as intradisciplinary separatism can put our study back into the framework of research paradigms that will not be easily shattered if under pressure from any of the feeder disciplines. On another note, seeking common ground in terms of discourse practice and procedure appears to be more efficient, as it does not need to be translated into the discourses of feeder disciplines. In any case, it certainly keeps the communication channels between the disciplines open, a role one would hope applied linguistics could take on more often.

Projects and their management

Having identified research areas within a CALL development project will necessarily raise the need for structural adjustment. What seemed to be one project, did in effect become four: one development and three research projects, which are described in the following paragraph. None of the subprojects could be neglected, which is why they all needed to be managed separately. For the academics, who are obliged to produce evidence of effective research, separate project management can help focus on the research issues more clearly and tailor their publications to reflect primarily the research component, thus flattering the tastes of theory/ practice separatism. However, the management of the whole cluster will become more complex, which is what happened in this case too.

The research cluster consisted of two university funded research projects carried out by academics and a masters' research project carried out by a postgraduate student, all complementary to a university funded course material development project. The projects do not exactly overlap with the development phases identified as bearing a research potential. They do, however, cover all the identified research areas to a satisfactory extent. Let us start with the chronologically least recent one: the one contrasting the features of native speaker written academic discourse and NESB student academic writing. The research was conducted on electronic corpora, LOB and Brown for model academic writing and a locally compiled corpus of NESB student writing. This study informed the development greatly about the standard features of academic English and those that the NESB students seem to have difficulty to master. Thus, the content of the on-line package could be defined within these parameters. The next project relied on error analysis to gain a better understanding of how to design the Intelligent Tutor module. The final project in the needs analysis phase examined the students' preferred learning styles as well as their attitudes to CALL. The information obtained was conducive to designing the student and tutor modules of the Intelligent Tutor as well as to justifying the entire endeavour. Evaluation in its research capacity was to be conducted within the development project.

Separate research project funding is another matter to consider. Isolating separate research objectives, which would go beyond the specific development goals, did get these projects recognition from the funding bodies. Most research bodies would refuse funding a research activity primarily aimed at improving particular teaching materials (McDonough & McDonough, 1997). For example, this EAP project has three research components. If these three activities had been conducted mainly to satisfy the criteria of the current development project, it would have been unlikely that they would have elicited support as stand-alone research projects. However, they were extended to provide more general answers to questions such as 'how a certain learner type linguistically responds to academic writing tasks', etc. which enabled them to stand on their own merits, no matter what specific information they were to feed into the current development project.

All the research projects as outlined above found favour with research funding bodies and participants. Thus, the author was able to survey the learning needs of the prospective population with the help of an amazingly keen research student from Thailand, Piphawin Suphawat. This project is described in Chapter 5 of this book. The target language and interlanguage of the learning population were examined in two stages and are also described in Chapter 5. The research proved to be of enormous importance in understanding and sometimes redefining the development goals. It also raised our awareness of any possible discrepancies or inconsistencies in the original model. Finally, it ultimately improved the quality of the software developed.

In the following we shall focus on the description of the research and development steps as they eventuated in this particular cluster of projects. The first important consideration was the choice of an appropriate and up-to-date medium for the delivery of a computer based course in academic English. This chapter has merely mentioned the Web and natural language processing as the author's choice. The following two chapters will elaborate on these choices, revealing the underpinning ideas for the selection of the above technologies.

Note

1. First published in a similar version in the *CALICO Journal* (1998), 15 (4), 27.

Chapter 3

Why the Web?

A question that is on every developer's mind is the one of choosing the right technology for the next generation product. At the time when the electronic learning environment for academic English was being planned, the multimedia CD was the most common choice and perhaps we would have opted out for it, had it not been for an enlightening talk by a guest speaker from the USA and his publication (Geoghegan, 1998), which had challenged us to choose the Web instead. This study noted an evident upsurge in the use of the Internet, email and the Web for educational purposes and offered some lucid explanations. A year later, when our funding proposal was being assessed by the funding body, Fidelman (1998) reported a growth of Internet use among the language professionals. In the same year, an entire conference (Cameron, 1999a) was dedicated to the effects of computer mediated communication (CMC) on creating a new type of learning community. Levy (1997b: 79) defines CMC as being 'concerned with communication between two or more participants via a computer'. Here he refers to a very broad meaning used generically in social sciences to describe email, bulletin boards, discussion lists, list servers and computer conferencing. According to Paramskas (1999: 14) the term originates in the linguistic domain of discourse analysis, which needed to distinguish this mode of discourse from more traditional types. Warschauer (1999: 5) points out that its strength is in the provision of 'time- and place-independent' environment for the interaction of not only one-to-one, one-to-many or many-to-one, but basically many-to-many. This chapter advocates the value of the Internet, Web and CMC in flexible course delivery, supported by more recent evidence and publications related to the subject. In particular, it justifies the use of the Web for the delivery of the Intelligent Tutor of Academic English, the CALL software package which is in the focus of this book.

Metaphor

Relying on a metaphor seems to guarantee the acceptance of an innovation, claims Frank Borchardt (1998a), one of the pioneers of CALL. In his keynote speech at the conference *Theory and Practice of Multimedia CALL* in Exeter, UK, Borchardt (1998a) pointed out how important it was for a number of successful innovations to have retained certain features of the technologies they were meant to replace. So, for instance, the early printed books were designed to look like manuscripts, thus preserving the metaphor of a hand-written document. Similarly, the graphic user interface, which contributed largely to the widespread acceptance and popularity of personal computers, revived the metaphor of a printed page. According to Borchardt (1998a), the concept of hypertext, which among other things constitutes an interactive multimedia encyclopaedia, is based on the metaphor of a library. What he did not mention is a striking resemblance of the World Wide Web to a global interlibrary service, which might indeed be the underlying metaphor responsible for the recent breakthrough of this technology in computer assisted language learning.

The term 'breakthrough' may require some clarification. In this text it denotes a major change in the number and category of CALL users. The Internet seems to have attracted more language teachers to CALL than any other predecessor technology. Not only is there a change in numbers, but also in the type of user. Whereas the early CALL supporter tended to be a risk-taking entrepreneur, sometimes even giving the impression of being more interested in the technology than in the language teaching aspects of it, the new type appears to represent the mainstream, whose interests lie primarily in the discipline related issues. While the former represents the technology driven approach to CALL software development (Levy, 1997b), the latter can be associated with the SLA views of CALL (Chapelle *et al.*, 1996).

A logical question to ask would be: Why has the Internet, and not another instance of IT technology, attracted this new type of user? Borchardt's (1998a) metaphor theory based on Lakoff and Johnson (1981), would suggest that it was strikingly similar to something they already knew and liked. Borchardt (1998a) is not isolated in this view. Another independent study (Geoghegan, 1998), which is based on general educational computing, claims that Internet, World Wide Web and email are accepted by the mainstream user because, among other things, they appear to be compatible with the current beliefs and practices of the teacher population. In other words, in order for an innovation to become widely accepted, it is not only important that it has a definite advantage, but it also needs to be embraced on a social and psychological level.

Quantitative research attributes importance to significant changes in numbers (Brown, 1988; Lewins, 1990; McDonough & McDonough, 1997) and such a change seems to have occurred in the area of CALL usage. This chapter will examine its implications in the light of an innovation diffusion theory arguing that what might appear to be just another increase in user population is actually a final step in the general acceptance of CALL. This important change will be viewed in the context of Internet driven growth in computer assisted learning (CAL) in general with an attempt to point out the specific difference of CALL, in particular its relevance to the project under development, the Intelligent Tutor of Academic English.

CALL and its Diffusion

CALL is computer assisted language learning in a very broad sense. It has always included a multimedia component, either as separate devices (cassette recorder, film projector, etc. switched on and off by the computer) or as a part of the computer hardware and software (digitised sound and video). As such, its potential has been recognised from the very beginning, which, however, was not enough to secure it diffusion. The term 'diffusion' is borrowed from Rogers (1983) and is defined below.

CALL now has a respectable history well exceeding a quarter of a century. From the very start, there has been a need to justify its presence and appease the mistrustful spirits of the language teaching community. In the course of the past 30–35 years, the benefits of CALL have been sought in quite different features of information technology and distinctly incompatible teaching methods, which were used to promote a range of language skills in populations with extremely diverse needs. Although research has proven many aspects of CALL beneficial to both learners and teachers, the use of computers remained restricted to the people who had always been convinced of their value in education. In the late 1990s, however, positive signs started emerging that something was happening on a much wider scale, by far exceeding any success known before: the use of technologies like email, the Internet and the World Wide Web in the classroom seemed to have increased hugely over the last few years of the 20th century (Geoghegan, 1998). Fidelman (1998) finds the same steep cline in the use of Internet by language professionals of the period.

This may be regarded as the diffusion of an innovation (Rogers, 1983). According to Rogers (1983: 5), diffusion is 'the process by which an innovation is communicated through certain channels over time among the members of a social system'. Computer assisted language learning has always been an innovation that has caused a lot of uncertainty (Rogers, 1983: 6) within the professional group of language teachers, especially with respect to its efficiency in language teaching, the extent to which it is consistent with traditional values (such as the teacher's personality as a role model), its user friendliness and availability, and reports of success or failure from other teachers (see Salaberry, 1996; Wresch, 1993). These concerns reflect the five characteristics of every innovation (Rogers, 1983: 14): (1) *relative advantage* (the extent to which an idea is perceived as better than the ones preceding it), (2) *compatibility* (perceived consistency with existing values and past experiences), (3) *complexity* (how difficult it is to understand or use), (4) *trialability* (how easy it is to try it out), (5) *observability* (visibility of results achieved). An innovation that does not satisfy one or more of these criteria is not likely to be widely accepted, which is probably what was happening to CALL for decades before the advent of the Internet and CMC.

A survey by Geoghegan (1998) showed a significant increase in the use of Web and email in comparison with CD-ROM and multimedia usage for all educational purposes in the last two years. In these results, Geoghegan (1998) saw a positive sign that email and the Web are easier to adopt and more appealing to students and teachers than the rest of IT achievements. To prove this point he conducted a survey of his own in which the participants were required to score adoptability of these technologies on a five-point scale, accounting for _relative advantage_, _complexity_, _trialability_, _compatibility_ and _observability_. Apart from the leading word processors, which were used mainly to prepare the teaching materials, the next three items on the rank list were 'the use of email to facilitate interaction and teamwork, the use of Web as a learning resource, and the use of a class Web page . . . as a means of organizing and presenting class material . . . ' (Geoghegan 1998: 9).

While multimedia scored much higher than these on _relative advantage_, it did poorly on _complexity_, _trialability_ and _compatibility_. The latter three criteria for the adoptability of an innovation are derived from Rogers (1983) and may require some elaboration. _Complexity_ is a measure of how easy or difficult it is to use a certain product. A car with manual gearshift is more difficult to utilise or adjust than the car with an automatic one, and therefore more _complex_ in terms of adoptability. A Web page is less difficult to adjust or update (a change in a file) than CD-ROM based software (a change in a file plus mastering a new CD) and therefore less complex. _Trialability_ is the second important criterion and indicates how easy it is to try out an innovation. Given that the user has the necessary hardware platform, a CD-ROM is less trialable than email or a Web page because it is a physical storage unit existing in real space, taking real time to physically obtain, either through a visit to a shop or through a mail order. Trying out email or a Web page is, on the other hand, a matter of seconds: it only takes a press of a button, because Internet does not require physical intermediary storage which is transported only as fast as the conventional transportation means would allow. Instead, it uses the electronic communication links capable of transferring a large amount of data at an incredible speed. Recent development of the wireless transmission makes even the cable link redundant. Finally, the third criterion is _compatibility_ or perceived consistency with existing values and past experiences. This takes us back to Borchardt's (1998a) hypothesis, based on Lakoff and Johnson (1981), about the power a metaphor has in the acceptance of an innovation, for _compatibility_ is essentially the capacity of an innovation to feature as a metaphor of something known and already accepted. So, for instance, email draws on both the older letter writing and the newer telephoning convention. The

Web has all the convenience of a powerful library interlending service combined with an incredible speed and quality of access.

History

Before the advent of the Internet, the diffusion of CALL had managed to accumulate only two of the five characteristics of an innovation (Rogers, 1983), these being the *relative advantage* and *observability*. The other three characteristics, *complexity*, *trialability* and *compatibility*, found by Geoghegan (1998) to be essential for the successful diffusion of an innovation, seemed to have been low in the pre-Internet era.

When the first sophisticated system for computer assisted instruction, PLATO, was launched at the University of Illinois approximately 40 years ago, the computer was considered to be a time and labour saving machine, where the immediate availability of feedback was seen as the main qualitative advance (Higgins & Johns, 1984). In terms of diffusion, there was a case of *relative advantage* (Rogers, 1983) of mainframe computer technology over its predecessors, the conventional media in instruction. In other words, computer assisted learning was perceived as better than traditional ways of learning in the area of feedback access.

In spite of the demonstrated benefits of mainframe PLATO, which had its own authoring system, and in spite of the fact that it did not require programming skills to author a lesson, the system did not appear very *trialable* (Rogers, 1983). Firstly, it needed an extremely expensive hardware platform, which hardly any average school could have afforded. Secondly, the general computer literacy of the population was far lower than it is today, so that what nowadays may be perceived as a relatively simple task of authoring a PLATO unit, may have seemed almost unfeasible for an average teacher in the 1960s. In other words, one of the obstacles to the *trialability* of CALL was its *complexity* (Rogers, 1983), regarded at the time as very high. An apparent lack of *compatibility* (Rogers, 1983) with existing ideas, especially in the humanities (e.g. Wresch, 1993), which are traditionally mistrustful of machines and automation, further inhibited the diffusion of CALL in the language teaching community. In addition, the behaviourist underpinnings of programmed learning that plagued a lot of early drill-and-kill CALL (Keobke, 1999) were no longer compatible with the evolved beliefs and practices of the language professionals.

The introduction of relatively affordable, user-friendly PC has allowed unrestricted access to computers to anybody who was willing to make the investment and spend some time on basic computer literacy. The computer was no longer confined to the selected audience of a few hand-picked organisations. Instead access was available to anyone who wanted to see how it works – the innovation had become *observable*. In terms of innovation diffusion, the results of CALL had become directly visible to the public.

Although CALL authoring packages for the PC were a later development, the early PC offered some relatively user friendly dialects of BASIC programming language, which appealed to the pioneers of CALL, such as John Higgins, Tim Jones, Graham Davies or Tony Williams, all of whom were originally language teachers. As a result, programs such as ECLIPSE or SEQUITUR, simple in terms of hardware platform and software coding, but clever in terms of instructional design, began finding their way to the target audiences.

Unfortunately, the _trialability_ of CALL still depended on the existence of at that time quite scarce computer labs, so that even though it was easier for teachers to get to see and experiment with CALL programs, they were still not able to try it out on a larger scale, in the classroom. The notion of relative _complexity_ of CALL compared with more traditional means of instruction seemed to persist (Herdina, 1991). Moreover, there were still a number of concerns regarding the _compatibility_ of CALL with the widely accepted communicative language teaching theory and practice (Herdina, 1991; Koebke, 1999).

Nevertheless, the PC era did bring about a certain popularisation of CALL. Whereas in the mainframe era CALL had a mainly experimental character (see Chapelle, 1997), the advent of PC resulted in its commercialisation followed by the founding of the first CALL specialised publishers like Wida Software or Camsoft. The emerging of a distinctive CALL market suggested that there was a recognisable user type, who must have undoubtedly found CALL very beneficial. An attempt at establishing a user typology and its relevance to the diffusion of CALL will be discussed later.

Great Expectations

If a fairly simple PC with a mainly monochrome screen supporting text only was so beneficial, what mightn't multimedia and CD-ROM provide? In the late 1980s and early 1990s much hope was put in these two technological advances. Funds were directed into production of interactive multimedia language learning programs, which came on laser videodisc first. The problem with videodisc, however, was that it was rather awkward to use, since it required not only a videodisc player, but also a separate TV screen to monitor the videos. A confused user, after having spent at least half an hour setting up the whole system, had to cope with dividing his or her attention between two screens, a computer screen with the program and a TV screen showing video sequences. This complexity explains its lack of popularity.

CD-ROM soon replaced videodisc as a storage medium, giving rise to great expectations in CALL achievement. Here, at last, was a device capable of storing what was regarded as essential in modern language teaching: samples of native speaker discourse visually presented with an appropriate cultural background, which could be interactively manipulated by computer programs, and, most importantly, all coming from the same device with only one screen. Indeed, this new multimedia technology was relying on one of the most innovative aspects of personal computing – the split screen. According to Borchardt (1998a), the split screen showing at least two different types of content was the relative advantage the PC had to offer. In addition, the CD-ROM technology was less complex to use than its cumbersome predecessor.

Entrepreneurs gave it every chance of success. Development funds, such as the European LINGUA or Australian CUTSD, were directed worldwide into the production of multimedia CD-ROM based language teaching materials. Publishers of conventional teaching and learning aids released language CD-ROMs. So great was the belief in the new gadget that even entertainment electronics went for it. Philips invented Compact Disc-Interactive (Barker, 1993: 118), a mouse-driven CD based device enabling interactive television of programs which were non-linear and could pursue any aspect of the story relying on user instructions as to how to continue. Educational technologists projected a lot of their hopes onto this particular device, but the instructional CD-ROM failed to deliver.

Why do Innovations Get Accepted or Rejected?

Why did the CALL world not accept a product with such apparent advantage? What was wrong with the CD-ROM technology? One problem stemmed from its limited capability. The ROM part of CD-ROM is an acronym for Read Only Memory, meaning that the disc is a storage medium from which data can normally only be read. In that respect it is reminiscent of a gramophone record, which did not reach a very high profile in language learning. Unlike the magnetic disc which is as easily writable as it is readable, a CD-ROM needs to be mastered using a special device, which until recently has been very expensive and not at all a part of standard configuration like it appears to be nowadays. Besides, the CD mastering procedure may still require some IT training, especially with novice users. However, this constitutes only a part of the overall CD-ROM production and distribution complexity. The other and more serious obstacle is the necessity to possess and know how to use either a programming language or an authoring system in order to develop the software in the first place.

What a language teacher wants, on the other hand, is an easily adjustable tool, something dynamic that can be changed often and easily, a kind of process material (Breen, 1979 cited in Levy, 1997b: 11) in other words. The email, the Internet and the World Wide Web seem to possess that feature. Internet design has been made extremely user friendly, in that it is now possible to develop a Web page without even the minimum requirement of HTML (Hypertext Markup Language) command. Programs like Front-Page, Dream Weaver or even MS Word and PowerPoint will insert the appropriate code automatically, so that the user only has to concentrate on visual design. No wonder then that the research indicates a remarkable increase in the use of Internet based technologies for teaching (Geoghegan, 1998).

User Categories

Not surprisingly, email, the Internet and the Web beat the CD-ROM and stand-alone multimedia in *complexity, trialability* and *compatibility*. They are easier to use or try out and appear to be more compatible with what the user already accepts. However, the 'user type' also plays an important part in the diffusion of an innovation (Rogers, 1983).

Due to the diversity present in every professional group, to which language teachers are no exception, CALL as an innovation has been differently perceived and responded to by the language teaching community. Some may have been involved from the very earliest stage and have become convinced users long before the majority were even familiar with the concept, while others are still not convinced. Rogers (1983: 22) distinguishes five adopter categories on the basis of how people respond to innovations: (1) *innovators* (2–3% of the total population ready to experiment with every idea), (2) *early adopters* (10–15%, those who use the innovation to achieve a major improvement), (3) *early majority* (a more conservative group which accepts an innovation after its value has been established), (4) *late majority* (a more sceptical group which accepts an innovation when it is quite safe), (5) *laggards* (a group resistant to change). Categories 3–5 are sometimes referred to as the *mainstream* (Geoghegan, 1998). It has been observed (Geoghegan, 1998) that the transition between early adopters and the mainstream is critical. Quite a few innovations have vanished in the 'chasm' between those two categories, failing to diffuse any further.

As an example of an innovation not accepted by the mainstream of a certain population, Rogers (1983) discusses the failure of an attempt to popularise disinfection practices in a village untouched by modern civilisation. Thus, for instance, boiling water as a germ killing measure did not impress the mainstream population, because for them the germs were not observable, and therefore not existent. The procedure was not trialable from their point of view, because to their mind there were no immediately visible effects. Finally, the whole concept was not compatible with the current beliefs, according to which boiled water was given only to the sick and was therefore unacceptable as a means of disease prevention. As a result, only the outsiders or marginalised individuals in the village accepted the new practice, because they had no social status to lose over this issue. This one, like many other innovations elsewhere in the world, failed to diffuse into the mainstream because it lacked *compatibility* and *trialability*.

Over the 'Chasm' and into the Mainstream

Geoghegan (1998) argues that computer assisted instruction has finally bridged the 'chasm' between early adopters and the mainstream. Whereas surveys (Geoghegan, 1998; Fidelman, 1998; Blin, 1999) show that during the 1980s the 'chasm' limit of 15% IT diffusion in higher education was reached, after which things came to a halt, they (Geoghegan, 1998; Fidelman, 1998; Blin, 1999) also indicate that the use of computers in education is on the rise, growing rapidly in some areas of use, such as email.

This general tendency is reflected in CALL, too. Although Geoghegan (1998) does not indicate how individual disciplines participate in the increase of educational Internet use, there are some other parameters which relate more specifically to CALL. Fidelman (1998) notices a steep cline in the number of language professionals using the Internet in the mid-1990s. In addition, the 1997 CALL conference in Exeter (Cameron, 1998) shows that the Web was used much more than two years before, when this biannual conference was previously held. The Web proved to be easier to use and program than most conventional authoring packages; it proved capable of accommodating multimedia and seemed perfect for independent learning, where simultaneous access has to be provided for a large number of students. A study by Pugh (1997) confirms that, given the right proportion of guided self-study on the Web, the students can find the experience very useful and the teachers can reduce the number of their contact hours.

It may be worth while looking at the factors which have contributed to this major breakthrough of the Web in CALL. The Web has a great potential in multimedia use, which is particularly important in language learning. The use of multimedia on the Web is technically and procedurally different from that on a single machine and provides a great advantage. While the use of pictures, video clips and sound files on a single machine is largely restricted by the copyright laws and may become extremely expensive, the Internet makes it possible to circumvent this problem by establishing hot links to other Web addresses and use somebody else's Web page as a reference from within one's own file, thus giving the user access to the generally cost-free original, not an illegal or an expensive legal copy. Besides, the traditional IT borders between data files and applications are being swept away in the latest generation of object oriented software such as Microsoft Office, especially regarding the Web design. What used to be a programming process in CALL software development is now becoming an editing process, not very different from word processing. This way the teachers can transfer their text editing skills to CALL development and concentrate on the linguistic and cultural rather than on primarily technological aspects.

In addition, the surge in the use of the Internet, the Web, CMC and even word processing means a massive introduction of computer as a tool into the language learning process. The computer no longer controls the learning process, but is rather controlled by the teacher or the learner, a perspective possibly much more comfortable to accept for the language teaching and learning communities. This CALL transformation from the tutorial program dominated scene in the 1980s to a tool dominated one in the late 1990s is noticed by Bradin Siskin (2004) and possibly indicates a trend toward more blended forms of learning.

The Web has now become a standard infrastructure element, containing a lot of information, which was not originally planned to serve language teaching purposes, but which can nonetheless be integrated into the curriculum without extra costs or great effort. Whereas the multimedia handling qualities as well as the simplicity of development process correspond to Rogers' (1983) *low complexity* and *high trialability*, the Web, being a part of infrastructure (Kramsch *et al.*, 2000), and its design increasingly relying on skills transfer may be associated with *compatibility*.

The specific advantage of Internet in language learning can be seen in the availability of different genres and media. Some of the Web materials have a tutorial structure whereas others are purely informational sources. Others yet are a combination of the two. The informational sources provide something which is regarded as highly important in language learning: guaranteed up-to-date authentic language. Moreover, the flexible hypertext links between files or parts of files make it relatively easy for the language learner to find explanation of new terms. Instead of producing separate teaching materials available on the Web, resourceful teachers prefer to provide links to sites they regard as useful for their students. Accompanied by a quiz and an email link to the teacher, such pages take a minimum effort to create while providing a maximum of targeted exposure to authentic language along with a high degree of interactivity and different feedback options. Thus, the Web makes it possible to organise an enormous amount of linguistic and non-linguistic information in an instructional way, suited to the needs of a particular language learning population.

While the Web had a significant place at the Exeter conference (Cameron, 1998), email was hardly mentioned. However, the next conference (Cameron, 1999a) paid it due tribute as did a number of other publications (Warschauer, 1995; Penningthon, 1996; Cameron, 1999b, Debski and Levy, 1999; Kramsch *et al.*, 2000). Regardless of the publicity email in education has received, many teachers have been using it for some time as an instructional aid, especially in distance education. In the late

1980s and the early 1990s collaborative email projects between schools and universities around the globe proved very successful and extremely motivating. The links were mostly established in such a way that both participants could act as either learners or native speakers of a language, for example a partnership between a German class learning English and an English class learning German (Leahy, 1999), where both languages were used in turns, tandem learning was promoted, learner autonomy fostered and both cultures explored. Such projects also provide greater motivation due to the presence of a real target language speaking recipient, the individualisation of the learning process, a reduction in the gap between written and spoken language (Kramsch *et al.*, 2000) in that writing is used to fulfil a highly informal communicative function, a growing awareness of the target language and an incentive to do more independent reading and self-study (Schmidt & Kornum, 1991).

Today, using email in language teaching is no longer considered to be a sign of technological prestige, but it may well be a sign that at least one form of CALL has been accepted as quite normal. In fact, an impressive number of publications on both the use of the Web and CMC is now available to a keen explorer, indicating that these technologies have become almost as ubiquitous as the press, which speaks to their compatibility with the beliefs, values and practices of the user population. The following section examines the phenomenon of compatibility in more detail.

Compatibility of CMC with Various SLA Theories, Practices and Beliefs

The Internet, Web and CMC have managed to gain the approval not only of language teachers, but also of language learners (Healy Beauvois, 1997; Warschauer, 1999; Gu & Xu, 1999; Kramsch *et al.*, 2000). They are being used in distance (Goodfellow *et al.*, 1999; Buckett *et al.*, 1999; Shield & Hewer, 1999) as well as in on-site education (Mills, 1999; Chiao, 1999, Warschauer, 1999), in class (Healy Beauvois, 1997; Crompton, 1999; Gitsaki & Taylor, 1999) as well as outside class (Söntgens, 1999; Peterson, 1999; Blin, 1999). Increasingly, they have been used to teach and learn both grammar (Felix, 1999; Dodigovic & Suphawat, 1999; Dawson, 1999) and vocabulary (Greaves & Yang, 1999; Allen, 1999; Lessard & Levison, 1999), while simultaneously being reasonably open to the practice of the four skills: reading (Martinez-Lage, 1997; Ganderton, 1999; Hunter, 1999), writing (Healy Beavois, 1997; Warschauer, 1999; Mills, 1999), listening and speaking (Buckett & Stringer, 1998; Cortes & Galindo, 1998; Buckett *et al.*, 1999).

Thus, these technologies seem to have become all things to all people, used with equal fervour even by the proponents of often conflicting SLA theories. These technologies are perceived as compatible with the values, beliefs and practices of the SLA theorists discussed at length in the first chapter of this book: behaviourism, comprehensible input hypothesis, Piagetian constructivism (Levy, 1998), comprehensible output hypothesis and social as well as sociocultural theories, including the social construction of knowledge. They also comply with the notions of learner autonomy, tandem and task-based learning, while simultaneously touching on issues such as language awareness, focus on form and inductive learning.

Conclusion

The Internet based technologies seem to have brought about the long awaited change in the number and profile of teachers using CALL. Whereas prior to the advent of the Internet, CALL, and computer assisted learning (CAL) in general, appeared to linger in the chasm between the pioneers and the mainstream, without being able to reach its final acceptance, this new technology has attracted a diversity of users, thus securing the diffusion of CALL and CAL among the broad population of teachers. The specific potential of Internet based CALL is in its ability to provide an almost unlimited free source of authentic language in context with opportunities for authentic tasks. The Internet has the marvellous ability to ignore the limitations of physical space and time and thus perfect the metaphor of a smooth running interlibrary service. In so doing it realises a metaphor, and maybe an archetypal dream of mankind to be able to move from place to place in an instant. Even though Internet is not magic, the opportunities it presents to a language teacher seem to have the appeal of it. These are some of the reasons which have guided the author in her choice of the Internet and the Web for the flexible delivery of a university course in academic English.

Chapter 4

Can Computers Correct Language Errors?

Error Correction

This chapter is an attempt to answer the question whether computers can correct language errors, especially those made by L2 learners. For this purpose we will examine the handling of such errors proposed in SLA literature. We will especially focus on the concepts of feedback and reinforcement within this context and will then view it from the perspective of CALL. Subsequently we will examine the technologies capable of evaluating free-style student output and identifying and correcting NNS errors. While it will become quite clear that the computer cannot substitute a human being at whole language processing, some strengths of artificial intelligence in partial language processing will be pointed out and their suitability for L2 error correction highlighted. The chapter will conclude by discussing some obstacles in the way of more efficient application of these advantages in practice.

In Chapter 1 of this book we examined some theoretical views regarding L2 errors and possible ways of handling them. We noticed that different SLA theories may hold radically different views of the meaning of language errors produced by second language learners. Thus, for example, the behaviourist theory views errors as a path to acquiring the wrong item and therefore an effect to be avoided at all cost, i.e. through overlearning. In contrast, interlanguage theorists see errors as idiosyncrasies in the learner's L2 system and therefore no errors at all in respect of the learner's IL, but only in regard to the target language, which is not quite what the learner produces (see James, 1998: 16).

A middle way was briefly supported by Pit Corder (1967), who was instrumental in the short-term revival of error analysis (EA) before subscribing to 'idiosyncratic dialect' close in concept to IL. He held errors to be the evidence of the learner's internal syllabus and the imminent difference between *input* (what is being taught) and intake (what is being learnt). While errors to him reflect the L2 competence of the learner (Chomsky's I-language), mistakes are self-correctable and reflect performance (Chomsky's E-language).

Thus, to the error analyst, errors are significant in three respects (James, 1998: 12): they inform the teacher about what should be taught; they inform the researcher about the course of learning; and they are an outcome of the learner's L2 hypothesis testing. The sources of error are deemed to be the redundancy of the code (intralingual), various sources of interference (interlingual) and unsuitable presentation (George, 1972). While error types will be examined in more detail in the following chapters, here we will focus on error treatment. Consciousness raising (see Chapter 1) is a proper response to L2 errors, the one which will help the learner notice the target linguistic features and give them the necessary time to reflect. This trend is noticeable in both the Language Awareness (LA) approach and focus-on-form (FonF). The latter refers to an occasional shift of focus on linguistic form in an otherwise meaning-focused lesson. An example of this is a recast of an erroneous utterance made by the learner, which conforms to the learner's intended meaning. Long and Robinson (1998) report a great effectiveness of this procedure, especially with adult learners. Focus on form is sometimes incorrectly confused with focus-on-FormS (Long & Robinson, 1998; Doughty & Williams, 1998a). The latter denotes a syllabus that is organised around linguistic forms. Long & Robinson (1998) categorise consciousness raising (CR) and language awareness (LA) as a part of the language rule tradition and therefore focus-on-formS bound. Margaret Allan (1999), however, stipulates that language awareness has a strong emphasis on inductive learning with the aim of going beyond grammar in the traditional sense. She defines LA as one's sensitivity to the nature of language and its role in human life, while together with Ellis (1997) and James (1998) distinguishing between language awareness and consciousness raising. While consciousness raising (CR) refers to focusing on what the learner does not know, language awareness (LA) refers to making explicit what the learner may already know implicitly (James, 1998). Therefore, correcting errors (Corder, 1967) would concur with CR, while correcting mistakes (Corder, 1967) would concur with LA.

On the other hand, Chomskyan concept of native speaker (NS) competence has given rise to the so called Incompleteness Hypothesis, a term used in reference to the NNS L2 competence in contrast with NS competence. Chomsky (1965) claimed that there can be either strong or weak equivalence between two grammars. Weak equivalence allows for both grammars to produce the same sets of sentences. Strong equivalence, however, enables the same sets of sentences to have precisely the same meaning. The issue of whether the NS and NNS grammars can be weakly or strongly equivalent has not been resolved (James, 1998: 54) and with it the L2 learnability issue in UG (Gregg, 2001). It has, however, opened the door to doubt that an NNS can ever master an L2 fully, or in other words achieve the ultimate attainment, which has also been shared by some of the connectivists (DeKeyser, 2001).

Chomskyan largely nativist view of language learning allowed in fact for very little influence of linguistic evidence in language learning, especially in first language learning (Mitchell & Myles, 1998). Krashen (1987), just like the behaviourists however believes in the power of positive evidence in language learning. Positive evidence here means exposure to well-constructed utterances (Gregg, 2001). In the context of interactionism and language awareness respectively, it can mean either implicit (FonF) or explicit instruction in grammar or vocabulary (focus-on-FormS) (Long & Robinson, 1998; Doughty & Williams, 1998), which we discussed in Chapter 3. In contrast, Gregg (2001) draws equivalent lines of distinction between positive evidence and language use on the one hand and negative evidence and language mention on the other hand, thus claiming that the use of linguistic metalanguage constitutes negative evidence, whether it confirms the learner's hypothesis, precedes it or disconfirms it.

Gregg (2001) however concedes that negative evidence in SLA most commonly means being alerted to one's linguistic errors. This can happen in many different ways and to a variety of degrees. Some interactionists for example believe in recasts as a corrective measure (Long & Robinson, 1998; Doughty, 2001) claiming that this is the least disruptive cognitive intrusion likely to have the desired repair effect. Lyster and Ranta (1997 in Mitchell & Myles, 1998) on the other hand argue that despite the valuable negative evidence they offer, recasts do not compel the learners to self-correct. Apart from recasts, research and theory on correction types and their effectiveness include stating the relevant linguistic rule, error type indication without recast, mere underlining and mere error count per line, the comparison between which currently seems inconclusive (James, 1998). Learner preferences for correction types also seem to vary, while it is not certain that the preferred method of correction is the most useful one (Oxford, 1995). It is however quite clear that the learners want to receive correction (Willing, 1988).

Individual learner differences also seem important in deciding how to execute the error repair or correction (Maingard, 1999; James, 1998; Gregg, 2001; Sawyer & Ranta, 2001; Oxford, 1990, 1995), but there is no consensus among the researchers in this matter. In any case, as discussed in Chapter 1, there is a body of research evidence in support of the hypothesis that error correction is beneficial, needed and may lead to learning (Doughty, 2001; James, 1998; Willing, 1988; Schulze, 2003; Gregg, 2001; Oxford, 1995).

Most SLA theorists however agree that noticing is the crucial event in language error correction and learning. To James (1998) it supports consciousness raising, which is equated with explanation of the unknown leading to what Krashen (1987) and Ellis (1997) call (explicit or conscious) learning or the kind of learning that is responsible for accuracy. Practice, on the other hand, which had been favoured by both the audio-lingual teaching method and the communicative language learning, requires actional attention and is therefore thought to lead to acquisition or uncon-scious (implicit) learning and therefore fluency, which was much valued by the audio-lingual approach and is in high regard by the proponents of communicative language learning. Thus noticing the error invites a cognitive comparison (Doughty, 2001; Ellis, 1995 in James 1998) between IL and TL. While to Doughty (2001) this is a cognitive intrusion designed to enable mapping between a conceptual representation and a new linguistic form under the influence of new pragmatic, semantic, syntactic and phono-logical information, James (1998) identifies this comparison as a form of error analysis, a procedure normally associated with the teacher's or researcher's and not the student's activity.

Whereas interactionists seem to be using the terms, 'noticing', 'attention' and 'awareness' interchangeably, James (1998) and Ellis (1997) differenti-ate between noticing, consciousness and awareness, a distinction we touched on in Chapter 1. Most of these terms have been associated with a special strand of cognitive psychology and their genesis will be discussed later in this chapter. Suffice it to say for now that according to James (1998) raised awareness of L1 is another element of success in L2 learning. As indicated in Chapter 1, language awareness is brought about through explication, i.e. of something that the learner already implicitly knows, while consciousness can be gained of something previously unknown to the learner. James (1998) believes that a coordinated focus on both L1 awareness and L2 consciousness can lead to an effect he calls interfacing, or a better understanding of L2 in terms of its parallels with L1. Understand-ing how language works in general seems to be the purpose of this activity. This brings it close to UG or to Slobin's Operating Principles (Gregg, 2001; Doughty, 2001), which refer to the way learners perceive, store or organise linguistic information. This procedure is supposed to lead to positive transfer, a method which seems to complement contrastive analysis (James, 1998). The consciousness raising or the explanation, e.g. as given in case of an error is according to James (1998) best provided by supplying the relevant rule that firstly allows insight into the structure described and secondly is delivered in simple language and if necessary through several propositions forming a decision-tree or an algorithm. In this respect, James' (1998) thinking is similar to Anderson's (1988) ACT model (Cook, 1993; Doughty, 2001, DeKeyser, 2001) and Chamot and O'Malley's (1994, 1990) cognitive learning, where the structure of procedural knowledge resembles a series of IF . . . THEN decision trees or algorithms.

We can summarise the preceding discussion of error correction in the following way. While nativists simply provide more positive evidence in response to error, interactionists support recasts as a way to correct errors; some cognitivists (DeKeyser, 2001) on the other hand support citing lin-guistic rules as a way to gain declarative knowledge, the application of which will eventually lead to procedural knowledge. In anticipation of the ensuing procedural knowledge, the rules given to the student mimic what is supposed to reflect the structure of that kind of knowledge. Both interactionists and cognitivists believe that focusing the learner's attention to the correct form or the rule will trigger learning. What we have not mentioned so far is the apparent agreement of all (or the lack of disagreement) about the requirement that the correction should be sensitive and non-threatening. Sometimes (James, 1998) explicit references in this context are made to Krashen (1987) and the danger of students raising their affective filter in case of harsh criticism, which would render them incapable of language acquisition. Oxford (1995), Garrett (1995) and James (1998) point out that individual differences between learners may play a major role in determining what kind of feedback is effective.

We have already discussed the methods of error remediation and the assumed learning mechanisms they are expected to trigger. In this paragraph we shall briefly review the extent to which such a procedure may go. To James (1998) error correction has three different degrees. The first one is intervention feedback, which informs the learner that there is an error, but leaves her to discover and correct it herself. This is similar to Doughty's (2001) recommendation to first provide the learner with some guidance as to what element of her (erroneous) utterance to focus on, e.g. by way of the 'isolated interrogative recast', which repeats the learner's utterance with rising intonation to signal the error. Spada and Lightbown (1993) offer two of the three types of overt or explicit feedback in this category, namely repetition, which corresponds to isolated interrogative recast, and focus on error, where the teacher draws attention to error by using stress or extralinguistic signals such as snapping her fingers. As in James (1998), this may give the learner a chance to self-correct. The next level or degree of correction is what James (1998) calls correction proper. It provides treatment that leads to revision and correction of that particular instance of error without aiming to prevent the same kind of error from occurring again. This comes very close to what Doughty calls 'corrective recasting', which provides a direct contrast of forms and is supposed to follow a failed self-correction subsequent to isolated interrogative recast. While Spada and Lightbown (1993) do not seem to advocate a direct recast, they propose what they call covert or implicit feedback. According to Schachter (1986 in Ellis, 1997), this can be some sort of indirect negative evidence, where correction is integrated in a communicative response (e.g. S: 'Yesterday I go . . . ', T: 'Yesterday you went . . . ?'). The third level or degree or error correction is called remediation by James (1998). It provides the learner with information that allows her to revise the linguistic rule she had been applying. Spada and Lightbown (1993) call this overt metalinguistic feedback, which is instantiated either asking a metalinguistic question or by the provision of a metalinguistic rule.

James' (1998) criterion for the division depicted in the preceding paragraph is the diagnostic power of error treatment. James (1998) defines diagnosis as the task of inferring the sources of errors, while accurate description of errors is regarded as a separate task. In terms of diagnosis, feedback or isolated interrogative recast does not provide information on how or why the learner's attempt is wrong, which is a point of concern for Garrett (1995). For Corder (1967) explanation is the ultimate goal of error analysis. Correction or corrective recasting, on the other hand, describes the nature of the wrongness, whereas remediation carries out both error analysis and contrastive analysis, making the learner aware of the reason why her output was wrong. It seems that what James (1998) is saying here can be translated into the language of cognitive psychology (Bigge & Shermis, 1999) in the following way: by understanding the underlying principle or the reason for the wrongness, the student has gained an insight which can guide her in the future when approaching similar tasks.

The review of the key attitudes toward error and correction has made us aware of a multitude of competing psychological, philosophical and other theoretical underpinnings to the research and practice of error treatment. Analysing some of the key terms used in this context by both SLA and CALL might help us place the various discussed proposals within a much broader framework of the history of human ideas. For this reason the next section is devoted to key terminology related to error correction in CALL.

Terminology

Feedback and reinforcement

In the following we shall look at some of the crucial terms within the context of learner errors, in particular as far as they are relevant to CALL. The term feedback in this context for example has been viewed differently in various sources. James (1998) restricts the scope of the term feedback to a specific type of response to error, i.e. to the type of intervention which informs the learner of the fact that there is an error, but gives no specifics of description or diagnosis. In contrast, other SLA theorists (Spada & Lightbown, 1993; Ellis, 1997; Doughty, 2001; Gregg, 2001), like the majority of CALL specialists (Heift & Schulze, 2003; Cowan *et al.*, 2003; Maingard, 1999; Kreindler, 1998), seem to extend the meaning of the term to include any type of information returned to the learner after accomplishing a production or comprehension task. Mathias Schulze (2003) very helpfully summarises the evolution of the term from its origin in technical sciences, the course of which we will recapitulate and interpret in this section.

The origin of the term seems to be far beyond the realm of language learning. According to Schulze (2003) feedback is a term originally used to describe a principle in self-regulating control systems in mechanics, where the information about what is happening in the system is fed back to the controlling device. The feedback is compared to what should be happening in the system, so that suitable action can be taken. This notion is often associated with servo-systems, e.g. those that can be found on aircraft. As Kramsch (1995) points out, discourse from prestigious disciplines is often borrowed in SLA or applied linguistics, which seems to be the case here too. Schulze (2003) further elaborates on how the term is frequently used in psychology and pedagogy in a way similar to that in mechanics and we will pursue the same course for a while.

There is a significant link between the origin of the term feedback and its subsequent use in psychology. The fact that the metaphor of a servo-system principle had been adopted from mechanics, a subdiscipline of physics, is no mere coincidence. Behaviourism, the psychology responsible for the introduction of the term into the description of learning processes, derived its philosophical underpinnings from logical empiricism, a philosophy subscribing to an objective representation of physical reality, in whose hierarchy of sciences physics and chemistry ranked first (Bigge & Shermis, 1999: 56). This kind of psychology looked upon the human being in a rather mechanistic way of cause and effect. Built upon the foundation of Thorndike's (1932) work (see also Bigge & Shermis, 1999: 78–9), instrumental conditioning theory defines feedback as the link between the stimulus, e.g. a reward, and response, which in contrast to classical conditioning precedes the stimulus. It is through the feedback principle that desired responses are connected with the reinforcing stimuli in a mechanical way, thus enabling an otherwise passive organism to learn or in other words change its observable behaviour. Feedback through reinforcement is thought to be crucial to learning since an organism is not viewed as purposeful or capable of insights, but as an entity discovering the desired outcome largely through trial and error. Frequent feedback is supposed to be capable of eventually establishing the routine of the successful trial thus reducing the amount of time necessary for the desired response.

Cognitive psychology, the other major pattern competing with behaviourism in contemporary learning theories, on the other hand, draws its philosophical underpinnings from positive relativism, a philosophy that denies the tangibility of an objective reality and the absolute truth. Instead, it stipulates that each organism creates its own reality and replaces the absolute truth with many individual truths. The empirical verifiability of theories is here replaced by the predictive power of a theory (Bigge & Shermis, 1999). Thus a successful theory has a greater predictive power than a less successful one. Within the framework of cognitive psychology, an organism learns by developing insights or understandings, sometimes through the testing of hypotheses. This is certainly the case in the cognitive-interactionist framework (Bigge & Shermis, 1999: 91–2).

Although the term 'feedback' does not seem to have the same significance in cognitive psychology, which understandably avoids any parallels to its rival theory, behaviourism, Schulze (2003: 443) observes that its related term, 'reinforcement', continues to be productive even in this context. Indeed, literature (Bigge & Shermis, 1999: 8–9; Schulze, 2003: 443) shows that the term 'reinforcement' is used in cognitive-interactionist psychology to describe the process of testing and verifying the hypotheses the learner has formulated about a problem. Within Bandura's linear-interactionist social-cognitive theory cognitive reinforcement plays an important part in human learning as a process within which personal cognitive factors and environmental factors are considered mutually interdependent (Bigge & Shermis, 1999). It consists of people developing self-activated, cognitively-activated expectations through gaining insight into what the consequences might be, which is a process where attention features in a major way. Rather than being entirely externally reinforced and thus shaped by its environment, an individual can administer self-reinforcement based on beliefs and not the immediate physical reward or punishment (MacWhinney, 1995).

This explains why innovators do not give up in the face of the frequent initial rebuff received externally. A person can also experience vicarious reinforcement based on the observation of others and the consequences they attract through their behaviour. Vicarious learning in particular requires the cognitive processes of attention, retention, motoric reproduction and observational reinforcement. The latter is instrumental in translating a person's ideas gained by the observation of others into action. Therefore, it must be said that 'reinforcement' has immensely different definitions within the two theoretical frameworks: behaviourism and cognitivism. Whereas to the behaviourist it is connected with the imposed external stimulus, to the cognitivist it is the confirmation construed as such by the learner in the process of testing an internal hypothesis or making an observation. The emphasis here is very much on the purposeful, engaged, creative and interactive nature of the learning person, which is in stark contrast with the behaviourist belief in the passive and erratic nature of learning organisms.

A number of SLA theorists nowadays believe that language learning occurs in both ways: some on an unconscious, involuntary level, in a mechanical way as surmised by the behaviourists, and some in a conscious, purposeful and insightful way (N. Ellis, 2002). This dialectic synthesis of approaches is best noticed in James' (1998) hierarchy of responses to L2 error, whereby the lowest level is occupied by feedback or information whether the produced form is correct or not. Other forms of corrective action are correction and remediation (James, 1998), both of which draw the learner's attention to the problem (Ellis, 1997; Mitchell & Myles, 1998) and may offer overt (explicit) or covert (implicit) ways to the solution or an insight. Hence James' (1998) emphasis on giving the reason why an error has occurred and on the ensuing remediation.

Finally, in SLA, feedback is seen as a feature of classroom discourse (Van

Lier, 1996: 149). As such, it is a part and parcel of descriptive, non-interventionist approach (McDonough & McDonough, 1997) to SLA research, in which discourse analysis plays a major methodological role. Thus feedback is the evaluative part of the IRF (initiation-response-feedback) paradigm or verbal exchange (Van Lier, 1996), within which both initiation and feedback are performed by the teacher, sometimes with a controlling and stifling effect on the student's production. As a result, the student does not get to produce full, meaningful or authentic utterances and may be apprehensive of the publicly delivered evaluation in the form of feedback.

Feedback and reinforcement in CALL

In CALL, the emphasis may have initially been on the behaviourist sense of the term 'feedback'. As Kreindler (1998: 243) correctly points out, simple correct/incorrect feedback has been the type of response that CALL programs offered most frequently and students learnt to expect from such programs in terms of 'canned praise/blame responses'. This is the programmed learning inheritance in CALL, which put trial and error learning back on the agenda by introducing information in small (easily digestible) steps and provided reinforcement of good habits via feedback at every step of the way. Like James (1998), Tschichold (2003: 550) believes that such feedback is useful only to a limited extent.

In contrast, Kreindler (1998), whose approach indicates fair closeness to cognitivism, advocates flexibility of feedback formats, from giving hints to correct answers without trying to 'bribe' the student with inflated praise (Schulze, 2003) and if necessary pointing the student to a variety of on-line resources that networked and hypertext-based multimedia enable. Such resources could well be dictionaries, glossaries, encyclopedias, concordances or the Internet (Kreindler, 1998). The criteria for providing good feedback in CALL are according to Kreindler (1998) the following: (1) focusing on content and meaning, (2) supporting learning rather than testing, (3) being communicative and low-key, (4) eliciting personal involvement, (5) promoting cognitive skills (e.g. inference), (6) providing cultural enrichment, (7) differentiating between students, (8) being simple, clear and economical. Thus, it is obvious that to Kreindler (1998) feedback represents a constituent part of teaching and learning in a predominantly cognitive way.

All of the above however reflect and encourage the students' involvement in receptive rather than productive language skills. On the contrary, Tschichold (2003: 550), who equally resents correct/incorrect feedback type, is interested in promoting some real L2 output, which does not seem to be espoused by Kreindler's (1998) approach. While Kreindler (1998) is silent in regard to feedback on the form of L2 output, Kuettner's (1998) view on feedback is more catholic. In his opinion (Kuettner, 1998: 146) the purpose of learning software is to convey information, repeat and reinforce information and analyse information. While the former sounds suspiciously behaviouristic, the latter seems closer to a cognitive approach and would allow for feedback on form. Kuettner's (1998) analysis of writing support software reveals that the teachers tend to believe that one of the virtues of good software packages is to make the students analyse in order to understand, especially when it comes to 'non-rote and more creative language learning' (Kuettner, 1998: 146) of computer savvy students. This is in agreement with Chapelle (1997), who is against mere clicking as an output activity, which is unfortunately often the case in CALL programs.

Thus, feedback in CALL as well as in its feeder disciplines has developed to mean information returned to the learner about the outcome of some action taken, which can assume a number of shapes or forms. The term 'reinforcement' also seems to be used quite loosely. Kuettner (1998), for example, uses it in collocation with 'information', even though originally it was associated either with behaviour or cognition. Maingard (1999), on the other hand, introduces the term 'reinforcement' into CALL within the framework of evolutionary epistemology, a concept that will be briefly examined in the following. This approach, derived by Donald T. Campbell and Gary Cziko on the basis of Popper's epistemology of science, 'sees knowledge in the first place as a product of the variation and selection processes characterizing evolution' (Heylighen, 1995). As knowledge is held responsible for the survival of species, it is deemed that 'the phylogenetical evolution of knowledge depends on the degree to which its carrier survives natural selection through its environment' (Heylighen, 1995). Since ontogenesis is seen as a replication of phylogenesis, knowledge is also believed to be a result of selection, which in this context refers to ideas rather than organisms. According to this theory (Heylighen, 1995), knowledge is acquired in three different stages supported by three different processes, the lowest of which is similar to behaviourist explanation of learning and therefore allows for a link with 'reinforcement'. The three stages or levels are described below:

(1) The principle of blind-variation-and-selective-retention, which notes that at the lowest level, the processes that generate potential new knowledge are 'blind', i.e. they do not have foresight or foreknowledge about what they will find; out of these blind trials, however, the bad ones will be eliminated while the good ones are retained.

(2) The concept of a vicarious selector: once 'fit' knowledge has been retained in memory, new trials do not need to be blind anymore, since now they will be selected internally by comparison with that knowledge, before they can undergo selection by the environment; thus, knowledge functions as a selector, vicariously anticipating the selection by the environment.

(3) The organization of vicarious selectors as a 'nested hierarchy': a

retained selector itself can undergo variation and selection by another selector, at a higher hierarchical level. This allows the development of multilevel cognitive organization, leading to ever more intelligent and adaptive systems. The emergence of a higher-level vicarious selector can be seen as a metasystem transition. (Heylighen, 1995)

Maingard (1999) seizes in particular on the hierarchical organisation of knowledge as presented by evolutionary epistemology and the fact that without the bottom level, which constitutes the foundation for all subsequent learning, no progress can take place. She sees the lack of solid foundation in L2 learning, the lack of 'nuts and bolts of language' as the main problem, especially at lower levels of proficiency and is enraged by the call of social interactionists in the area of CALL for more communication and 'creativity'. Her argument is that without the main elements of language, its nuts and bolts, creativity has nothing to work with. She therefore extends a plea for reinstating the lowest level of learning, at which automaticity takes place through practice and reinforcement.

Maingard (1999) is joined in her plea by DeKeyser (2001) who also believes in progressive automaticity and automatisation of certain linguistic and communicative tasks. He supports the idea of a three-dimensional L2 curriculum, which would move along the central diagonal from low complexity of form, low complexity of meaning and low social pressure toward a higher complexity of form and meaning and the increased pressure of linguistic performance in socially demanding communicative situations. He believes that automaticity at each level of progression, which he sees in a continuum, rather in a certain number of distinctive points as the evolutionary epistemology does, can be achieved through error feedback. Thus, error feedback here assumes a meaning similar to Maingard's (1999) interpretation of reinforcement, an action enabling the learner to eliminate the incorrect perceptions and thus achieve automaticity of knowledge.

When speaking about linguistic errors in learner free-style output, CALL publications often feature terms such as 'error detection', 'error identification', 'error correction' or 'error diagnosis'. Clear definitions of such terms are rarely provided, which unfortunately testifies to the poor theoretical underpinnings to a large body of CALL writing, as we are reminded by Chapelle (1997), Oxford (1995) or Bailin (1995). Rare examples of laborious term definitions and etymologies can be found, for instance in Schulze (1999, 2001, 2003), but this is rather an isolated case, not a general rule. It is therefore very difficult to establish links between SLA, pedagogy, learning psychology and CALL. In the worst case scenario they are non-existent. In the best case scenario they are implicit and not always consistent. This should not however deter us from our cause and that is exploring the situation and casting a verdict as to whether computers can correct L2 learner errors.

L'Haire and Faltin (2003: 481) make the following observation about contemporary CALL and its potential for handling errors:

> Computer assisted language learning (CALL) is a field in high demand of natural language processing (NLP) tools. Voice recognition software and speech synthesizers are certainly the most prominent sellable features of current commercial CALL software. However, the need in CALL for error diagnosis and for both intelligent and real-time feedback is great. Reliable error diagnosis systems would allow users/ authors to overcome the limitations of multiple choice questions and fill-in-the-blanks types of exercises and to present the more communicative tasks to learners.

Even though this is not explicitly stated in the text, the operating assumptions here seem to be those of Piagetian constructivism (Levy, 1998). The learner is seen as an individual working on her own, with the computer as a tutor, rather than as a mere tool. 'The success, therefore, of the computer in the tutorial role, hinges on how reliably the program manages the student's learning and on how timely, accurate and appropriate is [*sic*!] the feedback' (Levy, 1998: 90). It would also seem that the above kind of feedback would not be nearly as face-threatening as is the publicly delivered teacher feedback within the IRF (Initiation-Response-Follow-up) framework, even though on the surface its purpose and structure may appear the same. Besides, the preceding text clearly indicates a code switch. While the terminology used in the above and similar articles may or may not have a clear link to SLA, pedagogy or learning psychology, it certainly seems to be well and truly anchored in a range of computational disciplines, some of which we shall explore below.

Parsers, ICALL, NLP, AI, ITS and CL

Holland *et al.* (1993) argue that the benefit of parsers, or programs capable of analysing human language, in CALL is the opportunity it opens for students to practise productive, not only receptive language skills with the help of computers. While traditional CALL indeed lends itself to supporting the receptive skills of reading and listening, the 'intelligent' CALL would in theory allow students to practise the productive skills of writing and speaking. It would do what good human tutors frequently do: point out obvious linguistic errors and provide individualised feedback, correction and remediation. That this is, however, easier said than done can be seen from the still incoming complaints of the CALL specialists (Heift & Schulze, 2003) that this feature is grossly underutilised. Inman's (n.d.)

illustration of the general ability of contemporary computers to process human language is both witty and accurate:

> Science fiction has also been too optimistic in estimating progress towards NLP. An example from over 30 years ago, '2001: A Space Odyssey', made predictions for computers used at the turn of the century. One of these, HAL, was able to have meaningful dialogues with the astronauts. Speech recognition and understanding together with psychological advice were packaged into a friendly mentor. Interestingly whilst chatting with HAL, the astronauts would use a clip board and pen to monitor the state of the space ship. Today microprocessors, invented 5 years after the book was written, monitor and control car engines thousands of times a second and yet our PC cannot understand a sentence such as 'Can you delete this file?' We may get the infuriating reply 'Yes' if we intended a polite command, or worse the reply 'Done' to a genuine question about a possibly locked file.

In line with the general beliefs of the late 20th century, there might have been hope in the world of CALL that the program capable of 'understanding' human language would become the 'killer app', 'that is, an application so obvious, so time-saving, so directly usable as to be both irresistible and enough reason for the died-in-the-wool yellow-pad person to go over to computing' (Borchardt & Page, 1994: 3). However, as Borin (2002) points out, the CALL 'killer apps' have become email, chat and the like, a phenomenon we examined in Chapter 3 of this book.

Yet, creating intelligence comparable with their own has been one of the oldest dreams of mankind, starting from the legend of Golem, a man made of clay and summoned to life through Kabala, or Galatea, a sculpture so life-like that even gods felt it should be made alive. All the way down to the 19th century gothic story of Frankenstein by Mary Shelly and the more recent appearance of sci-fi android robots on the silver screen, the human spirit has expressed hope to be able to repeat the creation act traditionally attributed to God alone. It does not therefore surprise that the 1950s and 1960s saw the projection of this dream onto the quest for a linguistically intelligent computer, capable of machine translation. Even though machine translation was eventually negatively assessed in the 1960s (Matthews, 1998), the efforts to create a computer interface capable of communicating in human language, also known as natural language, have gone on with undiminished enthusiasm. In second language learning, the prospect of having a machine serve as a tireless language model, interlocutor and error correction or grading authority, seemed inviting. However, obstacles on the way toward attaining this goal were many, while successes remained few and far between. This chapter in its own way pays a tribute to the same kind of effort by depicting the research, development and evaluation undertaken to create intelligent language tutors.

In our definition of 'intelligent' as applied to the realm of machines, we will adhere to the Turing Test outcome. Alan Turing, after whom the computer was named 'Turing Machine', discovered that because of the nature of the computational process, in which decision making is conducted in a series of binary trees, almost any content that could be classified as either true or false could be logical and therefore accessible to computation (Borchardt & Page, 1994). As logic is also a human feature, he hoped that:

> ... one day, his 'machine' should be able to act as a human being might act, insofar as such a human being was acting logically. The 'Turing Test' posits an observer – denied visual access to the source of an utterance – unable to tell for sure whether the originator was human or mechanical. (Borchardt & Page, 1994)

According to Schulze (2001), Turing's way of demonstrating 'intelligence' consisted in the computer's ability to play various games, e.g. chess, bridge or poker, the learning of languages, the translation of languages, cryptography and mathematics. Thus language has played a significant part in the birth of the concept of artificial intelligence. The idea of 'machine translation' emerged shortly after the advent of the first computer programs and received much attention and funding in the then leading nations of the world (Schulze, 2001). It was perhaps due to the very enthusiasm of the researchers and the respectively high expectations of the funding bodies that the failure to materialise of the nowadays ridiculous seeming predictions were met with strong condemnation and abandonment of machine translation research (Matthews, 1998). However, the research in natural language processing (NLP) went on and so did the efforts in general artificial intelligence, leading up to the advent of intelligent CALL.

In literature (Levy, 1997b; Reeder & Hamburger, 1999; Hamburger *et al.*, 1999; Borin, 2002) on intelligent CALL (ICALL), we find that this concept often includes the following ingredients besides CALL itself: computational linguistics (CL), language engineering (LE), natural language processing (NLP) and artificial intelligence (AI). Lars Borin (2002) subsumes the first three under the common denominator of language technology (LT). In the following we shall attempt to clarify these terms and their interdependencies.

Computational linguistics is 'the application of computers to the study of linguistic problems' (O'Grady *et al.*, 1997: 660). Thus it seems to be a hybrid discipline, located at the intersection of the fields of linguistics and computer science. O'Grady *et al.* (1997) further explain that it has two goals: firstly to use the computer as a tool to build programs that model and test a particular linguistic theory or approach, and secondly to build working systems that use linguistic information. Its subdisciplines are computational phonology, morphology, syntax, lexicology, semantics and pragmatics.

Computational phonology covers two concepts: speech recognition or analysis and speech synthesis. While speech recognition has the challenging task of recognising sounds and words reduced and changed in casual pronunciation, speech synthesis is used to do the reverse, especially in systems designed for the disabled or for answering large database queries.

Computational morphology on the other hand uses the knowledge of morphology to perform stemming, that is finding the often graphically and phonologically differing word stems, or recognising parts of speech. Some problems computational morphology runs into include words that cannot be broken into component parts although they contain graphemes found in typical part of speech endings.

Computational syntax, which is used both in natural language analysis and generation, arose from two sources. The first source is the practical need to analyse natural language, e.g. in machine translation or database query systems, while the second one is linguistic theory testing. Within the framework of computational linguistics, this area is really responsible for natural language processing (NLP) or analysis. The way it tackles it is by designing grammars and parsers. Grammars are sets of rules defining a language, while parsers are engines responsible for applying the rules. Parsers can be deterministic or non-deterministic. Whereas a deterministic parser has to follow the path it has chosen, even though it may turn out to be wrong, the non-deterministic parser can retrace its steps in a procedure called back-tracking. In addition, parsing can be performed top-down, starting from the sentence rule, or bottom-up, starting from individual words and connecting them according to the rule. A grammar is said to have a strong generative capacity when it is capable of describing a language well. Natural language synthesis or generation has to rely very strongly on the lexicon and make more and more difficult choices than parsers do.

Computational lexicology is responsible for generating electronic repositories of lexical information needed in NLP and language generation. They are called lexica and consist of lexical entries that carry the morpho-semantic and syntactic information about each word. They can be generated in three different ways: manually, from machine readable dictionaries, or through corpus analysis.

The next component part of computational linguistics is computational semantics. While the previously discussed areas were mainly focused on structure, semantics is concerned with meaning. Each lexical item contains a field of semantic information, which has to be defined not only accurately, but also thinking of every possible context of use.

The final component of computational linguistics is computational pragmatics. It arises from general pragmatics, which studies the way language is used in communication. It remains controversial whether it is a subfield of computational semantics or not.

Practical applications of computational linguistics can be found in the organisation and searches performed on large electronic language corpora, information access and retrieval, machine translation, speech recognition, speech synthesis and computer assisted language learning or testing. The applications of computational linguistics in the sphere of electronic corpora are indexing, used in word frequency listing, and concordancing. Information access and retrieval relies heavily on computational semantics while including synonyms or restricting the semantic field in searches and language synthesis in displaying the sought information. Machine translation relies on both semantics and syntax very strongly, while speech recognition and speech synthesis use all of the available components. CALL is similar in that it can rely on all components, even though this is apparently not often the case. This concludes our brief review of the basics of computational linguistics in its potential service to CALL.

The next ingredient in intelligent CALL is thought to be artificial intelligence (AI). AI is an interdisciplinary area of knowledge and research, whose aim it is to understand how the human mind works and how to apply the same principles in technology design. Coordinated movement, vision, reasoning and language are the key features of intelligent organisms, in which AI takes a keen interest with the purpose of replicating them artificially. Thus, the key areas of technology development within AI are: robotics or coordinated movement, computer vision, expert systems or reasoning and natural language processing, speech processing and voice recognition. Thus from the point of view of AI, processing both written and spoken language, a task computational linguistics sets for itself, is seen as part and parcel of artificial intelligence. Thus AI is a much broader term than CL.

Whereas traditionally computer science, robotics and engineering have been largely involved in the design of robots, computer vision systems and expert systems, computational linguistics and phonetics have been involved in creating systems capable of processing human language, both written and spoken. The former is referred to as NLP, whereas the latter, although it often entails some NLP, is generally known as voice recognition or speech processing. While Jager (2001), Hamburger *et al.* (1999) and Reeder and Hamburger (1999) view NLP as an integral part of AI, Levy (1997) and Chapelle (2001) seem to imply a stronger link to computational linguistics. Schulze (2001), on the other hand, puts NLP into the much broader context of human language technologies (HLT), including typewriters, ball-point pens, spell checkers, grammar and style checkers, thesauri, terminology databases, print, photocopier, laser printer, fax machine, etc. The listed devices become a part of HLT when they contribute to natural communication with machines, i.e. using the natural human communication skills (Schulze, 2001: 112). The term itself was officially introduced by the European Commission in 1999 to replace the term 'Language Engineering'.

NLP is only one of the possible ingredients of intelligent tutoring systems (ITS). Holland *et al.* (1993: 28) suggest that the term 'parser-based CALL' be used to describe this kind of CALL software to distinguish it from the more general term 'intelligent CALL (ICALL)':

> The use of parsers in language instruction is commonly referred to as intelligent CALL or 'ICALL'. It might be more accurately described as parser-based CALL, because its 'intelligence' lies in the use of parsing – a technique that enables the computer to encode complex grammatical knowledge such as humans use to assemble sentences, recognize errors and make corrections.

ITS, on the other hand, refers to a system with a threefold architecture, consisting of an expert model, a tutor model and the student model (Matthews, 1993). The expert knowledge pertains to the content to be taught and in the case of CALL describes the language taught, which according to Matthews (1993) is equated with NLP. The student model reflects what the student knows about the target language, in other words the student's interlanguage, plus a number of other facts regarding the personality, language attitude, learning style and information processing modality of the student. The tutor model compares the first two and decides what is to be taught, when and how. Thus the term ITS seems to subsume NLP, although one could imagine an intelligent CALL program that offers the knowledge of language, but not in the NLP format. Some examples of such programs are described later in this chapter.

In fact the earliest attempts at what looked like natural communication with the computer, Weizenbaums' ELIZA, was a program mimicking a counsellor that gave the impression of intelligent natural language communication with the machine, whereas it did not really use what is considered NLP today. Instead it used most common chunks of language and was capable of reusing new language in cliché phrases. Its linguistic ignorance notwithstanding, anecdotal evidence suggests that the program passed the 'Turing Test' with flying colours, as its users could hardly distinguish it from a real human counsellor.

Automated essay grading

The earliest known program designed for educational purposes that was dealing with human language was Page's 'Project Essay Grade' (PEG), developed as early as 1966 (Borchardt & Page, 1994). NLP was not a part of the original package. However, the program could grade high school student essays with the reliability similar to that of human graders. What this program examined were some approximate variables (proxes) as indirect measures for intrinsic values or 'trins'. While trins were features of intrinsic interest such as fluency, diction, grammar and punctuation, their corresponding proxes were length of essay, variety of word length, count of relative pronouns, subordinating conjunctions and prepositions, as well as the number of grammar errors and commas. This program had to be trained on a large number of teacher-marked essays. While the program's grade resembled very strongly that of human graders, its lack of semantic analysis and focus on length lent themselves ideally to cheating strategies such as inflating the essay length or submitting a long string of words, unrelated to the topic. The controversy (Wresch, 1993; Hearst, 2000) this program seemed to have sparked off, continued as its successors emerged, equipped with always better yet undisclosed technical features, which have recently been enriched with a parser.

In addition to the numerous versions of PEG, alternative solutions emerged over the years. In the following we shall examine Slotnick's model, latent semantic analysis (LSA), IEA, e-rater, Short answer scoring and Question answering system. Very few of those systems use NLP as a representation of expert knowledge.

Slotnick's model (Wresch, 1993) seems stunningly similar to the early PEG. Thus it surprises that Wresch (1993) presents it with some enthusiasm while at the same time being guarded against PEG. In any case, the model entails the following:

(1) Fluency measured in total number of words, different words, commas and sentence counts.
(2) Spelling with a difference between common and uncommon words.
(3) Diction based on word length.
(4) Sentence structure represented by the number of sentences and mean sentence length.
(5) Punctuation expressed as frequency of punctuation signs.
(6) Paragraph development as indicated by the number of paragraphs and mean paragraph length.

The only new improvement in this model in relation to PEG is the paragraph development, which is based on values that in essence correspond with the mathematical outworking of PEG. Hence this system is equally prone to misuse and cannot distinguish an essay on global warming from a cooking recipe book.

Latent semantic analysis (LSA) tries to overcome the problem of not being able to automatically assess the content of writing. It is an automated, statistical technique for comparing the similarity of words or documents (Miller, 2003). In essay grading it is used to measure comprehensibility, coherence and comprehensiveness of writing. Its main advantage is that it captures transitivity relations and collocations, thereby accurately judging the semantic relatedness of words, sentences, paragraphs or texts (Kukich,

2000). The particular advantage of using LSA in essay grading is its ability to assess knowledge in terms of semantic similarity between the source readings and the student writing (Miller, 2003). It also seems to correlate well with human graders. However, while LSA is perfectly suitable for the assessment of semantic similarity, it completely ignores morphology and syntax, which when it comes to second language writing becomes a significant disadvantage. Moreover, the usage of the right vocabulary in a text is not enough. The vocabulary also has to be used in the correct way, i.e. LSA cannot tell whether a student writing about the brain is referring to the left hemisphere in the context which should be reserved to the right hemisphere.

Intelligent essay assessor (IEA), developed by Knowledge Analysis Technologies, uses LSA to provide essay scoring and tutorial feedback. The grading includes content, dealt with by LSA; mechanics, dealt with by corpus-statistical measures; and style, derived from both previous analysis modes. It also checks for plagiarism and flags papers that are nonsensical or otherwise unusual. Because of its massive memory requirements, IEA is currently offered on the Web only. The students can enter their essays into an on-line form and receive almost immediate feedback, including the grade and suggestions for revision. The mechanics module indicates grammatical and spelling errors, while the style module points out which sentences may be redundant and which parts need to be reorganised. Finally, the content module identifies the material which may not be relevant to the topic or even subtopic under discussion. The grade assigned for content is based on the comparison with the pre-entered textbook material. The essays entered to calibrate the system do not need to be pre-rated by human graders. The system automatically aligns them on a continuum of quality. If pre-graded essays are used, however, then only one half as many are needed for calibration. Miller (2003) reports that students like getting instant feedback and consequently being able to improve their writing.

The third prominent program that commands attention is e-rater, developed by Educational Testing Service (ETS). Some of the qualities ETS researches wished to evaluate were syntactic variety, topic content and organisation of ideas (Kukich, 2000). Some of these were translated into linguistic features, used to measure similarity between documents. Even arguments and rhetorical structures are being evaluated using NLP techniques, which makes it similar to PEG. Like PEG, e-rater also uses proxy features or proxes. For example, the textual coherence is measured by using a technique known as centring theory, whereby the syntactic referents are tracked across successive sentences, thus allowing the detection of abrupt shifts in topicality. To measure the semantic content, e-rater uses a vector-space model, which was originally developed for use in information retrieval. The features currently used by the system are syntactic features, discourse cue words, terms and structures, topical analysis, in particular vocabulary usage in two different contexts: firstly within the context of the whole essay and secondly within a single argument. The syntactic assessment module encourages syntactic variety by using a syntactic chunker, a kind of parser that identifies features such as subjunctive auxiliary verbs (e.g. could, would, should), complements, infinitives and subordinate clauses. Discourse organisation module follows the discourse markers such as 'firstly', 'for example' or 'in conclusion' as its organisational clues in order to separate the essay into its component arguments for further topical analysis. Topical analysis, as indicated before, is conducted at two levels, essay and argument, and relies on the vocabulary frequency lists extrapolated from the model essay (Burnstein & Chodorow, 1999).

Unlike with PEG, explicit details about the internal outworking of the system have been published (Miller, 2003). One of the big advantages of e-rater over PEG is its modular design, including an independent module for syntax, discourse and topicality analysis, thus being better able to adapt to new data and new purposes, such as summarisation and scoring of short answers. However, PEG can provide a better holistic assessment of essay quality. Finally, like PEG, e-rater requires a sample of pre-graded essays. In comparison with LSA, e-rater scores poorly on recognising lexical synonyms, while it is able to track down what is known in functional linguistics as cohesion by reference. Despite its shortcomings, the system has obvious values and is being used in practice to score Graduate Management Admission Test (GMAT) exams, thus contributing to a significant reduction in human grader workloads.

Moreover, e-rater has been successfully used in the grading of non-native speaker writing within the framework of Test of Written English (TWE). The differences between scores given by human graders and e-rater to speakers of Arabic, Chinese, Spanish, US-English and non-US English were not significantly different, even though they existed. In the case of the Chinese speakers, e-rater seemed more lenient than the human grader, whereas exactly the opposite could be found about the native speakers of Spanish. With the speakers of Arabic, a major difference showed between the scores on two different topics. On the other hand, there were significant differences between e-rater and human graders regarding the scores given to native and non-native speakers of English. Burnstein and Chodorow (1999), however, find that overall GMAT and TWE scoring models overlapped very well, opening the way to the conclusion that e-rater was not confounded by non-standard English either in terms of syntax or in terms of discourse features.

Many of the features that affect essay writing can be used to judge text comprehension. Thus for example lexical and grammatical errors, rough topic shifts and inappropriate discourse markers can even be used to assess short answers to questions and thus question difficulty (Kukich, 2000).

There is also a lively interest within the NLP community in automatic answering of questions. This could be successfully used in information retrieval systems. The two can even be used together in educational systems for feedback and teaching purposes. However, scoring short answers posits a greater challenge for NLP than does automated essay scoring. While the length of the essays allows for statistical averages to be used as acceptable measures, in short answers much greater precision is needed. One of the main justifications of using short answers rather than the easily graded multiple choice tests is the fact that more direct measures can be applied to the former than to the latter (Hirschman *et al.*, 2000). The main reason for creating short answer generating systems is the argument that the machine needs to pass the comprehension test before taking on the more complex task of answering user queries, which is expected of such systems, for example in library catalogue or Internet searches. The two systems, the answer evaluation and answer generation, are sometimes used to match the student's answer against the computer-generated one and look for overlap in key words (recall) and sentence correctness. More work is needed to bring the system's judgement in line with that of human judges.

On the other side of the Atlantic, University of Cambridge Local Examination Syndicate (UCLES) is developing another essay grading program based on NLP technology which so far has remained undisclosed. What they are hoping to achieve is to be able to use this apparently sophisticated technology paired with extensive learner corpora to place essays into broad bands, based for example on well-known testing systems such as ALTE (Boyle & Booth, 2000; Corcoran, 2000).

Thus, automatic essay grading seems to be on its way into the standard practice of large examination boards, with several products also being commercially available to a multiplicity of users. While this is an opportunity for the researchers to consider what it is that they want to accomplish, the potential backwash of such testing practices on the on-line learning communities may also be enormous (Potter, n.d.). On the one hand the automatic writing assessment has clear efficacy advantages over human rating. On the other hand it has the potential to redefine the learning activities it is designed to measure. Potter (n.d.) pleads for utmost caution in deciding on what is wanted from these innovations, realising that there are two kinds of pressure: the one to modernise and make mass procedures cost effective, and the other to preserve a humanist approach to learning and assessment.

Rudner and Gagne (2001: 1) describe the lure of the advantages in the following way:

> Computers and artificial intelligence have been proposed as tools to facilitate the evaluation of student essays. In theory, computer scoring

can be faster, reduce costs, increase accuracy and eliminate concerns about rater consistency and fatigue. Further, the computer can quickly rescore materials should the scoring rubric be redefined.

Automatic essay grading is, however, not appreciated in the same measure by everyone. Two types of concerns have made themselves noticeable throughout the history of this endeavour. The first one came from the efforts to introduce creativity into writing and move away from the grammar and punctuation (Wresch, 1993). It is related to similar concerns regarding the possible backwash of automatic testing and the good or bad practices it could teach the students (e.g. artificially inflating their essays or using the kind of words the program expects whether appropriate or not). The other type of concern arises from the social theories of learning that have espoused communicative language learning and community writing practices (Deacon, n.d.). The supporters of such practices are reluctant to see the writing process pushed out of the community and back into the isolation of pre-internet writers. The general concern is, however, about the process and outcome of writing that may be thoroughly redefined if the computer takes charge (Potter, n.d.).

An interesting aspect of automated essay grading is put forward by Wresch (1993). While this author was unable at the time to anticipate the giant leap in this fast-growing technology, he pointed out that one of the advantages of developing such programs is in analysing the processes good human essay graders engage in while grading essays. Even though Wresch (1993) was referring to mental and psychological processes, we can agree in principle that an analytical approach to grading techniques has had a momentous significance. In fact, the amount of linguistic research underlying such development projects seems to have been truly remarkable. It is a pity that a lot of it is unavailable for confidentiality and product protection reasons. One thing, however, does not seem to be tackled by automated essay grading research and development, and that is non-native-like error correction. The next section of this chapter is devoted to this subject.

Computers and error correction

Two trends become obvious from the previous discussion: firstly, the inconsistency of automatic essay graders in scoring NS writing on the one hand and NNS writing on the other; and secondly the apparent inability of parsers designed to support NS writing to deal with non-native-like language errors. Indeed, a number of CALL authors pinpoint the latter as a major problem with robust or probabilistic parsers, such as those that one finds in machine translation or word processing programs (Tschichold, 2003; Tschichold, 1999; James, 1998; Bolt, 1993; Liou, 1991). Tschichold (2003: 551) in particular identifies the lack of semantic, pragmatic and contrastive linguistic knowledge in such parsers as the root of their inadequacy in L2 assistance. This knowledge is, however, quite common and often taken for granted in a human teacher. She further elaborates on the issue:

> Due to this lack of highly formalized linguistic knowledge, what is left for computers to do, at least at the moment, is to focus on low-level errors of spelling, morphology, and certain parts of syntax. The robust computational grammars used for this purpose often produce superficial and incomplete analyses that are then supplemented by a number of error detection strategies. Similar grammars can be found in some of the grammar checkers integrated in today's word-processing software. The intended users of such software are native speakers who have made a minor mistake while typing but otherwise have a good command of the written language and enough linguistic intuition to critically evaluate grammar checker's response to their writing. Tschichold (2003: 551)

Commercially available grammar checkers indeed have another weakness. They cannot evaluate the semantics or the full syntax of the given text and as a result allow text like the following:

> Their are know miss steaks in my pepper be cause my word processor includes soft wear witch checks my spelling. The problem is that it doesn't correct errors in punctuate and it will not fined words that have bean miss used but that are spelled write. An if I write badly constructed sentences it won't correct them four me. (Sanders, 2000)

The reason why the latest version of MS Word grammar check program has not noticed that 'punctuate' in the second sentence should be a noun, 'punctuation', rather than a verb, as evident from the text, is because it most likely looks at two or three adjacent words at a time and calculates the statistical probability for their simultaneous co-occurrence in a text. It does not look at the sentence as a whole. This kind of parser is called a probabilistic parser (Smith, 1991). As a number of ESL students, in particular our EAP students including Eric and Jean, make the mistake of substituting one part of speech for another, such haphazard grammar checking is of no value to them. As Liou (1991) points out, the feedback can be misleading, because, as anecdotal evidence shows, the students tend to trust the computers and what they perceive to be their ultimate intelligence (Holland *et al.*, 1993). Therefore, ICALL looks for other ways of dealing with NNS errors. In the following we shall describe some of these approaches and while trying to give them a comprehensive coverage, we shall also try to remain comprehensible for a wide range of audiences, explaining the technical detail deemed relevant in very simple language.

Modern computing allows the students to practise and get feedback on both their written and spoken output. While the spoken output requires the kind of evaluative technology that is not necessary for the assessment of written output, it often includes elements of parsing that characterise some of the writing support software. We shall therefore start our analysis by identifying the major trends in written error identification and treatment within the framework of CALL.

Written errors

There are basically three ways in which a computer can identify and treat a written linguistic error produced by an L2 learner in what is supposed to be the target language. It can either perform a pattern matching operation, use a parser or a hybrid system in which parsing is combined with string matching in an efficient way. Parsing itself can be performed by a variety of parser types, which we will identify in further text. It can also vary according to the way it recognises and responds to errors. In addition, the system can have a modularity, which allows it to tackle the linguistic levels of the student's output separately and therefore perhaps more efficiently. These and related issues will be discussed in the following.

Pattern matching (Yoshii & Milne, 1995) is based on matching string patterns in the student's output with a list of expected and pre-recorded answers. Strings are 'contiguous sequences of characters the instructional designer wants to find in the student's entry' (Yoshii & Milne, 1995: 64). For example, if the question is 'What happens with the air temperature at night?', the computer might have been instructed to check whether the student's answer contains one of the following strings: 'FALL\COOL\DROP\ REDUC\DECREAS\DOWN\LOWER'. Notice that the string patterns sought allow the system enough flexibility to tolerate slightly different wording, a free choice of speech part and the inflection of the student's choice. The question is, however, whether this could be considered ICALL, as there is no parser or other device usually associated with intelligent behaviour. Since the system is nevertheless capable of great flexibility and is unhampered by the variance in lexical choice, part of speech or inflection, it may give the user the impression that it does 'understand' her input, in which case it passes the Turing test and can be classified as intelligent.

In fact, pattern matching or the identification of key words is one of the three essential procedures that characterise Weizenbaum's ELIZA (Weizenbaum, 1966), mentioned earlier in this chapter as one of the pioneering works of artificial intelligence. String pattern matching has been a part and parcel to a number of educational software programs in mathematics and sciences (Yoshii & Milne, 1995). An example of a CALL program which uses this technology is Understanding Spoken Japanese (Yoshii & Milne, 1995). It includes an Answer Pattern Manager (APM), a device responsible for the analysis of the student's free-form answers, that in fact, like ELIZA (Weizenbaum, 1966) is not language specific and can be used with any CALL program. In its analysis of the student's answer, APM allows for a wide variety of spellings, detects important mishearings of the spoken text played to the student, picks up spelling errors, identifies incorrect word order, detects missing sentence parts and handles a combination of the above. While the program has to have access to a list of anticipated errors, it also acknowledges student input that is not explicitly listed as correct or anticipated as an error and therefore counts as unrecognised entry. While this system is actually being used for the purpose of practising listening comprehension as its main strength is in content evaluation, its use in grammar correction may not be of universal value. Whereas it seems to be capable of handling predictable errors in languages that rely on word order, in languages that rely more on inflection, a more sophisticated kind of analysis may be needed. Parsers are generally held to be the next step toward analysing natural language and their use in CALL will be described in the following.

Holland *et al.* (1993) define parsers as NLP engines that compose and decompose natural language utterances by using the rules which represent syntax thus addressing the sentence structures in a language. 'Parsers take sentence-length input, break it down into components, and map these against a computational grammar. The output is a structural analysis that tells whether and to which rules the sentence fits' (Holland *et al.*, 1993: 29). Thus parsing is based on encoded 'complex grammatical knowledge such as humans use to assemble sentences, recognize errors, and make corrections' (Holland *et al.*, 1993: 28). The parsers do not include some further elements that would enable full natural language processing. These elements are semantics, pragmatics and domain, i.e. the knowledge of meaning in general, the knowledge about discourse and interactions and the knowledge about the topic of discourse. A system that has a claim on analysing the connections between sentences and paragraphs must have the knowledge of discourse and pragmatics, as we have seen in some of the automated essay graders above. We will address these issues in more detail later in the text.

The primary purpose of a parser is to tell whether a sentence is grammatical, i.e. whether it conforms to the rules contained in the parser's grammar. The applications of parsers are varied, including ICALL, grammar checkers and other writers' aids, translation programs, dialogue systems, information retrieval and automatic gist extraction, some of which we discussed in the context of automated essay grading. Even though more sophisticated systems use semantic, pragmatic and topical analysis in addition to parsing, Holland *et al.* (1993: 30) believe that 'it is the abstract linguistic rules that give the natural language processing the power to handle an enormous range and variety of text input'.

Even though the parsers in CALL can enable language production rather than mere reception, and can analyse a variety of sentences that do not have to be pre-wired in the system, as would have to be the case in string matching, which is quite remarkable, they also have a number of limitations. First, parsers rarely go beyond syntax, thus focusing on form rather than on meaning (Holland *et al.*, 1993), which seems to subvert the goals of communicative language learning, currently the prevailing SLA theory. Second, parsers are not foolproof and can well fail to detect errors or to acknowledge a perfectly correct sentence as such. Finally, parsers and systems capable of using them are expensive to develop, which may be the main reason why we see relatively few of them in actual use as far as CALL is concerned.

But how do parsers work? Well, there is a wide variety of types, depending on which abstract grammar model they are built. Some can analyse utterances in great depth, others can consider a number of parallel parse possibilities (breadth); some are focused on syntactic structures, others are preoccupied with lexis; some need a large number of rules, others can be efficient with only a few principles. Of course, not all the parsers developed for general purposes are useful or efficient in CALL. Thus, an early transformational parser, MITRE, took 36 minutes to analyse an 11 word sentence (Matthews, 1993), a time-frame that would nowadays disqualify it from any serious technological application, let alone CALL. It might be helpful to review the types of parsers used in CALL.

Well over a decade ago, Matthews (1993) compiled a list of eight parsers most commonly used in CALL, which included:

(1) Various Augmented Phrase Structure frameworks, including Definite Clause Grammar (DCG).
(2) Augmented Transition Networks (ATN).
(3) Lexical Functional Grammar (LFG).
(4) Systemic Grammar.
(5) Tree Adjoining Grammar (TAG).
(6) Incremental Procedure Grammar (IPG).
(7) Word Grammar.
(8) Preference Semantics.

Years later, Schulze (1999) adds to the list what had been Matthews' (1993) desideratum: Head-Driven Phrase Structure Grammar (HPSG). If the reader is not familiar with the above terminology, she will be pleased to know that the review of the most recent literature on parser-based CALL has revealed the following pattern, which will be subsequently discussed in more detail:

(1) Context Free Phrase Structure Grammar (CFPSG).
(2) Augmented Phrase Structure Grammar (APSG) including Definite Clause Grammar (DCG).
(3) Shift-Reduce Parser.

(4) Principles and Parameters Theory (PPT), Principle-based parsing and Chunk parser.
(5) Lexical Functional Grammar (LFG).
(6) Head-Driven Phrase Structure Grammar (HPSG).

We see that some types have been dropped and others have been added. For example, ATN (Augmented Transition Network) has been used in CALL since (Loritz, 1995), although it is not on our list. The reason it has been omitted is that even though this kind of algorithm, which treats each grammatical pattern as a network consisting of a node and different types of arcs (Allen, 1995), can process linguistic input (Eiselt & Holbrook, 2002), it is not based on the representation of the grammar knowledge as such (Gazdar & Mellish, 1996). While most of the parsers on our list are called a 'grammar' of some sort because they are based on declarative knowledge of linguistic rules, ATNs are procedural programs, executed in a sequential manner, which do not rely on a linguistic knowledge base (Eiselt & Holbrook, 2002). Therefore their application is limited to the task at hand as is the case with the bulk of procedural computer programs (Gazdar & Mellish, 1996). Although their popularity soared in the 1970s (Gazdar & Mellish, 1996) and even the LUNAR query module was based on one (Allen, 1995), contemporary knowledge representation approaches have very much pushed them out.

The ranking in our list of parsing methods applied in CALL is not based on frequency with which the respective parsing strategies seem to be used, but on their inherent characteristics, which make the explanation easier to follow if placed in the above order. I will now explain each of the above terms and give examples from the CALL literature.

The simplest thing to do is to start with phrase structure grammars. Such grammars consist of non-terminal symbols such as S for sentence, which can then be rewritten as NP VP or a combination of a noun phrase and a verb phrase and further subdivided into similar component parts until a terminal symbol is reached that is no longer available for such analysis. Such grammars are of course highly abstract and do not reflect the particularities of natural languages, nor are they concerned with meaning. They are best applied to artificial languages such as computer languages. They are often called context-free grammars (Matthews, 1998).

Nagata (2002) describes the implementation of 14 context-free phrase structure rules to process input in Japanese within the system called BANZAI. The purpose of the parser is to establish whether the student's input is well formed or not. This particular parser uses a bottom-up processing technique, which starts from identifying the parts of speech for individual words in a sentence and then tries to match them up with one of the possible rules (Allen, 1995). Thus, one of BANZAI rules identifies a verb as a verb phrase (VP$\rightarrow$ V^{*5}), while another one identifies a higher level rule

for a sentence, which in Japanese can by constituted by a verb alone (S →
VP). This very simple algorithm is used after the initial pre-processing of
words into morphemes, which is often necessary to complement the simple
syntax that does not account for word forms or inflections.

Definite Clause Grammars (DCG) are a special case of Augmented
Phrase Structure Grammars (APSG). If phrase structure grammars, which
are context-free, are furnished (augmented) with lexical or morphological
features, e.g. the terminal symbol N for a noun receives number, gender
and case (sg, fem, nom), these features can be used to check language
specific agreements between parts of speech in a sentence. We say that such
grammars are augmented phrase structure grammars. Definite clause
grammars use such features and are implemented in PROLOG, a programming language that uses the logic of the predicate calculus to formulate
knowledge in a series of statements. The notation is simple (e.g.: s → np,
vp), simpler than the original PROLOG syntax (s(Sentence,Text):-
np(Sentence,Rest), vp(Rest,Text).).

ILTS is an intelligent Greek tutor using DCG. It was designed to provide
interactive practice of grammar and vocabulary and error specific
feedback, thus contributing to individualised learning.

> The NLP component consists of a grammar, lexicon and parser. The
> grammar and lexicon use typed feature structures in an ALE style ex-
> tension of Prolog [see Carpenter and Penn, 1994]. The grammar and
> lexicon are processed by LOPE, which is a phrase structure parsing and
> definite clause programming system. A distinguishing feature of
> LOPE is the manner in which it supports the parsing of phrases con-
> taining conflicting values in their feature structures. Definite Clause
> Grammars (DCGs), like other unification-based grammars, place an
> important restriction on parsing, that is, if two or more features do not
> agree in their values, a parse will fail. However, in a language learning
> system, these are the kinds of mistakes made by learners. To parse un-
> grammatical sentences, the Greek grammar contains rules which are
> capable of parsing ill-formed input (buggy rules) and which apply if
> the grammatical rules fail (see also [Schneider & McCoy, 1998], [Liou,
> 1991], [Weischedel, 1983], [Carbonell & Hayes, 1981]). The system
> keeps a record of which grammatical violations have occurred and
> which rules have been used but not violated. The latter is an indication
> of the successful application of a grammatical concept. This informa-
> tion is fed to the Student Model. (Heift *et al.*, 2000)

While Holland *et al.* (1993) assure the reader that a specific focus on
grammar can be a result of a needs analysis for a particular learner population, Matthews (1993) warns against excessive focus on agreement which is
facilitated by the use of DCG, speculating that this may not be the most
frequent type of error L2 learners make. In support of this, literature (James,

1998; Singleton, 1999) provides evidence that lexical errors seem to be the highest in frequency. However, this does not prove the infrequency of agreement errors or the inadequacy of focusing on agreement in parser-based CALL. We will see in the next chapter that in certain student populations a high ratio of agreement errors can be present. There seems to be a general agreement regarding the advantages of DCG (Allen, 1995; Matthews, 1993): they are easy to implement in PROLOG, and with the advance in compiler technology can be very fast and precise.

'One way to improve the efficiency of parsers is to use techniques that encode uncertainty, so that the parser need not make an arbitrary choice and later backtrack' (Allen, 1995). Earlier, we said that backtracking is a procedure whereby a parser can return to an earlier state in analysis if the chosen path does not seem to lead to a satisfactory parse. With shift-reduce parsers, the uncertainty or the ambiguity is passed forward up to the point where all possibilities but one can be eliminated. This technique was developed to complement context-free grammars designed for artificial languages that have no ambiguities and therefore only one interpretation is possible at the time. Because of the ambiguity ridden nature of human language such techniques help avoid either the wrong parse or the need to retrace a number of steps thus slowing down the process. Shift-reduce parsers have the ability to look ahead for information that can resolve ambiguities and are therefore fast and efficient.

Weinberg, Pennington and Suri (1995 in Reeder & Hamburger, 1999: 324) included a shift-reduce parser in their ICALL system called MILT, whose purpose is the tutoring of German and Arabic. The use of the shift-reduce parsers seems to have enabled it to conform to a particular linguistic theory, arising from Chomsky's work. This is called the X-bar theory, the fundamentals of which will be explained shortly. Reeder and Hamburger (1999: 324) call this application 'a powerful and linguistically motivated NLP system'. Weinberg *et al.* (1995) describe a predecessor of MILT, called the BRIDGE, which also uses an X-bar theory based shift-reduce parser for German and Arabic. Rather than relying on numerous rules, like a DCG does, this parser operates on a small set of rules, which are accompanied by a set of constraints that must be met before a rule can apply. For example, in the clause 'X – > YZ, f(X,Y,Z)' (Weinberg *et al.*, 1995: 33) the left side of the predicate is the rule, while the right side contains the constraints. The latter indicates that YZ can be rewritten as X, given the criteria of the formula f are satisfied. It may be interesting to mention that this parser is also implemented in PROLOG, an artificial language that seems accommodative of the most diverse linguistic approaches.

As pointed out in Chapter 1, the principles and parameters theory, more recently known as X-bar (X') theory is based on language universals (Cook, 1993). It seeks the universality of a few common principles in all languages. One of these principles is, for example, that all languages have phrases of some sort and each phrase has a head. What is different across the languages is how the parameters of these principles have been set. Thus the position of the head within the phrase may be to the left or to the right, depending on the specific language. Phrase structure is handled through X-bar syntax, which symbolises the structure of each phrase as containing a head and having three levels: X'', X' and X. In a noun phrase, 'her fear of flying' for instance, the whole phrase is N'' (X''). When the determiner ('the') is removed, 'fear of flying' becomes N' (X') and can be further subsegmented into 'fear', which is N (X) and 'of flying'. The latter then becomes the next phrase for analysis, P'' or prepositional phrase.

Clive Matthews (1993) sees a lot of merits in using the X-bar syntax and the principles and parameters theory (PPT) in parsing. His advocacy of this approach is based on three distinct advantages: grammar size, grammar specificity and handling ungrammaticality. As we have seen, PPT is based on very broad universal principles and thus a parser based on this theory would not have to have nearly as many rules as is the case with DCG. Next, even though the principles seem too broad to satisfy the language specificity criterion, this is achieved by the use of parametric variation. Finally, the ungrammatical input can be at least recognised and assigned an X-bar structure by a PPT based parser, whereas a rule based parser in fact needs a new rule for each type of ungrammaticality or relaxing the existing rules, both of which can slow down the system significantly. At the time when Matthews (1993) wrote this article, there was a gaping shortage of PPT based parsers, in particular in CALL. Nowadays, the trend seems to be toward having more and more such parsers. We will examine an example in the following.

The FIPS syntactic parser is an NLP device based on the Principles and Parameters Theory (PPT). It is a part of the FreeText system for learners of French, consisting of a learner corpus, from which it derives its knowledge of most common errors, a spell checker, a syntactic parser (FIPS) and a sentence comparison diagnosis system (Granger, 2003; L'Haire & Faltin, 2003). It performs parsing in three main steps: (1) identification of X-bar phrases based on the lexical analysis, (2) combining the phrases, and (3) application of constraints for the purpose of rejecting ungrammatical structures (L'Haire & Faltin, 2003). Thus it seems that FIPS is a bottom-up parser because it starts from the individual words, moving on to building phrases and then sentences (Allen, 1995). As bottom-up parsers are faced with more choices than top-down parsers, taking the wrong decision and having to backtrack would be enormously time-consuming. For this reason, the efficiency of bottom-up parsers is much improved if alternative parses are stored in a chart and a full analysis can then take advantage of the most likely stored candidate. Such parsers are called bottom-up chart parsers (Allen, 1995). FIPS follows exactly the same procedure (L'Haire & Faltin,

2003). When a full parse fails, FIPS has the advantage of being able to work with the so-called chunk parse (Allen, 1995), i.e. partial input analyses.

In NLP literature (Allen, 1995) the above procedure is sometimes called partial parsing and constitutes the most radical approach to ambiguity problem. Because of the frequent learner errors, the ambiguity of IL utterances is normally much higher than the ambiguity level in L1 utterances. Thus, attacking ambiguity seems such a worthy cause for NLP in CALL. As explained in the previous paragraph, the partial parser looks for phrases and performs what is called local disambiguation. One of the disadvantages is of course that it returns a sequence of syntactic segments, which have to be disambiguated from without the parser itself. For this purpose, an appeal is often made to semantic (Allen, 1995) or lexical interpretation (Tschichold, 2003). FIPS however relies on: (1) its knowledge of the world (eliminates highly implausible analyses), (2) knowledge of French as L1 (uses word frequency ranking to select the best solution), and (3) knowledge of IL (uses error frequency from a learner corpus). Such parsers are sometimes also called principle-based parsers (Abney, 1991 in Tschichold, 2003) or chunk parsers (Tschichold, 2003).

The next parser type used in contemporary CALL is based on the theory of lexical functional grammar (LFG) and can be said to attach particular importance to the lexicon and the way it is described, usually in much semantic, morphological and semantic detail. As a computational representation of language, LFG assumes two levels of description: (1) constituent structure (c-structure), which similarly to X-bar grammar uses a context-free phrase structure representation producing a tree, and (2) the functional structure (f-structure), which 'encodes the syntactic predicate argument structure and is represented as an attribute-value matrix' (Butt *et al.*, 1999: 3). If c-structure may bear some familiarity for an X-bar theory proponent, the f-structure according to Butt *et al.* (1999) may to such a person appear quite baffling. It represents a series of constraints imposed on the context-free environment of the c-structure and contains attributes such as SUBJ, PRED, OBJECT, whose values can integrate other f-structures thus being pointers to the more elaborate lexical semantics of the item.

An example of LFG application in CALL is described by Veit Reuer (2003) within the context of error recognition. This interactive ICALL system uses an Early-based chart parser to identify four different types of errors: insertion, omission, misplacement and spurious replacement. Based on the article (Reuer, 2003: 500), only two of them seem to be working: omissions and misplacements. In order to identify omissions, the chart-parsing component relies on a part-of-speech list which consists of functional categories 'that restrict possible insertions of apparently omitted items in the sentence'. Misplacement errors are handled by storing the word sequence into the chart, where it is corrected at an appropriate stage. The advantage of this system is according to the author (Reuer, 2003) fast identification of errors, rather than just robust parsing, as is the case in chunk parsing.

The next kind of parser, which seems to find wider and wider application in CALL (Schulze, 1999), is HPSG or Head-driven Phrase Structure Grammar. While trying to provide enough lexical detail like LFG, it sometimes operates on one level only, rather than on two syntactic levels, which is the case with LFG applications. HPSG sometimes uses the approach of encoding linear precedence explicitly within the feature system of the lexical items. This linear uni-modular coding avoids too much modularity within the system (Butt, 1999). It also takes advantage of classes and their inheritance properties. Thus, it capitalises on what is known as object-oriented programming.

Trude Heift (2003) describes the application of an HPSG parser within a German tutor which provides error specific feedback. While the correct knowledge of language is encoded in the Domain Knowledge system (HPSG parser), the error types, in particular agreement errors, are also added to the regular lexical entry features. The error encoding is specific, which has the advantage that very specific feedback can result directly from this error recognition. It can be applied to a variety of linguistic phenomena, practically leaving no error unattended to. Finally, this mechanism ensures that the well-formed and erroneous input are not treated differently and that neither the parsing route nor the grammar itself have to be altered in order to achieve this goal.

In his CALICO article, Matthews (1993) postulates three different criteria for the evaluation of grammar formalisms in NLP. They are computational effectiveness, linguistic perspicuity and acquisitional perspicuity. Computational effectiveness would simply mean the best possible output with the minimum of input and time. Linguistics perspicuity means adequate description of language, while acquisitional perspicuity refers to the adequacy of explanation they can provide, which compares well with James' (1998) diagnostic power discussed earlier in this chapter. We can apply these criteria to evaluate the ICALL grammar formalisms enumerated so far.

Context Free Phrase Structure Grammar (CFPSG) is easy to develop, but may lack the necessary linguistic detail, which can be compensated for by using additional morphological pre-parsers or similar mechanisms called finite state automata (Allen, 1995). This, however, reduces their computational efficiency, leaving the explanatory power uncertain and very much language type and problem dependent. Definite Clause Grammar (DCG), as mentioned above, tend to necessitate a large number of rules in order to have both linguistic and acquisitional perspicuity, thus making them potentially less efficient than other formalisms. However, since they are implemented in PROLOG, which according to Matthews (1998) is reasonably fast, they might be a clear-cut and not altogether inefficient solution. Shift-Reduce Parser has a comparative strength in that it can efficiently resolve ambiguities. Principles and Parameters Theory (PPT) application results in Principle-based parsing and Chunk parsers, which seem to have the necessary linguistic and acquisitional perspicuity, but are rather complex and operate on multiple levels, which in the long run might affect their computational effectiveness. Lexical Functional Grammar (LFG) is similarly multimodular. Head-Driven Phrase Structure Grammar (HPSG) finally emerges as a system with many advantages, including all of Matthews' (1993) criteria.

Schulze (1999: 121) lists the following advantages of HPSG systems:

(1) They enable an eclectic approach, incorporating a number of insights from LFG and other linguistic theories.
(2) They make a great use of inheritance principles.
(3) They drastically reduce the number and detail of linguistic rules.
(4) They integrate syntactic and semantic information on one level in a single representation.

While it would seem that we have a winner in HPSG, we need to consider the criteria of needs analysis and cost-benefit ratio. At the end of the day, the system that addresses the learner's need in an efficient and cost-effective way will be the best system in a given situation. To gain a better understanding of what the needs may be and how various systems fulfil them we shall look at how some of the above systems identify the targeted learner errors. In order to do that, however, we need to start from the error coding strategies most generally applied in parser-based CALL.

According to Matthews and Fox (1991), in order to be able to detect learner errors, an ITS or a parser based system must have some sort of a student model. While the rules of the correct language constitute the expert model (EM), the rules of the learner interlanguage represent the student model (SM). The student model can be based on three different principles: (1) overlay or rule relaxation (Matthews & Fox, 1991; Menzel & Schröder, 1999), (2) mal-rules or bug rules (Matthews & Fox, 1991; Manning, 1991; Menzel & Schröder, 1999; Heift, 2003), (3) L1 grammar + L2 grammar, and (4) robust parsing accompanied by semantic and pragmatic disambiguation. The four approaches will be described in the following in more detail.

An overlay model is based on the notion of 'missing conceptions' (Matthews & Fox, 1991: 165). This means that the learner's grammar is considered to be incomplete in relation to the complete TL grammar, i.e. be a subset of it (Yip, 1995). Consequently, the student model will either omit entire rules or parts of rules. The latter is the case when we relax some constraints, as the subject-verb agreement in number for example. If this constraint is relaxed, the parser will accept structures such as '*they likes', in which the subject is the plural and the verb in the singular. (Matthews & Fox, 1991) provide evidence from first language acquisition (FLA) theory

(Brown & Hanlon, cited in Matthews & Fox, 1991: 165) according to which there is a basis for treating some of the language acquisition errors this way, but they also indicate their awareness of the inability of this model to account for all IL errors, especially as far as adult learners are concerned.

Another way to present the student IL model is by introducing the erroneous rules applied by the students, which are referred to in the literature as mal-rules (Matthews & Fox, 1991; Manning, 1991; Menzel & Schröder, 1999), bugs or buggy rules in NLP (Matthews & Fox, 1991) and incompetence rules in the broader FLA framework (Matthews & Fox, 1991). Not all types of parsers will of course support this approach. The one that is, however, perfectly matched with this approach is definite clause grammar (DCG) because of its strong focus on explicit rules (Matthews, 1993). An example of such an incompetence rule is faulty word order (Schwind, 1990 in Matthews & Fox, 1991). Matthews and Fox (1991) object to calling such systems 'intelligent', as apparently they 'know' what errors to expect. This, however, indicates that the term 'intelligent' in this paper is an undefined term or at least a term which has a very different meaning from the one we agreed on earlier in this chapter. That meaning is related to the Turing Test or the fact that a machine, when observed externally, can give an impression of being intelligent. Matthews and Fox (1991), however, may be thinking of the decision-making process built into a machine. If a machine is programmed to perform expectable tasks, then it is an automaton. Otherwise it is deemed to be intelligent.

Further to the subject, Matthews & Fox (1991) find two major faults with the mal-rule approach. The first fault is apparently that any unanticipated errors may go undetected. The second one is that there is no account for the underlying cause of the incompetence rules. In answer to the first objection, it can be said that the mal-rules are added to the rules of correct grammar within a rule based system such as DCG. This means that there is a double check of each utterance, performed once against the correct grammar and the second time against the faulty grammar. A faulty utterance should at least be identified as erroneous in the first check, even if it is not fully recognised and labelled in the second check. Thus it is not likely that an error would remain totally undetected, unless the supposedly correct grammar had a major flaw. Matthews & Fox (1991) themselves provide an answer to the second charge, namely that of not addressing the underlying cause of incompetence rules. In doing so they refer to the work of Menzel (1988, in Matthews & Fox, 1991), which uses a general error diagnosis procedure that can be applied to any domain of knowledge. More recently error diagnosis systems have used large learner corpora to study learner errors in order to be able to recognise and diagnose them (Tschichold, 2003; Heift, 2003).

The next solution to the problem of identifying learner errors is presented in the form of combined L1 and L2 grammars. Matthews and Fox

(1991) point out that such systems are not technically buggy or faulty since they do not contain any incompetence rules. The underlying theory is therefore that of mother tongue interference. Errors within this framework are not seen as competence errors, since incompetence is not explicitly encoded in the system. Rather they are seen as performance errors or mis-application of L1 rules in L2, comparable to the effect of bilingual aphasia (Matthews & Fox, 1991).

A fourth way of dealing with learner errors by way of NLP is based on robust parsing and external disambiguation methods (see earlier this chapter). This is done in order to satisfy two seemingly contradictory requirements on any learner error diagnosis system (Menzel & Schröder, 999). The first of these requirements is the determination of structural interpretation of the student's utterances even in the face of 'considerable local ambiguity and the possible existence of unexpected or unacceptable constructions' (Menzel & Schröder, 1999: 20). This requirement indicates robust parsing as a necessity. The second one is the requirement of fault diagnosis, associated with the need to identify and explain 'ungrammatical constructions and inappropriate communicative behaviour' (Menzel & Schröder, 1999: 20). The system proposed by Menzel & Schröder (1999) as an answer to both requirements performs multilevel parsing, using different description levels for syntax, semantics and domain specific relations. Structures on different levels 'are mapped onto each other by means of graded constraint and are disambiguated simultaneously' (Menzel & Schröder, 1999: 25). Thus this system uses loose syntax rules paired with more constrained semantic and propositional rules. In a way it is a combination of rule relaxation, which happens at the syntactic levels and introducing extra rules, i.e. by adding new levels of constraints in terms of semantics and domain knowledge.

We have so far examined the ways in which a parser can identify an error as such. The next step in the process is giving feedback in regard to the iden-tified error. While some ICALL authors believe in giving feedback to only one error per utterance at a time, others feel more relaxed about this issue. Holland *et al.* (1993), for example, very much support the former, in that they distinguish between the primary error and all other errors. The primary errors within the BRIDGE system are considered communica-tively significant and receive feedback per default, while secondary errors are not considered communicatively significant and therefore feedback to those errors is optional. BRIDGE also includes different levels of error indi-cation, ranging from indirect (caution light or frown face) to explicit metalinguisic description ('verb and subject don't agree') often accompa-nied by explanation in a separate proposition ('The reader might get confused as to whether you mean singular or plural'), as advised by James (1998). In addition, errors can be fed back intermittently or at the end of the dialogue.

Trude Heift (2003) identifies Schwind's (1990 in Heift, 2003) solution to the problem of multiple errors as the reason why BRIDGE and a number of other ICALL systems avoid giving feedback to all of them. Pedagogically (Heift, 2003) too much instructional feedback is thought to have the capacity of overwhelming the student. Instead, specific grammatical phenomena should be focused on from the outset. This principle also underlies one of three recommendations regarding ICALL feedback made by Van der Linden (1993 in Heift, 2003): (1) feedback needs to be accurate, (2) one error message at a time should be displayed, and (3) explanations for a particular error should be kept short (not more than three lines at a time). In a German tutor described by Heift (2003) the student model module keeps track of the student's proficiency level, including the types and frequency of errors made, which has an impact on the instructional content of the messages. In addition, the filtering module determines the order of instructional feedback displayed to students. More precisely, an error priority queue is directly responsible for that order, based on the frequency and the importance of the error within a given exercise.

While Holland *et al.* (1993) offer a variety of feedback styles and levels, Delmonte (2003) takes a different stance. His point of criticism is a feedback taxonomy by Lyster and Ranta (1997 in Delmonte, 2003), which includes explicit correction, recast, clarification request, metalinguistic feedback, elicitation and repetition. Delmonte (2003) believes that recast, clarification request, metalinguistic feedback, elicitation and repetition are inadequate as feedback from the computer. He also believes that explicit correction, which is identical with James' (1998) correction proper, is best suited for grammatical drills. Thus metalinguistic feedback remains the only type of feedback acceptable to this author as a parser's response to L2 errors. No theoretical explanation is provided for this view.

Granger (2003) bases her error descriptors for feedback purposes on Dulay, Burt and Krashen (1982 in Granger, 2003). These authors suggest two major descriptive error taxonomies, one focusing on linguistic categories (e.g. lexis, auxiliaries, passives, etc.) and the other focusing on the way surface structures have been altered (e.g. omission, addition, misformation, misordering). Granger (2003) like James (1998) believes that these two approaches should be blended into one and even adding a third dimension to the thus achieved bidimensionality. Granger (2003) is also in favour of providing error correction. Thus, the feedback would be something like 'Gender error on pronoun' + correction (L'Haire & Faltin, 2003: 489).

Reeder *et al.* (1999) believe that error feedback in ICALL should be more conversational. They consider it a disadvantage that many ICALL systems respond to learner errors with a template based explanation. These authors believe in contrast that the system should respond in a way that acknowledges both error recognition and its correction.

We have seen that there are a number of approaches to computer generated feedback in ICALL, ranging from natural communication and emulation of communicative style to correction and metalinguistic comment. We have thus explored the role of different types of parsers in language error identification and correction as regards the written output. What remains to be mentioned is a hybrid approach in which a parser is combined with the string matching approach in a special kind of template. We shall then examine how other types of knowledge bases can aid parsers in diagnosing errors.

Chen and Tokuda (2003) describe what they call a template-template-enhanced ICALL system available to teachers to design their own lessons. Template-template means an expandable template, one that can be easily converted into a range of other templates. This system uses a visual authoring tool with which the teachers can create new parse trees or indicate the most likely ones. This system is trained on what the authors call templates, but what seem to be examples of correctly and incorrectly used language within the context of translation. The system itself is quite complex and includes a part of speech tagger (POST), a template automaton structure for knowledge representation and a diagnostic engine based on the heaviest common sequence matching algorithm (HCS), a parser based learner model and a visual template authoring tool.

Thus, complexity is the nature of systems that want to deal with human language successfully. Parsers alone can often handle a lot of language in terms of structures, especially in case of LFG and head driven phrase structure (HPSG), but they may not be able to check whether, for example, an answer provided by a learner was not only syntactically correct, but also included the right content. While some systems build artificial constraints as to what input to allow, other systems use domain knowledge to perform the content check. Two such examples are described in the following.

Domain knowledge enables ICALL systems to better analyse language and secondly to make better decisions overall. Knowing the intention of the learner can narrow down the scope of interpretation and considerably reduce the level of ambiguity in a learner's erroneous utterance. O'Brien (1993) describes the advantages of at the time planned linkage between eL, a parser based system and a multimedia scenario based application. Constraining the communication context to one 'room' with a plausible limited scenario would considerably constrain the semantic scope and therefore disambiguate a lot of the language the learner might produce. What eL appeared to have at the time were knowledge bases, which could be used to enhance semantic checks. Thus in a lesson about animals, the knowledge taught to the system could be for example that a gorilla is bigger than a chimpanzee, etc.

An error diagnosis system described by Menzel and Schröder (1999) deals with ambiguity on a multi-level basis: syntactically, semantically and domain-wise. Structures on the various levels are mapped onto each other and are generally disambiguated simultaneously. Rich syntactic representation allows for example to specify that the verb 'visit' is transitive and therefore requires a subject and a direct object. Sortal restrictions further ensure that the semantically right categories of words are matched together. Finally, the domain knowledge considers whether an utterance is true or false within the domain.

This author's favourite example of a parser based ICALL system which works at multiple levels and certainly captures an array of learner errors is Amber Productions' murder mystery game Herr Kommissar, designed for intermediate learners of German (DeSmedt, 1995). The role of the learner in this game is to interrogate the suspects in a murder case. According to DeSmedt (1995) this is not only a communicative immersion task, but it also enables task based learning, where language is used meaningfully to accomplish an extralinguistic mission. The very fact that the focus is on meaning, as actually suggested by Doughty and Williams (1998b) or Long and Robinson (1998), may bring about the automatism in using the linguistic form deemed necessary by connectionists (N. Ellis, 2001; MacWhinney, 2001).

Not only is Herr Kommissar realistic and fun to use, but it also has some truly sophisticated AI and language processing features. Apart from performing both natural language analysis and synthesis, it utilises a rare form of underpinning grammar as well as several other forms of world knowledge representation complete with a discourse tracking facility. The grammar it uses is case grammar which restrains the number of permitted semantic relationships between words (Allen, 1995) and thus making sure that a formally correct utterance also makes sense. Besides, the semantics of the system is supported by three different ways of representing knowledge of the world: concept ontology, predication constraints and postulation. Concept ontology represents possible relationships between terms (e.g. murder and weapons), while predication constraints tell the system which words cannot go together (e.g. 'drink' and 'wood'). Postulations, on the other hand, are positive rules complementing predication constraints (e.g. that it is more likely that a dog bit a man rather than vice versa). Finally the system remembers not only what questions the leaner has asked, but it also tracks the learner's mistakes in terms of spelling and grammar, thus performing a sort of learner profiling which is a part of the student modelling process in ITS.

Thus, intelligent error identification and diagnosis systems, as far as written language is concerned, can be quite sophisticated and use a number of subsystems combined with a variety of processing levels, making them almost human and truly intelligent. There are some constraints that we will consider in the concluding remarks to this chapter. Next however, we will turn toward the speaking skill and the way it can be articulated and assessed using the speech processing technology.

Speech processing

Speaking is a language skill that has particularly gained in significance within the communicative language learning framework (Egan, 1999). According to Ehsani and Knodt (1998: 46) 'foreign language curricula focus on productive skills with special emphasis on communicative competence'. This is why Eskenazi (1999: 62) makes the following statement: 'Below a certain level, even if grammar and vocabulary are completely correct, effective communication *cannot* take place without correct pronunciation (Celce Murcia & Goodwin, 1991 in Eskenazi, 1999) because poor phonetics and prosody can distract the listener and impede comprehension of the message.' However, attaining a native-like pronunciation as an adult L2 learner is not an easy task (Ehsani & Knodt, 1998). Looking at the sheer physiology of speech and hearing, connectionists claim that auditory nerves specialise for the auditory tasks early on in a person's life, thus restricting the range of sounds heard and interpreted (N. Ellis, 2001). This makes the task of recognising and subsequently repeating speech sounds of another language correctly more difficult. Therefore, an adult L2 learner must take a series of time-consuming steps in order to improve her pronunciation. These steps include producing a large number of sentences, receiving pertinent corrective feedback, hearing many different native models, emphasising prosody (amplitude, duration, and pitch) and feeling at ease in the language learning situation (Eskenazi, 1999: 62).

Thus, the adult L2 learner needs to perform a difficult task with limited learning capacity without feeling ill at ease or lacking confidence, which is a sort of contradiction in terms. Ideally, the sheer amount of output needed for this endeavour would be attained in one-on-one interactive language situations (Eskenazi, 1999: 62), which are often both impractical and too costly. The situation lends itself perfectly to computer assisted language learning. For this particular purpose the upcoming speech processing technology offers a promise (Wachowicz & Scott, 1999; Egan, 1999). However, Ehsani and Knodt (1998) are concerned about the limited acceptance the new technologies have received within the language teaching community. The reasons they list for this situation are not unknown to us: the absence of a unified theoretical framework, the absence of conclusive evidence and the current limitations of technologies are among the most frequently cited ones (Nerbonne *et al.*, 1998; Chapelle, 1997; Salaberry, 1996; Holland, 1995). Ehsani and Knodt (1998), just like Nerbonne *et al.* (1998), identify a major flaw in the reasoning of some of the fiercest opponents of CALL. While Nerbonne *et al.* (1998) use the terminology of formal logic to identify the fallacy of division, Ehsani and Knodt (1998) use catchy everyday language to coin the phrase 'all-or-nothing reasoning'. The point made is that what is true of technology as related to human language in its totality is hardly true of technology as related to restricted domains of language, e.g. such as those often encountered in language teaching and learning. If the current technology does not have the potency to deal with the former, it can certainly be successfully used to handle the latter. Ehsani and Knodt (1998: 46) put their claim forward in a very eloquent manner:

> Salaberry (1996) demands nothing short of a system capable of simulating the complex socio-communicative competence of a live tutor—in other words, the linguistic intelligence of a human—only to conclude that the attempt to create an 'intelligent language tutoring system is a fallacy' (p. 11). Because speech technology isn't perfect, it is of no use at all. If it 'cannot account for the full complexity of human language,' why even bother modeling more constrained aspects of language use (Higgins, 1988, p. vii)? This sort of all-or-nothing reasoning seems symptomatic of much of the latest pedagogical literature on CALL. The quest for a theoretical grounding of CALL system design and evaluation (Chapelle, 1997) tends to lead to exaggerated expectations as to what the technology ought to accomplish. When combined with little or no knowledge of the underlying technology, the inevitable result is disappointment.

In order to make our own assessment of the value of speech processing technology in CALL, we need to examine the current theory and practice underpinning the effective teaching and learning of L2 pronunciation. Celce Murcia and Goodwin (1991 in Eskenazi, 1999) report that a 'listen and imitate' technique is often used drawing the student's attention to minimal pairs such as the English *pin* and *bin*. Their research suggests that noticing L2 sounds is the most effective way for the students to learn how to pronounce them. If a sound does not already belong to a student's repertoire of speech sounds, it may be associated with the closest equivalent in the learner's native language. For example, if a native speaker of Arabic who is just starting to learn English hears the sound /p/ in *pin*, she will most probably associate it with the sound /b/ of the English *bin*, since the student has no awareness of /p/ as a separate phoneme. Eskenazi (1999: 63) further reports:

> Teaching techniques in the past have followed the principle that in order to *hear* foreign sounds, categorize them, and produce them, students must be given specific instruction on how to *articulate* them. It was believed that learners must physically experience the articulation of the sound and be able to produce it before they can hear it as a separate, significant element in the target language. In the above example, teaching students to round their lips would be more effective than repeating a minimal pair. Yet recent research by Akahane-Yamada,

Tohkura, Bradlow, and Pisoni (1996) shows that perception training alone may be just as effective.

What seems beneficial in any event is that the learner be exposed to a large number and a wide range of native speakers (Eskenazi, 1999; Wachowicz & Scott, 1999), which in most educational settings does not seem to be a viable option. In addition to the phonemes of the target language, the student also needs to master the prosodic features of L2 utterances, since as Eskenazi (1992: 64) puts it 'intonation is the glue that holds a message together'. Feedback and correction of speech errors seems to be a very sensitive area with adult learners, as they appear to lose confidence if criticised in front of their peers (Laroy, 1995 in Eskenazi, 1999; Wachowicz & Scott, 1999). One-on-one instructional situation seems to work best in this case, with emphasis on the amount of interruption a learner can tolerate, avoidance of negative feedback and focus on positive reinforcement. Kenworthy (1987 in Eskenazi, 1999) advocates contrastive analysis of L1 and L2 sound systems as a way of avoiding errors in the first place, which if undetected can fossilise.

The profile of the instructor that ideally matches the requirements outlined above can be found in the latest speech processing systems as nowadays slightly more daringly applied in CALL (Wachowicz & Scott, 1999). In order to understand the unique advantages and some of the disadvantages of such systems, we need to understand the basics of the underlying technology, which we will review in the following.

As mentioned earlier in this chapter, the linguistic discipline involved in the design of speech processing technology is the subdiscipline of computational linguistics known as computational phonetics and phonology. While phonetics is concerned with speech sounds in general, phonology or phonemics is concerned with phonemes or ideal sounds of a natural language. Computational phonetics and phonology are applied in two distinct approaches to speech: speech synthesis and speech analysis. Of the two, the former has a much longer tradition and was initiated well before the advent of computer. Thus in 1939 Bell Laboratories piloted a device called 'vocoder', whose purpose was to reconstruct the human voice. It used a sound source and a set of filters whose values were derived from the analysis of human speech (O'Grady et al., 1997). At the background of this or any subsequent technology is the fact that each sound can be broken down into its fundamental wave forms. This procedure is known as spectrographic analysis and the graphic representation of sound waves is called spectrogram. A spectrogram is a diagram representing the duration of an utterance on the horizontal axis and the different wave frequencies on the vertical axis. The main frequencies or formants are marked for vowels because they have more intensity than other frequencies. Such acoustic analysis is used to isolate and represent typical speech sounds. This is not an overly easy task since visually similar waveforms do not necessarily indicate similar sounds (Jelinek, 1997). Some of the reasons are indicated below.

In theory, speech synthesis should be a simple procedure whereby thus extracted speech sounds would be concatenated into words and utterances. Unfortunately, this is not the case because speech sounds are not fixed, but vary according to the sounds that surround them. Adjacent sounds can modify each other on what is known as the segmental level (sounds). In addition to these local changes, suprasegmental features such as pitch, stress and intonation can have an effect on individual sounds. Therefore there are many steps involved in speech synthesis. The text to be synthesised has to be analysed syntactically, semantically and orthographically. Subsequently, pronunciation for exceptional words needs to be found and contrastive sounds have to be assigned based on the information available. After the correct sound is chosen, the system must look at the environment to select the most suitable allophone. A syntactic analysis then identifies the words that may have to go together and appropriate prosodic features need to be assigned (O'Grady *et al.*, 1997).

The task of speech recognition on the other hand is to take speech sound waves and decode them (O'Grady *et al.*, 1997). This task is much easier for human beings than it is for computers (Levow & Olsen, 1999). Broken down into steps, a human being has no problems coping with fast, informal and muffled speech, including faulty utterances in a continuous stream of sound, even under exacerbating conditions such as background noise. For a computer, all these things create problems (Wachowicz & Scott, 1999), which is why some systems require slow input with pauses between words, a limited vocabulary, speaker dependency and the exclusion of outside noise by using special microphones.

When dealing with the speaking skill within the L2 learning paradigm, especially as related to CALL, and in particular if thinking of error diagnosis and correction, speech recognition and its quality become the critical issue. Recognising and understanding human speech requires a considerable amount of linguistic knowledge at the phonological, lexical, semantic, grammatical and pragmatic level. While the linguistic competence of an adult native speaker covers a broad range of recognition tasks and communicative activities, computer programs perform best when designed to operate in clearly outlined sub-domains of linguistics. Ehsani and Knodt (1998) identify four different speech recognition tasks: that of a court reporter transcribing a court session, a voice activated dictation system, a computerised reading tutor highlighting difficult words and providing reading assistance, and finally that of a toddler being asked to fetch mum's slippers and getting a different type of shoe. The argument is that a human being, e.g. the court reporter, would perform all four tasks with similar competence whereas the computer is best used for a task for which it has been programmed or specialised. This is how they summarise the differences and similarities between human beings and computers at the same speech recognition task:

> Humans and machines process speech in fundamentally different ways (Bernstein & Franco, 1996). Complex cognitive processes account for the human ability to associate acoustic signals with meanings and intentions. For a computer, on the other hand, speech is essentially a series of digital values. However, despite these differences, the core problem of speech recognition is the same for both humans and machines: namely, of finding the best match between a given speech sound and its corresponding word string. Automatic speech recognition technology attempts to simulate and optimize this process computationally. (Ehsani & Knodt, 1998: 47)

One of the most successful and widely used techniques of automatic speech recognition is Hidden Markov Modeling (HMM) (Ehsani & Knodt, 1998; Jelinek, 1997; Allen, 1995). Markov Models are a way of representing and predicting patterns of activity within a system. They are based on the Markov assumption, i.e. the assumption that the state of the model depends only upon the previous states of the model. This is recognised as an oversimplification of any complex system in which components depend upon each other and change over time. Markov assumption ignores these possibilities and treats deterministic and non-deterministic systems in the same way. Deterministic systems always behave in the same way (e.g. traffic light changes) whereas non-deterministic systems do not (e.g. weather patterns) (Boyle, n.d.). The reason why Markov Models are called 'hidden' is that they use one accessible system to asses a related one which is hidden. For example, by analysing the acoustic properties of incoming sounds one can determine their articulatory or phonetic properties. The mathematical representation of HMM is simple: it includes two states and a transition between them represented via a matrix of probabilities. This principle can be used for phonetic, morphological, lexical and syntactic analysis of natural language to avoid exploring all possible hypotheses and facilitate a fast selection of the few most likely choices. According to Ehsani and Knodt (1998) a HMM based approach to speech recognition is an effective, even though not the most effective, method of high-performance speaker independent acoustic speech recognition.

Before continuing with HMM, it needs to be pointed out that speech recognition systems in general vary in type. They can be suited for the recognition of isolated words or for continuous speech recognition (Wachowicz & Scott, 1999). To use the former, one has to pause after each word, whereas with the latter one speaks normally (Allen, 1995). Isolated word recognition is older and has found application in issuing voice commands to computerised systems and in vocabulary focused

(Wachowicz & Scott, 1999) CALL. Another distinguishing feature of speech recognition systems is vocabulary size. Low end recognisers are often limited to not more than 30 words, while large-vocabulary systems can contain tens of thousands of words. Systems also vary from speaker-dependent (only recognising one speaker) to speaker-independent (recognising a wide range of speakers). Some speaker-independent systems can be additionally trained to suit one person for more efficiency. Training involves speech sampling at a certain rate and sound modelling, which will be described in more detail below.

Ehsani and Knodt (1998) give the most accessible description of a HMM based speech recogniser, which we will try to paraphrase here in order to illustrate the outworking of such systems in general. This is a complex system based on five components: (1) an acoustic signal analyser based on the spectral speech representation; (2) a set of phone models (HMMs) trained on large amounts of speech data; (3) a lexicon used for converting phone sequences into words; (4) a statistical model or grammar that supports the recognition task at the sentence level; (5) a decoder, which is a search algorithm responsible for finding the best possible match between a spoken utterance and a word sequence.

Automatic speech recognition begins with the analysis of the incoming speech signal. When a person speaks into a microphone the computer samples the input and creates a precise description of the speech signal. Next, a number of acoustic parameters such as the information on energy, spectral features, and pitch are derived from the speech signal. This information is used differently, depending on whether the system is in the training phase or the recognition phase. In the training phase, it is used for the purpose of modelling the speech signal. In the recognition phase, it is matched against the already existing model of the signal.

To train a computer program to recognise spoken language means to model the basic sounds of speech or phones. They are subsequently used in the recognition phase to identify words. An incoming speech signal can be said to be recognised when it is successfully matched with a set of HMM models. A HMM can either represent phones (monophones) or other sub-word units (biphones or triphones), whole words or even sentences. For example, a system can either have a representation of /d/ or /di/, /de/, / da/ or /dim/, /din/, /dig/ etc. Each approach has advantages and disadvantages. Following the comparison of the incoming acoustic signal with the HMMs, the system forms a hypothesis based on the sequence of models that most closely matches the signal itself.

Training necessitates a large amount of speech data representative of the type the system is expected to recognise. Generally speaking, an automatic speech recogniser is not capable of processing speech that differs significantly from the speech it has been trained on (Ehsani & Knodt, 1998). Thus, speaker-independent continuous dictation systems with large vocabulary are normally trained on tens of thousands of utterances read by a variety of speakers, including different dialects and age-groups.

> The lexicon, or dictionary, contains the phonetic spelling for all the words that are expected to be observed by the recognizer. It serves as a reference for converting the phone sequence determined by the search algorithm into a word. It must be carefully designed to cover the entire lexical domain in which the system is expected to perform. If the recognizer encounters a word it does not 'know' (i.e., a word not defined in the lexicon), it will either choose the closest match or return an out-of-vocabulary recognition error. Whether a recognition error is registered as a misrecognition or an out-of-vocabulary error depends in part on the vocabulary size. If, for example, the vocabulary is too small for an unrestricted dictation task—let's say less than 3K—the out-of-vocabulary errors are likely to be very high. If the vocabulary is too large, the chance of misrecognition errors increases because with more similar-sounding words, the confusability increases. The vocabulary size in most commercial dictation systems tends to vary between 5K and 60K. (Ehsani & Knodt, 1998: 49)

The language model is stochastic and predicts the most likely continuation of an utterance on the basis of statistical information. This information concerns the frequency in which words usually occur in a sequence in the target language. For instance, the sequence *A peace of pie* will have a very low probability, while the sequence *A piece of pie* will have a higher probability of occurring in standard English. An efficient language model must be trained on a large amount of text data collected from the target domain (Ehsani & Knodt, 1998; Egan, 1999).

The last piece of the jig-saw puzzle is the decoder or an algorithm that maximises the probability of a match between the speech sounds and the corresponding utterance. This can be described as a search problem, whereby particularly in large vocabulary systems questions of efficiency and optimisation must be carefully considered. The crucial question is whether to settle for the most likely hypothesis or to work with several solutions in parallel (Ehsani & Knodt, 1998). While the latter might be more accurate, the former could be much faster. Like in NLP systems we have discussed before, compromise might be necessary to achieve the best possible result within an acceptable time-frame.

Ehsani and Knodt (1998) further point out that task definition, i.e. specifying what the system is going to do (e.g. dictation vs. issuing system commands), is the most important step toward designing a viable speech recogniser. This is how they formulate it:

> Delimiting the performance domain imposes constraints on both the vocabulary size and what is referred to as 'perplexity,' which is usually

defined as the average branching factor within any given grammar network. A small vocabulary recognizer with limited perplexity (e.g., of the type used in automatic voice dialing), tends to be much more robust than a high-perplexity large-vocabulary dictation system. (Ehsani & Knodt, 1998: 50)

It is further pointed out that 'recognizers perform faster and more accurately when the incoming speech is enunciated clearly and in a noise-free environment, when the task perplexity is low, and when the dictionary is small' (Ehsani & Knodt, 1998: 50). Thus, precise task definition, appropriate acoustic modelling and input quality are essential features of a successful speech recognition system. Acoustic modelling has to take into account a sufficient number of representative speakers and can be augmented by single speaker features if need be. Input quality requires a good sound card and amplifier and a microphone that shuts out the background noise and is mounted at a constant distance from the speaker's mouth. Thus we have concluded the basic description of a voice recognition system. In the following we shall look at how such systems are being used in CALL.

Speech recognition in CALL

Voice-interactive systems have only more recently started being used in CALL (Ehsani & Knodt, 1998; Levow & Olsen, 1999; Egan, 1999) to teach pronunciation, reading aloud and some limited conversation skills (Holland, 1999; Wachowicz & Scott, 1999; Egan, 1999). Of the three, teaching pronunciation places the most demands on the system in terms of feedback. However, this is ultimately also the answer to the question posed in this chapter, namely whether computers can correct language errors. It would appear that also in the area of pronunciation computers can capture deviations from the expected and provide feedback that does not depend on the student's own perception (Ehsani & Knodt, 1998). This is possible on both segmental level (phonemes) and suprasegmental level (sentence prosody). In the following we will briefly clarify the difference. Traditional theoretical linguistics in the past focused on speech sounds, that is the segmental level. For this reason the teaching of pronunciation used to focus on the segmentals or the articulatory phonetics of individual sounds (Chun, 1998). A number of early CALL programs also focused on the segmental level (Wachowicz & Scott, 1999). Note the task description for the segmental level feedback as provided by Ehsani & Knodt (1998).

> Technically, designing a voice-interactive pronunciation tutor goes beyond the state of the art required by commercial dictation systems. While the grammar and vocabulary of a pronunciation tutor is comparatively simple, the underlying speech processing technology tends to be complex since it must be customized to recognize and evaluate the disfluent speech of language learners. A conventional speech

recognizer is designed to generate the most charitable reading of a speaker's utterance. Acoustic models are generalized so as to accept and recognize correctly a wide range of different accents and pronunciations. A pronunciation tutor, by contrast, must be trained to both recognize and correct subtle deviations from standard native pronunciations. (Ehsani & Knodt, 1998: 51)

For the reasons stated above, eliciting speech data from non-native speakers is a very important task when it comes to training large vocabulary speaker-independent continuous speech recognisers (Levow & Olsen, 1999). The target data can be broken down into three major categories: read, planned/careful and spontaneous (Tamokiyo & Burger, 1999). Two examples of spontaneous speech are conversation and query. The distinguishing feature of spontaneous speech is its subconscious quality (Tamokiyo & Burger, 1999), which means that the speaker is not really paying attention to the act of speech. There are doubts as to whether this could be said of semi-fluent non-native speakers (Tamokiyo & Burger, 1999). Thus it is not clear whether and to what extent their speech is truly spontaneous. Such reasoning seems to be in line with the comprehensible output hypothesis (Swain, 1998), which depicts the process of NNS output generation as a series of conscious decisions and plans for hypotheses testing. There are, however, other observable differences between NS and NNS speech. While with native speakers spontaneous speech contains disfluencies, filler words, conversational devices and a choice of syntactic devices which are often characteristic of a particular speech style, non-native speakers may exhibit an extreme measure of disfluencies, pauses between words and errors without any signs of a developed conversational style. Read speech on the other hand contains reading errors and stumbling that may not occur in spontaneous speech. NNS may exhibit a larger number of reading errors, especially with unfamiliar vocabulary. For all these reasons, Tamokiyo and Burger (1999) recommend collecting read and spontaneous NNS speech samples, whereby read speech is based on a familiar content rather than a phonetic balance and spontaneous or semi-spontaneous speech is developed around prompts or scenarios.

Following this digression, we return to the discussion of segmental and suprasegmental features of speech. Suprasegmental features include pitch, intonation, stress and rhythm. Pitch or fundamental frequency is one of the main acoustic correlates of stress and intonation and is therefore used in systems monitoring the suprasegmental level of speech. Some other acoustic features used are loudness, duration and tempo. It is said that intonation is one of the first aspects of speech that infants attend to (Chun, 1998). While for an infant the acquisition of intonation is an easy task presumably due to the plasticity of the brain (N. Ellis, 2001), for an adult L2 learner it appears to be difficult (Chun, 1998). This problem has been ignored in language teaching for a number of years (Eskenazi, 1999; Chun, 1998) and almost exclusive attention paid to the segmental level (Wachowicz & Scott, 1999). A renewed interest in the area is, according to Chun (1998), due to three particular reasons: developments in theoretical linguistics paired with the availability of acoustic signal analysis, expansion of theoretical linguistics to include discourse and text analysis, and finally a focus on communicative function rather than linguistic form in applied linguistics.

Suprasegmental training systems in particular make use of four aspects of pitch: (1) direction (level, falling or rising), (2) the extent of pitch change, (3) speed of pitch change, and (4) place of pitch change (Chun, 1998). Visual displays of pitch, including the difference between NS and NNS pronunciation, have been used to give feedback to learners, but it is not clear how useful they are in terms of learning, retention and modality (Stenson *et al.*, 1992; Chun, 1998; Ehsani & Knodt, 1998; Wachowicz & Scott, 1999). One of the problems associated with such systems is the inability of voiceless speech sounds to carry pitch, thus it is recommended that practice material contain voiced sounds mainly (Chun, 1998, Eskenazi, 1999). While early systems focused on sentence intonation, there has been a recent call for assessing discourse intonation, e.g. pairs of learners having conversation, which has become feasible through the accessibility of signal analysis software tools (Chun, 1998). It has also been recognised that the learner would benefit from the exposure to a large number of authentic NS produced utterances, especially if the cultural and attitudinal aspects of intonation are explained to the learner (Chun, 1998). Furthermore, since voice-interactive training systems have the ability to record learner speech, they can be used for extensive research, for which Chun (1998) makes an emphatic plea. Such research data could be invaluable when making decisions of what kind of feedback a system should offer. This is how some of the intonation features are used to generate feedback:

> Experiments have shown that a visual F0 display of supra-segmental features combined with audio feedback is more effective than audio feedback alone (de Bot, 1983; James, 1976), especially if the student's F0 contour is displayed along with a native model. The feasibility of this type of visual feedback has been demonstrated by a number of simple prototypes (Abberton & Fourcin, 1975; Anderson-Hsieh, 1994; Hiller *et al.*, 1994; Spaai & Hermes, 1993; Stibbard, 1996). We believe that this technology has a good potential for being incorporated into commercial CALL systems. Other types of visual pronunciation feedback include the graphical display of a native speaker's face, the vocal tract, spectrum information, and speech waveforms (see Figure 2). Experiments have shown that a visual display of the talker improves not only word identification accuracy (Bernstein & Christian, 1996), but also

speech rhythm and timing (Markham & Nagano-Madesen, 1997). (Ehsani & Knodt, 1998: 52)

In the following we shall describe how such systems can be used for different pedagogical purposes of reading aloud, pronunciation and conversation (Ehsani & Knodt, 1998; Holland, 1999; Wachowicz & Scott, 1999; Egan, 1999). We will also look at the architecture of such systems and the interplay between their foregrounds and backgrounds. Subsequently we will examine how the elements described are being used in individual CALL applications. We will especially focus on the types of feedback available.

Reading aloud is an exercise of pronunciation and literacy skill (Ehsani & Knodt, 1998) which helps the students establish a link between speech sounds and writing. Much as this skill is important, the architecture of a speech recognition based reading tutor is very simple as there is only one possible correct answer. However, it is a more challenging task to recognise and respond adequately to disfluencies such as hesitation, mispronunciation, false starts and self-corrections. The objective of such systems is to measure reading fluency as represented by the variable such as reading rate, silence between words and the measure of disfluency, i.e. false starts, self-corrections and omissions (Ehsani & Knodt, 1998).

Conversation, on the other hand, is a more open-ended task than reading aloud. However, systems designed to recognise speech in a conversational setting can be designed in two different ways, i.e. to allow either closed response or open response (Ehsani & Knodt, 1998). The former allows the student to choose one of the presented answers (LaRocca *et al.*, 1999), whereas the latter does not disclose the response design to the student. Thus the differences between both architectures are not large, as both must have all possible correct responses in the network. The student, however, faces a greater challenge because she has to work out the answers on her own (Wachowicz & Scott, 1999), without any help from the system, which is an answer to Eskenazi's (1999) concern about the passive role of student with closed response systems, where the student either reads aloud one of the written choices or repeats a learned sentence in response to a question. Ehsani and Knodt (1998) distinguish between two different types of open response systems: stimulus-response queries and simulated real-life conversation. The former present the material in the form of stimulus-response pairs, while the latter emulate natural human to human communication. They recognise however the need for an intelligent open response tutor that would rely on NLP techniques and would be able to both understand and meaningfully evaluate true open ended student input (Ehsani & Knodt, 1998). Finally, one of the most valuable resources for building open ended systems are large corpora of transcribed non-native speech data (Ehsani & Knodt, 1998; Levow & Olsen, 1999; Wachowicz & Scott, 1999; Egan, 1999).

Ehsani and Knodt (1998) observe that most of the voice-interactive CALL systems are designed to teach and evaluate linguistic form, including pronunciation, vocabulary and grammatical structure. One of the reasons for this is that formal features can be clearly identified, which contributes to the system's robust performance. Another reason is that cognitive SLA theories and approaches such as language awareness (Allen, 1999; James, 1998) on the one hand and focus on form (Long & Robinson, 1998; Doughty & Williams, 1998b) on the other see the benefits of making the form an integral part of the language learning process.

To remain true to the fundamental question asked in this chapter, we must examine the ways in which speech recognition based CALL systems detect and respond to errors. To answer the question whether they can identify errors, it can be said that indeed such systems are capable of both diagnosing and correcting segmental as well as suprasegmental errors (Eskenazi, 1999), albeit with restrictions (Wachowicz & Scott, 1999; Egan, 1999; LaRocca, 1999). There is however a huge difference between the segmental and suprasegmental level. While the number and nature of phonemes as well as the acceptable pronunciation space for each phoneme vary across the languages and present a greater problem to the learner, prosodic features involving the pitch duration and intensity are the same in all languages with the variation occurring in the relative importance, meaning and variability of these features in different languages (Eskenazi, 1999). The methods of identifying the two types of errors also differ. While phones can be identified either directly (Levow & Olsen, 1999) by calculating the score for each word in an utterance/phoneme error rate or indirectly (Levow & Olsen, 1999) by matching the voice signal to a text and then compared with native pronunciation, prosody, including the duration, fundamental frequency and intensity, is measured in relative terms, between the syllables of the same speech signal. The feedback can then be presented to the learner in visual, auditory or written form. It is however important that the expected correction does not occur based on the student's opinion of what was wrong, since this can lead to fossilisation of errors. Thus the students will need not only errors being pointed out to them, but also the means of remediation. Phone errors can call for instruction in how to articulate a particular sound, while in regard to prosody errors the learners only need to be told when for example to increase the pitch. Learning style and modality can also play a decisive role in choosing the right kind of feedback (Eskenazi, 1999; Oxford, 1995).

Although commercial speech-interactive CALL systems, of which there are already a fair few on the market, often misjudge the student input thus impeding learning, several strategies have emerged to minimise the systems' weaknesses (Wachowicz & Scott, 1999). These strategies are input verification, persona of the conversational character, authenticity enhancement and task-based language learning (Wachowicz & Scott, 1999). Input verification means that, if in doubt, the system should present a possible representation of the utterance on the screen and ask the learner whether this is what she meant. To compensate for poor recognition of the students' utterance, the character who personifies the system and is the student's virtual interlocutor in conversational voice interactive CALL programs can feature absentmindedness or poor hearing as a personality trait. In this way the student might be more willing to cooperate by repeating utterances rather than getting frustrated by the shortcomings of the system. Authenticity enhancement means that the development of the conversation can depend on the student's answer and does not have to be hard-wired. Finally, integrating task-based learning would mean asking the student to complete a meaningful real-life task by speaking. According to Wachowicz and Scott (1999), the best available systems have some of the above characteristics in addition to giving implicit corrective feedback in multimodal formats. They also focus on relatively predictable conversations and give learners a chance to correct their own errors.

Some examples of voice-interactive CALL systems

An early example of a voice recognition based CALL system with a focus on both segmental and suprasegmental level of pronunciation is the IBM developed Speech Viewer (Stenson *et al.*, 1992). Originally designed for clinical work with patients suffering from various communication disorders, it provides a variety of visual displays designed to raise the awareness of various aspects of pronunciation and develop better pronunciation skills. Its three major modules are Awareness, Skill Building and Patterning, which are subsequently broken down into components as follows. The Awareness module monitors pitch, voice onset, loudness and voicing. The visual feedback for pitch is thermometer shaped and its mercury rises as the pitch increases. Voice onset is depicted as a train moving forward at each onset. Loudness and voicing bear the likeness of a clown whose nose increases with the amplitude and whose tie changes colour when the voice changes. Similar graphic devices are used in the Skill Building module to depict pitch, voicing, vowel accuracy and vowel contrasting. These two modules thus have a game-like design, whereas the third module, Patterning, is based on spectral analysis. It uses colour for pitch and loudness, provides waveform patterns for utterances and presents spectra for vowel formants. One of the strengths of the program is that it enables the learners to compare their utterances with either prerecorded or on-the spot produced NS speaker utterances. Used in an experiment with two groups of adult L2 learners to teach sentence intonation and the pronunciation of field related technical terms and phrases, it contributed toward the higher post-test scores in the experimental group, which were however not significant (Stenson *et al.*, 1992). The affective attitude toward the software was positive, but the hardware limitations at the time seemed quite restricting.

Subarashi is a system designed for the practice of conversation in Japanese. It is based on continuous speech recognition in an open-ended dialogue framework (Bernstein *et al.*, 1999). Students engage in interaction with the system in a series of situations, in which they have to converse with various characters. To make the interaction meaningful, the students are expected to tackle problems which can only be solved by speaking. Although the student is free to select the encounters in random order, the system is designed in the form of an adventure game, where each encounter builds on the preceding one. Depending on the objective of the encounter, either the student or the system can initiate conversation. If the student attempts to negotiate an outcome contrary to the encounter objective, she is reminded of her mission. For example, a student might be told that one of the characters is likely to invite her to an outing, but that her task is politely, but firmly to refuse. This system uses hidden Markov models (HMMs) for the speech recognition tasks and was trained on a large corpus of spoken Japanese. The latter approach makes it different from a number of CALL programs that use speech recognition, which are usually trained on a limited number of target language speech samples. Because of its extensive training on a large number of speakers and its sophisticated technology, the system is able to perform much better at the recognition of non-native speech compared to similar CALL applications. After the initial piloting, some situations were found difficult by learners, which prompted the authors to add several additional features: pronunciation training, closed response queries and constrained grammar exercises. These modules had the function of preparing the students for the encounters. The use of high quality multimedia gives the system a realistic feel.

Project LISTEN's Reading Tutor is a third type of voice-interactive CALL application. It is designed to facilitate the reading aloud practice of young children. It adapts the Sphinx-II continuous speech recogniser (Mostow & Aist, 1999). The user interface presents the young reader with a sentence at a time, while an animated persona watches the text closely, 'listens' to input and provides various types of response. The tutor high-lights the correctly pronounced words green, which is not the case with each and every word, but with those that are expected to be difficult. The system keeps track of the student's past performance, which helps it decide if a word is a problem or not. Because of the limited accuracy of the recogniser, the system does not provide clear negative feedback. If in doubt as to the student's pronunciation, it either reads the sentence aloud high-lighting each word yellow as it goes or says 'mmm?'. It can also provide a clue to the pronunciation by juxtaposing the difficult word with an easier rhyming item or just simply supply the pre-recorded word. The Tutor always praises the reader, but only after a longer portion of text. This is done for motivational purposes. In the case of hesitation and prolonged silence on the part of the reader, the system waits for 2 seconds and then offers a hint after 4 seconds. After a silence of 7 seconds the system either prompts the student to read the sentence or does so itself. For the purpose of adapting the recogniser to the task, it was trained on adult female voices, augmented by children's voices. It runs on a Windows platform and is being used at schools with positive outcomes.

Concluding Remarks

It follows from the preceding discussion of both NLP and ASR (Automatic Speech Recognition) in CALL that the computer has the ability to capture and correct errors in speech, grammar and writing, not only as far as NS output is concerned, but also in respect of NNS speech and writing. These abilities may be limited at the moment, especially in regard to the latter. However, it is hard to think of any innovation in the human history that was perfect and all-powerful in its very beginnings. Take for instance, the light-bulb, which we take for granted nowadays and which took years of dedicated labour and a number of competing projects to evolve to its current stage. Could we not say the same of airplanes and TV and even the computer technology itself? As with any innovation (Rogers, 1983) the perceived advantages can only be seen and admired by visionaries, pioneers in the field, whereas the rest of the world really insists that the innovation resemble in its ways to something they are already accustomed to and that does not shatter their system of values and beliefs. Did someone's grandmother perhaps think that the planes were of the devil, since her religion told her that man cannot fly? Do we nowadays share a hidden belief that intelligent computers are evil, because deep in our unconscious lurks the idea that there is only one Creator who can grant the gift of life?

Why do these obvious advantages of the current technology take so long to proliferate? Holland (1995) enumerates four problems associated with the development of ICALL systems. Thus, such projects take a long time to develop only to offer an NLP analysis which is inherently uncertain, does not produce large curricula and is out of favour with the dominant communicative language theory. Nerbonne *et al.* (1998) note that CALL, even though it is ironically an application of technology in language, actually uses very little of language technology itself. They point out that the expectations of technology might be too high, nothing short of a perfect replica of what a human linguist can do (Salaberry, 1996). As mentioned earlier in this chapter, such an expectation is based on the assumption that what is true of computers in respect of language as a whole is also true of computers in respect of specialised domains of language (Narbonne *et al.*, 1998). However, precisely the opposite is true: while computers have not yet mastered the whole of the human language, they are capable of effectively assisting with its parts. This on the other hand might be against the grain of the whole language approach in language pedagogy (Salaberry, 1996; Garrett, 1995; Bailin, 1995). Thus language technology does have some obvious advantages, but they do not match the beliefs and practices of the language teaching community (Oxford, 1995; Garrett, 1995), which according to Rogers (1983) would be a crucial step toward their general acceptance.

Echoing the thoughts of Holland (1995) on scattered and sporadic funding of ICALL projects and the reluctance of the commercial providers to take a risk with a technology which may or may not bring profit, Borchardt (1998b) develops the idea of 'Gatekeepers'. These are according to Borchardt (1998b: 220) the influences that 'seem to be at the moment retarding CALL development and dissemination'. They fall into three main categories: (1) university-based research projects, (2) small business environment, and (3) publishers without a clear understanding of the marketability of CALL technology. Borchardt (1998b) argues that these three forces united mediate between the user and the product in such a way as to keep the CALL technology regional, marginal and not particularly inventive. He applauds the advent of the Web, which seems conducive to establishing a direct link between the user and the technology, without the potentially harmful effect of various kinds of referees.

While Borchardt (1998b) seems cautiously optimistic about the breakthrough of unconventional CALL technologies through the Internet, not everyone seems to have the same confidence in this respect. Borchardt's (1998b) hope seems to be based on the assumption that the technology itself can bring about a revolution, if not artificially kept away from the user. The question is, however, how free the user is to make her own choice. Even though the referees may disappear from the radar screen, other forces may efficiently prevent the users from seeing the advantages of the offered technology. These forces may well be the beliefs about the technology they may have picked up from their parents, teachers and the society at large (Rogers, 1983). Warschauer (1996) and Murray (2000) argue very strongly that the technology itself cannot bring about social change, but that it is rather a social change that can launch a technology to the surface. This seems reinforced by the fact that one of the pioneers of NLP in CALL, Melissa Holland (1999) appears discouraged about pursuing this technology. However, her discouragement does not seem to be final and overwhelming, since she has enthusiastically accepted ASR technology within the context of CALL (Holland, 1999).

Salaberry (1996) poses the crucial question: do we allow the machine to do what it is capable of doing if this is not what we believe to be the best for the learners? His answer is much in favour of the latter. Such reasoning readily confirms Rogers' (1983) theory of the diffusion of innovation, according to which even the perceived advantages of an innovation are not accepted by the majority if the innovation itself does not reflect the current beliefs and practices of the affected social group. While parsers in tutors seem to defy the prevalent communicative SLA theory (Garrett, 1995), the researchers in ASR based CALL (Holland, 1999; Eskenazi, 1999; Eshani & Knodt, 1998) are doing their best to fit this approach within the framework of communicative language learning. On the other hand, more recently, voices calling for some ways of integrating form into the language learning process (James, 1998; Doughty & Williams, 1998b) give the more form focused NLP approach some legitimacy. Whereas the lack of theoretical foundation of ICALL systems in SLA theories is often pointed out (Oxford, 1995; Chapelle, 1997), MacWhinney (1995: 323) discovers that SLA may not have shown enough interest in ICALL in order to design suitable evaluation procedures which would do justice to the product and would not compare 'apples and oranges', nor would they be biased toward any particular pedagogical procedure.

We started this chapter by wondering whether computers can effectively correct language errors. The discussion has hopefully demonstrated that they can do that and more. The intelligent computers can even assess NNS writing and speaking. A proof of this is the fact that even large, international examination boards are gearing toward computer based assessment of these skills. To echo Bailin (1995) we must ask: is it all worth an effort? The answer is: we'll never know unless we try it. The author of this book has made an effort to try the computer out in its capacity of NNS error correction. This effort is described in the following two chapters.

Chapter 5

How to Develop an Artificially Intelligent Language Tutor?

Design Questions

When designing and developing an intelligent language tutor, one needs to consider many things. What are the needs of the target learner population (Decoo, 1993; Decoo & Colpaert, 1999b)? Can the learners benefit from human–computer interaction that closely mimics human–human interaction, as suggested by Chapelle (1997)? Are they adult, analytical learners like Holland's (Holland *et al.*, 1993) or Willing's (1988) subjects who prefer to understand their language errors? One also needs to know their language proficiency and language learning needs. What purpose are they learning English for? What kind of English? How good are they supposed to become and at what skill? Do they accept the medium computer? How do they learn best? Can their learning styles be flexed and learning strategies improved? Do these styles, needs and preferences match the technology's capacity? What is it that may be holding the students back in their interlanguage development? What are the specific linguistic challenges that they face and what may be causing them? How can they be overcome? What could be the particular role of computer in this process?

These and other questions need to be addressed before a suitable CALL program can be developed to serve the needs of a target learner population. In the first chapter of this book, we have briefly introduced the target student population. The next section will introduce the reader to the segment of that population that was given the chance to help the researchers answer some of the above questions. The focus will then shift to the kind of English and the degree to which it had to be mastered. The reader will subsequently be introduced to the students' interlanguage. The data obtained in these three studies will then be utilised for the purpose of CALL program design.

Who are the Target Learners in On-Line Courses?

We usually think of learners as a community (Kramsch *et al.*, 2000). With the advent of Internet, however, the concept of community began undergoing a radical change. Whereas in pre-Internet times a community was usually defined as a group of people pursuing common interests in a geographically restricted area (Dodigovic & Suphawat, 1999), nowadays this restraint is being lifted. Thus the whole world seems to be amalgamating into the global village. At the university at which this project was conducted there used to be an EAP community, composed mainly of but not restricted to first year on-campus students. In the first chapter of this book we met two particular representatives of this community, Eric and Jean. With the development of the new Web tutor of EAP (English for Academic Purposes) the EAP community concept was expected to grow and include off-campus, very often also off-shore students, whose learning purposes are not always the same either, a concern this text shares with Doughty & Long (2003). Some of the students may be enrolled on a full-time or a part-time basis in institutions overseas, bringing their very special needs into the learning environment. It was hoped that the flexibility of the Web as a medium would allow for successful learning in a heterogeneous EAP community. The following section will discuss the process of learner population survey and needs analysis under the above circumstances.

The Macquarie Dictionary defines *community* as 'a social group of any size whose members reside in a specific locality, share government and have a cultural heritage'. A new type of locality is increasingly emerging as a defining criterion for a new type of community. The locality is called cyberspace. It is governed more or less by its own rules, successfully defying in particular the trade barriers otherwise effective in the actual space. It may be still somewhat early to talk about the cultural heritage of the Internet, but it is easily foreseeable that this invention is likely to have a global impact on every aspect of human life, as pointed out by Kramsch *et al.* (2000). To name just one, the Internet has already given rise to a new breed of language learner who might be living in Hong Kong, studying in Sydney per email, conversing with dozens of people around the globe in virtual space and learning German off the Web. Such is a representative of a new community of learners being generated by the new technologies (Kramsch *et al.*, 2000). Moreover, her flexible environment calls for and allows a change of her identity as well as her apprenticeship in and subsequent mastery of a new type of literacy, the one that may prove very beneficial to a language learner who seems stuck on her way to L2 learning success (Kramsch *et al.*, 2000).

This change in the makeup of the concept of community will have a lasting effect on the way courses are designed and developed in general, as Doughty and Long (2003) already prove. In most instances of needs analysis, it is assumed that the learning population will live within reasonable distance of the provider, and will therefore be able to attend the classes. Thus, a large number of courses are developed relying on the audio-visual potential of the venue itself and the participants. It is true that the notion of programmed learning, and later CALL, brought about an increased awareness of the need to create the learning context rather than taking it for granted. However, CALL and traditional classroom learning went their separate ways. It was not until the advent of the Internet (Geoghegan, 1998) that the boundaries between the two started to blur. This was discussed at greater length in Chapter 3.

Recently, many courses have become offered both on campus and on the Web. When developing such courses, the author suddenly starts facing restraints which were not there when the courses were offered in the on-campus mode only (Kayser, 2002). Thus, new copyright laws for electronic media strongly restricts the range of documents to be available on the Web. Furthermore, the potential variety of client machines may impose restrictions on Web page design (Suphawat, 1999). In addition, a discussion component needs to be added to make room for human–human interaction on the Web (Salaberry, 1999). On the other hand, the type of interactivity characteristic for CALL (Salaberry, 1999) will influence the course materials even when delivered in the classroom. To begin with, the needs analysis becomes a more difficult task, simply for the fact that it is not easy to define the target population. Also, computer literacy and the motivation to use the computer for learning purposes have to be investigated, no matter what subject the course is in. Accordingly, the following section will explore the intricacies of the Web-induced learner community as related to the development of a course in English for Academic Purposes (EAP) to be offered both on-campus and on the Web. It will primarily focus on the stages of needs analysis.

Study Subjects

In 1998/1999, Piphawin Suphawat (1999), a postgraduate student of applied linguistics at Macquarie University, undertook the challenge of investigating the readiness of the EAP student population at this university to accept on-line learning materials as an integral part of their EAP courses. As briefly pointed out in Chapters 1 and 2 of this volume, the EAP courses included Academic English I (EAP100) and Academic English II (EAP101). While the former focused mainly on general academic writing and some study skills at the time of the survey, the latter was trying to expose students to a variety of discipline related written and oral genres. The requirements of both courses were based on a survey previously administered by Simmons and Thurstun (1995) to the academics on campus. Suphawat's (1999) study had the purpose of complementing the faculty survey and bringing in the students' take on what kind of academic literacy they needed. In addition, the survey was going to investigate the students' computer literacy and attitudes to CALL, seen as necessary prerequisites for successful on-line learning.

The study subjects were 45 students enrolled in EAP100. This was the number captured in attendance in the afternoon lecture and its evening repeat on the day the survey was administered in late 1998. Admittedly, this is not a large number of students, but it did certainly cover 62.5% of the total student population enrolled in the course that semester (72). It being the second semester of the academic year, the student intake was generally smaller than in the first semester of each academic year. The subjects, however, well represented the diverse strata of the university studentship, among whom not least the kind of student we described in the prelude to this study report. In other words, the students in the evening lectures were to some extent 'external', part-time students, often taking the benefit of the EAP100 course only. This population of students were often full-time employees in Sydney's multifarious industries, had families to take care of and seemed genuinely interested in a flexible delivery mode. It needs to be pointed out that this course was for administrative reasons not available in the traditional distance or correspondence mode. However, the increased availability of the Internet and Computer Mediated Communication (CMC) was likely to change that.

Due to the deadline pressures, Suphawat was not able to capture more students in repeated attempts, as the survey was administered shortly before one of the term breaks and prolonged waiting for the purpose of increasing the number of subjects could have resulted in her failure to analyse and write up her research in time for the submission. Late submission in turn would have caused a lot of administrative problems, which were not justifiable in light of the task ahead (a short thesis in a predominantly course-work focused MA degree). Thus, the potential gain in the reliability of research had to be traded off for an important personal goal, in which Piphawin was wholeheartedly supported by her supervisors. The subsequent expiry of her ethics approval for the survey and the inability to extend it due to the completion of her studies further exacerbated the author's chances of administering the same questionnaire to another group of students. Thus, the pragmatic approach had to be taken that some data was better than no data at all.

The 45 subjects covered by this survey could be described as follows: They were all NNS or non-English speaking background (NESB) students, either overseas students or migrants. Their English proficiency was generally a minimum of 6.5 on the IELTS scale or equivalent. The majority (57.58%) were female, aged 24 or younger (62.22%), and mainly from the School of Commerce, enrolled in programs such as Finance, Accounting, Marketing, Economics and Business Administration. The next largest age group was 25–39 (26.66%), followed by only 6.67% of students aged 40 or above. In terms of major, another significant group (11.11%) was enrolled in Computer Science, while the programs of Linguistics and Education were represented by 9.89% each. Chinese (either Mandarin or Cantonese) was the first language of the majority of students (31.11%), followed closely by Indonesian (20%), Japanese (15.56%) and Korean (8.89%). Other native languages also included Persian, Turkish, Arabic, Hebrew and Czech. In addition, the students also spoke a variety of second languages: Chinese, German, French, Italian, Spanish and Swedish.

Needs Analysis

The survey was conducted with the aim to find out more about students' needs for on-line EAP course delivery and complementing the faculty survey. Both types of information, the faculty and the student opinions, constitute the so-called 'soft' data (Moore & Morton, 1998: 67), and will in the final part of this chapter be joined by the 'hard' data gained through document analysis (Moore & Morton, 1998: 67) in order to obtain an objective picture by triangulation (Ellis, 1997).

The questions asked of students were about their needs in terms of communicative skills (reading, writing, listening, speaking), preferred academic genres and tasks (see also Candlin *et al.*, 1998), acceptable learning styles and computer literacy as well as motivation for learning EAP with computers. Some of the research goals were to find out whether the students would be interested in pursuing this subject on the Web, and if so, how their computer skills and preferred learning styles could be matched. The first goal, however, as pointed out above, was to understand what the students perceived to be their literacy needs.

The first two questions of Suphawat's (1999) questionnaire are accordingly designed to elicit responses about the literacy practices required of the students in the academia. Although Supawhat's (1999) questions pertain to reading and writing academic tasks mainly in order to complement the previous faculty survey (Simmons & Thurstun, 1995), the term literacy itself means more than reading and writing (Johns, 1997). It 'encompasses ways of knowing particular content, languages and practices' (Johns, 1997: 2). It also 'refers to strategies for understanding, discussing, organizing and producing texts' (Johns, 1997: 2). Johns (1997) additionally subsumes the discourse and its context as well as the learning process and product under the term. By querying both the soft and the hard data, at the end of this chapter, we will look for the immerging patterns that will tell us how to direct our pedagogical efforts.

Investigating taxonomies of academic tasks has already had a 20 year history, starting with Hawkey (1982) and Weir (1990) in the UK and Bridgeman and Carlson (1983) in the USA. According to a recommendation by Waters (1996), Suphawat (1999) has geared her instrument to the purposes of our research, listing types of reading and writing tasks that would be easy to operationalise within an on-line EAP course. Thus, in the reading section she listed textbooks, academic/professional journals, newspapers/magazines, leisure reading and documents as options. The question of how dominant a reading genre the textbook might be preoccupied Johns (1997) as well. Suphawat (1999) found that 60% of all tasks are indicated to be textbooks, followed by academic/professional journals (40%), newspapers (26.67%), leisure reading (24.44%) and various documents (17.78%). Thus her top category converges well with Johns' (1997) research, but the second category is in comparison relatively high. Suphawat (1999) confirmed that the EAP faculty had been right about devising the top two categories as EAP100 readings.

According to Johns (1997), articles in academic journals are more likely to reflect the complexity of thinking and community practices within a discipline. Textbooks, she claims, often simplify issues, presenting only matters about which there is some consensus in a community of practice. A community of practice is defined by Wenger (1999) as a community of meaning, learning and identity. Secondly, textbooks tend to talk down to the student, who appears to be their secondary audience, the primary audience being the teacher who selects the mandatory readings for her classes (Johns, 1997). Thus, Suphawat (1999) had made an important discovery when she identified academic and professional journals as likely sources of information for our population of students.

Unlike Moore and Morton (1998), who list a series of rhetorical functions as viable writing tasks, Suphawat (1999) had chosen to focus on text types or genres. According to Swales (1990), a genre is a class of communicative events, sharing a communicative purpose and constraints on context, positioning and form. However, the prototypicality of genre instances can vary (Swales, 1990: 49), which allows for some flexibiliy. The owners of genres are discourse communities (Swales, 1990). Discourse communities according to Swales (1990) have a set of common public goals as well as a mechanism of intercommunication between members, which is used to provide information and feedback. In addition to genres, discourse communities own specific lexis, used by a threshold level of members with a suitable degree of discoursal expertise (Swales, 1990).

Genre approach brings Supahwat's (1999) work closer to Johns (1997), the Australian genre approach (Derewianka, 1990) or Swales (1990), all of whom focus on genres. Like Johns (1997) and Swales (1990), who see genres as flexible and changing, Suphawat (1999) also structures her categories rather broadly, without trying to give them specific rigid definitions. Because of their pedagogical function these genres can also be referred to as tasks (Swales, 1990). In the limitations of her study Suphawat (1999) acknowledges the possibility that having loosely defined terms may have skewed her data. However, the shortness of her list was a virtue in terms of the amount of time and effort it demanded from the subjects. Her list is in some respects similar to that of Hale *et al.* (1986: 10), which includes essay, library research paper, report of observation with or without interpretation, summary, case study, plan, proposal, documented computer program, book review and unstructured writing. In the following I shall list Suphawat's (1999) genres followed by the percentage of students who deemed it important for their studies. Thus, her list included argumentative/discursive essays (53.33%), research reports (40%), summaries (37.78%), academic articles/papers (35.56%), reports (35.56%), instructions (31.11%), data commentaries (28.89%), CV/resume (26.67%), critical literature review (22.22%), annotated bibliography, letter (22.22%), memo (13.33%) and minutes (13.33%). We see that Suphawat's (1999) list includes some additional items compared to Hale *et al.* (1986). Annotated bibliography can also be found in Horowitz (1986: 449–52). Data commentaries are a category particularly highlighted by Swales & Feak (n.d.), whereas CVs, letters, memos and minutes are business genres often represented in literature on business English or writing for business.

It does not surprise that essay is the most common type of written academic task. This conforms very well with Johns' (1997) findings. Also the academics in Simmons and Thurstun's (1995) survey frequently bring up essay as the most common genre. The apparent relative importance of research paper, which seems to reflect the perceived importance of academic journal article as a reading task, may well be representative of the diversity of the EAP student community. Some of our part-time students were either graduates preparing for postgraduate studies or postgraduate students enrolled at another university that did not cater to their language development needs. In hindsight, it would have been helpful to allow the questionnaire to differentiate between graduates and undergraduates. Judging by the recorded responses, it would appear that three students had not been enrolled in any program of studies leading to a degree, whether graduate or undergraduate. The number of graduate enrollees from the same university would have been small, as this was a costly option, much less utilised than the free graduate workshops and individual tutorials. While the presence of part-time and postgraduate students may not have significantly influenced the data, their presence in the sample was valuable.

The next aspect Suphawat (1999) was interested in was learning style. 'The term "learning style" refers to a person's general approach to learning and problem-solving' (Reid, 1995 in Oxford & Nam, 1998). While a learner can be aware of her learning style, she does not make a conscious effort to implement it (Oxford & Nam, 1998). On the other hand, the action that she does consciously apply to enhance her own behaviour is called a learning strategy (Oxford & Nam, 1998; Oxford, 1990; Willing, 1988). Strategies are often related to style (Oxford, 1995). These definitions have hopefully helped resolve the difficulties theoreticians have had in the past (Willing, 1989; Suphawat, 1999) differentiating between the two. These features are different from individual to individual (Oxford, 1995). Reid (1998) believes that a learning style can also be 'flexed' or extended. However, generally speaking a quantum leap to a totally opposite learning style cannot be expected, at least not overnight.

Most learning style taxonomies are based on the distinction between the left and right brain, one of which seems to be dominant in most people (Anderson, 1988). Thus a basic division is the one between 'analytical' or left-brained and 'concrete' or right-brained (Willing, 1988, 1989). The way the analytical learner processes information is linear, sequential, rational, objective, abstract, verbal, mathematical, with focus on detail, engaging in reflective and cautious thinking, responding to selective, low-intensity stimuli (Willing, 1989). The concrete learner, on the other hand, processes information in a holistic, pattern-seeking, spatial, intuitive, subjective, concrete, emotional and visual way, focusing on overall impression, while being impulsive and trusting hunches, requiring rich, varied input (Willing, 1989).

Some of the learning strengths of analytical students are that they have control over sequential and structured thinking, analytical problem solving, predictable routines and familiar activities; they persist at unstimulating tasks and contend with the learning material that is abstract, factual, impersonal and practical. In contrast, the concrete learner exhibits the following learning strengths: intuitive and improvisational thinking, collaborative problem solving, varied and creative activities, withdrawal from unstimulating tasks and requiring a learning material with human and social content and cultural relevance (Willing, 1989). While an analytical learner uses focused and systematic instructional strategies, works independently or with a compatible partner, sets own goals and directs own learning and pursues narrow examples, trial and error, rules and definitions, a concrete or 'relational' (Witkin *et al.*, 1977) learner uses varied realistic and simultaneously managed instructional strategies, works with others to achieve common goals, prefers explicit structure, modelling, guidance and feedback for task completion as well as repeated exposure to association patterns (Willing, 1989). In interpersonal relationships, an analytical learner relies on a self-defined personal identity and social role, her self-esteem is less dependent on the opinion of peers, she is task oriented and inattentive to emotional cues in interpersonal interactions. A concrete learner, however, defers to social group for identity and role definition, her learning performance is improved if group or authority figure gives praise and support, she is people oriented and sensitive to verbal and non-verbal cues in interpersonal interactions (Willing, 1989).

Interestingly, Willing (1988, 1989) equates the analytical mind with 'field independence' and the concrete one with 'field dependence'. Both have been briefly mentioned in Chapter 1 of this volume. Ehrman (1998: 63) defines field independence (FI) as the 'ability to distinguish and isolate sensory experiences from the surrounding sensory input'. The same author also suggests that research often associates FI with certain personality traits such as being task oriented rather than people oriented, individualistic rather than compliant and interacting with others in a cool rather than a warm way (Ehrman, 1998). Field dependence (FD) is by contrast defined as a lack of field independence (Ehrman, 1998). The concept of FD has gradually been replaced with the concept of field sensitivity (FS). The latter is seen as a positive rather than negative descriptor, suggesting an array of skills including the ability to guess from the context and to work with incomplete data (Ehrman, 1998). It is interesting to note that FS has gradually developed its opposite – 'field insensitivity' (FN).

If field dependence (FD) does not mean the same as field sensitivity (FS), it is imaginable that a learner could be both: FI and FS. Thus Ehrman (1998) has developed a four type learner paradigm: (1) high independence and high sensitivity, (2) high independence and low sensitivity, (3) low independence, high sensitivity, and (4) low independence and low sensitivity. If FI is further equated with left brain activity and FS with right brain activity, the result could be Tyacke's (1998) four types ranging from the strongly left-brained studier, over diverger and explorer to the fully right-brained absorbers. Willing (1988, 1989) also distinguishes between four types of learning styles: communicative, concrete, authority-oriented and analytical.

The theoretical underpinnings for Suphawhat's (1999) investigation of learning styles are based on the work of Willing (1988), according to which all learners, as indicated above, can be categorised as one of the four learner types: (1) concrete, those who like games, pictures, video, talking in pairs, practising outside class, (2) analytical, those who like studying grammar, using books, reading, studying alone, being given tasks to work on by the teacher, (3) communicative, those who prefer listening to native speakers, talking to friends, using the target language in everyday situations or basically learning by listening, and (4) authority oriented, those who prefer teacher explanation, using textbooks and learning words by seeing them. These emerged as a result of survey data factor analysis and are seen as stages along the FI/FD continuum (Willing, 1988). While the analytical learner represents the extreme of the field independence end, the concrete is its opposite – the extreme field dependence case. The communicative learner on the other hand is predominantly field independent, with a tendency to use communication as a strategy toward analytical practices (Willing, 1988). The authority oriented learner is consequently a concrete learner with a need for structure provided by an authority, e.g. the teacher (Willing, 1988). The four categories have more in common with personality factors, and therefore individual differences, than with sociocultural factors (Nunan, 1992; Willing, 1988).

While the grouping in the above taxonomy is attributed to the interference of the active/passive variable with the FD/FI one (Willing, 1988: 161), the theoretical model underpinning the investigation is based on ways of information processing and their interaction with the management of learning process and human relations. Neil Fleming (2001) distinguishes between four information processing modalities sometimes referred to as VARK, i.e. Visual, Aural, Read/write and Kinesthetic. While Willing's (1988, 1989) concrete learner is clearly right-brained with a tendency toward kinesthetic information processing modality, the analytical learner is fully left-brained with a strong read/write information processing orientation. The communicative learner on the other hand seems to be aural in her information processing modality, whereas the authority oriented learner seems to rely heavily on her visual modality. This is at least a possibility for the interpretation of Willing's categories, which however does not seem to be suggested by the author himself (Willing, 1988).

This approach to eliciting information about the learning styles in the EAP class in its stage of candidacy for the on-line delivery mode was well suited to the purpose at hand. While the computer at the time was capable of catering to most of the information processing modality, especially visual, aural and read/write, it was really important to understand whether the learner would expect an analytical approach to error diagnosis and correction or whether a communicative treatment grounded in social learning theory would be more useful.

Suphawhat's (1999) questionnaire and a full set of results are fully available in her 1999 thesis deposited at Macquarie University Library. A partial report of the survey is also available in Dodigovic and Suphawhat (1999), included in the proceedings of the 1999 Exeter conference, edited by Keith Cameron. For reasons of copyright this volume will refrain from quoting large sections of either source. The questions pertaining to learning style were based on Willing's work (1988, 1989). Thus the questions related to communicative learning style asked the subjects whether they liked learning by conversations, talking to friends or watching TV. The questions related to concrete learning style asked the learners if they learned English well by talking in pairs, playing games and using cassette recordings. The questions related to authority oriented learning style asked the learners about their preference for learning by reading, from textbooks or the teacher. Finally, the questions about the analytical learning style were based on the assumption that these learners would like to find their own mistakes, studying grammar and problem-solving.

While almost 60% of students decided that they preferred some activities typical of the communicative learning style (learning by conversation), a strong 40% could identify with some of the typical analytical learning style patterns (identifying own errors). Overall responses indicate that there might have been overlaps between all styles and averaging out the counts for each group of questions shows that the communicative style leads with 50%, while the analytical lags behind with 26%, followed by authority oriented (18%) and concrete (17%) styles. This is in many ways different from Willing's (1988: 157) findings, although there is a similarity in that the communicative learning style seems to prevail. Thus in light of the strong lead of communicative and analytical learning preferences, at least as far as some of the practices are concerned, it became clear that the intelligent tutor under development should explicitly cater to these two learner types.

For this reason the tutor will have to utilise the communicative language learning approach which specifically focuses on enhancing students' autonomy and control over the language learning process. Therefore, obviously this particular group of students is more likely to employ the computer mediated communication or perhaps human–computer communication disguised as human–human interaction following the suggestion by Chapelle (1997). The tutor will however also have to approach the analytical learners the way they wish to be approached and that is by giving them problems to solve, helping them understand the nature of their own mistakes and giving them opportunities to learn grammar (Willing, 1989).

Insignificant and inconclusive though as the above results may seem to a statistician, they are still of tremendous importance to the developer on a mission to accommodate the individual learner, something SLA theories often neglect to do (Willing, 1988; Oxford, 1995; Gregg, 2001). Indeed a number of SLA theoretical texts seem to assume not only that all adult individuals learn languages in the same way, but also that there is no significant difference between a child learning its first language and an adult learning a language other than her first one (Gregg, 2001; Oxford, 1995). The universal grammar theory is the only nativist theory that explicitly claims that there is a difference between the former and the latter. It is however rather pessimistic about the latter and fails to see the strengths of the linguistic and non-linguistic knowledge the adult second or foreign language learner brings along. The other and final exception is the individual learning differences theory (Oxford, 1995) based on individual cognitive needs, beliefs, values, attitudes and skills.

Moreover, most SLA theories actually cater to a particular learning style. Thus the currently dominant interactionist learning theories (Vygotsky, 1997; Lantolf & Appel, 1994; Long & Robinson, 1998; Doughty, 2001) assume that most learners are extrovert, right-brained, possibly aural, visual and kinesthetic, communicative or concrete learners, to put it in Willing's (1989) terms, who happen to learn best in meaningful social interactions and have egos permeable enough to accept advice or correction in a social context (Larsen-Freeman & Long, 1991). Swain's (1998) comprehensible output theory, on the other hand, seems to assume that all learners make conscious decisions about the possible application of language rules during language production, which would make all learners left-brained and analytical (Willing, 1989). When the two theories are used mutually to confirm each other (Long & Robinson, 1998; Doughty & Williams, 1998b), the underlying assumption seems to be that all learners are both strongly left-brained and exceedingly right-brained, analytical and concrete or relational at the same time. From a number of studies (Willing 1988; Suphawat, 1999; Hatherley-Greene, 2003) we know that this is not the case. Therefore, designing CALL software to test an SLA theory, as suggested by Chapelle *et al.* (1996) and Chapelle (1997), on the tacit assumption that all learners foster the same way of learning, is bound to render inconclusive results, as seen from a number of studies (Dodigovic, 1995; de Ridder, 1999; Whistle, 1999), because what benefits one learner may happen to the absolute detriment of another. Therefore when developing CALL applications, it pays off to investigate the learning styles of the target population and then select a suitable SLA theory or elements of several matching theories, as has been the case in this study.

Computer literacy was the next variable under examination in Suphawat's (1999) study. Students were asked to self-assess on the level of their computer literacy and typing skills. Both categories were rated as good (44.44%). In addition, 84.44% of the students used computer before attending this university course and the majority of students used it for their studies (63.64%). While 75.56% of the students had their own computers, 41.94% of them had had computers for more than three years. Interestingly, female students seemed to have the lead in terms of computer ownership. Whereas 90% of all female subjects had computers at home, only about 62% of all male subjects could say the same. Neither gender nor computer ownership, nor even the course of studies seemed to influence the motivation to use the computer for EAP learning purposes, which was overall good. The results indicated that prolonged exposure to computers may lend itself to the conclusion that learning with a computer can be fun, which seemed a powerful motivator to a number of students (Suphawhat, 1999).

In terms of software type previously used, Suphawhat's (1999) survey correlated to some extent with the previously mentioned surveys by Geoghegan (1998) and Fidelman (1998), (Chapter 3 this volume). It appears that the largest proportion of computer activities that the students had engaged in were word processing, email and the World Wide Web, 75.56%, 68.89% and 62.22% respectively. While the top three applications largely remain the same, the ranking in Suphawhat's (1999) study is slightly different from the other two in that it puts word processing at the top of the list, which is elsewhere occupied by more interactive applications. This, however, makes it consistent with Pennington (1996), who describes word processing as a major facilitator of writing. Having help only an email away seemed in addition to be a strong motivator.

It was obvious from the survey that 42.22% of the students knew how to use a computer to help them learn English; 45.45% revealed that using the computer makes learning English more interesting; that computer programs are useful when learning English (56.25%), and useful to their studies in general (36.67%). In addition, 54.54% indicated that they would enjoy learning a language by using computer; 35.56% of the respondents said that they had used computer help learning a language before and the activities often used were word processing (23.63%), spelling exercises (21.81%) and multiple-choice exercises (10.91%). All of the above were generally well liked, whereby spelling and grammar featured prominently as reasons, confirming that a significant body of our learners are indeed analytical in their approach to second language learning.

When asked about their autonomy in using computer applications, 67.74% of the respondents indicated that they preferred to choose their own computer activities, practise something they had learned, and write English by using computers. When they do not understand a computer activity, 42.86 % of the students want the teachers to help, 26.19% need help from friends, while 21.43% believe that the computer is the only thing they need. However, 61.54% preferred to work alone on the computer, 17.95% wanted to work with teachers, and 10.26% liked to work in pairs or in a group. The fact that over 60% were confident in their own choice of CALL materials and preferred to work alone, again points either to the analytical learning style or to an introvert personality, both of which would be well served with intelligent computer–human interaction as a part of the learning process.

Thus, Suphawhat's (1999) study fulfilled an important purpose in the early development stages of the Intelligent Tutor, namely that of learner (or user) profiling, which is an essential step both in course development (Doughty & Long, 2003; Munby, 1981; van Lier, 1996; Willing, 1988) and software engineering (Pfleeger, 1998; Somerville, 2001). We have learnt from it that our learners would most likely have either a strong communicative orientation or an analytical one. We have also learnt that they could be expected to have familiarity with computers in general, including word processing, email and the Web. Some exposure to designated CALL software, i.e. tutor as opposed to tool (Higgins, 1988), was also existent, but word processing was most highly valued because of its perceived capacity to assist with grammar and spelling. While the latter speaks to the high confidence our students, like Liou's (1991), had in the authority of the computers to give an accurate ruling in matters of grammar, it also raises the same concerns Liou (1994) and Tschichold (1999) raise regarding the uncritical acceptance of commercial grammar checkers packaged with popular word processing programs. The higher the students' trust in the omniscience of the computer, the greater the developer's responsibility to produce a program that would address the real errors of a real L2 learner population. This was precisely the task of the intelligent tutor whose development is described in this chapter.

The Content: Academic Language

Written and spoken language

Suphawhat's (1999) survey has also shown that the readings required for the discipline courses attended by our EAP students were not restricted to textbooks, but included in many cases academic and professional journals, deemed to represent the academic discourse and language in its true nature (Johns, 1997). While the importance of the discourse itself and the community of practice (Johns, 1997; Swales, 1990; Wenger, 1999) plays an undeniably important social role in apprenticing a university student into the discourse of her discipline, both academics (Simmons & Thurstun, 1995) and students (Suphawhat, 1999) perceived grammar as a possible barrier to the delivery of the content in a manner accessible to the academic sitting in judgement of the student's writing. The findings seem to echo Halliday's thoughts (1994b; 1999) on grammar as the main vehicle of creating meaning in academic language. This section will try to explain the written practices of the academia, often in clash with our students' approaches to learning, which in the majority of Suphawhat's (1999) sample did not appear to be read/write oriented. As this text accepts the premise that academic language is predominantly written (Halliday, 1994b; 1999), we will start by examining the history and features of written language as opposed to spoken language and will then try to explain the phenomenon of specifically academic writing in linguistic, semiotic and epistemological terms.

Within the context of systemic functional linguistics (SFL), written language has a special place in the contexts of situation and culture (Butt *et al.*, 1997). This linguistic approach actively includes the semiotic theory in its description of language. It seems to this author that Hallidayan systemic view of language, as opposed to viewing language as a meaning empty structure, includes all aspects of the rich structure of Morris' (1938) sign: the signified (field), the sign users or the participants in communication (tenor) and the relationship between signs in use (mode) (Butt *et al.*, 1997). The field in SFL controls the content of linguistic communication, responsible for ideational meaning of the text. The tenor is responsible for the interpersonal meaning of a text or a sign within a text, whereas the mode accounts for the textual meaning of a linguistic sign (Butt *et al.*, 1997). Text in the jargon of SFL simply means a group of signs used together as a meaningful whole, be it language signs or any other signs including picture, motion or sound (Butt *et al.*, 1997). This complex interconnection between text, user and context is also at the base of Johns' (1997) notion of academic literacy. We will use this complex and yet articulate perspective to identify the specifics of academic use of language, which is an example of language used within a narrow field, with a particular tenor and in one dedicated mode – written.

Our investigation of the academic language starts with its preferred mode: writing. Halliday (1985, 1999) gives a thoughtful description of the difference between the written and the spoken language, anchored in his view of language as a semiotic system or a system used to express meaning. He starts by invoking a commonly held misconception, namely the one that the alphabet successfully represents all speech sounds and therefore all that can be said can be equally well represented in writing. This is true only to a certain extent. In fact, speech is the older of the two aspects of language (Halliday, 1994b). Writing, on the other hand, is a system that was histori- cally developed much later than speech to serve a different purpose, and it has maintained its own authentic purpose until this day.

> Writing itself arose from the impact between grammar and pictorial, non-linguistic semiotic practices; it evolved in contexts which required text to be made permanent – inventories, calendars, inscriptions, divi- nations and the like. Thus it never was 'speech written down'; from the start writing construed different domains of experience, and hence was naturally at hand to serve as the medium for a different construction of knowledge . . . (Halliday, 1999: 103)

According to Halliday (1985), writing evolved in response to cultural changes in the society. A predominantly hunting and a gathering economy supported a small, mobile social group which would not gain any advantage from writing (Halliday, 1985). Thus spoken language answered its needs. However, the transition to an agricultural economy brought more stability to the society and fixed a number of its patterns. Language also became an element of the increasingly complex cultural institution. The process of speaking as action limited in space and time had to be trans- formed into a written product for further reference unlimited by space or time (Halliday, 1994b). Thus writing took over the function of transmitting (and conserving) cultural knowledge.

In the modern-day academia much of the history of any discipline is tra- ditionally traced back to Aristotle (Vivenza, 1999; Pera, 1999). The main reason for this can be assumed to be the fact that this philosopher had left his thoughts not only in writing, but also in a format that has shaped much of the Western academic convention. It was thought grounded in certain principles of logic on the one hand, enabling it to carry an unchanging meaning in a changing world, and rhetoric on the other, convincing the reader to become a willing party to the acceptance of the propositional content of the text at hand. While the former is used for the benefit of the community but is largely structural and ideational, the latter is interper- sonal and speaks to the individual's sentiment and intuition (Dow, 1999). At least this is how we will define the boundaries of rhetoric in this volume, even though to Aristotle it might have combined both the art of linguistic expression as well as some elements of logic, especially that of argumentative or syllogistic reasoning. Following this duality, logic and rhetoric still overlap in modern use when it comes to describing rhetorical patterns or models of writing, which denote types of text organisation.

Much as the written practices of the contemporary academia are grounded in ancient Greek written discourse, some of its spoken practices also stem from ancient Greece, more precisely from its community oriented dialogic approach to teaching and learning (Sinclair, 1999; Hemp-Lyons, 2001). Thus the preferred form of examination in Britain and Europe until the late 19th century was oral, reflecting the elitist nature of the small academic community who could afford 'tutor-student dialogue and seminar-style debate' (Hemp-Lyons, 2001: 118). Interestingly, writing as a method of examination was introduced in the English speaking world as a response to the growing British colonial empire and the consequently growing need to educate an efficient administrative task force. This method had existed in China for about 3000 years to ensure impartiality, objectivity and reliability (Hemp-Lyons, 2001) and is likely to have been adopted by the colonial force in this country at the end of the 19th century. In the USA, Harvard was the first university to introduce a written composition as an entrance exam instead of the traditional oral examination (Hemp-Lyons, 2001). This has cemented the role of the written mode as the single valid and reliable assessment mode in the English speaking world, hence its importance to all university students.

According to Halliday (1985), writing as a product is different to speech as a process. The former, at least in the Anglo-Saxon tradition we would add, is basically linear, in that expressions follow one another in an exact order (Halliday, 1985), whereas speech can branch off and meander as it evolves (Halliday, 1999). In writing, a high level of order, standardisation and codification in terms of grammar, vocabulary and spelling is needed because language is the only channel of communication. The reader does not necessarily have access to the immediate physical context in which writing has taken place. Thus pointing to objects, gesticulation and mimicry are not available for additional clarification. The reader has to rely on text alone for clarity or to a set of commonly understood criteria according to which the text is designed (Halliday, 1999).

Comparing speech to writing, it must be said that writing leaves certain things out. For example, in speech we use features such as voice, pitch, intonation, stress, rhythm, which are called the *prosodic* features (Halliday, 1985; Halliday, 1994b). Punctuation can only represent some of these features in a limited way (pause represented by a comma, period, parentheses or dash; question mark and exclamation mark). Thus it needs to be noted that the question mark does not always represent the same type of intonation, which is either falling as in WH questions or rising as in yes/no questions (Halliday, 1994b). In fact, punctuation has not always accompanied writing. It was first introduced in ancient Greek (Halliday, 1985). The writing conventions in ancient Greece at first did not allow for any punctuation at all. The letters were written in sequence, following one another without any spaces between words or utterances. When the end of the first line written from left to right was reached, the line was simply continued below, this time going from right to left. Thus, the writing direction was alternate. Gradually, the punctuation system emerged as we know it today. Due to the occasional mixing and overlaps between speech and writing, nowadays there are two different styles of using punctuation (Halliday, 1985). One would be strictly grammatical, relying mainly on grammar as a feature of written language predominantly. The other follows the speech patterns. In highly formal documents (e.g. legal documents) punctuation does not follow speech patterns at all.

As pointed out above, a significant difference of writing as compared to speech, observed by many authors (Halliday, 1999; Arcaini, 1999; Pera, 1999), is the relative autonomy of the written scientific or generally speaking academic text from a physical context:

> . . . the written text (Ricoeur, 1977) induces a radical transformation in the relation of the subject to utterances, which would imply a sort of autonomy of the written text (in comparison to the spoken word) and give written communication a special status; all the more so in that certain fundamental marks of oral discourse are generally lost in transcription (this opens the great debate of paralinguistics) . . . (Arcaini, 1999: 117)

Thus, the field of an academic text is not necessarily the extratextual physical reality, but the ideational world of the semiotic system underlying the text (McDermott, 1999). It can be argued that this is the case because the written academic language has become a repository of accepted views about a number of possible contexts (Pera, 1999; Vilks, 1999). We will pursue this thought in more detail slightly later in this section.

In addition to making the immediate physical designata superfluous thus changing the nature of the field, a written text also revolutionises the tenor by making the simultaneous presence of the participants (reader and writer) redundant (Sinclair, 1999; McDermott, 1999). Yet, its basic function still remains communication (Halliday, 1999). Who is supposed to communicate with whom via academic writing and how? Pera (1999) claims that there are two diverging views concerning the participants in communication through academic writing: the Text view and the Trial view. The former is represented by Galileo and Descartes, for example, or shortly the Founding Fathers of the modern science, while the latter goes back to Aristotle (Pera, 1999). Whereas the Text view sees nature or the objective reality as a participant that can be queried or read like a book, the Trial view sees nature as the object of a dialogue between people. In the former, the nature itself clarifies, enlightens and issues verdicts on correctness or truth; in the latter, academics bring their views to the trial and judge among themselves which view should prevail (Pera, 1999). Thus the tenor of written academic discourse is monologic, with elements of internalised dialogue (Sinclair, 1999) to account for the performative or illocutionary aspect of discourse (Austin, 1962 in Sinclair, 1999). We will return to the topic of tenor in our discussion of rhetorical features of academic writing.

Overall, it can be seen that writing has a communicative purpose, which is entirely different from that of speech. Not only does writing conserve cultural knowledge (Halliday, 1985) over time, but it also represents knowledge in all the disciplines of the academia (Johns, 1997; Halliday, 1999) to the respective communities of practice (Swales, 1990; Wenger, 1999). In this function, it serves the purpose of exchanging precise information about professional matters between specialists in the same discipline (Hoffman, 1988; Halliday, 1999). The discipline provides the field, the specialists the tenor and the style of precision the mode (Butt *et al.*, 1999). The need for all participants in such discourse to share the same language conventions becomes evident when a person attempts to read a professional text from a discipline she is not specialised in (Pera, 1999). Two problems mostly occur. In the sciences most of the vocabulary may be borrowed from a dead language, i.e. Latin or Greek (Picardi, 1999) and therefore inaccessible to an uninitiated person. Secondly, in arts, sciences or humanities alike, even the words familiar outside the context at hand may become inaccessible due to a special singular meaning attributed to them by the discipline (Pera, 1999). Thus even though a text on sociology may be in English, I may not understand its meaning, even though I might have learnt all of its words prior to reading it and am fairly familiar with them outside the sphere of sociology. On the other hand, I may be able to understand a text in French or even Russian languages in which I have had little or no training, so long as it pertains to the discipline of my specialisation, linguistics.

General English vs. academic English

The example above should be enough to start the linguists thinking about the nature of academic language. Can we say that English for Academic Purposes is really English? Hutchinson and Waters (1987) obviously think that it is, or rather that there is hardly any difference between general English and English for Specific Purposes. Grabe and Kaplan (1996: 171) however point out that a 'scientific text belongs less to a particular linguistic system than it does to ... [a] ... community'. Disciplinary communities are however built for the purpose of communicating knowledge in a standardised way (Pera, 1999; Wenger, 1999), using language that is specifically standardised for this purpose (Halliday, 1999). That meaning is sometimes called systematic knowledge, due to its regularity of occurrence in the same form (Arcaini, 1999: 121). This sets it apart from everyday spoken language, which is based on a different kind of knowledge, that which Halliday (1999) calls commonsense knowledge and Arcaini (1999) chooses to label 'a-systematic' knowledge because of its partial vagueness or ambiguity. The issue of ambiguity will be discussed in more detail later in this section. Thus if communicating specific meaning in a standardised way is the purpose of written academic language, we must be talking about a semiotic system in its own right, built with the elements of an existing semiotic system, the English language for example (Halliday, 1999; Vivenza, 1999; Vilks, 1999; Petkovic; 1984). As Halliday (1999: 99) points out, the language of science is 'a subsystem, or rather a family of sub-systems, of the language as a whole'.

Indeed, English for Academic Purposes and English for Specific Purposes have become separate subjects, different from English as a foreign (or a second) language, because the kind of English language they encompass is distinctly different from the variety used in everyday situations. A lot of research has been undertaken (Dodigovic, 1993, Halliday & Martin, 1993; Halliday, 1999; Halliday, 1994b) for the purpose of discovering and describing these differences. This chapter will try to raise the awareness of the features specific to academic language and style, including its predominantly written tradition, its specific vocabulary (terminology), somewhat simplified grammar, logical reasoning and text and discourse structure. This may be what Johns (1997: 6) calls a 'traditional', 'positivistic' or 'factual' view of academic literacy. However, it will hopefully contribute to understanding the basis for academic and professional communication, and that is the semiotic system used.

To start with, at an Australian university, as at many other English speaking universities, a lot of communication going on between the student and the lecturer is written (Halliday & Martin, 1993; Johns, 1997; Grabe & Kaplan, 1996; Clanchy & Ballard, 1977; Peters, 1985). The students spend several hours a week listening and speaking in lectures or tutorials, but they also spend much more time reading books or other documents and writing essays or reports. This goes back to a centuries long academic tradition of writing down one's thoughts for the purpose of documenting them, reviewing them critically and communicating them across the barriers of space and time to other scholars (Pera, 1999). Thus by reading a book by Aristotle, an ancient Greek philosopher from the 4th century BC, we are able to overcome a gap of 23 centuries, with more or less success (Vivenza, 1999; Pera, 1999). Equally, if situated in Sydney, Australia, and reading a book published in London we have conquered the distance as large as thousands of kilometres. Imagine that this was possible at the time when there were no telecommunication satellites, no computers and no Internet. Writing is therefore a powerful device of academic language and we will soon discover how exactly its language is different from the spoken variety.

The following two sentences originate from Butt *et al.* (1997) and clearly demonstrate the formal and structural difference between the written and spoken language:

Examples of written and spoken language
Written, also called 'Attic' by Halliday (1999)
(1) Excessive **consumption** of **alcohol** is a major **cause** of **motor vehicle accidents**.

Spoken, also called 'Doric' by Halliday (1999).
(2) If you drink too much **alcohol** when you drive your **car**, you are likely to have an **accident**.

The first example comes from a written text. Comparing it with the second example, which is a product of spoken language, two distinct structural differences can be observed. There is a large number of content words (Halliday, 1985), or words which have a dictionary meaning, e.g. 'excessive, consumption, alcohol, cause, motor, vehicle, accident'. This is different in spoken language (example 2), where there are fewer content words, but instead a number of grammar words (Halliday, 1985) are used (e.g. 'if, you, too, much, when . . .'). In contrast with content words, grammar words do not denote objects found in the real world. Instead, they denote the relations between other words in a sentence. In speech we use a number of these words, partly because there is no time to plan our utterance, so that grammar words are used as fillers while we are thinking what to say next. Also we use deictics (Halliday, 1994b) or words that point to something, because we can point to things in an immediate context, which luxury the writing mostly does not allow for. In writing, on the other hand, time is mostly available to plan our utterances very carefully. The result is usually a high load of information, which is expressed through a large number of content words.

In order to be able to combine so many content words in one sentence, the structure of the sentence, its grammar, has to change. This is mostly achieved by means of the so-called nominalisation. Nominalisation means that processes, normally expressed through verbs (e.g. 'when you drink . . .') become objects (e.g. 'drinking') or 'things' expressed by way of nouns (Halliday, 1999). When verbs are transformed into nouns, the sentence tends to contain a large proportion of nouns or nominals, which is why it becomes nominalised (Halliday, 1999). In turn, since the verbs are no longer used to denote processes, they are reduced to a few items of very low object or process related meaning (e.g. 'be, become, form, mean, define . . .') (Halliday, 1993). Later in this section we shall discuss a number of reasons why this is so.

Another way of condensing the amount of information in a text is by using the passive voice. Instead of saying 'I performed the experiment' one can simply say 'The experiment was performed'. The effect of this transformation is that we no longer know who performed the experiment, but this is also no longer of interest from the point of view of science (Halliday, 1999). The important information is that it was performed. The passive voice here, and elsewhere, also has a somewhat nominalising function. The full verb 'perform' is turned into a participle ('performed') which is originally nominal in form (Jespersen, 1972), while its place is occupied by 'was', a merely relational word. Thus the use of the passive voice contributes to informational density of a text.

> Also with regard to the *passive*, we should not simply note its frequency as a syntactic phenomenon, but we should underline its cognitive function: the passive construction places greater importance on objects than subjects, and phenomena rather than processes, transforming action into existence and freezing events into situations. All these effects would be hard to conciliate with narrative or dramatic writing, but are exploited fully by scientific writing that flattens the chronological dimension of the event in the definition of the phenomenon, and highlights the object of the research rather than the subject performing it. (Altieri Biagi, 1999: 48)

An academic text usually follows a pattern of organisation which is best suited to express one's thoughts on a certain subject. One would think that this would give the authors an unlimited amount of freedom to organise their texts as they see fit, which was the view of a particular approach to literacy called 'personal-expressivist' by Johns (1997: 9). This is, however, only partly true. While there surely is a certain freedom to express one's own views, the way in which all views are organised is highly formalised and complies fully with the rules of logical thinking, which are inherently mathematical (Halliday, 1999: 101). This mathematics of language brings about the need for a new grammar, the one that transforms processes into 'things' (Halliday, 1999). Processes need to be transformed into things due to the forces of Aristotelian science, which rather than asking 'how things work' seeks to find out 'how things exist' (McDermott, 1999: 69). For example, there is a verse in a popular song saying 'to know me is to love me', meaning 'it is impossible for someone to know me and not to love me'. If we wanted to transform this sentence into the language of logic and science, we would most likely come up with something like: 'Knowing me is loving me'. The processes 'to love' and 'to know' have become objects 'loving' and 'knowing'. However, the transformation would not be complete with this merely grammatical change (Halliday, 1999), since there is no organised system of scientific knowledge (Arcaini, 1999) behind it to assure that 'knowing' and 'loving' always mean the same thing to the same community (Raccah, 1999). In the following text this phenomenon will be explained at length.

Logical superorganisation

In dealing with the representation of reality, logic is a general code used by every science or academic discipline for the purposes of creating order and organisation (Pera, 1999; Raccah, 1999) in its system of knowledge. This logic imposes certain requirements on the units of meaning at all levels. The reason why processes are best dealt with when they become objects, which is what happens in logic, is that they can be more easily classified (e.g. 'There are two different ways in which language is articulated: speech and writing') (Halliday, 1999).This classification is always organised around a topic and is therefore topical (Raccah, 1999). For this very reason, objects are also very well suited for establishing conceptual relationships (e.g. subordination – speech is an aspect of language; or coordination – 'knowing me is loving me'). These objects are called terms, and they can not only be classified (or build a taxonomy, e.g. 'Natural languages are Chinese, Thai, French, English, German . . . '), but also very precisely defined, which is not frequently the case with words in everyday language (Jespersen, 1972). A definition places a term into a relation with a class of similar objects (subordination, superordination), e.g. 'A square is a rectangle . . . ', but this is not all. The information crucial to identifying how this object is different from other members of this class follows immediately (e.g. 'A square is a rectangle with equal sides'). Definition and classification are very important in the knowledge systems of all academic disciplines. They are both logical categories and they both influence the academic language by turning processes into things or objects, which are easily defined or classified, thus turning semantics into an algebra of concepts (Weinberger, 1999).

One could say that verbs can also be defined and to some extent classified (Halliday, 1999). Thus one could build a taxonomy of movement by including the verbs *walk, run, fly*, etc. (Halliday, 1999). However, the verb has a dimension that is not particularly useful in precise logical knowledge representation, as required in all academic disciplines, especially in sciences, and that is its temporal function, the ability to unfold in time (Halliday, 1999). Even though fine literature may capitalise on time and temporality as its main devices (Lessing, 1854), academic language defies it. It upholds the illusion of expressing unchanging universal truths: 'it is holding the world still, giving it stability and permanence, while you observe it, measure it and experiment with it' (Halliday, 1999: 110). Thus the nominal is timeless. It enables the projection of an eternal unchanging world in which things exist rather than work (McDermott, 1999).

Nominal terminology, including terms and their definitions, is therefore very important in academic writing (Halliday, 1994b, 1999; Dodigovic, 1993, 1998; Graffi, 1999; Weinberger, 1999), especially when it becomes a pedagogic task. On the one hand, understanding the meaning of technical terms enables the analysis of an essay question. On the other hand, defining crucial terms is necessary in order to write a good essay or report. Needless to say, no reading comprehension is imaginable without it.

Language is obviously the main ingredient of academic writing. However, it is not the only one. The knowledge of language alone is not enough to understand or write an academic text on e.g. *tensile strength*. Knowledge of mechanical engineering is a further prerequisite for the comprehension of it. Yet, the respective discipline does nothing to explain why the majority of academic texts, especially in sciences, use very restricted and quite distinctive grammatical patterns like the passive voice or nouns instead of verbs. Research (Halliday, 1999; Dodigovic, 1998) has shown that these features have something to do with logic, i.e. the scientific method of reasoning.

In academic language, logic constitutes an additional code, superimposed to that of language (Petkovic, 1984). This is based on Morris' (1938) understanding of semiosis, i.e. the process of meaning making, according to which there are four levels of semiosis. The first level is the so-called 'objective' reality, also called the object world or Level 0. We will get back to the concept of objective reality shortly. The next level is Level 1 or that of natural language. Level 2 belongs to metalanguage or language about language, which is possible because natural language had been organised according to a new principle into a new, higher semiotic system. One of these systems, or indeed a family of such systems, is the language of the academia. The final level, Level 3, is the level of meta-meta-language or epistemology, which can be conceived of as the science about science (Petkovic, 1984; Pera, 1999). One would assume that logic, common to all academic disciplines, comes from Level 3 rather than Level 2, but this is not so much of consequence here. Suffice it say that its function is largely to ensure the validity of reasoning, but also to enable a precise linguistic representation of that reasoning. Since natural spoken everyday language is not always clear or precise, its potential for creating ambiguity needs to be highly restricted in academic writing (Allen, 1995; Vilks, 1999; Graffi, 1999). Logic is a mechanism which has been successfully applied for that purpose to an array of different natural languages.

The disambiguation effected by logic occurs at three levels (Dodigovic, 1998). These are the level of words, syntactic level (sentences) and the level of discourse (the whole text or a group of texts). The following figures illustrate the process which occurs at the word level. Out of a *word*, which is a linguistic unit covering a broad field of different meanings, logic creates a *term* with only one definition, using the definition of the respective science across all texts within the same discipline. So for instance the word **field,**

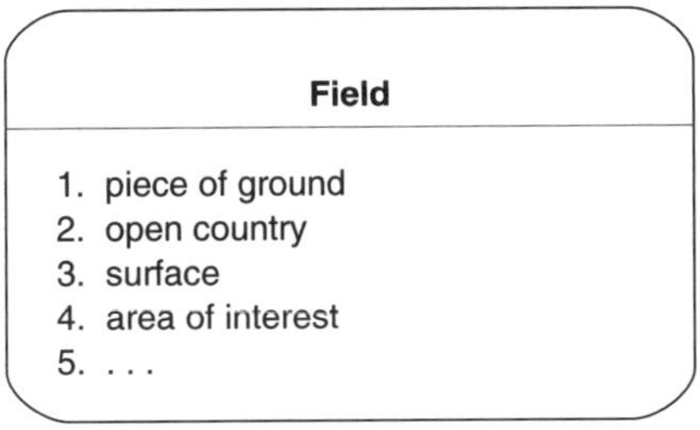

```
┌─────────────────────────────────────┐
│              Field                   │
├─────────────────────────────────────┤
│   1. piece of ground                 │
│   2. open country                    │
│   3. surface                         │
│   4. area of interest                │
│   5. . . .                           │
└─────────────────────────────────────┘
```

Figure 5.1 Word

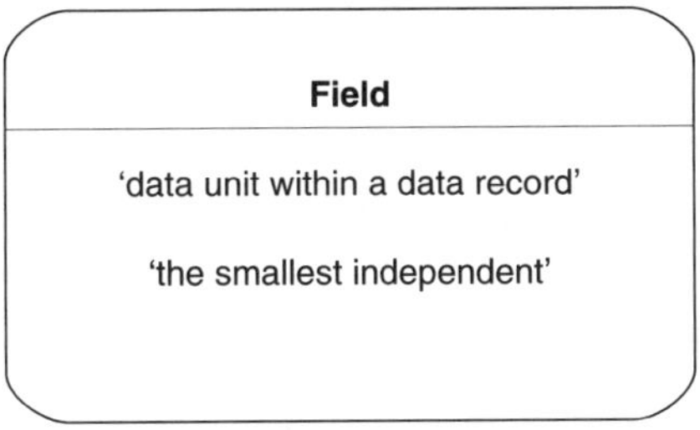

```
┌─────────────────────────────────────┐
│              Field                   │
├─────────────────────────────────────┤
│     'data unit within a data record' │
│                                      │
│       'the smallest independent'     │
└─────────────────────────────────────┘
```

Figure 5.2 Term

which can denote a number of concepts (e.g. **field** = 1. *piece of ground, 2. open country, 3. surface, 4. area of interest . . .*), will become a disambiguated term of information science meaning '*the smallest independent data unit within a data record*'. This definition, like any valid logical definition consists of two elements: a) the *class* of which the term is an element i.e. '*data unit within a data record*'; b) the *specific difference* of that element in regard to the class, i.e. '*the smallest independent*'.

The meaning of words, i.e. units of meaning in everyday language, can often be more than one, containing a range of concepts, frequently determined in context. Not even the context is sometimes informative enough to disambiguate a word, resulting in vagueness or ambiguity, lack of precision, allowing for an array of possible misunderstandings. These are hardly useful units of meaning in academic writing, which needs to be clear and precise, communicating the same meaning in any situation, over time, to any initiated member of the discipline (Halliday, 1999; Pera, 1999). Clearly, this raises the need for the one word-one meaning principle. The ideal unit of meaning in academic writing thus becomes a unit borrowed from formal logic, an ancillary discipline of philosophy and science that supplies its cognates with the norms of valid reasoning (Pera, 1999; Raccah, 1999). Thus logic affects language by creating terms out of words (Pera, 1999; Raccah, 1999; Weinberger, 1999). Terms, as opposed to words, have a formally precise definition. A definition gives two essential pieces of information: (1) the class the object belongs to (genus proximum), and (2) the specific difference or defining criterion (differentia specifica). Thus in the example 'A bit is the smallest unit of information', 'unit of information' is the class, while 'the smallest' is the specific difference, showing how this unit of information is different from any other unit of information.

Sometimes, dictionary entries are referred to as *words* and their *definitions*, which can be rather confusing. If a word happens to have more than one definition, then it is not a term (Petkovic, 1984). Most of the time, however, everyday words defy definitions and are best described by way of synonyms (words of the same or similar meaning, e.g *to cope = to struggle or contend*). We can speculate with Arcaini (1999) that this is a consequence of the a-systematic knowledge stored in a word, which Halliday (1999) would call commonsense knowledge.

To assure consistency (Arcaini, 1999), terms are fixed in two ways: (1) by definition *(setting defining criteria, boundaries)*, e.g. 'Language is a system of spoken or written symbols used in interpersonal communication', and (2) by classification *(dividing according to a principle, e.g. people according to their countries of origin)*, e.g. English, Chinese, Spanish, German, French. In academic writing one has to use both: definitions to define terms which are not clear or are subject to controversy (and sometimes such that seemingly are); and taxonomies to establish classification principles in order to analyse, compare, contrast or make inferences.

Both comparing and contrasting are unthinkable without a set of common criteria. One can only compare like with like, so one can compare two phenomena in what they both have in common. Thus every classification is built around one and the same principle (e.g. languages according to nation – English, Korean, Spanish, French).

Language and logical reasoning interact at many levels in academic writing (Halliday, 1999). We were able to see how a word, which is a unit of language denoting sometimes a vague field of various meanings, becomes a precisely defined term-object in academic language, thanks to the interference of the logical code. Just as we combine words into utterances in spoken language, logic combines terms into statements (e.g. 'Sparrows are birds'). Each statement consists of exactly two terms (e.g. 'Flying [T1] is dangerous [T2]'), which form several different types of relations with each other. The most important ones have already been mentioned: subordination (being a member of a larger class), superordination (being the larger class an object belongs to) and coordination (an object is a member of two different classes). Thus statements are complex logical units consisting of two terms each. In language they closely resemble sentences, which is why in academic writing most sentences are built according to the statement model (e.g. 'Excessive consumption of alcohol is a major cause of motor vehicle accidents'; 'The intensity of the observed radiation is in agreement with the thermal radiation'). From these examples it is obvious that the sentences are divided into two parts (terms) often consisting of several nominal content words each.

Apart from the above 'amiable' relationships between terms, including the relationship of equivalence, there are those less amiable. For example, terms can be disparate, i.e. not related at all, contrary or even contradictory (Tempest Media, 2002). It is relations like these that enable certain less monolithic qualities and practices of academic discourse, rather than just the quarrelsome nature of the community of academics, as tacitly suggested by Pera (1999) that allow for a certain measure of disharmony and dispute in written academic discourse, especially at the intertextual level. For the moment we will postpone further development of this topic, until we have concluded the discussion of what is recognised as the influence of formal logic on academic writing.

At the sentence level precision in academic language is achieved by transforming the linguistic unit *sentence* into a logical unit called *proposition* or *statement* (Pera, 1999). There are several differences between the two. Whereas a sentence can contain any number and type of words which are linguistically related (e.g. *Mary gave the book to the teacher yesterday afternoon after school*), a logical statement can only have two terms (e.g. 'Mary is unselfish'). The main difference is, however, found in the fact that a logical statement has to be either true or false (Vilks, 1999), whereas a sentence can be ambiguous even in that respect. While '*This man is both dead and alive*' is not a valid logical statement, being neither true nor false, it is an acceptable sentence, which can be taken figuratively (meaning 'this man is very sick' or 'this man is in a great distress' or even 'this man is socially functional, he sleeps, gets up, eats, goes to work, but he hasn't got a personality'), rather than literally. Logic, however, will not tolerate parallel interpretations, nor will it allow for more than a binary choice in regard to the truth of a statement. This is called 'the law of the excluded middle' (Vilks, 1999: 160), formulated by Aristotle to assure the 'two-valued' standard of mathematical logic in reasoning. Amazingly, this is the same principle used by modern cybernetics to produce computers capable even of natural language processing. As we saw in Chapter 4 of this volume, it is this very principle that underlies the Turing Test, used to decide if a machine is acting in an 'intelligent' manner (Borchardt & Page, 1994). At this point we will resist the temptation to enter a debate on how valid or necessary the binary tree logic is and what could possibly replace it. We will continue to pursue its powerful out-working in the written discourse of the academia, in particular at its syntactic level. Thus, in academic writing, the sentence patterns tend to conform to the following sentence forming rule: Term 1 + relational verb + Term 2. Observe the example below:

The intensity of the observed radiation (T1) is (verb) **in agreement with the thermal radiation** (T2).

Planetary radiation (T1) is (verb) **discussed by Burke** (T2).

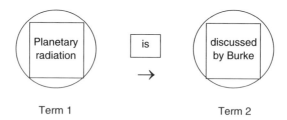

Term 1   Term 2

Figure 5.3

A sentence in academic English, most frequently in sciences, tends to group several words into one term (Halliday, 1999). This happens because one word is often too general to express the precise meaning of the author (e.g. 'radiation'), which is why this word receives further specification ('planetary'). This is how the term 'planetary radiation' is built. One term is, however, not enough to form a statement in logic or a sentence in a text. For this reason another term is needed to provide more information on the first one. Thus in a sentence of academic English, just as in a logical statement, a minimum of two terms is required: one to be described through its relationship with the other.

Thus not only are individual words and expressions nominalised, but whole sentences are made to conform to a certain pattern: 'thing' + relational verb + 'thing'. Halliday (1994b, 1999) calls this process a grammatical metaphor. Just as a lexical metaphor helps create a new lexical meaning by substituting one expression for another (e.g. 'my treasure' for a beloved person), the grammatical metaphor creates a new meaning by using one grammatical structure ('Excessive consumption of alcohol is a major cause of motor vehicle accidents') for another ('If you drink too much alcohol when you drive you are likely to have an accident'). This is how Halliday (1999: 105) sees the role of the grammatical metaphor in the process of writing science:

> In the construction of a scientific theory, two semiotic conditions need to be met. One is technicality: the grammar has to create technical meanings, purely virtual phenomena that exist only on the semiotic plane, as terms of a theory; and not as isolates, but organized into elaborate taxonomies. The other is rationality: the grammar has to create a form of discourse for reasoning from observation and experiment,

drawing general conclusions and progressing from one step to another in sequences of logical argument.

As pointed out by Halliday (1999: 105), in logic, statements are further combined into *arguments* or *syllogisms*, which roughly correspond to paragraphs in academic writing, of which we will give a brief account. Deductive arguments (progressing from the general towards the specific) usually contain three statements: one general one (All human beings are mortal), one specific one related to the preceding general statement (Nero is human) and a conclusion (Nero is mortal). This conclusion was possible, because we established a relation between an object and a class, and then we concluded about that object what we know to be true about the whole class. Furthermore, we were able to establish these relations because we only operated with a limited number of terms (3 – *human, Nero, mortal*). The three statements within an argument roughly correspond to the three parts of a paragraph: topic (introducing an idea in a general way), middle (giving specific detail in relation to the generally stated topic), conclusion (reaching a logical conclusion). In fact, the same triadic structure applies to the macrostructure of the whole text (introduction, body, conclusion), which seems repeated across different natural languages of the same academic subculture (Favretti, 1999), e.g. English and Italian. Thus, there is clear evidence of logical code strongly influencing academic writing at the paragraph and text level.

Moreover, at the text level, logic is present again, in the sense that most academic texts are usually organised around some form of taxonomy (Halliday, 1999). An example of this is an essay on the expectations of Australian academics of their students' writing. An essay answering this question would usually start out with an explicit classification: 'Australian academics expect several things of their students: independent learning, critical thinking, logical reasoning and good command of the English language'. Each subsequent paragraph would then discuss one of the above expectations. We can say that this essay is organised around the taxonomy or classification of the expectations Australian academics have of their students, with the latter as the guiding principle for the taxonomy (*principium divisionis*). Some academic texts are organised around various causes of a phenomenon or the consequences of an event, or even around a timeline of events. These are all examples of possible taxonomies.

What has made the above taxonomies possible are relationships of cause, consequence and sequence between terms. The latter may seem like the previously discarded temporality of a verb denoting a material process (Halliday, 1999), but is in fact time suspended and turned into a geometrical form, that of a line, on which the relationship of mathematical sequence can be comfortably analysed, thanks to logic. In fact logic underpins a number of other textual properties in academic writing (Halliday, 1999).

cause 1			consequence 1		70–75
cause 2	phenomen	event	consequence 2	time (70–99)	76–88
cause 3			consequence 3		89–99

Figure 5.4 Taxonomies

For example, a very important aspect of paragraph and text organisation is cohesion, which is discussed extensively in Halliday (1994a); Hasan (1994); and Halliday and Hasan (1986). Apart from the grammatical relationship that comes into being when words are put together into sentences or rather when terms are put together into statements or propositions, there are other relations in a text, and these are relations between sentences in a paragraph (i.e. propositions in an argument) or a longer text which connect the ideas or words and make the whole piece of writing seem unified. This is called *cohesion* (Hasan, 1994). Logic as the organising principle is here at work too and we will see how in the following paragraphs.

Cohesion

According to Halliday (1999), the Theme, or the structural beginning of a sentence, i.e. the part of it preceding the verb, has in academic writing become bonded with the Subject. In contrast, speech or fiction will very often have the Subject bonded with the function of Actor. In academic writing, however, the Theme is frequently used to introduce what is already known to the reader, often from the same text. Even long arguments can be 'destilled' or condensed into nominal groups (Halliday, 1999). Thus the Theme 'excessive consumption of alcohol' in our example sentence is possibly a 'summary' of a preceding sentence or perhaps even a paragraph dealing with quantities at which alcohol can no longer be safely ingested. The nominal group acting as a 'summary' of the foregone proposition or argument constitutes co-referentiality (Hasan, 1994) in text, i.e. the means of referring to the same thing. Consequently, nominalised Themes are often previous discourse accrued (Halliday, 1999), whether stemming from the same text or not. Nominal group thus becomes a grammatical way of representing the vast body of knowledge generally accepted within a discipline (Pera, 1999). When Themes within a text are combined from logical arguments containing no more than three terms each, chances are that the themes are going to be lexically and semantically related. Similarities in Themes (Martin *et al.* 1997) are related to *lexical* cohesion, as the similarities in Themes are basically to do with the words used in them. The similarity of wording, called *lexical cohesion*, is in academic writing closely related with the restrictive power of logic on the number of available terms.

Lexical cohesion is essential to the texture of written discourse (Hasan, 1994). It may occur in the form of exact repetition of a word, or it may involve the use of synonyms, i.e. words of similar meaning, or collocation, i.e. words which are closely associated and often occur together (such as *malaria* and *parasite*) (Martin *et al.* 1997). It can involve co-refentiality, co-classification or the mention of terms belonging to the same class, or co-extension, i.e. words from the same general field of meaning, more precisely synonyms, antonyms and hyponyms (Hasan, 1994). The repetition of words or use of words with a similar meaning is a very important way of binding a paragraph or whole text together so that we can follow it more clearly. Note that the logical relation between superordinate (disease) and subordinate (malaria) terms is often used to maintain lexical cohesion in academic texts. Cohesion, however, also includes *reference* and *conjunction*, which are described in the following.

Reference is a term used for the way in which certain words refer to other words used somewhere else in the text, and hence connect these ideas (Martin *et al.* 1997). We have already encountered the concept of co-referentiality (Hasan, 1994) that explains the general meaning of reference. Whereas in speech co-referentiality is sometimes used for items not previously mentioned in the text, but present in the immediate extralinguistic context (exoforic use), in a written text endoforic reference or reference to the already mentioned is the norm (Hasan, 1994). This explains the perceived autonomy of the written text in respect of the extralinguistic context. If a word takes the place of something which came earlier it is a repetition of sorts, called an anaphoric cohesive tie (Hasan, 1994). Otherwise, words may refer to something following the referent, which is called a cataphoric cohesive tie (Hasan, 1994). The referring words may also be making a comparison of some kind. To understand what is meant by a particular reference word, it is necessary to look somewhere else, and make a connection.

Words can create cohesive ties within a text either by similarity chains or by identity chains (Hasan, 1994). While similarity chains include co-classification and co-extension, enabled not only by word semantics, but predominantly by the logical superorganisation of language, identity chains include co-referentiality (Hasan, 1994). As the latter involve individual objects and persons rather than whole classes, they would not be expected in large amounts in academic writing, except when the preceding arguments are being referred to in short expressions. Thus, in academic writing reference words (e.g. 'this') may point to terms, propositions or even entire arguments, as is the case with thematic development which is mostly responsible for lexical cohesion.

Cohesion in academic language should be a reflection of a logical quality of the underlying reasoning, and that is called coherence. Thus, thematic development as well as cohesive devices are used to underscore valid reasoning rather than to create it. In other words, if the reasoning follows the rules of formal logic, according to which each term within the syllogism has to appear twice, the text will result in either lexical cohesion or cohesion by reference. The semantic relations between terms and statements (cause, consequence, addition, contrast etc.) will be reflected in conjunctions, thus accounting for its cohesive devices. These relationships have become the object of study of Rhetorical Structure Theory (RST). The latter identifies 23 different types of relationships between parts of text (Jurafsky & Martin, 2000). Some of these relationships are contrast, condition, purpose, sequence or result (Jurafsky & Martin, 2000).

Participants and circumstances

We have been able to see that written academic language serves an important purpose. This purpose is to be perceived as the lasting truth, unpolluted by the personality of the writer (Pera, 1999). For that purpose the text has to be formally logical and has to have the appearance of objectivity (creating precise formalised objects – terms), systemic organisation (defining and classifying terms) and seeming impersonality induced by 'the fuzzifying of the clear distinction between participants and circumstances' (Halliday, 1999: 105), e.g. through the use of the passive voice. Proper linking of terms and propositions according to logical principles is also a must, either by clear and obvious taxonomising of the terminology or through the appropriate use of linking words like 'thus', therefore', 'if', etc. Yet, we are also told that despite all the intended impersonality, expressing opinions is an important part of the written academic tradition (Halliday, 1994a; Dow, 1999), e.g. by using words such as 'surely', 'certainly' etc. Is this a contradiction in terms (the fallacy known as 'contradictio in adjecto')? The following paragraph will try to provide an answer.

Notice what I just did at the end of the previous paragraph: I told you that the paragraph would provide an answer, not the author thereof. In doing so, I have reduced the number of participants in the original sentence ('I will try to provide an answer in the following paragraph') from two (*I, answer*) plus a circumstance (*in the following paragraph*) to two without a circumstance (*the following paragraph, answer*). In other words, I have 'fuzziefied' the distinction between the participants and circumstances (Halliday, 1999: 105), as my previous circumstance (*in the following paragraph*) has become a participant (*the following paragraph*). In any other context one would undoubtedly wonder how on earth an inanimate concept such as paragraph is to perform a rather concrete action like providing an answer. Why is it necessary to say such a thing which defies our entire experience and our sense of word semantics? A possible answer can be found in the fact that the academic text is often viewed as discursive (Pera, 1999: 178). To put it in Pera's (1999: 178) words:

> As I see it, Aristotle conceived of scientific enquiry as a discourse in the literal sense, that is not so much a question of reading and deciphering

a text, but rather a question of discovering a law or a theory (a principle, in his terminology), by making observations and, what is more, by engaging in a discussion with other enquirers in order to compare different views about the same subject (hypotheses, in our vocabulary).

The above invitation of debate into the academic discourse opens the door to viewing it in a manner that largely defies the systematicity of logic we have just established to exist at its core (Pera, 1999). Pera (1999: 177) calls the latter the 'Text view', largely associated with the philosophy of empiricism and the logical positivism. The former he calls the 'Discourse view', which at its extreme can be associated with scepticism and deconstructivism (Pera, 1999: 178). We have seen in Chapter 2 of this volume how deconstructivism views academic discourse as subjective, localised, value laden and therefore relative. On the other hand, the Text view holds that scientific knowledge (and therefore its language) is universal, objective, rational, true and progressive (Pera, 1999: 177). One wonders whether the golden middle between the extremes is possible at all, and indeed, Pera (1999: 181) finds it in the dialectics, the logic of science.

Rhetoric

However, if the academic discourse means interaction between people rather than that between a person and the subject matter, it cannot be expected to be purely rational, as people are known to have both instincts and emotions in addition to the capacity for logical thinking. It follows that academic discourse must be subject to both sentiment and intuition (Dow, 1999), as pointed out by Smith and Keynes (Dow, 1999), prominent economic theorists separated by almost two centuries of history. Rather than ignoring these thoroughly human capacities, Dow (1999) believes to have found enough evidence in both Smith and Keynes to support the use of rhetoric, or the art of explanation and persuasion, in academic discourse for the purpose of appealing to both the sentiment and intuition of the reader. Unfortunately, very often, various rhetorical devices can create logical fallacies or errors in logic. Thus it could bring about a false analogy in its attempt to explain the unknown in terms of something familiar to the reader, or it can end up in sheer appeals to pity or authority. Thus rhetoric that defies logic in academic discourse may best be left out. Overall, it can be said that rhetoric belongs to tenor within the academic context of situation and is responsible for the interpersonal meaning, whereas logic is a part of mode directly creating the textual meaning, the quality that gives the academic text its internal coherence and perceived independence from any immediate context.

While Pera (1999: 182) insists that formal logic is only a part of the rules of debate, we would say that it is the most important part of it. Thus, the foundation for a valid debate is a set of propositions accepted as true within a discipline. The proponent of a new academic idea has the task to either prove that it conforms to the commonly accepted set or that some of the commonly accepted propositions need to change. She will be able to do either of the above by using terms and their mutual relationships as well as the relationships between propositions depicted accurately by Pera (1999: 183) in the predicate calculus, the mathematics of the academic reasoning. Therefore, though the moves of debate such as opening, conducting the debate, managing the interlocutor's commitments and terminating or adjudicating the debate (Pera, 1999) may be outside the sphere of formal logic, strictly speaking, it is that same logic that is crucial to the outcome of each move and has power against vocal and even numerous opponents. Thus logic governs the rules of communication in academic discourse above and beyond language itself.

As a result of the substantial influence of logic on the form and the meaning of words, sentences, paragraphs and texts, academic writing is generally made to appear very formal, objective and mostly impersonal (often through the use of the passive voice). It is required to be free of slang, colloquial language, biased personal involvement and logical fallacies. According to McRoberts (1981), sincerity, clarity and simplicity, decisiveness, and consistency are generally quoted as acceptable criteria for good academic writing, a worthy list representing perhaps the views of logical positivism. This is unfortunately a view of the world that appears fragmented (Halliday, 1999: 111) because of its refusal to rely on material process and its flow over time. The movement in time is, however, replaced by the movement through structure, from term to proposition, to argument, to text, to discourse.

Thus logic is active on an intertextual discourse level in academic writing as well. This is true due to the relatively permanent nature of knowledge organisation, to which, according to Halliday (1999), we only ever add new facts, never losing anything; stable term definitions within a discipline and the propositional structure of generally accepted scientific facts that can be relied upon even if not explicitly stated in a text. The latter is what gives the knower the power to unlock the secrets of a text that potentially holds a high level of entropy and therefore ambiguity for the uninitiated (Halliday, 1999). Thus it may not be the power of being a member of a social group that gives one the right to a certain discourse, as asserted by Benesch, (2001) and Murray (2000), but rather the power to control the entropy of natural language by understanding the rules of logic and one's own discipline. This power is otherwise known as academic literacy.

EAP Student Writing vs. Established Academic Writing

In the above we have enumerated an array of features displayed by the established, mostly native speaker written academic prose. We could agree that it differs from everyday language in terms of field, mode and tenor. While spoken language is the preferred mode of everyday language, the field of everyday discourse is rarely as intensely specialised as it is in written academic discourse and the participants are rarely all specialists in the same field, which opens the way for all sorts of logical fallacies based on the entropy and ambiguity of natural language (Graffi, 1999), but precision is less required than is empathy and cooperation (Scollon & Scollon, 1995). On the other hand, a fine line needs to be walked between monologic and dialogic discourse in academic writing, a skill requiring a high degree of understanding, not of the natural language only, but of the debate and internalisation rules (Sinclair, 1999). One wonders if withholding this information from EAP students, as suggested by Hutchinson and Waters (1987), would be of any benefit, considering the above demonstrated importance of writing in exams.

We have now come to a point where we can comfortably stop using opinion and speculation as a method of research, capable of yielding 'soft data' only, and look at some 'hard data' (Johns, 1981) obtained by document analysis. The documents to analyse will be representative of both established academic prose and EAP student writing. The possible difference in how language representative of the academic prose is used in the two kinds of writing will supply us with the necessary information about what it is that our EAP students may be missing out on and should therefore by all means be taught.

The features displayed by professional native speaker academic writers are tacitly expected of second language student writers (EAP students) as well. As the above features can be easily tracked down by using a computer, a corpus of EAP students' academic writing was compiled in order to compare its features with those of native speaker professional academic writing found in Brown (American) and LOB (British) corpora, in particular the section entitled 'Scientific and Learned'. For the purpose of EAP corpus compilation, two samples of academic writing were collected from 87 predominantly Chinese and Indonesian students over the period of one semester. Some of them had participated in the survey administered by Suphawhat (1999). The sample included a small proportion of native speakers of other languages, such as Norwegian, Portuguese, Spanish, Hebrew, Malay, Japanese, Arabic and Tagalog. All students had scored an average of 6.5 on the IELTS test or higher, which is equivalent to approximately 580 of the TOEFL scale, usually briefly before enrolling in the EAP course. This means that their English skills are theoretically not only reasonably high and a good predictor of favourable academic success, but that this should be a fairly homogeneous population in terms of language skills. However, in reality there seems to be a high rate of English skills divergence that the above standardised tests do not seem to detect very well. Thus the description of the respective interlanguages may yield a more

Table 5.1 Data on writing styles across the corpora

	LOB	*Brown*	*EAP students*
Words	142,977	142,753	14,035
Sentences	5,786	6,889	2,094
Content words	75,505	77,564	7,146
Nouns	69,010	70,692	5,494
Full verbs	6,495	6,872	1,652
Auxiliaries	7,159	6,889	479

reliable source of information about the actual language skills of these students than the numerical test scores do. The interlanguage data will then be used to create the blueprint for the Intelligent Tutor. Even though the multilingual setting had a strong leaning toward a cross-sectional study, the data was expected to capture various individual stages of inter-language development, since it was shown by Andersen (1978 cited in Larsen-Freeman & Long, 1991) that individual and group data correlate significantly. The findings have been most interesting. The researchers compared the number of content words in the three corpora. The results can be viewed in the Table 5.1

Table 5.1 shows that there is a difference between native speaker academic writing and EAP student writing. Although the EAP student writing corpus is approximately 10 times smaller than both other corpora, certain features can be very well compared. For instance, the EAP corpus has a proportionally far larger number of sentences, which means that the students tend to write short sentences, avoiding compound structures. While the number of content words appears to be similar across the three corpora, the distributions for nouns and full lexical verbs differ. Whereas the British and American corpora comprise a large number of relational verbs (i.e. *be, have, will, shall* ...) and considerably fewer full verbs, the EAP corpus demonstrates a lower number of relational verbs, complemented by a high number of full lexical verbs. Consequently, processes largely exist in EAP student writing, full verbs have not been replaced by passives or nouns, which leads to the conclusion that the active voice may be used with much greater frequency than normally found in native speaker academic writing. All these features render the EAP academic writing strikingly similar to spoken English, which does not surprise considering the oral teaching methods and communicative language learning methods these students would have been exposed to in their pre-university English classes. These findings really reinforce the need for raising the language awareness of the target student population.

Another feature important in academic writing investigated on the

Table 5.2 Cohesive devices in EAP student writing

Cohesive device	Number of occurrences
actually	10
also	44
Although	6
and	465
because	31
Besides	7
Finally	1
Firstly	3
including	4
Nevertheless	4
regarding	1
Therefore	21

EAP corpus was cohesion (Halliday, 1994a: 287) or the textual function (Martin *et al.*, 1997), including the linking words and signals. Cohesion fulfils the function of presenting academic discourse as logically coherent (Dodigovic, 2002). Based on a Hallidayan list of cohesive devices, previous research (Field, 1994) into the use of linking words by native speakers of Cantonese has shown that the patterns are not consistent with those found in native speaker academic writing. The test subjects (Field, 1994), who all came from Hong Kong, seemed to be overusing the conjunctions *moreover*, *besides* and *nevertheless*. The EAP student corpus, consisting to a large extent of contributions from Hong Kong born students, showed no sign of overuse. Compared to Field's (1994) study, it seemed to indicate an underuse of linking words. Thus *moreover* did not occur at all, whereas *besides* was used seven and *nevertheless* only four times. One possible reason for this difference may of course lie in the method used to teach cohesive devices to either group. Field's students appear to have had more targeted exposure to and explicit tuition in linking words than did our EAP students. A tentative conclusion is, however, that linking words in English are linguistically quite challenging for the native speakers of Cantonese, whether they have been explicitly taught, as documented by Field (1994), or not, as was the case in this study.

Since academic discourse serves as a vehicle of expressing opinions and being rhetorically persuasive, expressing critical opinions or what is known as interpersonal function (Martin *et al.*, 1997) in systemic functional

Table 5.3 Expressing opinions across the three corpora: number of occurrences

Opinion indicator	EAP	LOB	Brown
apparently	1	15	19
clearly	16	24	31
definitely	1	2	3
no doubt	5	14	6
maybe	1	1	3
obviously	1	15	24
positively	2	0	1
probably	2	44	52

linguistics (SFL) was also a subject of this study. Scollon and Scollon (1995) argue that the extent to which opinions are freely expressed is a matter of culture. Their next claim is that most Asian cultures see the imposition of one's own opinion on someone else as impolite. To test the readiness of the primarily Asian EAP sample to express opinions, a search was done on the so-called opinion indicators. These, according to Halliday (1994a), include words such as *clearly, apparently, no doubt*, etc. The results were then compared with those for native speaker writing corpora.

These results indicate that EAP students were using only eight out of 20 expressions listed in Halliday (1994a: 82). Table 5.3 compares the use of these eight items across the board. Apart from those eight, both British and American scholarly writing corpora showed a wide variety of other opinion indicators, including *certainly, surely, perhaps, possibly, evidently, presumably, of course*, etc. which were not used by EAP students. Table 5.3 brings into focus the contrastive expression poverty of the EAP population. Thus *clearly*, which seems to be the most widely accepted opinion indicator in the EAP corpus, tends to be overused in comparison with native speaker data. This of course can be brought back to general English skills of the EAP population.

In conclusion, EAP writing appears to compromise between the written and spoken style. The spoken style is reflected in the EAP student preference for full or material verbs (Martin *et al.* 1997), rather than for noun groups linked by relational verbs, which are otherwise so typical of written language. Short sentences, lacking clear linking words or definite opinion indicators, are a further feature that brings the EAP student writer style closer to spoken discourse than to academic writing.

Thus the question of what exactly constitutes academic writing became one of the most important questions for this study. According to Halliday

(1994a) there is a distinctive feature of written language, something that does not exist in speech, an element which in EAP teaching could be effectively used to raise the students' awareness of the difference between the two. That element is a sentence, so the argument goes (Halliday, 1994a), which is a unit beginning with a capital letter and ending in a full stop. This is really non-existent in speech, where clauses flow spontaneously from one another, building never ending complexes, let alone the lack of one-to-one punctuation equivalents. Thus a sentence has the potential of becoming a building block of written academic English, a starting point for research as well as for teaching. We have also seen from the discussion of academic language that one of the most potent transitions from colloquial to written academic style occurs at the sentence level in the form of grammatical metaphor (Halliday, 1994b; 1999). Accordingly, the rest of this chapter is devoted to firstly, EAP corpus sentence level profiling and secondly, developing an artificially intelligent sentence writing tutor, based on the student sentence profiles.

EAP corpus: Error analysis

Earlier on, student interlanguages, or rather their erroneous subsets, were identified as a research target for the purpose of developing the Intelligent Tutor of written academic English. Some quotations from Simmons and Thurstun's (1995) survey of academics' opinions regarding their students' writing indicate what concerns were prevalent:

> Grammatical weaknesses need to be rectified . . . Poor spelling and sentences without verbs are all too prevalent . . . They don't intend to plagiarise, but don't have the self-confidence to express the ideas in their own words . . . Overseas students tend to use too many redundant words; they are unaware of how to keep sentences short and precise; vocabulary is insufficient . . . Many students write essays that are unreadable because of poor grammar; ideas are confused and poor sentencing confuses the reader further . . . so much can be improved regarding language, argument, organization, grammar . . . errors of punctuation, grammar etc. (Simmons and Thurstun, 1995)

After a theoretical model described below for the interlanguages of Chinese and Indonesian learners of English as L2 was adopted from literature (Yip, 1995; Jones, 1999 in Dodigovic, 2002; Swan & Smith, 1987), the EAP corpus was analysed for grammatical and semantic errors. The non-native-like features were then categorised, thus generating a bottom-up description of the two systems. The results of the corpus analysis were mainly convergent with the theoretical models. However, as the models themselves could be better understood on the basis of actual data and their descriptions subsequently brought to a common denominator, the differences between the two interlanguages were found to be much less significant than originally anticipated.

Corder (1967 & 1974) identified a model for error analysis which included three stages:

1. Data collection: Recognition of idiosyncracy
2. Description: Accounting for idiosyncratic dialect
3. Explanation (the ultimate object of error analysis).

Brown (1994, pp. 207–211) and Ellis (1995, pp. 51–52) elaborated on this model. Ellis (1997, pp. 15–20) and Hubbard *et al.* (1996, pp. 135–141) gave practical advice and provided clear examples of how to **identify and analyze** learners' errors. The initial step requires the **selection** of a corpus of language followed by the **identification** of errors. The errors are then **classified**. The next step, after giving a grammatical analysis of each error, demands an **explanation** of different types of errors. Moreover, Gass & Selinker (1994, p. 67) identified 6 steps followed in conducting an error analysis: Collecting data, Identifying errors, Classifying errors, Quantifying errors, Analyzing source of error, and Remediating for [sic!] errors. (AbiSamra, 2003)

While for Corder (1967) explanation seems to be the main objective of error analysis, our purpose converges with that of Gass and Selinker (1994 in AbiSamra, 2003), that being error remediation. For this reason, our model of error analysis will be identical with the one described by Gass and Selinker (1994 in AbiSamra, 2003). Explaining the errors in terms of their sources is a paramount task and requires much more detailed profiling than we have done. Besides, theories vary in their identification of possible sources. Thus, Selinker (1972) identifies five sources of errors: (1) language transfer, (2) transfer of learning, (3) strategies of second language learning, (4) strategies of second language communication, and (5) over-generalisation of TL linguistic material. Richards and Simpson (1974 in AbiSamra, 2003) identify seven sources of errors: (1) language transfer, (2) intralingual interference, (3) sociolinguistic situation, (4) modality of exposure to TL and production, (5) age, (6) successions of approximative systems, and (7) universal hierarchy of difficulty. James (1998), on the other hand, believes in three main sources of errors: (1) interlingual, (2) intralingual, and (3) induced. His categories are fairly broad and subsume most of the above quoted types. While we have explained some of the avoidance errors, i.e. not using opinion indicators, in terms sociolinguistic situation and learning strategy with a tendency toward induced errors in terms of overuse (Field, 1994), we will rely on two very broad categories in further analysis: interlingual or native language transfer errors and intralingual or developmental errors. We will also marginally look at all errors in the light of cognitive psychology and its slant on learner age as a source of error.

According to Corder (1967), error analysis has a twofold purpose. Firstly, it is diagnostic, as it tells us about the state of our students' interlanguage, and secondly, it is prognostic because it can predict future language problems, thus being of high value to us as educators and learning software developers. This study is based on the error analysis of the cyber age, inspired by an idea of Gerard Dalgish (1991). In an article published in *CALICO Journal*, Dalgish (1991) describes an electronic database used to classify and catalogue errors in NNS writing. To some extent error typology used by Dalgish (1991) was helpful, but was not followed in its totality in this study. The former identifies the following error categories: vocabulary/idiom, subject-verb agreement, confused part of speech with several subcategories, tense and verb form. The latter was developed around parts of speech, but in a much broader sense than was the case in the Dalgish (1991) study.

In our study the part of speech was also used in the sense of a head word in a phrase, thus accounting for syntactic structures and the phrase structure character of the PROLOG programming language chosen for the implementation of grammar. Each part of speech allowed for several relevant subcategories. For example, as in the Dalgish (1991) study, a number of parts of speech allowed for part of speech confusion subcate-gory. In addition, missing part of speech was also a subcategory in some cases, including articles, nominals, conjunctions and verbs. Conjunctions also allowed a subcategory for the tautological use or doubling up, e.g. of conjunctions, as observed by Chang (1987) in Chinese-English Inter-language. With the parts of speech that have the category of number in English (nouns, pronouns, verbs), number of course became an eligible error subcategory. Apart from part of speech based morphological and syntactic error types, the database also allowed semantic, syntactic and clause related, word order and punctuation categories. Beside general semantic errors, a separate verb semantics subcategory was added to the verb category, including the information whether the verb is transitive, intransitive or ergative, whether it calls for an animate subject or not and whether its meaning has already been expressed otherwise (tautology). Table 5.4 shows some examples from the unsorted database with erroneous forms in upper case letters.

As could be seen from the example, sentence was in accordance with the point of departure in error analysis as it was the intended unit for practicing grammatical accuracy (Halliday, 1985). Consequently, the error taxonomy also reflected a sentence perspective, as sentence seemed to be the battle-field of error and possibly fossilisation. Two separate SLA theories feed into such reasoning, the one being the connectionist (N. Ellis, 2001; Cochran *et al.*, 1999) and the other the lexical chunking theory (Lewis, 2003) theory.

Table 5.4 Error database

Having a global language, which unites all nations in their diversity of languages and cultures, may have a good impact IN the relationship and exchange of information between countries.	Prep	Indonesia
Each country WOULD benefits if the information can be exchanged and work together in building an improved technology that can be beneficial for the country.	Vtaut	Indonesia
Each country would benefits if the information can be exchanged and work * together in building an improved technology that can be beneficial for the country.	ClMiss	Indonesia
Each country would benefits if the information can be exchanged and work together in building an improved technology that can be beneficial FOR the country.	Prep	Indonesia
It can be said that a global language is the language that is spoken and understood by * majority people all around the world.	DetMiss	Indonesia
It can be said that a global language is the language that is spoken and understood by majority * people all around the world.	PrepMiss	Indonesia
It is OBVIOUSLY that a global language is beneficial to the modern world, in order to conduct better communication between international businesman and develop new high technology.	AdvAdj	Indonesia
It is obviously that a global language is beneficial to the modern world, in order to conduct better communication between international BUSINESSMAN and develop new high technology.	Nnum	Indonesia
However, there are a lot of limitations of having * translator…	DetMiss	Indonesia
Furthermore, another RESULTS of surveys of European satellite TV audiences confirm the widespread understanding of English is over 70% of viewers claim they can follow the news in English and over 40% could do so inFrench and German.	Nnum	Indonesia
Furthermore, another results of surveys of European satellite TV audiences confirm the widespread understanding of English IS over 70% of viewers claim they can follow the news in English and over 40% could do so inFrench and German.	Vtaut	Indonesia

Table 5.4 (*cont.*) Error database

News is the central * of information from the whole world, so it is good by using a global language in media communication, because it will be understood by majority of people.	Nmiss	Indonesia
News is the central of information from the whole world, so it is good BY USING a global language in media communication, because it will be understood by majority of people.	Vform	Indonesia
News is the central of information from the whole world, so it is good by using a global language in media communication, because it will be understood by * majority of people.	DetMiss	Indonesia
On the other hand, it is good for people whose THE native language is not English but could follow the news in English, because it means that they can keep up with the latest news.	DetTaut	Indonesia
On the other hand, it is good for people whose the native language is not English but * could follow the news in English, because it means that they can keep up with the latest news.	PronRelMiss	Indonesia
International business WILL not be EXISTING if businessmen could not communicate each other.	Vform	Indonesia
International business will not be existing if businessmen could not communicate * each other.	PrepMiss	Indonesia

The meaning of classifiers and subclassifiers is as follows:
Det = Determiner
Pron = Pronoun
Rel = Relative
V = Verb
N = Noun
Form = Error of form
Miss = Missing part of speech
Cl = Clause
AdvAdj = part of speech confusion (adverb instead of adjective)
Taut = Tautological use

The former is an outcome of research in the cognitive science, which shows that adult language learners on the one hand have the ability to memorise and reuse large chunks of discourse (usually on subsentential level) and on the other hand lack the capacity of breaking down the same chunks of discourse into smaller units as effectively as do young children. The lexical chunking theory is interested in language as lexis, which does not exist in one word paradigms, but in collocations or chunks (Lewis, 2003; Tognini-Bonelli, 2001). Both converge toward subsentential lexical chunking, stipulating that adult learners have problems putting the chunks together into a sentence, thus making the sentence level the target level of remedial pro-duction. Thus our taxonomy is built around phrases with parts of speech as phrase heads. A number of other error taxonomies are of course possible, including the anonymous example from the Web cited below. However, the following needs to be considered when designing one:

> If we consider the approach from the proofed text and the sources of writer errors, we could classify errors in terms of their source in the writing process. A few obvious types in this classification, as men-tioned in the writer model, would be: slips of medium (typing errors, OCR errors, cut and paste slips . . .); dialect differences between the writer's language and some standard language; second language er-rors; concentration lapses resulting in 'derailed' sentences; and other performance errors. Such a taxonomy has the advantage that if we have a proper writer model, we cover all errors that result in ungrammatical text, and it may fit the writer's and end-user's categories of thought and thus permit easy mapping on to customer-reportable attributes, which is an important purpose of the taxonomy. However, our writer model would then have to be a detailed psycholinguistic model of language competence and performance, and this seems rather a tall order. In practice, the source of our writer model is likely to be an analysis of proofed and unproofed texts, that is, working back from the second type of derivation of the taxonomy of errors. (Eagles, 1995)

In our taxonomy or typology, we have referred to Standard English for the criteria separating error from non-error (Lengo, 1995), fully aware of the fact that the errors represented in writing could be errors of perfor-mance as well as errors of competence (Lengo, 1995). In order to capture the most relevant errors we therefore followed a set of criteria normally applied to make decisions about error correction. This seemed logical in view of the fact that the intelligent tutor for whose design the errors were being analysed was to be used precisely for error correction. Freiermuth (1997) enumerates the following criteria for error correction:

> Error correction can assist language learners to acquire structures in the TL if the language teacher consistently applies these criteria: (a) the learner's amount of exposure to the language structure or form, (b) the seriousness of the error, (c) whether or not the error has impaired com-munication significantly, (d) the frequency of the error, and (e) the needs of the students. (Freiermuth, 1997)

While the learner's exposure to the target language form means the extent to which the learner is familiar with the form and should conse-quently be accountable for it, the seriousness of the error means its gravity and is related to its communication impairment capacity. Thus global errors, or those that affect the meaning of larger expressions, are more serious than local errors that only affect one word in the utterance (Freiermuth, 1997; Lengo, 1995). What is meant by the needs of the students is personality traits such as self-confidence and the level of L2 mastery, both of which lead to profiting even from minor corrections (Freiermuth, 1997).

Parts of speech constitute a broad base of linguistics concepts that our learners should be expected to be familiar with (exposure) and therefore should receive correction in if required. In addition, parts of speech prominence (gravity) of the academic language rendered this approach useful. In academic language, decoding large nominal groups is essential to understanding the text. As part of speech confusion in such groups can impair communication significantly, part of speech error identification and correction also seems important for communication reasons. In a preliminary assessment of possible error types, based on the analysis of 10 short pieces of writing from the target sample, it was shown that a large number of global errors were speech part related in one way or another. Finally, the learning styles of our students being mainly communicative and analytical and thus basically field independent, allowed for the assumption that correction would be beneficial, thus addressing the criterion of need (Willing, 1988), especially if executed in the semblance of social interaction for the former (Doughty & Williams, 1998b) and in the form of problem solving and grammar rule citation (James, 1998) for the latter.

The broad coverage of errors that this typology allows caters to both contrastive analysis approach (Chang, 1987) and the interlanguage as a system approach (Yip, 1995). Both have proven useful in understanding Chinese-English Interlanguage. Of the categories found in our database, Chang (1987) has identified part of speech confusion, verb form error, time, tense and aspect, all due to Chinese not being an inflected language. In addition, determiner errors could be explained by the lack of this category in Chinese (Chang, 1987). Gender and number were found to be a frequent problem with pronouns, while word order, conjunctions and prepositions in addition to various lexical and semantic errors followed closely as a source of errors. Thus, Chang's (1987) analysis too seems to be very much speech part related.

Virginia Yip (1995), on the other hand, bases her analysis of the Chinese-English Interlanguage (CIL) on UG and typological paradigms. As UG theory is the only linguistic theory that also tries to account for language learning (Gregg, 2001), it certainly seems useful in the description of interlanguage as a linguistic system (Yip, 1999). In this chapter we will also rely on systemic functional grammar to provide the criterion of classification for the interlanguage grammar emerging from our own analysis. While Yip's (1995) approach, like ours, includes systematic errors generated by the grammar of interlanguage, she warns against potential pitfalls of error analysis as an instrument of IL research, in particular

Table 5.5 Error analysis

Part of Speech/ L1	Indonesian 72% students	Chinese 20% students	All students
Verb	27%	28%	27%
Noun	15%	14%	15%
Determiner	14%	9%	12%
Preposition	10%	10%	9%
Lexis	9%	9%	9%
Other (miscellaneous)	25%	30%	28%

related to the practice which describes learner errors in terms of target language only, of which we are guilty by our first typology, but not by our final error description. Thus Yip (1995) is anxious to include both L1 transfer or interlingual errors (James, 1998) such as those caused by the topicalisation in Chinese and developmental or intralingual errors (James, 1998) in her CIL description. We will pursue this cue further after examining the breakdown of errors according to speech part. In Table 5.5 the errors are classified according to source and type.

Significance was not calculated in recognition of a small sample and the absence of generality claims. It is quite obvious though that most errors in all groups, including representatives of nationalities other than Chinese and Indonesian, found the verb to be the most difficult part of speech. This does not surprise in view of the fact that the majority of these students' verbs were fully fledged lexical verbs, used overly generously in comparison with acclaimed academic writing. The result supports the idea of the relatively low learnability of verbs, which is in some languages caused by high morphological complexity (Singleton, 1999) and in English may be exacerbated by irregularities. Nouns, which are supposed to be more readily learnable because of being more imegeable (N. Ellis and Beaton, 1993 in Singleton, 1999: 142), surprisingly came second in the order of difficulty. An explanation for this may be that nouns in academic English are possibly less imegeable, as they most often represent terms referring to abstract definitions, rather than to physical objects. The most surprising finding though is the count of lexical errors, which did not amount to more than 9% of all errors. This is in stark contrast with the evidence from literature according to which lexical errors usually constitute the majority (James, 1998; Singleton, 1999). In academic English, however, as we have seen earlier in this chapter, much lexical complexity is lost in favour of strict definitions and terminological consistency. As the students were familiar with this principle, they in fact made an effort to transform their lexis into a range of logically valid and semantically less complex terms. The above raw errors were then classified according to the subcategory and those were matched to two alternative ways of error description, Yip (1995) and Jones (1999 in Dodigovic 2002) / Yong (2001).

As already pointed out, the majority of errors overall had something to do with the finite verb (aprox 30% of all errors). While Yip (1995) finds that Chinese learners use pseudo-passives (*These sentences can analyse many ways*), ergative construction (*What is happened with these verbs?*), tough movement (*Never easy to be learned . . .*), existential construction (*There are sentences cause learnability problems*), Jones (1999 cited in Dodigovic, 2002) and Yong (2001) report that Indonesian based interlanguage has the following features: malformed expressions of feelings / reactions / states (*Parents must take responsible*), missing copula (*Sometimes very easy to make mistake*), finite / nonfinite verb confusion (*I decided to cancelled*). Thus, expressed in terms of systemic functional linguistics (Halliday, 1994a), the Chinese learners would mainly seem to misjudge the verb transitivity, whereas the Indonesian learners appear to have difficulties with the Mood.

In the following, the above errors will receive some clarification, starting with the CIL pseudo-passives. Pseudo-passives (*These sentences can analyse many ways*) derive their name from their superficial resemblance to the English passive structure. Yip (1995), however, rules out the English passive as a possible IL target structure, since she finds that the contrastive difference between the Chinese and the English passive is not large or confusing enough for that purpose. She also rules out the English middle construction (*This car drives smoothly*) as a possible candidate and concludes that the pseudo-passives are an attempt at the topicalisation of the object or the patient in the sentence. This is motivated by the high productivity of topicalisation in Chinese and the existence of null subject in Chinese. Thus, this explanation has elements of textual and discoursal.

Ergative construction (*What is happened with these verbs?*) is the next typical CIL error on Yip's (1995) list. This construction consists of an attempted passive using ergative verbs. These verbs, though intransitive, take the patient rather than the agent for a subject. Since they cannot take a direct object, they are not transitive and therefore cannot build the passive. Yip (1995: 129) finds that this construction is found in speakers of first languages other than Chinese and that it is not a result of either English or Chinese influence, but rather a developmental IL error. In CIL, English passives are subset of CIL passives, whereas CIL ergatives are a subset of English ergatives. Using a semantic category (ergative) to describe a verb related error pushes this explanation into the lexical direction. Thus, what seems like a purely formal error on the surface might have a deeper lexical root.

Tough movement (*Never easy to be learned . . .*) is based on the UG notion of movement that is perceivable in structural transformations (Cook, 1993) and bears a superficial resemblance to the English tough movement (*This book is easy to read ← It is easy to read this book*). According to Yip (1995: 153) the CIL structure is really pseudo-tough-movement and like the ergative construction above involves overpassivisation. Yip (1995: 154) points out that real tough movement in English has been the stumbling block of linguistic analysis and has presented a difficulty for both L1 and L2 learners of various backgrounds. What Chinese learners seem to be doing in the case of pseudo-tough-movement is misapplying the English tough movement to the subject (agent) rather than object (patient) of the complement clause (Yip, 1995: 155). Yip (1995: 155) argues that this is not a simple over-generalisation of tough movement error, as the CIL speakers additionally passivise the dependent verb. The grammatical interpretations of CIL pseudo-tough-movement apparently vary and Yip (1995) herself does not claim to have resolved the issue of its correct analysis. She finds though that there is a similar structure in Chinese which requires the passivisation of the dependent verb for the purpose of disambiguation. She also points out that a similar construction is available in Indonesian (Yip, 1995: 160). However, the problem she identifies with the structutre is not the passivisation itself, but the raising of the wrong predicate. A possible cause is seen in the topicalisation typical of Chinese. Finally, Yip (1995: 170) decides that it is the interaction of L1, L2 and universal factors that are responsible for this error.

Existential construction (*There are sentences cause learnability problems*) refers to the overgeneration of sentences starting with 'there is' in CIL, accompanied by a pseudo-relative clause missing the relative pronoun. Yip (1995: 175) finds that this structure has its source in the Chinese pivotal construction and is therefore unrelated to the relative clause in either English or Chinese. In addition, it can be said that CIL undergenerates indefinite subjects in comparison with the English sentences containing the existential construction proper. Thus, this error can be described once in terms of a superset in relation to the English 'there is' type sentences and once in terms of subset in respect of the English sentences with indefinite subjects.

The description of the Indonesian-English interlanguage was confirmed by Yong's (2001) analysis, who claims that the verb phrase in English is most difficult for a native speaker of Indonesian. Yong (2001) demonstrated that the complex verb phrases in complex tenses do not allow for a clear distinction between the finite and non-finite verb. This is exacerbated by the non-existence of the non-finite verb form in Indonesian. As the copula *to be* is frequently optional in Indonesian, its English equivalent is often omitted, especially in sentences expressing 'a condition or a state of existence' (Yong, 2001: 287). In addition, some parts of speech seem confused with others, in particular adjectives and adverbs. Yong (2001) also mentions errors that seem to coincide with Yip's (1995) CIL errors. One of them is the unusual status of the passive voice in Indonesian, leading to errors in English comparable to those exemplified by Yip (1995) for CIL. While Yong (2001) does not specifically mention the existential construction as overused by Indonesian

Table 5.6 Transitivity related errors

• pseudo-passives
Malaria can find all over the world.
• ergative construction
The immune system can be failed.
• tough movement
More difficult to be realised...
• existential construction
There is a new problem occur.

Table 5.7 Mood related errors

• malformed expressions of feelings / reactions / states
*The disease had * dominant over human.*
• missing copula
*Secondly, communities * affected.*
• finite / nonfinite verb confusion
It will caused death of both mother and baby.

speakers, but in fact argues the opposite, she does isolate topicalisation as a typically Indonesian related feature of Indonesian-English interlanguage, which makes it similar to Chinese.

This study shows that in fact both types of errors, CIL and Indonesian related ones, are equally committed across the board and may be better described as transitivity and Mood errors respectively. See Tables 5.6 and 5.7 for the results of qualitative analysis.

The difficulties seem to arise from a variety of transitivity and Mood patterns in English as perceived by systemic functional linguists (Halliday, 1994a; Martin *et al.*, 1997). The terms 'transitivity' and 'Mood' have been selected to bridge the gap between the exceedingly formal description offered by Yip (1995) and Yong (2001) and the lexical and semantic implications that they seem to have. To be more specific, some transitive verbs can form sentences like: 'this commodity sells well', whereas others cannot (e.g. *'Malaria finds everywhere'*). Learners may simply overgeneralise from one group to all transitive verbs. Similarly, ergative verbs (e.g. *'the stone fell'*) may have a patient for a subject, which is why in an overgeneralising fashion the students may attempt to build passives with these verbs. Apart from the first example in Table 5.7, which can be interpreted as either the wrong choice of verb (i.e. the Finite part of the Mood element in SFL) or a mismatch between the Mood (i.e. *'the disease* *had'*) and the Residue (i.e. *'*dominant over human'*), the problems with Mood are mainly linked with the distinction finite–non-finite verb. Thus the need for a finite auxiliary in addition to a non-finite main verb may not be self-evident to an EAP learner, especially in view of the fact that a large number of sentences appear to need one verb only. The matter is further complicated by the fact that only one verb in a complex tense can be finite, which if not understood can lead to a rather arbitrary choice of verb or verbs to inflect. If a finite verb is not a workable concept in the learners' native languages, as is the case in Chinese and Indonesian (Yong, 2001; Yip, 1995; Jones, 1999 cited in Dodigovic, 2002), it would seem rather difficult to predict which of the several verbs in an English sentence should be inflected and why.

The purpose of this study is, however, not so much to offer unambiguous reasons for typical errors, but rather to identify the errors themselves and suggest some ways of making the underlying grammar transparent to the student. Structure explanation seems to help the learning process, especially with adult learners (McLaughlin, 1993), as is the case in an EAP environment. Thus, raising both consciousness and awareness, correcting and explaining, are some of the functions of the Intelligent Tutor. Its development is described in the next section.

The Intelligent Tutor of academic English on the Web

The above research has yielded what was required in the first place to construct a successful Intelligent Tutor, and that is a linguistic description of the students' interlanguages. Thus, in addition to being a sort of native speaker of academic English, the Intelligent Tutor also became a native speaker of Chinese and Indonesian based interlanguages. As a tutor, it was well equipped to respond to two different types of learners: the ones who like to experiment with their own linguistic hypotheses and those who prefer to be given the rules (Dodigovic & Suphawat, 1999). Since most students could be categorised as either communicative or analytical leaners (Willing, 1989), the Intelligent Tutor was to allow different approaches, typical of the learning styles. While the communicative learners had the benefit of engaging in the kind of interaction with the computer that highly resembles a conversational exchange between humans, the analytical learners had the opportunity to have their sentences parsed and their output analysed. The authority of the computer and its final verdict in language production matters was designed to appeal to authoritative learners, whereas to the concrete leaner the computer program might have had the appeal of a game (Willing, 1989). Thus, the program was designed to cater to a variety of learning styles.

Mike Levy (1999) advocates an approach to CALL design which he calls design space. The latter denotes parameters and purposes of a particular project or a problem (Levy, 1999). Three dichotomies are reportedly useful in clarifying the choices that have to be made by the designer: (1) holistic vs. discrete element approach, (2) tutor vs. tool role of the computer, and (3) theory testing vs. application (Levy, 1999). While the overall EAP on the Web project entails a holistic approach by including a number of skills, sources and methods, its NLP component, the Intelligent Tutor mainly focuses on sentence grammar in written academic English, thus favouring a discrete element approach. The difference between a tutor and a tool is that the tutor evaluates the student's input whereas the tool does not (Levy, 1999). Accordingly, the Intelligent Tutor is a tutor, since it evaluates the accuracy of the students' written sentences. Finally, the Intelligent Tutor is not designed to test a specific language learning theory, even though it does rely on several. Rather it is designed to be an application used by a real life population of students. Therefore, a fourth element, indicated by Levy (1999), becomes important, namely data about the learner characteristics and the learning context. We have amply covered this ground in our needs analysis.

In the prelude to its design and development and during these phases we relied on the proven procedures of software engineering. The latter, as pointed out in Chapter 2 of this volume, means using the knowledge of computers and computing to solve problems by developing quality software (Pfleeger, 1998; Sommerville, 2001). While the computer science fed theories of analysis, design, data structuring and programming into the enterprise, the intended users contributed their opinions and hard data that helped us understand their EAP learning problems. Thus with the help of the users, the developers worked out the needs for the new system in a phase called requirement/needs analysis/assessment or definition. It was followed by system design, a phase which converted the analysis data into a system-level description of what the system will do, which is described below. The programmers (the author and Alyson Fowler) then followed the design document, which contained the specifics on how to implement the system in computer code and finally came up with a computer program. Once the program was written (implementation phase), the testing at various levels commenced. This final step will be described in a separate chapter since it is a vital part of evaluation (Levy, 1999).

In the design document, the principles we abided by were the principles of structured programming (Butt *et al.*, 1999) which imply modularity, maintainability and transparency of the design and the ensuing code. In terms of computer science, maintainability pertains to the program or system itself, which is more easily maintained if each function is modularised and therefore any subsequent changes need only be global, not local. In the CALL literature (Armitage & Bowerman, 2002; Levy, 1999) maintainability is sometimes connected with reusability and extensibility in a way that exceeds the scope of the equivalent term used in computer science. Armitage and Bowerman (2002) seem to imply that CALL developers should make all parts of their programs accessible to a wide public. This principle is otherwise known as customisation. I would like to draw a clear line between a system's capacity to be customised by a user (e.g. through change of screen appearance and addition of new content) and maintainability. It does not follow that the latter necessarily leads to universal reusability. Thus our system passes the criteria of maintainability, modularity and transparency, in the sense that any other programmer familiar with the programming language in question will be able to change or extend it easily, or even reuse its modules to build a new system. This however does not mean that a wide array of language teachers will be able to do the same. However, modules for the customisation of the system have been developed, although not used in the pilot version, to help the system acquire new linguistic knowledge. The latter requires only linguistic skills and no knowledge of programming.

User interface design is another point of consideration for most systems. It is the shell that enables a successful exchange of information between the user and the computer (Thayler & Dorfman, 2000). Levy (1999) notes that commercial CALL programs, or at least those built for actual pedagogical use rather than theory testing, have more elaborate and user-friendly interfaces. Partly in contrast, our interface is quite simple, consisting of one window with a space for computer generated questions, student input and computer generated feedback. No audio-visuals are used at this stage. However, according to the purpose of the task, this is all that is required of the interface, which is always required to reflect the user, task and the context of use (Hackos & Redish, 1998).

PROLOG was chosen as indicated in Chapter 4 of this volume because of its predicate structure, which is conducive to representing logical rules, including linguistic rules. Moreover, it is based on predicate calculus, the mathematical representation of traditional formal logic (Bratko, 2001), a feature that brings it very close to the very nature of academic language. It also allows lists, which are ideal for the representation of written language, where linguistic signs are 'listed' in succession. Finally, recursion is one of the inherent virtues of PROLOG when it comes to natural language processing. As discussed in Chapter 4 of this volume, this shortens the programming time and makes the code more efficient.

> One reason for this choice is that it is one of the major programming languages used by NLP researchers. Consequently, implementation details in the literature are frequently stated in Prolog, so that it is useful to have some knowledge of the language in order to be able to follow the discussion. However, perhaps more importantly for our current purposes is the oft expressed view that Prolog is one of the more 'user friendly' programming languages to learn. Although this

claim is perhaps exaggerated – learning to program in any language is never easy – it is true that beginners can learn to write fairly interesting programs in a relatively short time using Prolog. This again, makes the learning process that much more enjoyable. (Matthews, 1998: ix)

While the author of this volume is responsible for the initial implementation of this program in an easily accessible version of the programming language called PIE-PROLOG, Alyson Fowler of the University of Kent has kindly provided the rendition of this program into the Web based SICSTUS PROLOG. Due to considerable differences in syntax between the two dialects of PROLOG, Fowler's work was considerable and of very creative nature. She also developed a user interface shell in PERL, which regulates the output, accepts student input and passes it on to PROLOG in an acceptable and consistent format. The author is deeply indebted to her for her enthusiasm, expertise and a willing spirit.

As indicated in some of the previous chapters of this volume, the type of parser used for NLP in this context is augmented phrase structure grammar. Logistically, the program, which is written in PROLOG, relies on two different knowledge banks: one representing a subset of the ideal, correct grammar of English and the other modelling the students' faulty grammar. Both are encapsulated in a user interface, called Dialogue, which is responsible for the communication between the user and the knowledge banks. The purpose of the former knowledge bank is to recognise and acknowledge a student's correct input. The latter identifies and corrects typical errors, based on the regularities observed in the above mentioned study. Each of the knowledge banks comprises a finite number of augmented phrase structure rules while both have simultaneous access to the same lexicon, a finite yet appendable list of words accompanied by relevant morpho-syntactic information.

The modest vocabulary of this very first pilot module is loosely related to the topic of malaria. It might be necessary to point out that the program does not perform simple string matching, so that the given vocabulary can be quite creatively used and re-combined. However, sentences using either the vocabulary that is not in the lexicon or the syntactic structures that are not covered by either knowledge bank cannot be successfully parsed, which is how NLP usually operates. Figure 5.5 shows the language input processing sequence in a highly simplified form.

These features make this a depth first, top-down, left-to-right (Matthews, 1998) algorithm, called so because its processing starts from the sentence as a whole, capable of parsing (1) any correct sentence for which the rules are recognised within the bounds of the given vocabulary, and (2) any erroneous sentence based on the same vocabulary provided they conform to the seven main types of errors depicted above. Below are the representations of these rules in PIE-PROLOG syntax:

Pseudo-passives: Malaria can find all over the world.

```
vp(K0,Kn,vp(VI,VT,PP),Num,Pers,Trans,Aux,Fin):- %
    verb(K0,K1,VI,Num,Pers,intr,aux,fin),%
    verb(K1,K2,VT,Num,Pers,trans,full,inf), % ERR
    pp(K2,Kn,PP).
```

Ergative construction: The immune system will be failed.

```
vp(K0,Kn,vp(VI,V),Num,Pers,Trans,Aux,Fin):- % ERR
    verb(K0,K1,VI,Num,Pers,intr,auxw,fin), %
    infinf(K1,Kn,V,Num,Pers,Trans,Aux,Fin).

infinf(K0,Kn,infinf(Inf1,Inf2),Num,Pers,Trans,Aux,Fin):- %ERR
    verb(K0,K1,Inf1,Num,Pers,Trans,Aux,Fin),
    verb(K1,Kn,Inf2,Num,Pers,Trans1,Aux1,Fin1).
```

Tough movement: The parasite is easy to become resistant.

```
vp(K0,Kn,vp(VI,N,IK,Inf,Adj),Num,Pers,Trans,Aux, Fin):- %
    verb(K0,K1,VI,Num,Pers,intr,cop, fin), % ERR
    adjp(K1,K2,N,Comp),
    infto(K2,K3,IK),
    verb(K3,K4,Inf,_,_,_,full, inf),
    adjp(K4,Kn,Adj,Comp).
```

Existential construction: There is a problem occur.

```
vp(K0,Kn,vp(VT,NP),Num,Pers,intr,cop,Fin):- %
    verb(K0,K1,VT,Num,Pers,intr,cop,fin),
    npe(K1,Kn,NP,Num,Pers,Trans,Aux1,Fin),
    nl,write('You need a sentence like this:'There is a problem'.'),
    nl,write ('Or: 'A problem has occurred'.'),nl.
```

Malformed expressions of states: Malaria causes a die.

```
npv(K0,Kn,npv(D,V),Num,Pers,Trans,Aux,Fin):- %
    nl,write('You need a sentence pattern like this: 'Malaria
    causes death'.'),nl,
    det(K0,K1,D,Num1),
    verb(K1,Kn,V,Num,Pers,Trans,Aux,Fin).
```

Missing copula: Communities affected.

```
vp(K0,Kn,vp(VI,N),Num,Pers,Trans,Aux,Fin):- %
    verb(K0,K1,VI,Num,Pers,trans,full,pap).
```

Finite/nonfinite verb confusion: Malaria will caused death.

```
vp(K0,Kn,vp(VI,VT,NP),Num,Pers,Trans,Aux,Fin):- %
    verb(K0,K1,VI,Num,Pers,intr,auxw,fin), % ERR
    verb(K1,K2,VT,Num,Pers,trans,Aux,Fin), %
    np(K2,Kn,NP,_,_,oblq).
```

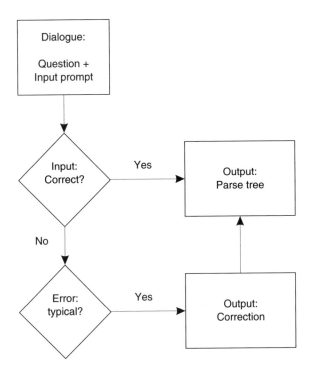

Figure 5.5 Input processing sequence

As can be seen from the above examples, PROLOG is a declarative rather than procedural language (Matthews, 1998; Bratko, 2001), which combined with its recursive power saves a lot of coding time and reduces the code length by many lines. Thus each of the above statements (ending in a full stop) will execute a number of times, until each of its terms has been assessed and a terminal symbol (a word) found in the lexicon (Matthews, 1998). In a procedural language more explicit coding would have been necessary to achieve the same result.

The above rules all pertain to verb phrase (vp), since this is where most errors in the sample had occurred. A noun phrase (np) in this system is often treated as a part of a verb phrase, representing the object or the verb complement. Apart from phrases, which make this a phrase structure grammar, the program is augmented by features, hence the name 'augmented phrase structure grammar'. Features of a verb are thus number (Num), person (Pers), transitivity (Trans), full verb or auxiliary (Aux) and finite or non-finite (Fin). For each of these features there are several choices, depending on the closed paradigmatic systems allowed for these categories in the English language. Each lexical entry has the features explicitly stated. Thus, the program can successfully discard the noun 'cause' in favour of the verb 'cause' if required by the input. It will also make sure that there is subject-verb agreement and that a number of other grammatical rules are abided by. In the case of the seven errors, the rules are not relaxed, but changed to reflect the specific error registered as frequent for the student population. Thus in the last example related to the missing copula, the verb phrase has been changed to allow the past participle as the only constituent of the phrase. Therefore, the use of the present participle ('communities affecting') will not incur error analysis, even though the entry will be recognised as faulty. The student however will not receive error specific feedback or correction, as this has not been a frequent and therefore important error (Freiermuth, 1997) in our sample. Some agreement and verb inflection errors can also be tracked and followed by meaningful feedback. These errors become recognisable by the relaxation of some of the features in the augmented rules.

For a number of reasons, the program was placed on the Web, though with a number of access restrictions. Some might see a contradiction in placing the software on the Web, which should render it universally accessible, and then restricting access to it. The universal availability of the Web, however, makes it easy for the authorised user to access the software, regardless of the time, place and hardware platform. Commercial considerations yet caution to restricting the access to those who have in some manner obtained a right to utilise this software.

The following text focuses on the user interface of the tutor, the module called Dialogue. Dialogue is a program that converses with the learner using a parser, a device for natural language processing (NLP), which we have described above in some detail. Dialogue functions in the following way: the learner is asked questions about an essay topic. The answers expected are in the form of a freely structured sentence at a time. The student enters her sentence into a text box. The parser activated in the background analyses the student input and either accepts it as correct, rejects it as incorrect without specific help, or comments on the type of error made while at request giving a hint as to how to correct the sentence. An example is shown in Figure 5.6.

In Figure 5.6 we see the opening screen of a lesson. This particular lesson is about malaria and the questions are based on three readings from different Web based sources about the disease. The content was deemed a familiar topic for the students, who are predominantly South-East Asian. The questions asked of students are specific leading questions, designed to guide them through the brainstorming and essay planning process. The questions also present scaffolding designed to help

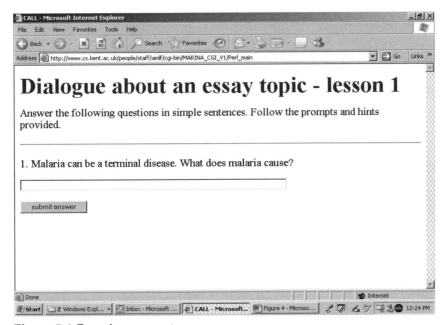

Figure 5.6 Question prompt

them come to terms with text structure and organisation. As pointed out in Chapter 2 of this volume, the idea of posing well sequenced generic questions as a guide to the planning processes is found in DIWE (Daedalus Interactive Writing Environment). Dialogue differs in that it asks specific topic and reading related questions, rather than generic questions, applicable to any topic, as does DIWI. While DIWI however uses an interpersonal communicative strategy and involves a number of users simultaneously, Dialogue relies on the human–computer interaction known in the computer world as natural communication (Marsic *et al.*, 2000). Another difference to DIWI is that the students' answers are parsed for grammatical correctness, which with DIWI could happen coming from another user logged in simultaneously, but cannot be taken for granted. If most other users are also learners, the corrections may be wrong, thus leading to further fossilisation.

In Figure 5.7 we see the result of a faulty entry that is recognised by the system as one of the seven specific errors, namely malformed expressions of states. In the current pilot version, the student has only two options after submitting a recognised faulty entry: 'try again', which may appeal to some analytical learners, and 'get a hint', which is a blend of two actions to be implemented in the future. The first one would be called 'get a hint'

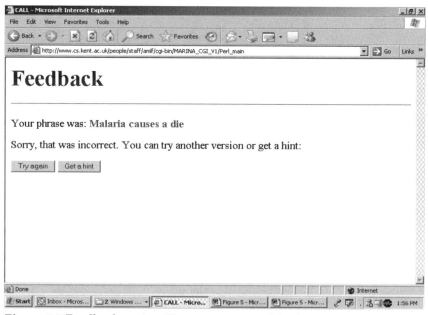

Figure 5.7 Feedback option 'Error type recognition'

and would give the student a sentence with the target structure, but with different vocabulary (e.g. 'Smoking causes cancer'), or offer an interrogative recast ('Does malaria cause death?'). The second one would be 'solution' and would actually give the correct version of the sentence the student has entered. The reason why they are merged at the moment can be tracked back to a desperate shortage in available resources at the time when the program was being developed. According to the original plan, the program was going to use natural language synthesis in addition to analysis, in order to 'recycle' the student's own words and generate recasts at varying states of completion. The less complete or interrogative recasts would have been hints as opposed to complete recasts that would have been solutions. Suffice it to say that this, unfortunately unfulfilled, good intention led to certain awkwardness in the layout of the user interface. Considering however the paramount nature of the underlying language processing task, we are certain that the reader will understand and pardon the current oddity of the pilot's interface, which is being repaired even as these lines are being written.

While the 'try again' and the future 'get a hint' option are designed for analytical and concrete learners respectively, the future 'solution' is designed for communicative and authoritative learners, where the former

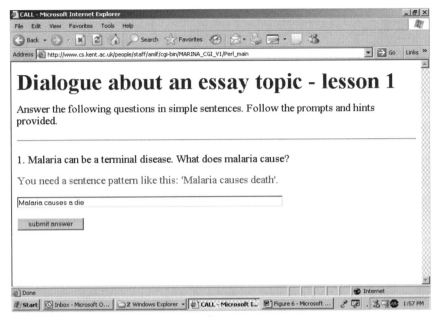

Figure 5.8 Feedback option 'Get a hint'

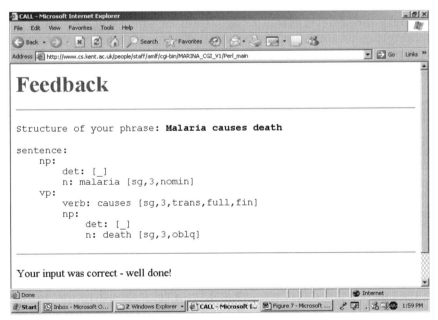

Figure 5.9 Feedback to a correct answer: full parse

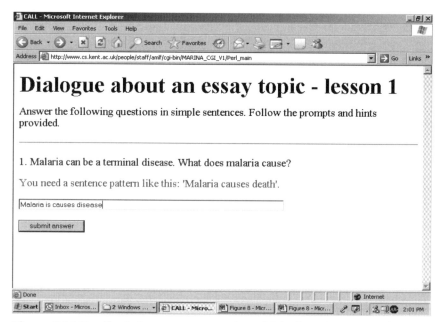

Figure 5.10 Feedback to an error type for which there is no specific error rule

will take the correction as a recast, while the latter will embrace it as coming from an authority. An analytical learner can then enter the correct version and obtain a parse tree which provides what this learner type needs – analysis. The parse tree is also likely to reinforce the correct language while raising the awareness of the structure. To return to the current version of the software, 'get a hint' for now actually delivers the solution.

Figure 5.10 shows what happens when the erroneous entry does not comply with any of the explicit error rules, whereas Figure 5.11 shows the kind of feedback available. While the same options, 'try again' and 'get a hint' pop up on screen, the outcome of pressing the 'get a hint' button is different, as can be seen in Figure 5.12. Thus correction cannot be given unless the error is recognised.

Figure 5.13 finally demonstrates how the Tutor can be used outside the scope of essay planning. Thus the student in this example has used it to try out a sentence for an essay in progress ('Malaria is a disease'), which does not answer any of the questions posed by the program. However, any correct sentence on the topic of malaria, recognised as such by the system, yields both the confirmation of the student's hypothesis that the sentence is correct and the parse tree, designed to raise her awareness of a rule that

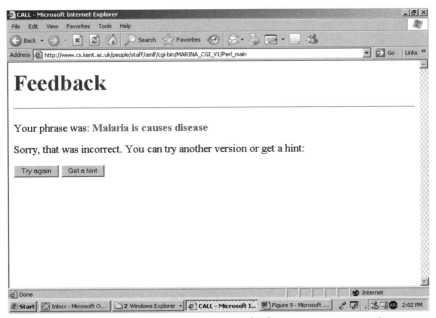

Figure 5.11 Feedback to an error type which is not recognised: correct grammar parse

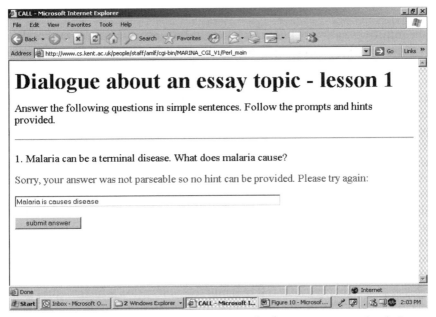

Figure 5.12 Feedback to an error type which is not recognised: inter-language grammar parse

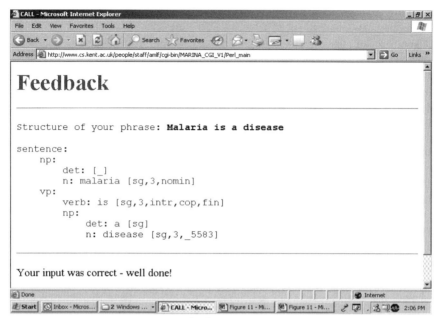

Figure 5.13 Feedback to input which is not an expected answer to the question, but is parseable

she intuitively already knows, although she may not be sure what makes it correct. This procedure caters especially to analytical and concrete learners.

The above pictures demonstrate how Dialogue works. If a grammatically incorrect answer is given, there are two choices. The student can either try again or obtain a suggestion as to how her input could be improved. The student who likes experimenting with language is free to try yet another variation to the answer. If the answer sentence is correct, a full parse is displayed and the student's correct input is reinforced. On the other hand, a rule or a vocabulary item unknown to the system causes the attempted parse to fail. Refining the grammar and appending the lexicon will make this system more flexible. However, in order for this to happen, more data analysis is necessary, in particular regarding the correct structures most frequently generated by the target population. Another possibility is appending the lexical entries with more features, thus adding to the parser's sensitivity lexically. This would introduce elements of head driven phrase structure grammar (HPSG) into this enterprise, which might prove beneficial in terms of the number of rules needed. It would also make it more in line with the current trends in instructional NLP, a more up-to-date intelligent tutor.

More examples

In the following, a user's route through the program is outlined, starting with the EAP Web page designed to house the Intelligent Tutor as well as the rest of the components enumerated in Chapters 1 and 2. Thus the Tutor is used here in the context of an entire learning environment conducive to essay writing. This is a provision for such readers who feel that more examples of how the program works would be useful. As pointed out, however, in Chapters 2 and 4, it may be more important to the reader to understand what the program 'knows', this being a declarative rather than a procedural type of program. This is the reason why research was such a substantial part of the development process and its proportion in this chapter should therefore not surprise.

We begin our journey through the program with the home page of the EAP programs, which is unfortunately not being officially used:

(1) The learner enters the EAP Web page (Fig. 5.14).
(2) The learner chooses the 'Courses' option (Fig. 5.15).
(3) Clicking on 'Writing Practice' brings the learner to the Intelligent Tutor (Fig. 5.16).
(4) Here the learner is greeted by the screen we are already familiar with from the previous section, and must answer the first of the 12 leading questions regarding the essay topic. Let's assume the learner has typed in the correct answer: 'Malaria causes death' (Fig. 5.17).

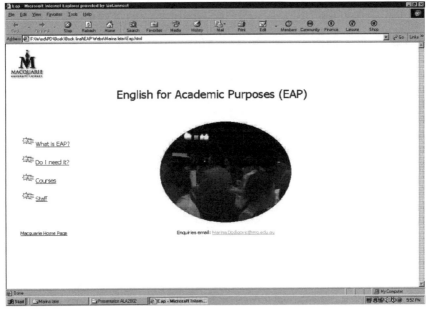

Figure 5.14 A possible entry to the program

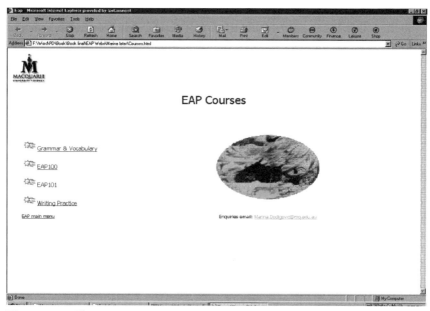

Figure 5.15 The next step

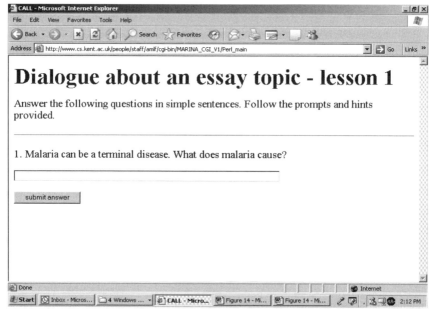

Figure 5.16 The first screen of the Intelligent Tutor (Lesson on Malaria)

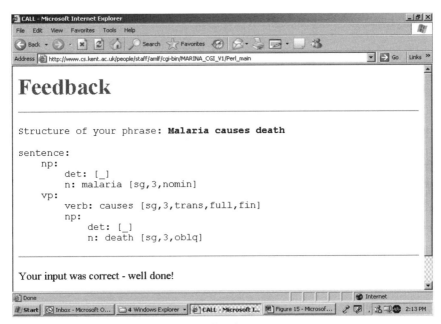

Figure 5.17 A correct answer – feedback

(5) The system executes a successful parse using the correct grammar only and the learner is given awareness raising feedback in the form of a parse tree. This sentence also introduces one of the subtopics in regard to malaria, namely malaria and mortality. After pressing the 'Next question' button, the system introduces the second leading question: 'A pregnant woman carries two lives: the baby's and her own. What happens when a pregnant woman gets infected?' This question introduces the second important subtopic – malaria and children (Fig. 5.18).

(6) In the above example the student has correctly recognised the subtopic, but has incorrectly inflected both verbs, so the system responds to the error and gives the student the choice of the course of action to take (Figs 5.19, 5.20, 5.21).

(7) Here after some experimenting with the sentence subject, the student has chosen to be led to the correction. Next, the computer asks the third question: 'For a number of reasons it has been very difficult to eradicate malaria. What is the current state of its eradication?' Human inability to eradicate malaria is the third subtopic the students will find facts about in their readings (Figs 5.22, 5.23).

(8) The student has provided a correct answer, having learnt from the feedback to answer number two. The next question introduces the subtopic of international travel as one of the factors facilitating the

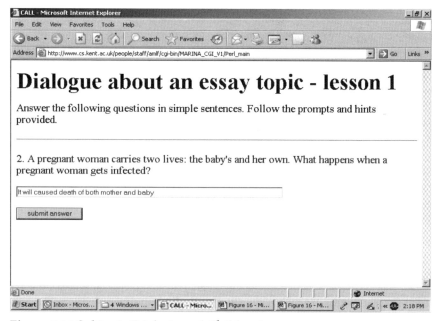

Figure 5.18 Subtopic 'Malaria and Children'

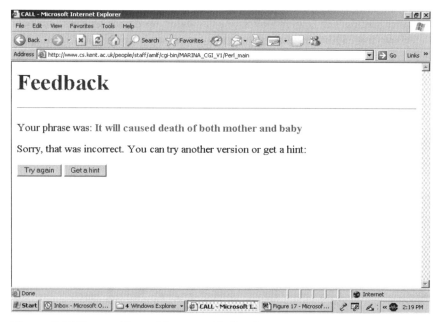

Figure 5.19 Recognition of incorrect inflection

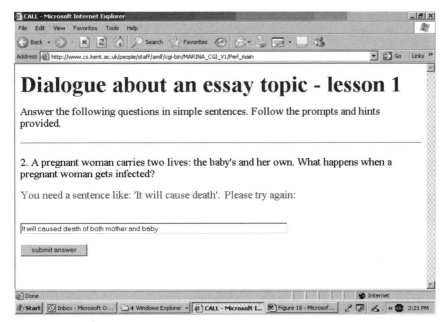

Figure 5.20 The error is recognised and feedback provided

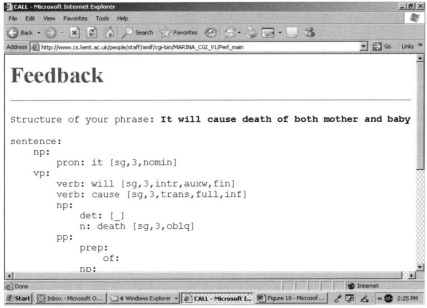

Figure 5.21 The correct input is rewarded with a parse

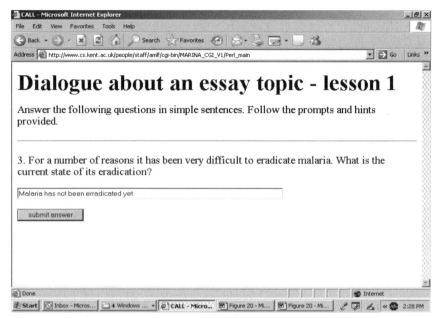

Figure 5.22 The student has provided the correct answer

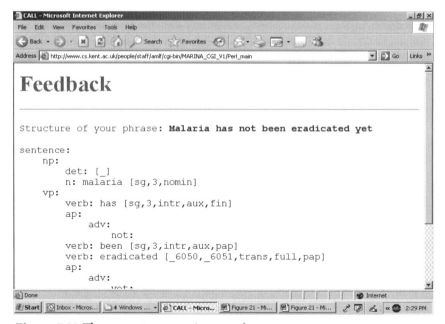

Figure 5.23 The correct answer is parsed

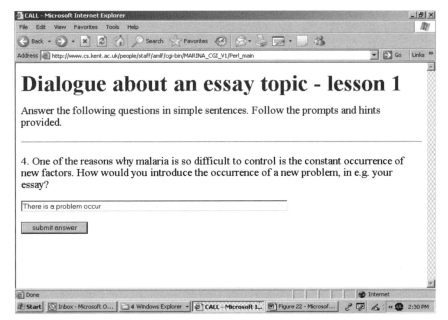

Figure 5.24 The student commits the 'Existential Construction Error'

spread of the disease, while expecting incorrect use of existential construction, which in fact happens (Figs 5.24, 5.25).

(9)   After the student has experimented with the article, the system helps her find the correct form (Figs 5.26, 5.27).

(10)   Having received feedback in the form of a successful parse tree, the student is now ready for the fifth question, which is designed to provide a causal link between international travel and airport malaria, while at the same time expecting (but not being restricted to) a verb inflection error. The error actually occurs (Figs 5.28, 5.29).

(11)   The student is guided by the system to the correct form and moves on to the next question. Here the subtopic addressed is malaria and the developing countries and the error she commits is a word formation one (Figs 5.30, 5.31, 5.32).

(12)   Having not received the correction of her error, the student looks up the word in the Cambridge learner's dictionary, which is conveniently also available on-line and retrieves the correct form, thus being able to correct her sentence (Figs 5.33, 5.34, 5.35, 5.36, 5.37, 5.38).

(13)   The student now proceeds with the rest of the questions, receiving meaningful feedback (Figs 5.39 to 5.68):

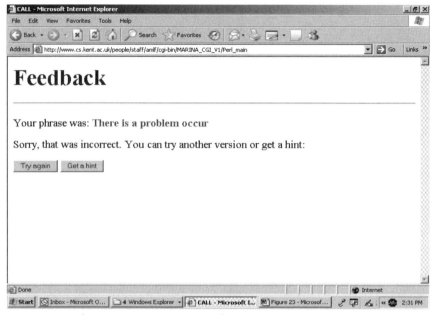

Figure 5.25 The first parse identifies the structure as incorrect

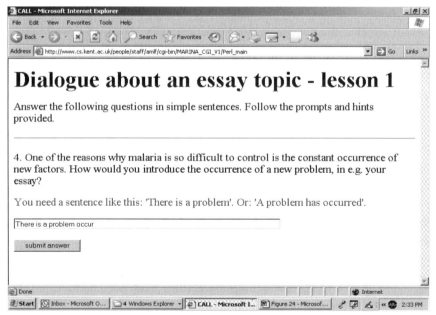

Figure 5.26 The second parse identifies the nature of the error and offers a solution

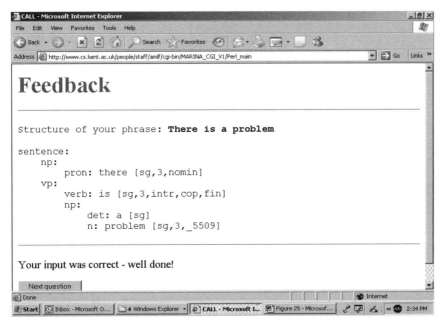

Figure 5.27 The system parses the corrected version of the student input

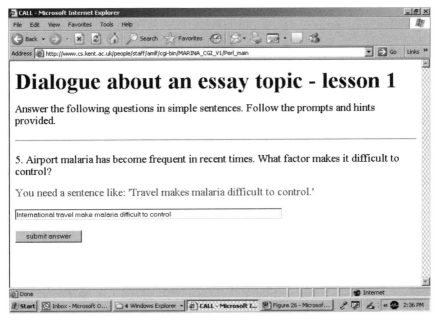

Figure 5.28 The inflection error is corrected by the system

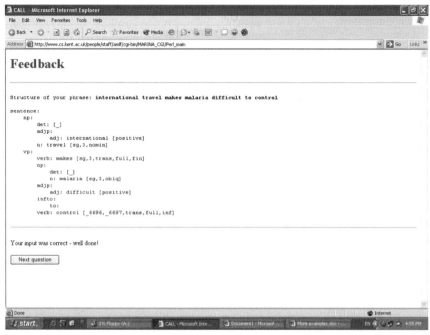

Figure 5.29 The corrected student input is parsed

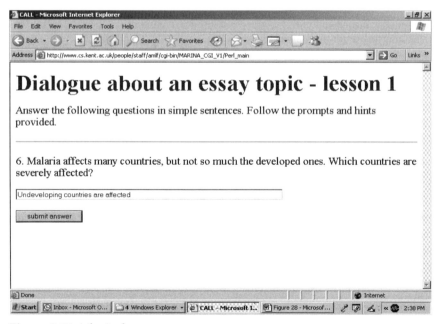

Figure 5.30 A lexical error occurs

Figure 5.31 The system is unable to find the word 'underdeveloping' in the lexicon

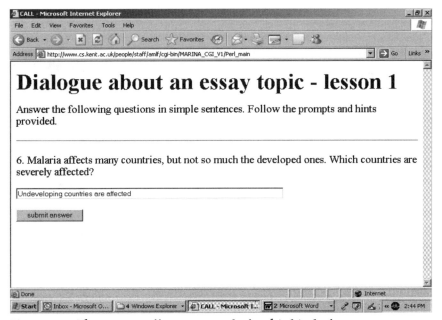

Figure 5.32 The system offers no remedy for this kind of error

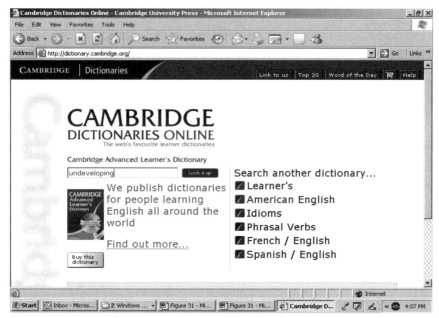

Figure 5.33 Consulting an on-line dictionary

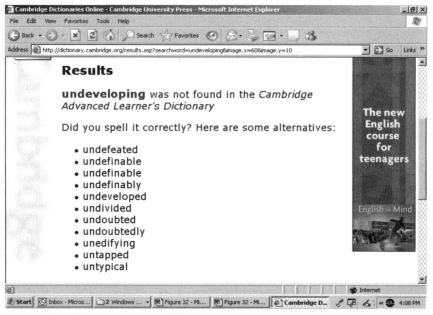

Figure 5.34 No entry is found in the on-line dictionary

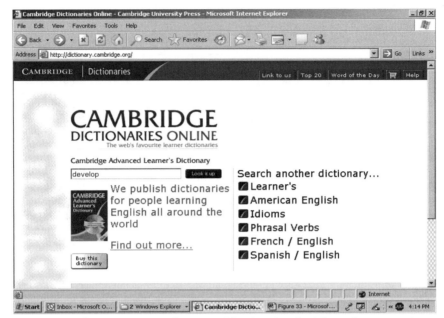

Figure 5.35 The student uses the root of the word to find the right expression

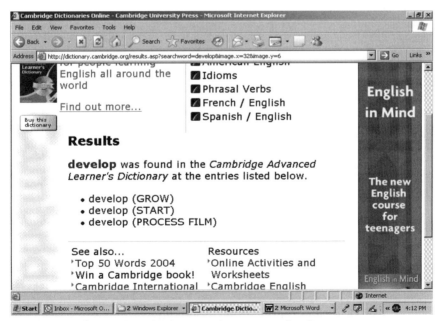

Figure 5.36 The student finds several entries in the dictionary

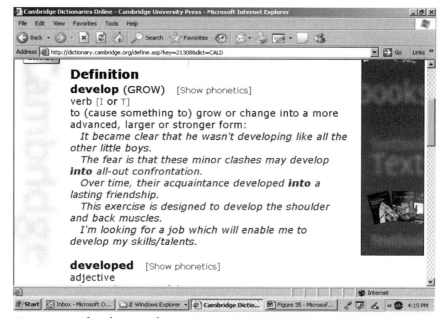

Figure 5.37 She chooses the most appropriate dictionary entry

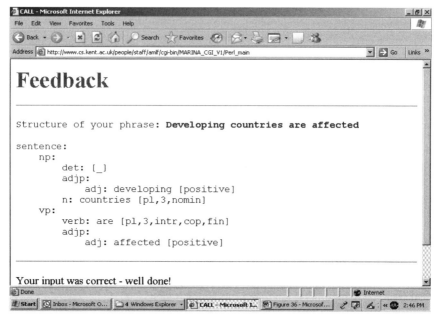

Figure 5.38 Using the output from the on-line dictionary, the student corrects her Intelligent Tutor input and is rewarded with a parse tree

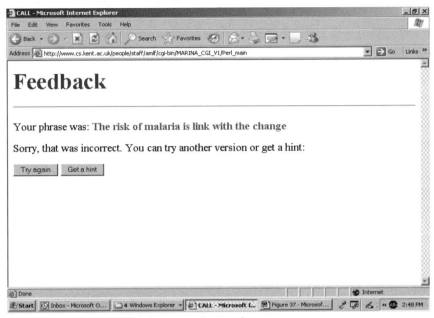

Figure 5.39 Rejection of the sentence by the correct grammar

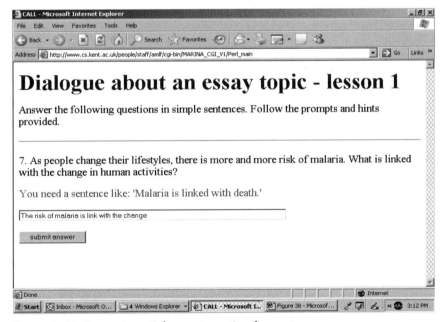

Figure 5.40 Correction of the sentence by the system

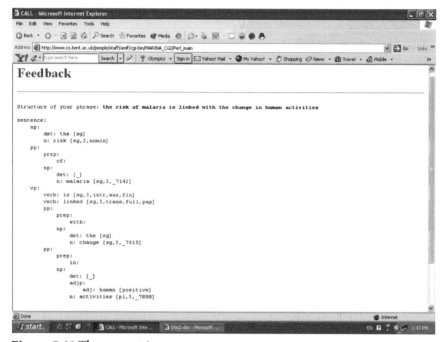

Figure 5.41 The correct input parse

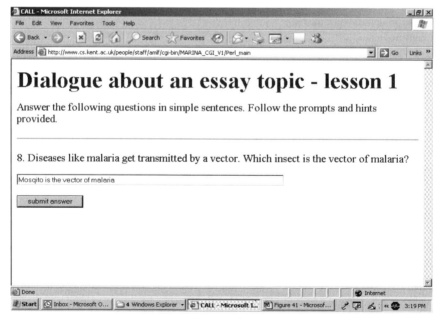

Figure 5.42 A new question is asked and an answer is attempted

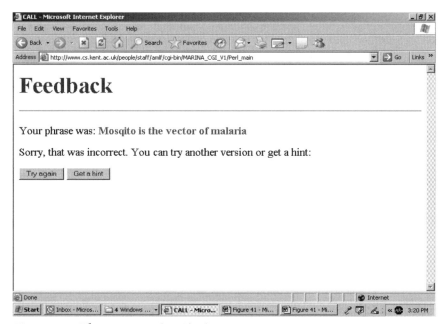

Figure 5.43 The input is identified as incorrect

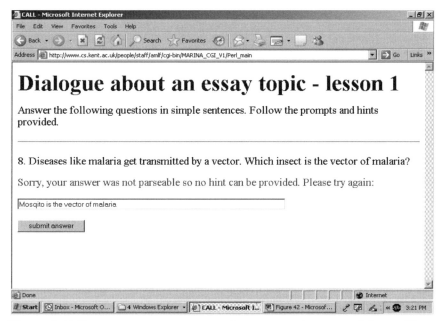

Figure 5.44 The system cannot correct the sentence because of the spelling error

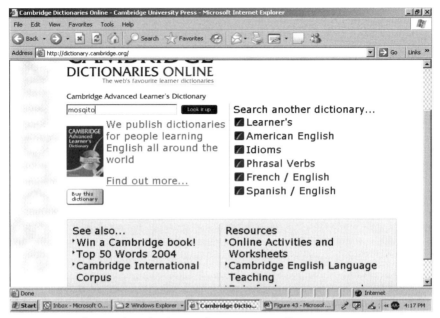

Figure 5.45 The student looks up the correct spelling

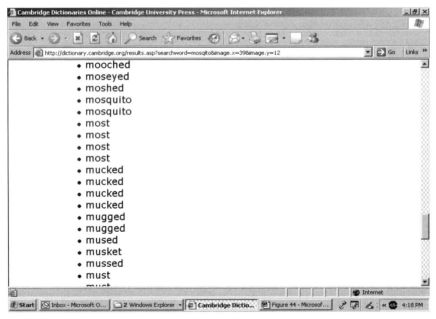

Figure 5.46 The student finds the correct spelling of the word 'mosquito'

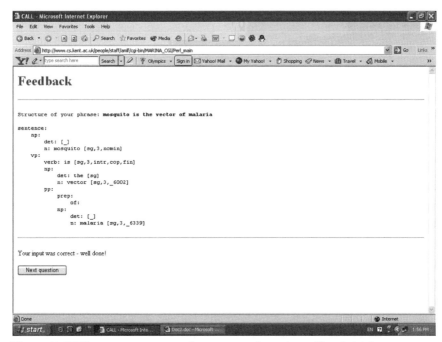

Figure 5.47 The system accepts the corrected version of her initial attempt

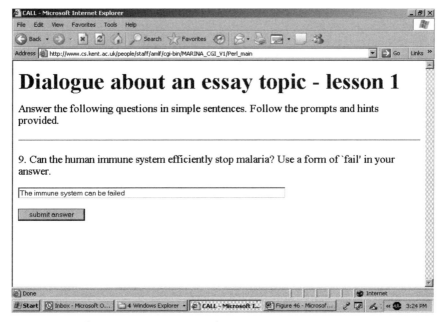

Figure 5.48 The student makes another common error

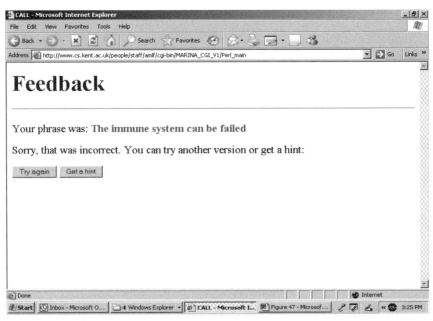

Figure 5.49 The system identifies it as an error

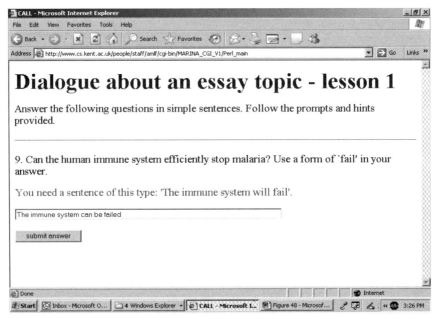

Figure 5.50 The system then specifies the nature of the error and provides help

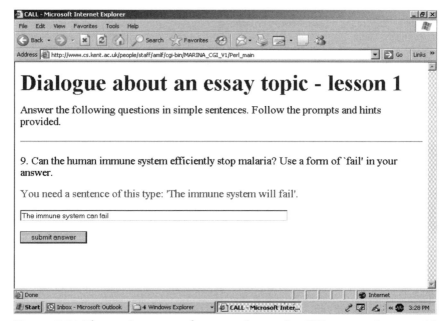

Figure 5.51 The student uses the same form of a different verb to avoid copying from the system

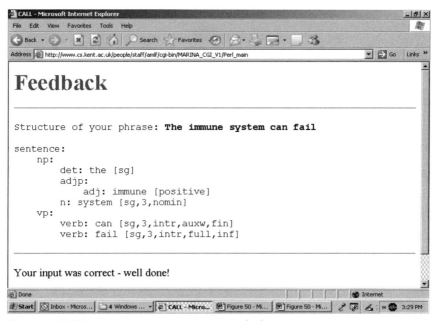

Figure 5.52 Her creative attempt is rewarded

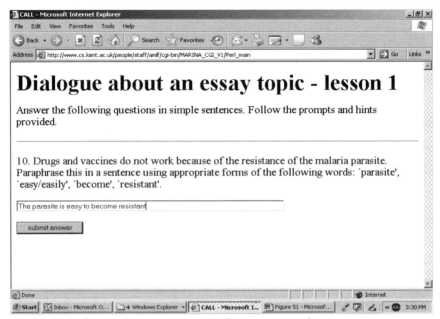

Figure 5.53 The student moves on to the answer to the next question

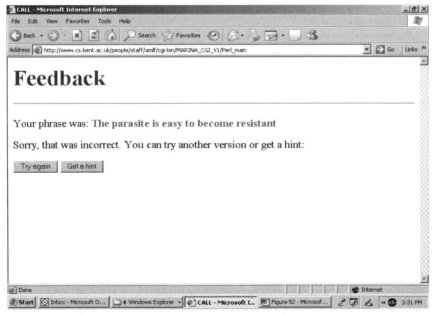

Figure 5.54 She makes a different kind of error this time

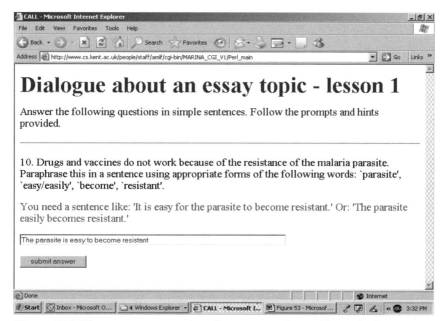

Figure 5.55 The system recognises the error and provides solutions

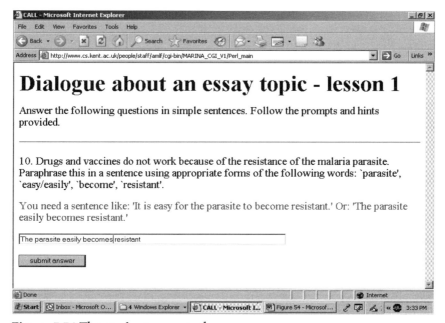

Figure 5.56 The student corrects the error

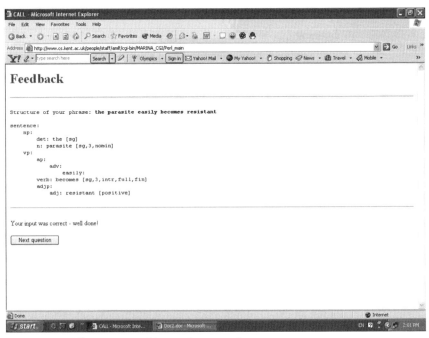

Figure 5.57 The corrected input is parsed

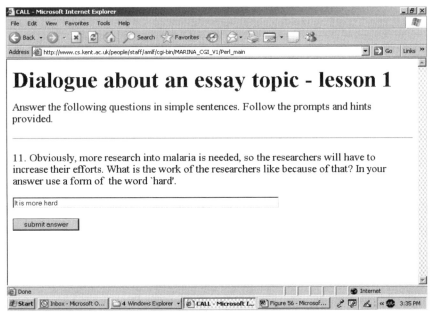

Figure 5.58 In response to question 11 the student incorrectly compares the adjective 'hard'

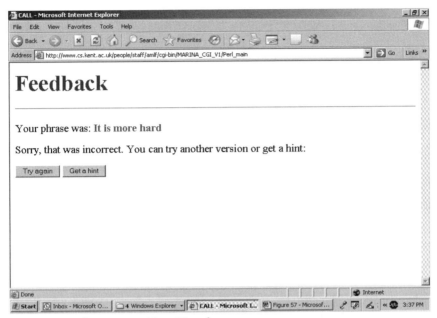

Figure 5.59 The system identifies the sentence as erroneous

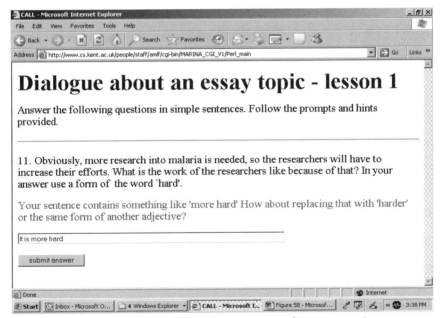

Figure 5.60 The system analyses the nature of the error and suggests a possible solution

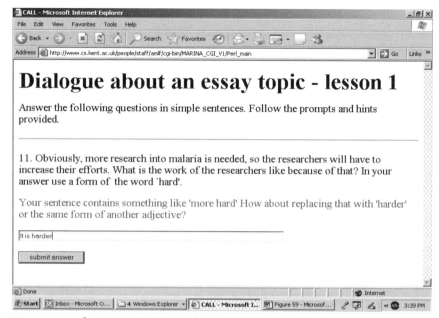

Figure 5.61 the student corrects her input

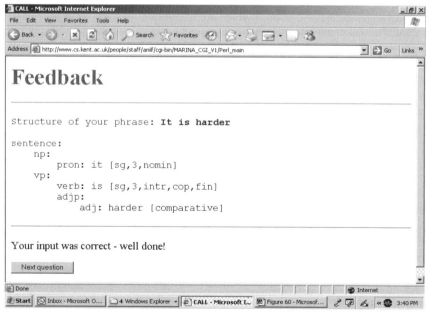

Figure 5.62 Her input is now correct and is parsed

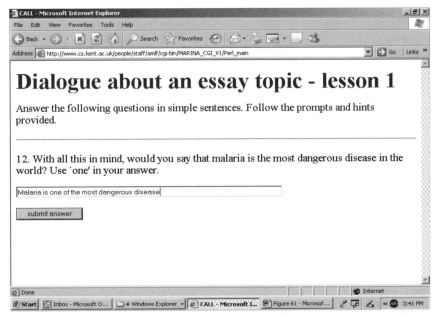

Figure 5.63 In her answer to the final question the student is unsure about the number of the noun 'disease'

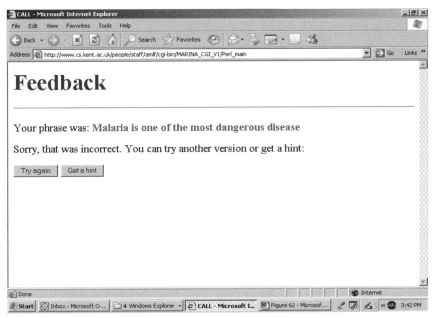

Figure 5.64 The system recognises the ungrammaticality of her input

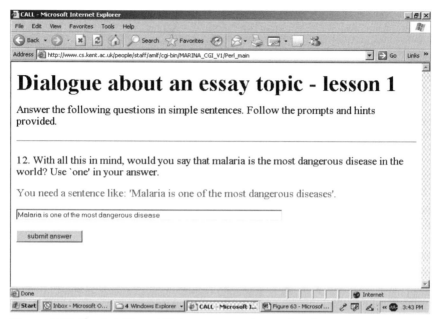

Figure 5.65 The Intelligent Tutor corrects the student's error

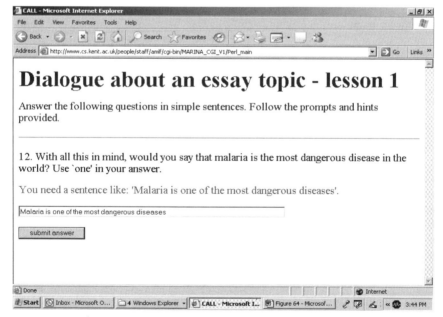

Figure 5.66 The student copies the solution

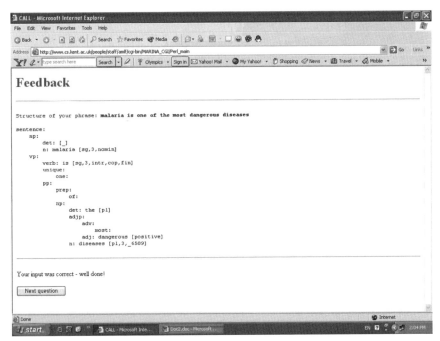

Figure 5.67 the correct input is parsed

(14) The student then decides that she has enough ideas concerning the subtopics of her essay topic. She therefore opens her word processor and starts composing the essay. She copies each sentence individually onto the system prompt and receives error messages as she does so. The system helps her correct her errors or, if uncertain, she changes her sentence to a format acceptable to the system. She copies the correct sentences into the word processor, which helps her with the punctuation, one of the aspects of writing that the Intelligent Tutor does not address (Figs 5.69, 5.70).

Thus the Tutor has played a dual role, the one of the teacher in a form of Socratic dialogue and that of the patient grammar checker, specially designed to recognise and respond to her particular error types.

Without the Intelligent Tutor, the topicality of her essay could have suffered, let alone the grammar. Only if she had been extremely lucky, would she have found a competent helper at this early stage of her essay to provide such multi-tiered, even though not perfect, help. Her teacher would have, unfortunately, intervened at the grading stage, a fact that would most likely have had negative affective repercussions on this student and possibly her overall success in this subject.

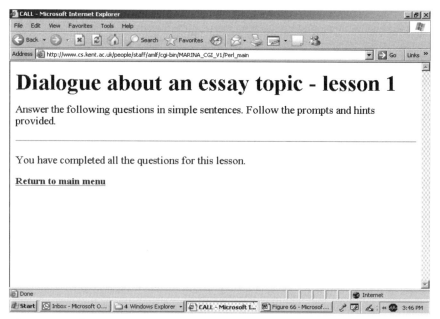

Figure 5.68 There are no more questions regarding malaria, but the student can go back and type any sentences on the prompt line. The only requirement for her input to be processed is that the system's lexicon recognises the vocabulary used

Conclusion

In this chapter we examined the needs of the specific learner population, we decided to call our EAP learners. Different learner styles were evident in the group, however the communicative and analytical learning styles were prevalent, influencing our approach to the ways errors are corrected by the intelligent tutor. We also found that these students needed a full command of the kind of academic language used not only in textbooks, but also in academic and professional journals. The EAP student writing was then compared to the features of professional academic writing and found diverging from that model toward the spoken language style. As material verb is one of the most common features of spoken language, it was found to be one of the most frequently used speech parts in our student writing. Consequently, most errors were also related to the use of verbs.

Thus based on the statistical regularity of certain error types, an interlanguage grammar could be devised and applied to develop an intelligent computer resource, capable not only of identifying the typical errors in L2 student writing, but also of making adequate corrections. The purpose of the corrections is in the first place to make the students aware of the

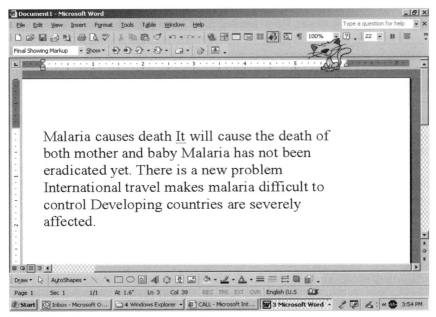

Figure 5.69 The word processor objects to punctuation errors

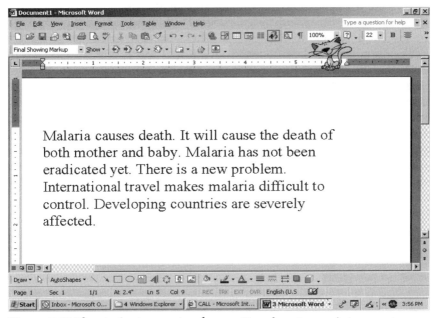

Figure 5.70 The student organises her scattered sentences into a neat paragraph

language used and then to sharpen the focus on form (Doughty & Williams, 2001; Long & Robinson, 1998) thus aiming for eradication and de-fossilisation (Selinker & Lakshmanan, 1993) of errors. What exactly is gained by this approach can be summarised in the following sentences. The students, left mostly to their own devices when writing academic assignments in English, which is not their first language, are frequently unsure of the grammaticality of their own sentences. Having an opportunity to have each sentence checked by an expert in both English and their particular interlanguage would not only contribute significantly to the readability of their assignments, but would also facilitate language learning.

Another advantage of the Tutor is the recognition of individual differences between students, especially concerning the learning style. With right-brained, concrete learners (Willing, 1989) as well as with the basically field independent communicative learners (Willing, 1988), the computer can mimic a game or the human-to-human mode of communication respectively. With the left-brained, analytical learners (Willing, 1989), the computer can be itself, an analytical device for taking language apart and making the rules clear. An authoritative learner can by contrast request and get the correct answer from the computer, the ultimate authority. Thus, all would feel that their particular learning needs are met.

Moreover, the intelligent tutor is designed to complement classes in academic English or be used for self-study, independent of any classes. It is conceived of as available in a global learning environment (Debski *et al.*, 1997 in Levy, 1999), including a number of links and resources, on the Web or the local server. In a situation where human language tutors are available only in the classroom and outside that only in rare individual consultations, all efforts to raise the language awareness of the students remain largely futile. Especially considering how little exposure to focus on form these students have previously had, it becomes clear that any artificially intelligent agent that serves the purpose can be of tremendous benefit. Following an introductory literature review, the research and development work led to the piloting of precisely such a resource, which reaches new frontiers in second language learning. The process of its testing and evaluation will be described in the next chapter.

Chapter 6

How Does it Work?

The Concept of Evaluation in CALL

In this chapter we will discuss the process of evaluating the Intelligent Tutor, the needs analysis for and the development of which was described in Chapter 5 of this book. In literature on CALL (Levy, 1997b; Goodfellow, 1999) or SLA research (McDonough & McDonough, 1997) we often find references to two types of evaluation: formative and summative. While the former can be said to accompany development projects, the latter is meant to follow them. This chapter will reflect on both concepts while trying to apply them to the Intelligent Tutor. It will also explore the research aspects of this evaluation. Having the software evaluated by a sample of student population other than the one it was designed for means that a lot of data will be presented about that population, which has no other purpose but to make sure that there is a good overlap between the two. Interesting as it is, this data will not be extensively commented on here, but may be explored in its own right within a separate publication, while the focus of this chapter remains firmly on the evaluation of the Intelligent Tutor. The findings indicate that there is a good match between the two populations and that the software itself is effective in terms of learning outcomes.

In Chapter 2 of this volume we discussed the potential for research in CALL development projects. It would appear that the evaluation phase in addition to the needs analysis phase provides ample opportunities for research (Fischer, 1999; McDonough & McDonough, 1997). However, the primary goal of CALL software evaluation is not necessarily research, but the quality assurance function (Thayer & Dorfman, 2000) as an integral part of the software development cycle (Levy, 1999; Sommerville, 2001; Pfleeger, 1998). Thus CALL software is subject not only to pedagogical standards, but also to those of software engineering. This is the reason why, as pointed out by Chapelle (2001: 51), CALL is scrutinised 'beyond what is expected of evaluation of other classroom activities'.

While saying that the tendency to view CALL as some sort of experiment, as Chapelle (2001: 51) did within the context of the above quotation, is a fair assessment, this reason alone does not justify the amount of scrutiny it is exposed to. It is rather a requirement imposed on it by its dual nature: (1) computational, by virtue of which it has to satisfy the standards of software engineering, and educational, by virtue of which it has to satisfy pedagogical standards. Furthermore, the need for a linguistic justification of methods and procedures implemented in CALL software packages adds another layer of complexity to their evaluation process, requiring that in addition to sound software engineering and sound pedagogy, sound linguistic principles be observed. Just how sound is 'sound' in the preceding sentence has been the bone of contention in CALL theory and practice. In the first four chapters of this volume we embarked on a quest for answers to that very question. It seems that universality is elusive when discussing CALL software, as the specifics of the situation, such as the learner, the content, the context of application as well as the linguistic and language learning theories, seem to dictate the values and therefore the criteria for evaluation (Levy, 1997b). Moreover, all these layers do not remain strictly segregated as they would in a clinical environment, but interact with each other often producing entirely new qualities, in view of which it is difficult to say that CALL software equates the sum of its elements. This chapter will accordingly lay out the principles selected for the evaluation of the Intelligent Tutor. Subsequently the evaluation process itself will be described, leading to the conclusion about the usefulness of the Intelligent Tutor.

As pointed out above, Chapelle (2001) assumes that CALL is a classroom activity, rather than perhaps a self-study activity complementing classroom learning or even being practised without reference to any classes. Another tacit assumption made by Chapelle (2001) is that CALL software as a rule comes off the shelf and has not been designed for a specific group of students, as has been the case in this book. A logical conclusion based on the above premises is that CALL software, being a classroom activity and not specifically designed for a particular class, has to be evaluated by teachers, as is indeed being proposed by Chapelle (2001). This view very much equates CALL software with a textbook (see Hubbard, 1996: 15), for which as argued very eloquently by Johns (1997), the teacher is the target audience, an intermediary (Hubbard, 1996) or a 'gate-keeper' to express this notion in the language of Borchardt (1998b). Another logical conclusion, provided this view is adopted, is that while the teacher should judge the appropriateness of the software for a particular class, the learner should be used only to provide empirical data concerning the effectiveness of a program. Given the premises, this is a neat division of labour. However, let us see what happens when these premises are altered.

Literature (Decoo & Colpaert, 1999b; Goodfellow, 1999; Gillespe & McKee, 1999) shows that CALL is often used outside the classroom. Based on that premise, one can take the approach of Mike Levy (1997b), namely that there are two basically different types of CALL software, tool and tutor, each of which requires a different method of evaluation. While a tool according to Levy (1997b: 203–4) should be evaluated in two stages, as it follows implicitly, the tutor can be evaluated in one stage. The reason for evaluating a tool twice is because of its primary purpose as a tool, e.g. a word processor or a database and its secondary purpose as a learning tool. In the former role the tool has to be compared to other similar products, while in the latter role it should be evaluated in its context of use. Levy's (1997b: 205) assumption is that the learners will as a rule use a tutor in self-access mode and that it therefore has to have an absolute reliability, as the teacher is presumably not expected to be available for help. This view is entirely opposite to that of Chapelle (2001), cited above.

The above views additionally have a huge impact on the concept of research and its relation to the development process. While the former view can be said to be theory driven (McDonough & McDonough, 1997; Levy, 1997b), linear (Lewins, 1990), top-down and deductive (McDonough and McDonough, 1997), the latter is at least to some extent data driven (McDonough & McDonough, 1997; Levy, 1997b; Decoo & Colpaert, 1999) and circular (Lewins, 1990), although not necessarily bottom-up or inductive (McDonough & McDonough, 1997; Levy, 1997b; Decoo & Colpaert, 1999). The former starts from the theory, sets a hypothesis, carries out a development and the subsequent evaluation in the light of the theory, without allowing for the mutual influence of the many variables involved in the process. This equals the assumption that in a system all variables are independent and none are dependent, which is questionable. The latter on the contrary willingly takes into account the expectation that some variables will be dependent on each other and will therefore change with the introduction of each new parameter.

> In this view, then, reality is seen not as fixed and stable but socially con-structed, so what Sevigny (1981: 72) calls 'social order' – in our case, of a classroom – is perceived as 'an emergent phenomenon'. This view is echoed by Ericson and Schulz (1981: 148) who describe social contexts as 'interactionally constituted environments' where there is a constant process of change and re-adjustment. (McDonough & McDonough, 1997: 46)

Although the above quotation refers to the classroom as the object of research, the nature of CALL research can be described in the same way, since its object is dynamic rather than static. Any new element, such as CALL and moreover a special type of it, ICALL, is likely to add more com-plexity to the observed phenomenon, and that not by mere addition, but also by mutual influence and ensuing change of the variables intended for observation. In continuation of the above quotation, McDonough and McDonough (1997: 46–7) do indeed bring up 'the problematic light' this view throws 'on standard research questions of validity and reliability'. This researched world that refuses to stand still is very different from the Aristotelian world (Halliday, 1999) which stands still suspended for obser-vation and measurement. In a world which is in flux, it is very difficult to isolate independent variables. Therefore, it is difficult to carry out interventionist research (McDonough & McDonough, 1997: 44; Ellis, 1997), the kind of research attempting to isolate the influences of one or more variables. Causality, largely sought to establish by experimental methods, which search 'for effects of certain treatments on given measures' (McDonough & McDonough, 1997: 157), depends on such control of variables. The key to such control is decomposition of a problem into details (McDonough & McDonough, 1997: 158).

However, in complex and ever changing environments it is very difficult to decide at what level to stop decomposing, as there are levels and levels of complexity underneath each seemingly simple phenomenon, such as native language, L2 proficiency, learning style and achievement, which are the phenomena observed in this study. With a truly bilingual student, the face validity of the native language concept fades away; in L2 proficiency, we are dealing with a complex term comprising two potentially undefined terms: L2 and proficiency, and so forth. When considering an ICALL program, it becomes unclear whether it is the theoretical underpinnings of the program or the familiarity of the topic that facilitates learning. Such variables that are difficult to separate from each other are called confounding variables and are often a stumbling block in an experiment (McDonough & McDonough, 1997: 159).

In view of such complexity, Goodfellow (1999) argues that an approach to both design and evaluation should be taken that does not try to separate the outcome of learning from the processes by which learning happens. He claims that the phenomenographic approach answers the above criteria, being essentially humanistic and taking the learner as the reference point for the assessment of outcome. According to Goodfellow (1999), CALL interaction can yield five types of data that would be useful in a phenomenographic study. They are quantitative performance data or scores, qualitative performance data or evidence of strategies applied, qualitative learning approach data or evidence of learners' assumptions as to what they are doing and why, and finally quantitative and qualitative introspective data. This is indeed an alternative to the experimental model, which separates performance from the learning approach (Goodfellow, 1999).

In recognition of the complexity of both the learning process and the context in which it happens, this study will use some of the experimental principles, without the fully fledged experimental model. This is called a quasi-experiment (McDonough & McDonough, 1997: 162) and will be discussed later on in this chapter. This method of research will be complemented with two interpretive research techniques: participant observation and verbal report as a method of introspection (McDonough & McDonough, 1997; Goodfellow, 1999). In addition, document analysis will be used in connection with contrastive and error analyses, supported by literature research and review. Finally, a survey will be used in learning style analysis. While the quasi-experiment is likely to yield some numerically analysable and therefore reduced or 'thin' data that can possibly answer the question 'why', the interpretive techniques are likely to yield a lot of rich or 'thick' data that are likely to answer the questions 'how' or indeed any questions arising from the data. Evaluation is a type of case study, in which the researcher investigates one entity (i.e. the interaction of a population of students with an ICALL program), looking at the entity from various angles and hence combining different research approaches, which is a usual procedure in similarly oriented SLA (McDonough & McDonough, 1997). We will now return to the question of CALL evaluation.

Having seen the two extreme positions in regard to CALL software evaluation, one assuming the use in the classroom, the other the use in self-study mode, we will now consider a more conciliatory view which allows for both situations. In order to achieve this, we must remember that CALL software, much as its application is specific and different from any other type of computer programs, is first and foremost software. Thus, it has to be first evaluated in terms of software engineering and then in terms of its pedagogical value. In fact, Allen and Periyasamy (1997) strongly advocate the application of software engineering principles to all phases of CALL software development. According to these authors, there are six systemic principles of software development: (1) requirements gathering and analysis, (2) specifications of requirements, (3) architectural and detailed design, (4) coding, (5) testing, and (6) maintenance (Allen & Periyasamy, 1997).

I have quoted similar principles in some of the previous chapters. In this context following the above steps is a part of quality assurance, which is a much broader term than evaluation. In software engineering, quality assurance means checking that the correct procedures are being followed (Thayer & Dorfman, 2000) all the way through the development process and beyond. The quality of a product is determined by the degree to which it conforms to the stated requirements or, in other words, fits the purpose (Thayer & Dorfman, 2000). Thus, the integrity of a product is required at the external level (following the general software engineering principles) as well as at the internal level (following its own stated purpose). Testing is one of the crucial steps in ascertaining the integrity of a software product for the client and is a part of the development process (Thayer & Dorfman, 2000).

While in traditional software engineering the client is seen as a monolithic entity (Thayer & Dorfman, 2000; Sommerville, 2001; Pfleeger, 1998), in CALL two obvious choices are teachers and learners. Since it is unusual for the learners to commission CALL developers to design a program for them, we can agree with Allen and Periyasamy (1997) that teachers (or perhaps institutions) fit that profile better. However, this by no means indicates that the learners should be excluded from any of the stages of the development process or indeed from the evaluation. Thus testing should be performed by both teachers and learners.

Having identified the client, at this point we also need to identify the 'stated goals of the program' for CALL. At one level, that of software engineering strictly speaking, the testing should prove no more than that the lines of code execute as they are intended to. At another level, the program will also have educational goals and objectives, against which it should be checked. This is known in the literature as effectiveness testing (Holmes & Leney, 1998; Dodigovic, 1995; McDonough & McDonough, 1997). In the past this has more frequently included language learning outcomes, or in Chapelle's (2001: 67) words 'the product' of learning rather than the process. According to Chapelle (2001), both are covered by empirical evaluation. By empirical evaluation Chapelle (2001) means collecting evidence that the program has a language learning potential, especially regarding the target forms. Evidence further has to corroborate the learner fit of the program, the focus on meaning, the authenticity of task, the pedagogical impact and practicality (Chapelle, 2001). Clearly, the focus on meaning and authenticity of materials are specific to a particular learning theory and could be more generally replaced by the criterion of conformance to a theory used as a point of departure.

In his CALL methodological framework, Hubbard (1996) highlights this flexibility to choose the preferred theory. Thus he sees a CALL package emerge in a triangle between the development, evaluation and implementation. While he makes the learner responsible for the developmental input, the classroom teacher and the reviewer are responsible for the evaluation, which is the exact reverse of the order suggested by Chapelle (2001). This view, however, implies that the software package does not come off the shelf, but is being developed for a specific learner population and the evaluation is therefore closely related to the development. The development module in Hubbard (1996) further breaks down into approach, design and procedure, the three stages of course design in Richards and Rodgers' (1986 in McDonough & McDonough, 1997: 94) model. 'This model is intended to show how "theory" becomes "practice" through a process of increasing specificity and concretization' (McDonough & McDonough, 1997: 94). Approach according to Hubbard (1996) includes the theoretical underpinnings such as linguistic and SLA assumptions as well as the ensuing approach to teaching. Design is seen as an organic part of the institutionalised education, in which respect it is very similar to Chapelle (2001), and includes learner profiles as well as references to the syllabus. What Hubbard (1996) calls procedure is very similar to what is in the language of software engineering called user interface design (Hackos & Redish, 1998) and entails designing the screen layout, activity types, control options, input processing, presentation scheme, feedback and help options.

In Levy's (1997a) words, the above approach runs a risk of being seen as hierarchical and linear, if it is not understood as a network of inter-relationships and a checklist, rather than as a strict sequence of events to occur always in the same order. Levy's CALL survey (1997a, 1997b) identifies two main points of departure in the CALL development process, the theory (educational, linguistic, SLA) or the technology. However, Levy (1997a, 1997b) recognises that whatever the point of departure, it has to be changed and reshaped by the other factors in the development process. Thus it helps to be aware of the intrinsic quality of the development process, i.e. that it is not a state and therefore cannot be represented statically; that it is non-hierarchical and therefore neither top-down nor bottom-up; and finally, that it is radically transformational (Schneiderman, 1987 in Levy, 1997a).

> The development process is first and foremost a dynamic one. Any theoretical point of departure needs to be seen in that light. The initial theoretical orientation has to be reconciled with the technological environment in which it is realized, and the end result, the working CALL program, must be validated within this context. The 'fit' is resolved through the development process: this implies early considerations of the technology to be used. (Levy, 1997a: 53)

It does help to think of the development process as a cycle or a spiral (Thayer & Dorfman, 2000; Levy, 1999), the way it is viewed in software engineering. Evaluation, both formative and summative, is a part of that cycle (Levy, 1999). While formative evaluation stretches throughout the cycle, the summative evaluation is supposed to follow the completion of the development stage (Levy, 1999). This however does not mean the breaking of the development cycle, as the summative evaluation may lead to revision, not just in the implementation, but also in conceptualisation. The release of the software on the other hand does not mean the end of the evaluation. The users will continue to evaluate it against their (predictably changing) context of use, which will eventually lead to a major revision and the release of a new version (Pfleeger, 1998; Sommerville, 2001). And so the process continues.

The development of the Intelligent Tutor described in this book has very much been a process. Even though its sequence might appear linear (Lewins, 1990), since one event seems to follow another, a different one, without any apparent recursion, this is just an impression gained by the insight into one cycle. In reality, the process of analysis, development and evaluation is far from over. Insights gained at all levels will be incorporated in a new revision and renewed evaluation will follow, which will also have some aspects of analysis thus enabling the next cycle.

In the development of the Intelligent Tutor we started from a problem –

erroneous grammar obscuring the meaning – pointed out to us by discipline lecturers at an Australian university. Levy (1997a: 47) calls this 'lower level task or problem'. Early on in the process we decided that the intelligent CALL had a lot of potential to handle this problem and that subject to further investigation we would give it a go. We subsequently performed learner profiling (Hubbard, 1996) including the learning styles, particular learning problems and the context of learning. Further we consulted 'higher theoretical frameworks' (Levy, 1997a: 47), including linguistic and sociolinguistic theories, SLA theories and the CALL literature. Theories were reviewed with a full awareness of their limitations and bias toward a particular learner type or a situation. Therefore, upon discovering that we were dealing with predominantly two groups of learners, the communicative and the analytical (Willing, 1989), it was decided that the interaction SLA theory (Long & Robinson, 2001) would best match the communicative learner, whereas the language awareness theory (James, 1998) would be best suited for the analytical learners. The linguistic and sociolinguistic theories chosen reflected the learner profiles too. Thus the community of practice theory (Wenger, 1999; Swales, 1990) was chosen to represent academic English to the communicative learners, whereas the semiotic system theory (Petkovic, 1984; Halliday, 1999) was chosen to clarify the underlying structures and mechanisms of the academic language to the analytical learners. While the former initiates the user into essay planning by constructing a scaffolding (Bigge & Shermis, 1999), the latter parses her sentences and in the process exposes the simple structure of the sentence grammar encountered in academic English.

It can be expected that a number of variables mutually influenced each other in the process. Thus, while the initial considerations did influence the choice of technology, the ICALL technology further narrowed down the range of applicable learning theories. The choice of the learning theories was further influenced by the range and prominence of the learning styles identified. Thus they should be viewed as confounding variables, or such variables that cannot be separated from each other in a satisfactory fashion (McDonough & McDonough, 1997).

Formative Evaluation

Formative evaluation started early on in the process, in that both the theoretical underpinnings and empirical needs analysis was written up and submitted to peers for review and publication (Dodigovic, 1998; Dodigovic & Suphawat, 1999; Dodigovic, 1999), which is an important step in attaining research status and credibility (McDonough & McDonough, 1997: 60). The same principle was applied to the design and development process (Dodigovic, 2000; Dodigovic, 2002), especially in regard to needs analysis (McDonough & McDonough, 1997). While Alison Fowler of the

University of Kent examined the design documents and the early code, and found that they were largely plausible, both Fowler and the author of this book performed the initial testing, i.e. the check that the code executes as it should. For that purpose, a list of test case sentences (Thayer & Dorfman, 2000) was devised, which can be found in Appendix 1. Test case here and elsewhere in this chapter refers to a specific set of test data and associated procedures (including the population) developed to verify a program's compliance with a requirement (Thayer & Dorfman, 2000: 520).

The program successfully passed that test. Next, two international specialists in both ESL and CALL, were asked to review the program in the context of academic English. Again, the program passed with flying colours. Both reviews are included in the Appendices. Finally, two representatives of the student population, whose profiles were very similar to Eric and Jean, described in the first chapter of this volume, were asked to test the program extensively. They did experience some frustration using the program on-line on their own, from home, without previous training, one even not familiar with the associated readings on malaria. This is reflected in the comments they made (also included in the Appendices). Especially the latter two represent written down verbal reports used in introspective research methods (McDonough & McDonough, 1997: 191). The user reports were unstructured, capturing anything that seemed important to the users while working with the program and recollected later, including evaluative observations. Thus these reports are retrospective, produced slightly after the fact (McDonough & McDonough, 1997). The program was then presented to a broader academic audience through a series of publications (Dodigovic, 2002; 2003a; 2003b). In addition to some truly constructive suggestions, the response has been overwhelmingly positive.

The students who tested the program found it very useful. However, their desire to experiment with language seemed to go far beyond the limitations of the program in terms of topic, vocabulary and grammar range. Some found it frustrating that they could not try out just any language construct that came to mind. Here is the feedback from one student that seems to encapsulate all the relevant points:

> It is quite useful as all the topics link with our reading. Some little improvement could be made though . . . It might be too difficult for a computer to judge student's own sentence I think. Actually, I tried several times and could hardly get the right answer. (Dodigovic, 2003c)

A reviewer, however, noted the following:

> This is a good quality suite of software with a substantial innovative component based on language processing technology. Such software is really needed in both language and literacy learning and one can only

hope that more developers will turn to producing this sort of tool. (Dodigovic, 2003c)

Thus, the obvious needs for improvement of this pilot program seem to be its limited grammar that may have to be extended to accept more structures, the way the computer generated questions are phrased, which could be made clearer and the instructions given by the system to the student, which can be made more explicit and available at different levels from a help menu. All these caveats, however, do not make this program a failure, as many of them do not pertain to the concept, but to the characteristics of the user interface, which is often known to suffer in non-commercial and research oriented CALL software (Levy, 1997b). An obvious problem in the academia of course, as pointed out in Chapter 2 is the limited availability of time and resources to resolve such issues (Holland, 1995). In addition, it does not help when academics for various reasons change the place of work and residence. However, it is clear that with some modest additional funds and other resources, such as the software platform, time and personnel, this program could become a useful learning partner bookmarked by many EAP students. Moreover, this prospect motivates to make further improvements and eventually render the much needed tutor available to a broad public in a user friendly form.

In Lieu of Summative Evaluation

Summative evaluation is usually carried out after the development work has largely been completed (Levy, 1999). This cannot be definitely said of the Intelligent Tutor in this book. There are several reasons for this state of affairs that seems to plague projects in ICALL (Holland, 1995). They are the change of the research agenda at the original institution, the discontinuation of funding, the relocation of the author to another institution in a different country and with it a change in the author's set of research agenda.

Still, the formative evaluation seemed incomplete without evidence of pedagogical impact of the program. So far, namely, we only had the so-called 'smile coefficient' (Levy, 1999) or one could rather say the 'frown coefficient' caused by the program. This refers to the amount of satisfaction or dissatisfaction derived by the students from the program. Research (Levy, 1999; Levy, 1997a) has however shown that this is not necessarily a true indicator of the quality of the product. Thus collecting evidence of the learning outcomes of the program seemed indicated (Chapelle, 2001). Unfortunately, for all the above mentioned reasons, it was impossible for the author of this book to test the learning outcomes of the program in the exact context for which it was designed. Given this obstacle, the available learning context, which was in many respects already similar to the target context, was further approximated to match the target criteria. The following text describes this effort in detail.

Rationale

The rationale for this study is the evaluation of the Intelligent Tutor, the Web based writing and grammar correction aid which we followed through its needs analysis and development phases in Chapter 5 of this volume. While the formative evaluation described above provided information pertaining to the user interface issues, this study is expected to deliver data pertaining to the effectiveness of the program in terms of the learning outcomes. What is crucial for the developer to find out at this stage is whether the program has any learning effect at all. For this reason the effect of the program will not be compared with any other procedures or resources. The study will measure only the statistical significance of the states before and after the use of the program by a group of students roughly matching the profile for which the program was developed. If the program is to be recommended for self-study or indeed any other mode of study, it is essential for it to demonstrate some effectiveness. Other variables such as retention or comparative difference to compatible resources or procedures can be measured at a later stage, the stage of summative evaluation proper, when the faults of the program have been removed and its basic usefulness established. This is, however, not the purpose of the current study. Similarly, this chapter will not elaborate on the findings regarding the confounding variables in the test case sample, including the learning styles and typical errors. It must be remembered that the primary purpose of investigating these two areas in the test case sample is to establish whether there is a significant qualitative difference between the population for which the program was originally developed and the one it is being tested on. The hypothesis made here is that the two samples are similar enough, which will enable us to draw conclusions about the success of the program with the original target population based on its success with the test case population.

Study: Methods and design

The evaluative procedure underlying this section of the chapter is based on a quasi-experiment and some participant observation (McDonough & McDonough, 1997). This means that it has some characteristics of the more rigorous experiments, but lacks others. The elements of experiment are the features that make it replicable, including the research question, the literature review, the hypothesis, the experimental task, the design and method, controls and counterbalances, subjects, results and statistical analysis, discussion and interpretation (McDonough & McDonough, 1997: 165). In the following we will identify each of these elements for this study.

Before proceeding ,however, the terms 'experiment' and 'quasi-experiment' will be briefly clarified. While some SLA authors claim that both an experiment (Nunan, 1992; Larsen-Freeman & Long, 1991) and a quasi-experiment (Nunan, 1992) must be performed with two groups, the experiment and control groups respectively, McDonough and Mc-Donough (1997) make no such claim. In fact, other sources (Muzic, 1986) allow for the existence of an experiment with one group and two treatments, pointing out the importance of comparison and the solid base for it. We will therefore select the definition offered by McDonough and McDonough (1997) and will continue by identifying the main elements of experimental approach as identified by these authors.

In a nutshell, the research question in this study is very simple: does the exposure to Intelligent Tutor have an effect on learning in the given context which is similar to the context of development, as demonstrated by achievement outcomes? The literature review pertains to the most prominent disciplines featuring in this undertaking, i.e. language and linguistic theory, SLA, CALL research, Web based learning and the social learning theory, ICALL, CALL software design and evaluation, and is scattered throughout the chapters of this book. The hypothesis is that the Intelligent Tutor has a significant effect on the learning outcomes. Thus the null hypothesis to be rejected is that there is no significant difference between the states of pre-treatment and post-treatment with the same subjects. This calls for a very simple design including only one group and one treatment procedure, preceded by a pre-test and followed by a post-test. The treatment procedure equals the experimental task and that is the work with the Intelligent Tutor. The number of participants is greater than 30, which in statistical terms is likely to produce a normal distribution and is therefore conclusive in terms of parametric statistics (Mosteller *et al.*, 1983). The subjects are not taken from the exact same target population, which is where we depart from the traditional experimental setup, but is subjected to observation and approximation to make sure that it conforms to the characteristics exhibited by the target population. Similarly, there is no randomisation or pair matching, since only one treatment is indicated. However the matching with the target population in a number of confounding variables provides some controls and counterbalances (McDonough & McDonough, 1997: 160). Results, statistical analysis, discussion and interpretation follow.

Before describing the procedure, let us briefly discuss the kinds of variables involved in this quasi-experiment and their significance in answering the research question. This setup would have ideally included a moderator variable, i.e. the variable that could have affected the outcome of the procedure (McDonough & McDonough, 1997: 159). This could have been the learning style (i.e. concrete vs. analytical). However, learning style differences were not very pronounced in individuals, even though trends were visible in the population. Besides, as indicated above, certain variables such as learning style, ICALL use and learning theory chosen, were seen as confounding variables (McDonough & McDonough, 1997: 159), difficult to separate from one another, because they were treated as a plethora since the inception of the program. This leaves us with one independent variable, i.e. the treatment (Intelligent Tutor), and one dependent variable, i.e. the learning outcome measured as achievement.

Subjects

The context of evaluation had some similarities with the original context of design. Thus, the original target population was predominantly female, aged 24 or younger and spread across various disciplines throughout the curriculum at an English speaking university. Their learning styles were mainly communicative and analytical. They were computer literate, had experience with CALL and felt comfortable with learning EAP with computers. The test case student population also consisted of female university students, aged 20 years and above at an English speaking university. Their preferred learning styles showed similar trends to the original target population. This group was exceedingly computer savvy, had had ample exposure to CALL and enjoyed doing most things with computers. Their first language was on the list of minority first languages in the original study by Suphawat (1999). The test samples were of similar sizes: 47 in Suphawat's (1999) study and 46 in the more recent one. Both populations were enrolled in some sort of an EAP course.

The differences between the two populations included the fact that the test case population was homogeneous, monocultural, all female, all Arabic speaking, while the original population was heterogeneous, in terms of language, culture and ethnicity with a number of truly bilingual and bicultural participants. Furthermore, the Arabic language spoken as the first language by all of our test case students was not on the majority list in Suphawat's (1999) original survey. Most importantly, the English speaking university is located in a country in which Arabic is spoken as the official language, although English has a privileged status and is used for many private and official transactions on a daily basis. Finally, none of our students came from the College of Business, which was the most numerous population in the original study. Rather, the majority was in the General Education program (36 students) in their first year of university studies, while a minority (11 students) were enrolled in the College of Information Systems. None of the test case students were part-time students or employed outside the university, whereas a few students in the original sample matched that profile. Table 6.1 summarises the similarities and differences between the two samples.

To make sure that the two samples had more similarities than differences, two distinct studies were conducted: firstly the study of learning styles and secondly a mixture of contrastive and error analysis. These are

Table 6.1 Samples – similarities and differences

Suphawat (1999)	Dodigovic (2003)
• English speaking university	• English speaking university
• English speaking country	• Arabic speaking country (English has privileged status)
• Age 20+	
• M + F	• Age 20+
• TOEFL 550/580	• F
• Chinese, Indonesian, Norwegian, Arabic…	• TOEFL 500/550
	• Arabic
• Bicultural	• Monocultural
• College of Business, etc.	• General education
• Good computer skills	• Good computer skills
• Strong preference for CALL	• Strong preference for CALL
• Communicative learning style	• Communicative learning style

some of the counterbalances (McDonough & McDonough, 1997: 160) included in the quasi-experimental procedure to make it more exact. In the following, I will describe the learning style analysis. The contrastive/error analysis is extensive and requires a section of its own.

Learning styles

Since the age, the English language proficiency (TOEFL 500 and above), the program of study and the first language of the test case students was known, as well as their computing skills and motivation to learn English with computers, the only unknown in terms of Suphawat's (1999) study were the learning styles. For this reason, a short questionnaire was administered to the target population, or rather the 36 students enrolled in the General Education program. The 11 students enrolled in the College of Information Systems did not have the opportunity to participate in this study, as the questionnaire was not available at that stage, which was a few months before the trial with the General Education students. The questions asked were the same questions asked of the original EAP population; however, they were available in an on-line format with numerical values substituting a rating scale (Bachman & Palmer, 1996: 242) as answer options. The format is shown in Table 6.2.

This questionnaire was administered in the form of an Excel spreadsheet to 36 students in the General Education program in December 2003. The sum of the responses turned out as shown in Tables 6.3 and 6.4:

A clear preference for communicative learning style comes through in this population as well. While the average percentages in Suphawat's

Table 6.2 Learning styles

1.	I like to learn English by reading.
2.	I like to listen and use cassettes.
3.	I like to learn English by playing games.
4.	I like to learn English by conversations.
5.	I like to learn English by talking in pairs.
6.	I like to study English from my own textbooks.
7.	I like the English teacher to explain everything to us.
8.	I like the English teacher to give us problems to work on.
9.	I like the English teacher to let me find my mistakes.
10.	I like to study grammar.
11.	At home, I like to learn by watching TV in English.
12.	I like to learn by talking to friends and teachers (outside class) in English.

How to fill this in?
For each question in column A, insert a number (0–3) in column B.
The meaning of the numbers is as follows:
0 = Not at all
1 = A little
2 = Fairly well
3 = Best

Table 6.3 Learning style responses

1. I like to learn English by reading.	55	authority oriented
2. I like to listen and use cassettes.	35	concrete
3. I like to learn English by playing games.	54	concrete
4. I like to learn English by conversations.	72	communicative
5. I like to learn English by talking in pairs.	55	concrete
6. I like to study English from my own textbooks.	45	authority oriented
7. I like the English teacher to explain everything to us.	73	authority oriented
8. I like the English teacher to give us problems to work on.	61	analytical
9. I like the English teacher to let me find my mistakes.	66	analytical
10. I like to study grammar.	41	analytical
11. At home, I like to learn by watching TV in English.	71	communicative
12. I like to learn by talking to friends and teachers (outside class) in English.	70	communicative

Table 6.4 Learning style summary

analytical	168
authority oriented	173
communicative	213
concrete	144

(1999) study indicate a slightly different order of preference (communicative, analytical, authoritative, concrete), this study, similar to Willing's (1988), shows that on the average the authoritative learning style is the second favourite learning style, which may be explained in terms of the authority oriented culture (Smith, 2001). It was followed very closely by the analytical learning style. The concrete learning style remains the least favourite one. Looking at individual questions, all questions related to the communicative learning style scored the highest marks, while two out of three questions related to the analytical learning style came second. Only one of the authority oriented questions scored very high marks, whereas the others received a more moderate response. Thus we can say that there is some similarity in learning style preferences between the two learner samples. The next section describes the other issue crucial to the usefulness of the Intelligent Tutor to the test case population, this being the learner errors.

Errors of Arabic speakers in written English

While the phonetic challenges of spoken English to Arabic speakers are interesting (see Smith, 2001; Thompson-Panos & Thomas-Ruzic, 1983), we will focus on the difficulties the test case population has in written English. The reason for this restriction is the Intelligent Tutor itself, the piece of CALL software to be tried out by this population of students. This program is not only restricted to the written mode, but it can also correct only a limited number of grammar errors at the subsentential level. It was however designed for a different population of students, unfortunately not fully available for the program evaluation purpose. For this reason, the compatibility of the available Arabic speaking student population needs to be assessed in terms of written English errors.

Unfortunately, even though an extensive corpus of test case population writing was compiled, there was no time to analyse it thoroughly for all sorts of errors. Instead, three steps were taken to find out whether the test case population was likely to make errors similar to the original learner population. The three steps were literature based contrastive analysis, literature based error analysis, and limited error analysis on a sample provided by the 36 General Education students.

Contrastive analysis (James, 1998) means comparing the features of L1 and L2 for the purpose of predicting the areas of possible difficulty for L2 learners. In addition to literature based contrastive analysis (AbiSamra, 2003; Smith, 2001; Thompson-Panos & Thomas-Ruzic, 1983), some limited knowledge of Modern Standard Arabic and some information about two colloquial dialects of Arabic (Levantine and Gulf) has been of great help to the author. The following problem areas could be identified: verbs, prepositions and articles (Scott & Tucker, 1974 in Thompson-Panos & Thomas-Ruzic, 1983). This overlaps nicely with the findings of the error analysis on our original EAP population sample, where the main areas of difficulty were found to be verbs, nouns, determiners (or articles) and prepositions. In fact, contrastively, one would expect that English nouns would also be very difficult for the speakers of Arabic, since the Arabic category of nouns is very broad and includes adjectives and adverbs as well as nouns (AbiSamra, 2003).

One might speculate that some of the above similarities may arise from the fact that the majority of the original population were Indonesian. Even though it is not being implied that there are typological similarities between Arabic and Indonesian, what is being alluded to is the fact that Indonesia is the largest Muslim country in Asia. Consequently, many Indonesians would be familiar with the classical Arabic, the language of the Koran and daily prayer (Smith, 2001). Languages in contact, so it seems, usually have influence on each other (O'Grady *et al.*, 1997: 292) and therefore one would expect the Classical Arabic to have reflected in some way on the expression of the Muslim Indonesians, although this is just a speculation by the author. Thus, overall, there seemed to be enough common ground to pursue further investigation.

The next task was to examine the literature for the seven typical errors of the original EAP student population. They are pseudo-passives (*These sentences can analyse many ways*), ergative construction (*What is happened with these verbs?*), tough movement (*Never easy to be learned . . .*), existential construction (*There are sentences cause learnability problems*), malformed expressions of feelings/reactions/states (*Parents must take responsible*), missing copula (*Sometimes very easy to make mistake*) and finite/non-finite verb confusion (*I decided to cancelled*).The most obvious one to look for was the missing copula, quoted in AbiSamra (2003), Smith (2001) and Thompson-Panos and Thomas-Ruzic (1983). This is explained by the fact that the verb *to be* in Arabic does not have the present tense and is therefore not used as a copula (Smith, 2001). This error's frequency has been confirmed in the author's practical experience. A number of occurrences were also found in the mini-corpus of test case student writing (e.g. *She * happy*).

The confusion of finite with non-finite verb is quoted in Thompson-Panos and Thomas-Ruzic (1983: 615). This may be partly due to the non-existence of some non-finite verb forms as well as to the total lack of modal verbs in Arabic (Smith, 2001). Instead, particles and conjugated auxiliary verbs can be used to express some complex tenses or modalities (Thompson-Panos & Thomas-Ruzic, 1983). As a result, sentences like 'I didn't went to school' are possible (Thompson-Panos & Thomas-Ruzic, 1983: 615). The author's investigation confirms these findings.

Another predictable error was malformed expressions of feelings/reactions/states. This type of error is based on the part of speech confusion (Yong, 2001). Since Arabic groups nouns, adjectives and adverbs into one large part of speech class (AbiSamra, 2003), mutually confusing these parts of speech in English would be expected. In addition, the capacity of Arabic to build verbal nouns (Smith, 2001) must add further confusion. In fact, both the author's personal classroom experience and the mini-corpus confirmed the hypothesis that part of speech confusion would occur frequently.

The above error types were originally associated with the Indonesian English interlanguage (Yong, 2001). We found them quite easily identifiable in Arabic English Interlanguage, which seems to justify the languages in contact hypothesis. The remaining four errors (pseudo-passives, ergative construction, tough movement and existential construction) were originally associated with the Chinese English Interlanguage (Yip, 1995), although they were subsequently found in the Indonesian part of the corpus as well (Dodigovic, 2002). We will now look into the likelihood of identifying these errors in the Arabic English Interlanguage.

Since the passives in Arabic are very similar to active forms (Smith, 2001), three of the above errors of passive form become likely: pseudo-passives, ergative construction and tough movement. Errors of the pseudo-passive type are reported by Smith (2001: 205): 'He hit by a stone', although the Chinese topicalisation that apparently causes them in CIL is reportedly not very productive in Arabic. However, the word order in Arabic is much more flexible than it is in English, which may allow for topicalisation as a partial cause of tough movement in Arabic-English interlanguage. Ergative construction is not mentioned in the cited literature. However, some limited errors of the type are also found in the mini-corpus ('. . . it will be happened . . .'). The students who produced this error were not able to explain the reason for their confusion very clearly. A possibility is that 'happen' is mistaken for a part of speech other than a verb. Thus, part of speech confusion may be responsible for this error in Arabic-English interlanguage, but there is no definite proof for this assumption. Tough movement is only found to a limited extent in the mini-corpus. However, Yip (1995: 162) reports that Arabic speakers experience difficulties with this structure because of the lack of tough movement in Arabic. Cooper *et al.* (1979 in Yip, 1995: 172) on the other hand note that there is some sort of tough movement counterpart in Arabic with passivised complement clause, but no mention is made as to whether pseudo-tough-movement is found in spontaneous English production.

Existential construction stands on its own and has no theoretical framework to support it in regard to Arabic-English interlanguage. By contrast, 'there is', which plays a major part in the existential construction, is reported to be a difficult structure for Arabic speakers (Smith, 2001). One occurrence of the redundant use of 'there is' is registered in the mini-corpus. We hypothesise that difficult constructions may be either under-used (avoidance) or misapplied, as is the case in the existential construction error (James, 1998).

So far, we have discussed the errors of the test case population mainly in terms of L1 transfer (James, 1998; Mitchell & Myles, 1998; Larsen-Freeman & Long, 1991) or the influence the first language has on the learners' interlanguage. It is however often argued that L1 transfer does not necessarily account for all of the learner errors (Corder, 1967; Ellis, 1985). In fact, research seems to suggest that only about one-third of all errors are traceable to L1 (Mitchell & Myles, 1998; AbiSamra, 2003). However, we will take these findings with a grain of salt and take a closer look at what are considered to be developmental or intralingual errors (James, 1998), in other words, errors not caused by L1 transfer. While intralingual errors seem to resemble the developmental errors in L1 (Larsen-Freeman & Long, 1991; Mitchell & Myles, 1998), one must bear in mind that a child learning its L1 and an adult learning an L2 bring into the learning process a completely different level of knowledge, skills and cognitive development. While their errors may on the surface seem similar, even identical, there is nothing to guarantee that they were made for precisely the same reasons. Let us, however, first examine some thoughts on intralingual errors.

Larsen-Freeman and Long (1991: 58–9) acknowledge four types of intralingual errors: overgeneralisation (Richards, 1971), simplification (George, 1972), communication-based errors (Selinker, 1972), and induced errors (Stenson, 1974). While learners overgeneralise when they fail to observe the boundaries of a rule, e.g. assuming that all verbs are regular (Richards, 1971), they simplify when they do away with some of the system redundancy in L2, e.g. omitting the ending –s in third person singular present tense verbs (George, 1972). Communication-based errors, on the other hand, entail incorrect language use, but successful communication (Larsen-Freeman & Long, 1991), whereas induced errors are often a result of a new language item introduced by the teacher but insufficiently explained in terms of contextual requirements (Stenson, 1974). James (1998) sees ignorance as the main cause of intralingual errors and identifies four broad sources: learning strategy (comprising overgeneralisation and simplification), communication strategies, induced errors and compound or ambiguous errors. The latter allow for a combination of sources or even inability to determine the true source of error (James, 1998). This is the first hint we get that it may not always be possible to identify a single source of each learner error. Given this uncertainty regarding the source of error, we may justifiably question the statistics of studies showing an overwhelming majority of intralingual errors.

The second hint comes from Yip (1995), who has an interesting take on some of the overgeneralisation errors. Thus she discusses over-generalisation in its intralingual context, but also introduces some evidence from which the reader can deduce that some of the overgeneralisation errors may be interlingual in type, i.e. caused by the native language inter-ference. An example of this is the CIL ergative construction (e.g. '*it will be happened'). The IL rule underlying this construction is that ergative verbs are transitive rather than intransitive, since they seem to require a patient (even though they do not necessarily have an agent). While Yip (1995) attempts to account for this error in terms of overgeneralisation within the IL system, she also quotes a study by Li (1990 in Yip, 1995), according to which there is a difference between English and Chinese ergative verbs. While Chinese ergative verbs allow for the NP (noun phrase) argument to be in either the subject or the object position (Li, 1990 in Yip, 1995), the English language only allows for the subject position. This may give rise to a compound error, in which an overgeneralisation of the Chinese object position of the NP accompanying an ergative verb allows for the interpreta-tion that ergative verbs are per default transitive verbs. This is then extended to English, since English verbs that allow for an object are per def-inition transitive. Hence, all English ergative verbs are treated as though they were transitive. Since no introspection data are available from Yip's (1995) study, it is hard to tell whether the source of ergative construction error is intralingual, interlingual or compound. We can further hypothesise the same about most error types discussed in Yip's (1995) and other studies where error sources had been determined without consulting introspection data. Thus, it may be premature to say that the majority of learner errors are indeed intralingual. Let us now return to the test case population and their respective errors.

While the typically Indonesian errors seem very likely to be found in Arabic-English Interlanguage, the CIL errors are found, but seemingly not very systematically. This is interesting, as Yip (1995) explains two out of the four typical CIL errors, ergative construction and tough movement, in terms of overgeneralisation, i.e. as potentially intralingual or develop-mental errors. In theory, such errors should be a part of learners' IL in general, regardless of their L1. In support of this theory, all four of Yip's (1995) CIL errors were also found in Indonesian English Interlanguage (Dodigovic, 2003b). The only way to establish whether the four CIL errors are a part of our test case population's interlanguage is to administer a grammaticality judgement test (Ellis, 1997). In this test, the takers have to judge the grammaticality of utterances. Their performance on this test is then taken to reflect their competence or command of these structures (Ellis, 1997; Yip, 1995). According to Ellis (1997), this kind of test is often associated with the universal grammar theory. Yip (1995: 8) argues that certain aspects of grammatical knowledge cannot be understood by mere analysis of production data. One of the reasons for this is frequent avoidance of difficult structures in NNS production (Yip, 1995: 5). An example of this is the avoidance of relative clauses in English by Chinese learners, which is the reason for a low count of errors in this area (Yip, 1995; 5–6).

While Cook (1993: 237–41) sees the benefits of the grammaticality judgement test as evidence of language competence, he pinpoints several concerns regarding its use. The first objection is that grammaticality judgement test is skewed toward the native speaker. The second one is that it is not clear to what extent this test measures competence rather than some kind of performance. The third one is that such tests are not stable or reliable, as L2 learners often perform differently on the same grammaticality judgement test. However, the latter seems to reflect the nature of learner interlanguages, which often allow for concurrent existence of the correct and the erroneous form (Yip, 1995; Ellis, 1997). Another, more general concern comes from the possibility that the elicitation task type might influence the type and frequency of errors (Larsen-Freeman & Long, 1991: 32). Larsen-Freeman & Long (1991: 32) however report on several studies that found no significant differences between the rate and type of errors elicited through different tasks. Thus, having found some plausible answers to the concerns raised, a grammaticality judgement test was indeed administered to the test case population to establish their familiarity with the seven typical errors found in the original EAP writing sample. According to a recommendation by Cook (1993: 241), this test also elicits and is combined with other types of error evidence. This is done for extra reliability, an instance of which is the mini-corpus error evidence available in this study. In the following the test itself will be described in more detail. A full version of the test is found in the Appendix.

Quasi-experiment

There were altogether 12 questions in the grammaticality judgement test, which was designed as a multiple choice test. Each question was very similar to those asked of the Intelligent Tutor users. Thus the students had to find one or more correct paraphrases of the initial statement in each question. This assured that in addition to grammaticality judgement, the students would have to select the correct answer based on comprehension and appropriateness, as suggested by Cook (1993: 241). The first question had to do with parts of speech confusion. There were two correct answers and five distracters. The second question had only one correct answer and one distracter and pertained to finite–non-finite verb distinction, as did the third and the seventh question. The fourth question targeted the existential construction, while the fifth question merely tested verb inflection. The sixth question was of lexical nature, while the eighth question tested subject verb agreement. The ninth question had the ergative construction as the target, while the tenth question pertained to tough movement. The eleventh and the twelfth question tested the comparison of adjectives and the inflection of nouns respectively. It has to be pointed out that in certain cases all of these structural problems can be recognised by the system. Some of them, e.g. the inflection of verbs and nouns as well as subject verb agreement, are found difficult by the speakers of Arabic in general (Smith, 2001; AbiSamra, 2003). Thus, a range of grammatical items were included in this test to take the focus of attention off the seven target structures. The rationale behind this was to prevent the students from noticing anything unusual about the seven error types or the procedure itself, in which case they are deemed to perform in an out of the ordinary fashion. This effect is called 'Hawthorne effect' (McDonough & McDonough, 1997: 166).

The results of the test demonstrated that four errors were consistently made by the test case students: tough movement (TM), part of speech confusion (PSC), finite–non-finite verb confusion (FNV) and ergative construction (ERC). It is not clear whether such grammatical misconceptions as tough movement and ergative construction had a pre-existence and were concealed by avoidance or whether they were test-induced (AbiSamra, 2003; James, 1998). While some evidence of pre-existence was found in the mini-corpus, the performance showed quite clearly that the students did not have a native-like intuition regarding those particular structures. A total of 53 errors (1.47 errors per student) were made: 19 TM, 12 PSC, 9 FNV and 13 ERC. Thus unexpectedly, the tough movement and the ergative construction became the strongest pronounced errors. Based on the combined findings of the contrastive analysis / error analysis and this grammaticality judgement test, it can be said that the test case sample is comparable to the original sample in the types and gravity of errors.

In two subsequent class sessions stretching over a period of a week, the students had an opportunity to work with the Intelligent Tutor in the first one and complete a post-test in the second one. This separation was introduced to avoid the effects of rote learning. The context in which the students were expected to work with the Intelligent Tutor was configured to resemble that of its intended use, as a medium used in the process of learning about an essay topic and taking the first steps toward writing the essay itself. Thus the students were given several texts on the topic of malaria, originally envisaged to be retrieved on-line. The texts were adjusted to match the students' slightly lower level of English proficiency (TOEFL 500–550 as opposed to TOEFL 550–580 or equivalent in the original population). The students worked in self-study mode, but were not prevented from consulting with their colleagues or the teacher. Other on-line resources originally envisaged for the on-line version of the EAP materials were not readily available in the same format, although the Blackboard materials for the particular General Education course these students attended contained ample references to such resources on the Web.

After having read the initial pre-reading activity questions, which encouraged the top-down approach to reading, the students were given the two simplified readings and asked to look for answers in the two short texts. The texts were naturally so designed that each answered a number of questions, complementing each other in informational value with partial overlaps. The students could then ponder again how they would answer the questions and would then receive the answer key to check their understanding of the readings. Although similar to the questions asked by the Intelligent Tutor, the pre-reading questions were different in wording and the elicited information. While these questions were analytical, in that they required one piece of information each, the Intelligent Tutor generated questions were synthetic, encouraging the students to return or evaluate several pieces of information in one answer. The questions were also designed to encourage summary and paraphrase rather than plagiarism, which is often found in NESB student writing (Ballard & Clanchy, 1984; Simmons & Thurstun, 1995).

After completing the reading activities, the students were asked to start the Intelligent Tutor and to work with the pilot lesson on malaria. At this stage, the quasi-experimental process was joined by another method of educational research, namely that of observation (McDonough & McDonough, 1997). Observation is often performed in CALL evaluation (Dam et al., 1991; Dodigovic, 1991; Higgins, 1995). A mixture of open-ended and structured observation was applied (McDonough & McDonough, 1997: 101). What is meant by open-ended is the chance to notice any data (i.e. not to exclude anything that seems significant because of a preordained scheme of observation). Systematic meant that some behaviours were consistently taken note of at regular intervals, i.e. the interaction of the students with the program, the interactions of the students with each other, the interactions of the students with the teacher. The teacher was the observer.

The process of working with the Intelligent Tutor was obviously not easy for the students, for which reason the teacher and fellow students had to be consulted for help. It seemed that the questions were at times unclear and that the system did not provide the user with sufficient instruction or help on how to proceed in certain situations. The often experienced frustration was that the student's error was identified as such, but since it was non-systemic, no hints were available as to how to correct it. No spell-check was available through the system, even though the students were encouraged to try out their sentences in MS Word first. Thus, incorrect spelling slowed down the process most of the time. However, all students completed the work with the tutor successfully.

In the final session, the students were given the post-test (found in Appendix 3) to complete. While the questions in the post-test were similar to those in the pre-test and much more so to those in the tutor, the method of answering was radically different to both. Not only did the students have to answer these questions without selecting a ready-made answer from a list of multiple choices, as was the case in the pre-test, but they were also free to choose any style or wording, needless to say without receiving any help or criticism from anyone, which was not the case when working with the tutor. The questions were nonetheless framed to induce the error if it was a part of the student's repertoire. Amazingly, this time the students produced only a total of 14 errors (0.38 errors per student): 5 TM, 5 PSC, 2 FNV and 2 ERC. Thus, the number of errors was slashed by over 70%, which proved statistically significant. The statistics are shown below. This means that it is unlikely that this event has occurred by chance (McDonough & McDonough, 1997; Mosteller *et al.*, 1983), and that it is highly likely (with 99% reliability) that it is related to the introduction of an independent variable, which in this case was the Intelligent Tutor.

Results

Table 6.5 shows the results of the pre-test and post-test as well as the values needed for the test statistics, which help establish whether, given the circumstances, the improvement in results is statistically significant. Statistical significance refers to the likelihood that the investigated event could have happened by chance (Mosteller *et al.*, 1983). If the reduction in the number of errors is statistically significant, this means that it is un-likely that the result is the product of mere chance. The procedure chosen was t-test, which is applicable to both small samples (30 or less) and large samples (Triola, 1997). Brown (1988) finds that this type of test statistic is most frequently found in language acquisition studies, while Triola (1997) calls it a traditional approach. Both of these statements contribute to the feeling that this is a very appropriate method. The formula shown below is specifically suited for two different measurements taken on the same population (Brown, 1988). It is thus called 'test statistic for matched pairs of sample data' (Triola, 1997: 450). It is used in its mathematically simplified format (Muzic, 1986: 566), which yields precisely the same re-sults as the more explicit and somewhat redundant formula cited in Triola (1997: 450).

Table 6.5 Pre-test

Subjects	TM	PSC	FNV	ERC	Total
S1	1		2		3
S2	1			1	2
S3					0
S4	1				1
S5	1				1
S6	1				1
S7	1		1		2
S8	1				1
S9	1				1
S10	1				1
S11		1	2	1	4
S12	1			1	2
S13				1	1
S14	1			1	2
S15		1			1
S16	1				1
S17					0
S18					0
S19	1			1	2
S20					0
S21	1				1
S22	1				1
S23	2	1			3
S24	1				1
S25	1		3	1	5
S26	1			1	2
S27	1				1
S28					0
S29			1		1
S30		1			1
S31			1	1	2
S32		1			1
S33		1			1
S34					0

Table 6.5 (*cont.*) Pre-test

Subjects	TM	PSC	FNV	ERC	Total
S35	1				1
S36			1	1	2
S37					0
S38	1	1			2
S39	1	1			2
S40		1		1	2
S41	1	1		1	3
S42		1	2	1	4
S43	1	1		1	3
S44	1		1		2
S45					0
S46	1	1		1	3
S47					0
Total	28	13	14	15	70

Table 6.6 Post-test results

Subjects	TM	PSC	FNV	ERC	Total
S1					0
S2					0
S3					0
S4					0
S5					0
S6					0
S7					0
S8					0
S9					0
S10					0
S11			1		1
S12					0
S13					0
S14					0
S15	1				1
S16			1		1

Table 6.6 (*cont.*) Post-test results

Subjects	TM	PSC	FNV	ERC	Total
S17		1			1
S18					0
S19					0
S20					0
S21					0
S22		1		1	2
S23					0
S24		1			1
S25					0
S26					0
S27					0
S28					0
S29	1				1
S30					0
S31					0
S32					0
S33					0
S34					0
S35					0
S36					0
S37					0
S38					0
S39	1				1
S40			1		1
S41	1			1	2
S42					0
S43	1	1			2
S44		1			1
S45					0
S46					0
S47					0
Total	5	5	3	2	15

The t-test formula used is found below:

$$t = \frac{\left|\overline{dX}\right|}{\sqrt{\dfrac{n\sum D^2 - \left(\sum D\right)^2}{n^2(n-1)}}}$$

The meanings of the symbols in the formula are as follows:

$\overline{dX}$ = Difference between the arithmetic means of the two sets of results.
$\sum D^2$ = Sum of squares of differences between individual results on the two tests.
$\sum D$ = Sum of differences between individual results on the two tests.
n = Number of subjects in the study.

Table 6.7 Comparison between pre-test and post-test data

Subject	Pre-test	Post-test	x_1-x_2	$(x_1-x_2)^2$
S1	3	0	3	9
S2	2	0	2	4
S3	0	0	0	0
S4	1	0	1	1
S5	1	0	1	1
S6	1	0	1	1
S7	2	0	2	4
S8	1	0	1	1
S9	1	0	1	1
S10	1	0	1	1
S11	4	1	3	9
S12	2	0	2	4
S13	1	0	1	1
S14	2	0	2	4
S15	1	1	0	0
S16	1	1	0	0
S17	0	1	−1	1
S18	0	0	0	0
S19	2	0	2	4
S20	0	0	0	0
S21	1	0	1	1
S22	1	2	−1	1
S23	3	0	3	9

Subject	Pre-test	Post-test	x_1-x_2	$(x_1-x_2)^2$
S24	1	1	0	0
S25	5	0	5	25
S26	2	0	2	4
S27	1	0	1	1
S28	0	0	0	0
S29	1	1	0	0
S30	1	0	1	1
S31	2	0	2	4
S32	1	0	1	1
S33	1	0	1	1
S34	0	0	0	0
S35	1	0	1	1
S36	2	0	2	4
S37	0	0	0	0
S38	2	0	2	4
S39	2	1	1	1
S40	2	1	1	1
S41	3	2	1	1
S42	4	0	4	16
S43	3	2	1	1
S44	2	1	1	1
S45	0	0	0	0
S46	3	0	3	9
S47	0	0	0	0
Σ	70	15	55	133
$\overline{dX}$	1.489362	0.319149		
σ	1.16459	0.587327		

Table 6.8 Values for the equation

$\overline{dX}$	1.170213
n	47
Σd^2	133
$(\Sigma d)^2$	3025
t	6.567641

$$t = \frac{1.170213}{\sqrt{\dfrac{47 \cdot 133 - 3025}{2209(47 - 1)}}} = 6.567641$$

The value for t was then located in the relevant table. As the sample is larger than 30, z-distribution table, normally associated with larger samples, was used for this purpose. This is the only option, as the t-distribution table normally holds critical scores for up to 30 subjects (or degrees of freedom), which is why sources on test statistics (Triola, 1997; Mosteller *et al.*, 1983) refer to z-distribution table for the evaluation of statistical significance. As the t-score exceeds the largest value in the z column of the table (3.10), the relevant area (0.4999) by far exceeds the critical value for the degree of confidence of 99% (2.575). Thus the results show that there is not only a huge difference in raw scores between the pre-test and post-test, but that the results are positively statistically significant with the highest degree of confidence.

Discussion

To play the devil's advocate, it could be said that the results are too good to be true. We will therefore examine the possible pitfalls in this case study and decide together to what extent they may be responsible for the result. Doubt could be raised of course as to whether the errors were simply avoided in the post-test, which was open-ended, by choosing alternative grammatical structures. This has however not been the case. The students attempted the same structures they were struggling with in the previous two sessions, the pre-test and the Intelligent Tutor one, this time with a much higher rate of success. Another probable pitfall is the possibility that the students might have memorised whole sentences while working with the pre-test or the Intelligent Tutor. Their post-test responses were however mostly creative and different in many ways from the example sentences presented by the pre-test and the Intelligent Tutor. Finally, the likelihood that the students copied from each other was small, as the answers differed substantially from student to student. Thus, the results seem to suggest genuine improvement in grammar.

Several other factors might have contributed to the extraordinary improvement in grammar recorded in this study. The first one is called 'Hawthorne effect' (McDonough & McDonough, 1997: 166) and was mentioned in a previous section of this chapter. This refers to a substantial improvement in student performance under study conditions due to their noticing the uniqueness of the circumstances. While the quasi-experimental procedure was introduced in a fairly low-key manner and the target errors were mixed with a few other inflection errors to conceal their significance, it is still possible that the students might have sensed something out of the ordinary about it. Since the entire procedure was conducted by the author of this book, who is also the author of the software used in the treatment, it is of course possible that her enthusiasm contributed to the success of her students. Finally, the pre-test itself might have contributed to learning as well, thus enhancing the effect of the treatment. For instance, Ellis (1997: 161) reports that some tasks can significantly raise the learners' consciousness concerning some linguistic property of the target language. Judgement of well-formed vs. deviant linguistic data, or in other words our grammaticality judgement test, is precisely such a task that could help a learner arrive at an explicit understanding of the linguistic item in question. However, no studies come to mind where the extraordinary success of treatment was totally unrelated to the treatment itself. Replicating the study in different environments may shed some more light on this.

Another fact that needs to be clarified is that the Intelligent Tutor was not compared to any other method or resource, as is usually the case in an experiment proper (McDonough & McDonough, 1997; Mosteller *et al.*, 1983; Larsen-Freeman and Long, 1991), where under strictly controlled conditions one kind of treatment is compared either to another kind of treatment or to the absence of treatment. In our wish to avoid comparing radically different categories with one another, such as the textbook and the computer, an incompatibility criticised in CALL literature (MacWhinney, 1995; Goodfellow, 1999), we have not sought to prove that the Intelligent Tutor is better than the textbook or a teacher or indeed any other incompatible resource. We have simply demonstrated that the Intelligent Tutor is the most likely cause of a considerable improvement in learning outcomes and that it hence most probably achieves its purpose of eradicating some of the typical errors in a certain type of student population. This means that it can be successfully used either in class, or with some interface improvement in self-study mode. It could therefore be said that the quasi-summative evaluation has been successful and the program has demonstrated effectiveness in terms of more immediate learning outcomes and learner fit.

Improvement in interface design and the addition of grammatical knowledge would of course positively change the affective effect the program has on learners. Because of its important implications for the affective factors, the new and improved interface design itself needs to be based on a systematic study of feedback, the students' reaction to it and its effectiveness. McDonough and McDonough (1997) report that this is one of the areas where introspection as a method would make much sense, but has been hardly used. Thus the next step would include giving students different types of feedback and asking for either a think-aloud protocol or a retrospective statement regarding how they made sense of the feedback. The feedback induced success could then be correlated to the affective and cognitive reactions toward the feedback style and content. More testing of course in the context for which the program was designed, including the learner's first language, the culture, the language of everyday interactions and the overall learning environment would constitute the next step toward summative evaluation. The learning environment in this case would be defined by the availability of the rest of the Web Tutor, including the readings on-line, the lessons on academic writing techniques as well as the dictionaries, spell checkers and grammar glossaries, all of which were not available to the test case population as one meaningful on-line whole. Finally, retention should definitely be one of the traced variables. Overall, however, the future of this particular development can be faced with optimism due to the promise that this study holds.

Conclusion

In this chapter we have described the evaluation of the Intelligent Tutor. The procedure has included formative evaluation and some methods and elements of summative evaluation, even though summative evaluation is typically conducted at the completion of a development project, whereas our project was notably far from completed. Given, however, the fact that there usually are quite unique circumstances accompanying most ICALL development projects (Holland, 1995), it is not unusual to have such projects evaluated at an inconvenient point in time. A similar situation, although not quite to the same extent, is reported in Holland *et al.* (1993). This chapter recognises that it is a little premature to talk about the 'summative evaluation' of the Intelligent Tutor and therefore calls the equivalent procedure 'in lieu of summative evaluation'.

Although CALL software evaluation is a complex affair due to the complex nature of the software itself and the many different variables that mutually influence each other in the process of development, two main approaches could be isolated. The first arises from its computational nature and is called quality assurance. In this respect, testing for internal and external integrity, i.e. the integrity of the development process and product was conducted in accordance with that requirement with satisfactory results. The second approach has to do with the educational value of the program. For this purpose, the Intelligent Tutor was reviewed by teachers and verbally reported on by students. While the teachers were positive, the students were confused by the interface. The Tutor was then introduced to a group of learners similar to the original population. While the effect of its interface was still confusing, the learning outcomes of the program were met with statistical significance. Thus the Intelligent Tutor met its pedagogical objectives, although its interface was found in need of improvement.

The cyclic nature of software development was reflected in the cyclic nature of research, conducted with mixed methods and sometimes generating questions, such as in participant observation and verbal reporting, other times answering them, as in the quasi-experiment. Contrastive analysis and error analysis were used in the approximation of the confounding variables of the quasi-experiment while literature research and publication of project segments were used in support of overall evaluation. In addition, a questionnaire was disseminated to investigate the learning styles of the test case sample. The many layers and considerations hopefully demonstrate the complexity of ICALL software development and evaluation.

Conclusion

Do your overseas students cry their hearts out over an insensitive remark made by their lecturers concerning their L2 errors, as did the student I briefly introduced to you at the beginning of this book? If they do, or worse, if this kind of reality becomes too harsh for them to accept, just as it was for the second student from my introductory example, hold on to your hope – because there is a new kind of remedy designed to help in situations such as these. The remedy is called artificial intelligence.

Learner errors can be successfully addressed and corrected by intelligent CALL programs. This book has taken us through a series of steps required to prove that the above statement is both true and valid. We started by describing the problem of a population of non-English speaking background students studying at an English speaking university in an English speaking country. Their lecturers required better accuracy in their students' writing and the students themselves were painfully aware of the fact that they did commit errors in English. We gave our learner population a profile by describing an Indonesian and a Chinese student, Eric and Jean respectively. Students such as Eric and Jean participated in the needs analysis and evaluation of the Intelligent Tutor of Academic English on the Web this book has set out to describe.

The discussion in this volume moved from querying the SLA theory and the existing body of SLA research about the learnability of a second language. Having concluded that adult L2 learners have a fair chance of eradicating their L2 errors with raised awareness and practice, we set out to develop an intelligent learning aid for our EAP students. We started by examining the theoretical approaches to CALL and the role of research in the development cycle. We than elaborated on the two key technologies selected for this development: the Web and artificial intelligence. Subsequently, we described the needs analysis preceding the development and the development process itself. Finally, we engaged in evaluation, which convincingly supports the hypothesis that an intelligent error correction oriented CALL program can be of significant help to learners such as Eric and Jean.

When faced with the perceived need to identify the most important aspect of Computer Assisted Language Learning (CALL) and the development of CALL programs, most CALL theorists will zoom in on either SLA theory or the power of the modern technology (Levy, 1997a). Some authors, on the other hand, identify the learner as the mandatory main point of departure in the design of CALL programs (Decoo, 1993; Decoo & Colpaert, 1999b). While one would agree with the concerns some authors (Chapelle *et al.*, 1996; Salaberry, 1996, Chapelle, 1997, Salaberry, 1999) have in regard to purely technology driven CALL (Levy, 1997a), one could be equally sceptical about purely SLA theory driven CALL. Thus Armitage and Bowerman (2002) argue that pedagogy as the driving force behind CALL software development may lead to simple transfer of classroom practices to the digital medium, without recognising and utilising the full potential of the technology in a particular area of learning.

Whereas purely technology driven design invites the risk of leaving both the learner and the theory far behind, the latter may turn CALL into a sheer vehicle for testing SLA theories, while potentially neglecting the needs of real-life students. It could also neglect to provide the link between what the students need and what the technology can supply, which would be truly regrettable. To accommodate all the listed caveats, it would be fair to say that CALL program development, just like any curricular development, should rest first and foremost on an analysis of student needs (Doughty & Long, 2003). This analysis should be informed by the knowledge of what the state of the art technology is capable of doing for the student. It should also be rooted in SLA theories, while being allowed to take an eclectic approach, the one that is often taken in successful classroom practice (Harmer, 1998).

Doughty and Long (2003) point out the importance of needs and means analysis in course development, in particular concerning the technology mediated distance learning. Davis *et al.* (1992) make the link between the general good practices of software development and needs analysis, saying that the user (learner) should be involved at every step of the way, which is echoed by Decoo (1993). Similarly, in her design considerations for a multimedia development project Liou (1994) stresses the importance of knowing the media, the institutional needs or constraints, which includes the learners, and finally the design principles, which include the knowledge of teaching and learning. Thus, even a superficial analysis of CALL literature in the last decade or so reveals a concern for and an awareness of the three main factors to be considered in CALL development projects: the learner, the technology and the language learning theory. It is therefore not quite fair to say that CALL has avoided the SLA theory issues (Chapelle *et al.*, 1996). The only thing it has not turned into is a vehicle for pure SLA theory testing, even though it has been found guilty of focusing on one of the three main factors rather than all three.

This book presents at one level the research and development work invested in the Intelligent Tutor of Academic English. As discussed in

Chapter 2 of this volume, both the phase of needs analysis and that of software evaluation in the resource development cycle present opportunities for research. In Chapter 5 we focused on pre-developmental research and the resulting development effort. We argued that needs analysis can provide the crucial pieces of information needed to put together the jig-saw puzzle of effective CALL software. We then described the steps taken to obtain the information about the learners and the subject required for the development. Since academic language in some of its aspects is the subject the Intelligent Tutor is supposed to teach, its nature was critically examined. Special emphasis was placed on sentence in this context, partly due to the propositional nature of academic language and partly because according to Halliday (1985) it is a true unit of written language, sharply distinguishing writing from speech. Both in this chapter as well as in Chapter 1, we seriously looked at language itself and divided linguistic and acquisitional theories according to where they see the ownership of language: outside an individual, inside an individual or within a social group. We have discovered not only that SLA theories differ greatly among themselves, but also that they may be designed for different types of learners altogether.

We then examined the features of what is supposed to be the L2 learners' academic English, again with the focus on sentential and subsentential level. The reason for the latter is firstly the general sentential orientation and secondly the nature of errors frequently made by the students and reacted to by their lecturers. We found that there were a number of differences, making the students' academic prose more similar to speech patterns in terms of sentence development and verb use. Thus the model of student interlanguage slowly emerged through theoretical and practical research and was translated into a computer language to build the much needed electronic learning aid. Thus interlanguage and learner errors were SLA concepts that we strongly exploited in this book.

For all the above reasons, pre-developmental research is crucial to successful CALL development. In this particular context it is known as needs analysis. However, this is not where the marriage between research and development in CALL ends. To the contrary, good CALL evaluation practice will also include research. Thus, research is a *sine qua non* of every successful CALL program, in other words a program that delivers on what it sets out to do, in ways which are both linguistically and pedagogically sound. In this book, the program under construction, called the Intelligent Tutor, was evaluated using both qualitative and quantitative or interventionist and non-interventionist methods. Much care was devoted to the approximation of the confounding variables in a quasi-experimental procedure and non-parametric statistics were used to test the significance of the results, which confirmed the usefulness of the Tutor to the intended or similar audience. The following paragraph gives some of the reasons for the Tutor's success.

Since language errors mostly result from ignorance (James, 1998), language learners need to engage in what they are promised would take place in their language classes, and that is language learning. In the first chapter of this book we have deliberated on the kind of instruction that learner errors call for and have come to the conclusion that explicit instruction or correction is the right answer (James, 1998; Ellis, 1997). In light of this explicitness in instruction, one can only assume that any knowledge resulting from such instruction would by default be explicit (Ellis, 1997). In fact, McLauglin *et al.* (1983) as well as Anderson (1983) argue that all knowledge is initially declarative or controlled, in other words explicit, and then gradually, through repeated practice becomes procedural or automated, in other words implicit. This is well in accord with the cognitive approach in psychology, which stipulates that insight or understanding is the way living organisms learn (Bigge & Shermis, 1999). Be that as it may, the eradication of language errors is a matter of language accuracy, which is deemed to be a result of conscious learning (Ellis, 1997).

If explicit knowledge is what we expect from the process of error correction, then any learning conducive to this can only happen with the increase of language awareness and consciousness. Intelligent computers are ideally suited to the task of raising the language awareness of students, who vary in terms of learning needs and habits. Such computers, by virtue of being machines, can similarly allow for tireless practice required for the retention of new knowledge (N. Ellis, 2001). Indeed, as far as the correction of learner errors is concerned, a course of action eagerly expected by a large body of adult learners (Willing, 1988), artificially intelligent computer programs do have definite advantages over other means of instruction. They are constantly available, analytically insightful, adaptable to different users and do not require even a wink of sleep.

Even though artificial intelligence as such is not yet at the point of covering the whole language, this does not mean that it cannot successfully address its parts, especially those that learners seem to have the most problems with. This book has to a large extent been devoted to one such program.

Our Intelligent Tutor has taken several years to research and complete, as it was required to be proficient in both standard academic English and the students' interlanguages, English-Chinese and English-Indonesian. When it was finally first piloted, it proved far less then perfect. And a bit of a Quasimodo he was, an intelligent mind trapped in a somewhat malformed user interface. Or perhaps the metaphor of the ugly duckling provides a better fit, because it gives hope, the hope that our unseemly tutorling will some day learn to fly and rise to the realm to which at present only our imagination can take it.

The book has in addition addressed very broad issues closely related to the Intelligent Tutor. These issues are the learnability of L2, the purpose of research in CALL development projects, the attraction the Web holds for L2 learners and the ways in which artificial intelligence can address learner errors. In respect of L2 learnability, this book very strongly supports the view expressed in some of the previously published research that it is never too late for a learner to make further L2 progress. It is also assumed that adult L2 learners are very different to infant L1 learners and should therefore be approached in a way that capitalises on their experiential and cognitive resources while minimising the effect of aging on their information processing systems. Intelligent tutors seem to be an excellent device to deliver just that.

In order to achieve the perfect fit between a learner and an intelligent tutor, much analysis research is needed. To evaluate the fit, more research is needed, which will this time be effect oriented or post-developmental. Hopefully this book has demonstrated very clearly and by example what is meant by either. It has also attempted to place the tutor in an environment designed to be optimally accessible to the learner. This kind of environment was deemed to be found on the Web, partly because of its trialability and partly because of its conformance with the current beliefs and practices of the SLA circles.

In conclusion, this book does not advocate the artificial intelligence technologies for their own sake. It does so carefully balancing out what we know about learners in general, especially about the target learner population, about the learning environment and about the development process itself. The Intelligent Tutor whose development and evaluation is described here is intended to exemplify the CALL development practice in its most comprehensive approach, the one that will hopefully find resonance with the reader, should he or she wish to embark on a similar journey of discovery.

Appendices

(1) Test Case Sentences

[Malaria causes a die.]*
[Malaria cause death.]*
[Malaria caused death.]
[Malaria caused a die.]*
[Malaria causes die.]*
[Malaria causes people to die.]
[Malaria caused a death.]
[It will caused death of both mother and baby.] *
[It will cause the death of both mother and baby.]
[Malaria has not yet been eradicate.]*
[Malaria has not yet been eradicated.]
[Malaria has not been eradicate yet .]*
[Malaria has not been eradicated yet .]
[There is a new problem occur.]*
[There is a new problem.]
[A new problem has occurred.]
[International travel makes (airport) malaria difficult to control.]
[International travels makes (airport) malaria difficult to control.]*
[International travel make (airport) malaria difficult to control.]*
[Undeveloping countries are severely affected.]*
[Undeveloped countries are severely affected.]
[Developing countries are severely affected.]
[Increasing risk of the disease is link with the changes in human activities.]*
[The increasing risk of the disease is linked with the changes in human activities.]
[Mosquito is the vector of malaria.]
[Mosquitos is the vector of malaria.]*
[The immune system can be failed.]*
[The immune system can fail.]
[Parasite is easy to become resistant.]*
[It is easy for the parasite is to become resistant.]
[The parasite can easily become resistant.]
[It is more hard.]*

[It is harder.]
[Malaria is one of the most dangerous disease.]*
[Malaria is one of the most dangerous diseases.]

(2)   Intelligent Tutor of Academic English: Software Review 1

I have seen a presentation of the Intelligent Tutor of Academic English by Marina Dodigovic and have found the idea novel and quite exciting. In my career as an English teacher, instructional designer and language software developer, I have seen and created a number of computer programs to teach languages. Many of these were technically quite sophisticated and made use of the leading edge technology: however, I have not yet seen an application using what we know about student errors to evaluate free style input the way Marina's software does. This, of course needs to be the overall objective of evaluating language competency.

The foundation of this program seems to be quite substantial research into student interlanguage and error analysis. Such research is frequently omitted in educational software development, leading to results which are poorer than they could be if time were taken to investigate. Gathering, analysing and evaluating data in the light of recent literature in the field, as it was conducted in this case, is a remarkable piece of research in itself. In particular it guarantees high standards in implementation.

The parser has two different grammars: the ideal or the 'correct grammar' which is used to evaluate student input and the erroneous grammar which the students seem to follow consistently. The latter is used to correct errors and clarify grammar patterns. Both grammars are described in surprising detail, thus providing a sophisticated and highly sensitive parsing device. Especially the correct grammar is capable of very fine distinction using a number of features such as parts of speech, inflection, morphology and syntax with a number of varying sentence patterns.

The computer language used in the parser application is PROLOG, the language of artificial intelligence. I understand that until recently it presented a considerable challenge to integrate PROLOG files into an HTML environment. Marina seems to have found an answer to this challenge, thus avoiding a costly and cumbersome procedure of translating the software into another computer language, which might work well in a HTML environment, but may not necessarily be ideal for processing natural language.

I believe that the pedagogy behind the program is right. In particular, the parser presents prompts, thus creating sufficient linguistic context to elicit the most typical errors in student response and correct them, while at the same time giving the user the freedom of linguistic choice. The prompts also serve the purpose of delimiting the scope of the parser, keeping the conversation bound to a topic. This is extremely important in educational software, which as a rule focuses on a particular level and register.

I also am convinced that the use of the program will develop the learners' metacognition relating to common errors and increase the efficiency of language learning.

I am convinced that this program will become a real asset in academic and general English at Macquarie University. A user friendly design paired with an excellent response to student needs will make it a tool likely to be used with preference for both research and practical applications. Finally, I applaud the developer for her innovative ideas, diligent work and perseverance in the midst of changing technology.

(3)   Intelligent Tutor of Academic English: Software Review 2

Intelligent Tutor of Academic English is a combination of software tools to be available on the Web, even if to a limited audience. I will focus on the most interactive part of the suite – a program called 'Dialogue' which converses with the learner using a parser (a device for natural language processing). The program functions in the following way: the learner is asked questions about an essay topic. The answers expected are in the form of freely structured sentences. The parser analyses the student input and either accepts it as correct or it comments on the type of error made (hints can be given as to how to correct the sentence).

It must be said that the application of NLP technology in computer assisted language learning (CALL) is at a pioneering stage worldwide. Any efforts in this area are to be regarded as important steps in advancing CALL and taking language learning in general to the next level. I believe the same can be said about Dialogue.

It might be of interest to mention that parsers developed in linguistics laboratories with considerable support in terms of funding, personnel and equipment are usually capable of dealing with correct grammar only. In order to be able to classify and correct student errors, Dialogue relies on two separate grammars: a correct grammar of English and a grammar model that the learner is likely to follow. The former acknowledges correct input while the latter classifies and corrects errors. This valuable addition to a conventional parser has been developed using extensive research data collected from a representative student sample. Thus it can be said that Dialogue, while being highly flexible and interactive is at the same time tailored to the specific needs of the student population at whom it is targeted.

Another feature of Dialogue deserves mention – in order to be manageable a parser has to have a limited vocabulary bank. In Dialogue this has been successfully achieved by setting limits in terms of a conversation topic. While each question prompts the user to produce a sentence in which he or she is likely to make typical mistakes, the whole framework of questions provides a possible structure for an essay on the topic. Thus the learner is practising two skills at a time, writing at both sentence and text level - which seems to correspond very well with the desired learning outcomes of the program.

The screen design (Web interface) is simple and user friendly. This is a good quality suite of software with a substantial innovative component based on language processing technology. Such software is really needed in both language and literacy learning and one can only hope that more developers will turn to producing this sort of tool.

Student response 1

Hi Marina

I have been to the website and attempted some of the questions.

It is quite useful as all the topics link with our reading. Some little improvement could be made though. Wouldn't it be more clear if all the questions are Multiple-choice instead of making sentence ourselves. It might be too difficult for a computer to judge student's own sentence I think. Actually, I tried several times and could hardly get the right answer <?_? >

That's my personal view and if you've got any other problems, please don't hesitate to contact me.

Merry Christmas

Xxxx

Student response 2

Marina

I found it very frustrating as it kept on coming back with 'your answer is not parseable', no hints and wouldn't let me get on. The question about malaria is ambiguous, not sure if the question is asking about the symptoms of malaria or what.

Xxxx

Pre-test

Which of the sentences below each question are correct answers to the question? There may be one or more correct answers per question. Tick or encircle the correct answer(s).

1. Malaria can be a terminal disease. What does malaria cause?

    [Answers]

    a. [Malaria causes a die.]
    b. [Malaria cause death.]
    c. [Malaria caused death.]
    d. [Malaria caused a die.]
    e. [Malaria causes die.]
    f. [Malaria causes people to die.]
    g. [Malaria caused a death.]

2. A pregnant woman carries two lives: the baby's and her own. What happens when a pregnant woman gets infected?

    [Answers]

    a. [It will caused death of both mother and baby.]
    b. [It will cause the death of both mother and baby.]

3. For a number of reasons it has been very difficult to eradicate malaria. What is the current state of its eradication?

    [Answers]

    a. [Malaria has not yet been eradicate.]
    b. [Malaria has not yet been eradicated.]
    c. [Malaria has not been eradicate yet.]
    d. [Malaria has not been eradicated yet.]

4. One of the reasons why malaria is so difficult to control is the constant occurrence of new factors. How would you introduce the occurrence of a new problem, in e.g. your essay?

    [Answers]

    a. [There is a new problem occur.]
    b. [There is a new problem.]
    c. [A new problem has occurred.]

5. Airport malaria has become frequent in recent times. What factor makes it difficult to control?

    [Answers]

    a. [International travel makes (airport) malaria difficult to control.]
    b. [International travels makes (airport) malaria difficult to control.]
    c. [International travel make (airport) malaria difficult to control.]

6. Malaria affects many countries, but not so much the developed ones. Which countries are severely affected?

    [Answers]

a. [Undeveloping countries are severely affected.]
b. [Undeveloped countries are severely affected.]
c. [Developing countries are severely affected.]

7. As people change their lifestyles, there is more and more risk of malaria. What is linked with the change in human activities?

    [Answers]

a. [Increasing risk of the disease is link with the changes in human activities.]
b. [The increasing risk of the disease is linked with the changes in human activities.]

8. Diseases like malaria get transmitted by a vector. Which insect is the vector of malaria?

    [Answers]

a. [Mosquito is the vector of malaria.]
b. [Mosquitos is the vector of malaria.]

9. Can the human immune system efficiently stop malaria? Use a form of 'fail' in your answer.

    [Answers]

a. [The immune system can be failed.]
b. [The immune system can fail.]

10. Drugs and vaccines do not work because of the resistance of the malaria parasite. Paraphrase this in a sentence using appropriate forms of the following words: 'parasite', 'easy/easily', 'become', 'resistant'.

    [Answers]

a. [Parasite is easy to become resistant.]
b. [It is easy for the parasite to become resistant.]
c. [The parasite can easily become resistant.]

11. Obviously, more research into malaria is needed, so the researchers will have to increase their efforts. What is the work of the researchers like because of that? In your answer use a form of the word 'hard'.

    [Answers]

a. [It is more hard.]
b. [It is harder.]

12. With all this in mind, would you say that malaria is the most dangerous disease in the world? Use 'one' in your answer.

[Answers]

a. [Malaria is one of the most dangerous disease.]
b. [Malaria is one of the most dangerous diseases.]

Post-test

Write your answer below each question:

1. Malaria is sometimes a terminal disease. What does malaria cause?

_____

2. A woman who is pregnant is more at risk from malaria than a woman who is not pregnant. This is because two lives are involved: that of the woman and that of the baby. What happens when a pregnant woman gets infected?

_____

3. It is very difficult to eradicate malaria. What is the current state of its eradication?

_____

4. Malaria is so difficult to control because of the constant occurrence of new factors. How would you introduce the occurrence of a new problem, in e.g. your essay?

_____

5. Airport malaria is becoming more and more common. What factor makes it difficult to control?

_____

6. As people change their lifestyles, they are more at risk of malaria. What is linked with the change in human activities?

_____

7. Malaria is transmitted by an insect serving as a vector. Which insect is the vector of malaria?

_____

8. Can the human immune system prevent malaria? Use a form of 'fail' in your answer.

_____

9. The resistance of the malaria parasite counters the effects of drugs and vaccines. Paraphrase this in a sentence using appropriate forms of the following words: 'parasite', 'easy/easily', 'become', 'resistant'.

---

10. Malaria researchers will have to increase their efforts. What is the work of the researchers like because of that? In your answer use a form of the word 'hard'.

---

11. Is malaria the most dangerous disease in the world? Are there other diseases that are similarly dangerous? Use 'one' in your answer.

Bibliography

AbiSamra, N. (2003) *An Analysis of Errors in Arabic Speakers' English Writings.* (http://abisamra03.tripod.com/nada/languageacq-erroranalysis.html, 10 March 2003).

Allan, M. (1999) Language awareness and the support role of technology. In R. Debski and M. Levy (eds) *WORLDCALL. Global Perspectives on Computer-Assisted Language Learning* (pp. 303–18). Lisse: Swets & Zeitlinger.

Allen, J. (1995) *Natural Language Understanding.* Redwood City: Benjamin/Cummings.

Allen, J.R. and Periyasamy, K. (1997) Software engineering principles applied to Computer Assisted Language Learning. *CALICO Journal* 14 (2–4), 35–50.

Altieri Biagi, M.L. (1999) A diachronic view of the languages of science. In R.R. Favretti, G. Sandri and R. Scazzieri (eds) *Incommensurability and Translation* (pp. 39–52). Cheltenham: Edward Elgar.

Anderson, J.R. (1983) *The Architecture of Cognition.* Cambridge, MA: Harvard University Press.

Anderson, J. (1988) Cognitive styles and multicultural populations. *Journal of Teacher Education* 39, 2–9.

Arcaini, E. (1999) Linguistics, hermeneutics and analysis of scientific discourse. In R.R. Favretti, G. Sandri and R. Scazzieri (eds) *Incommensurability and Translation* (pp. 117–30). Cheltenham: Edward Elgar.

Armitage, N. and Bowerman, C. (2002) Knowledge pooling in CALL: Programming an online language learning system for reusability, maintainability and extensibility. *CALL Journal* 15 (1), 27–54.

Asdjodi, M. (2001) A comparison between *ta'arof* in Persian and *limao* in Chinese. *International Journal of the Sociology of Language* (148), 71–92.

Bachman, L.F. and Palmer, A.S. (1996) *Language Testing in Practice.* Oxford: Oxford University Press.

Bailin, A. (1995) AI and language learning: Theory and evaluation. In V.M. Holland, J.D. Kaplan and M.R. Sams (eds) *Intelligent Language Tutors* (pp. 327–44). Mahwah: Lawrence Erlbaum.

Ballard, B. and Clanchy, J. (1984) *Study Abroad: A Manual for Asian Students.* Kuala Lumpur: Longman.

Barker, P. (1993). *Exploring Hypermedia.* London: Kogan.

Bedell, D.A. and Oxford, L.R. (1996) Cross-cultural comparisons of language learning strategies in the People's Republic of China and other countries. In L.R. Oxford (ed.) *Language Learning Strategies around the World: Cross-Cultural Perspectives* (pp. 47–60). Honolulu: University of Hawaii Press.

Beebe, L. (1983) Risk-taking and the language learner. In H. Seliger and M. Long (eds) *Classroom-Oriented Research in Second Language Acquisition* (pp. 39–66). Rowley: Newbury House.

Benesch, S. (2001) Critical pragmatism: A politics of L2 composition. In T. Silva and P. K. Matsuda (eds) *On Second Language Writing* (pp. 161–72). Mahwah: Lawrence Erlbaum.

Bereiter, C. and Scardamalia, M. (1987) *The Psychology of Written Composition*. Hillsdale, NJ: Lawrence Erlbaum.

Berkenkotter, C. and Huckin, T. (1995) *Genre Knowledge in Disciplinary Communication*. Hillsdale, NJ: Lawrence Erlbaum.

Bernstein, J., Najmi, A. and Ehsani, F. (1999) Subarashii: Encounters in Japanese spoken language education. *CALICO Journal* 16 (3), 261–384.

Bigge, M.L. and Shermis, S.S. (1999) *Learning Theories for Teachers*. New York: Longman.

Blin, O. (1999) E-mail and the students, the social price of access to innovation. In K. Cameron (ed.) *CALL & The Learning Community* (pp. 15–22). Exeter: Elm Bank Publications.

Bloomfield, L. (1933) *Language*. New York: Holt, Reinhart & Winston.

Bolt, P. (1993) Grammar checking programs for learners of English as a foreign language. In M. Yazdani (ed.) *Multilingual Media* (pp. 140–97). Oxford: Intelect Books.

Borchardt, F. (1998a) On the history and aesthetics of screen design (or why do most screens put learners to sleep?). In K. Cameron (ed.) *Multimedia CALL: Theory and Practice* (pp. 3–10). Exeter: Elm Bank Publications.

Borchardt, F. (1998b) For, against, for the development and dissemination of CALL. In J. Nerbonne, S. Jager and A. van Essen (eds) *Language Teaching & Language Technology* (pp. 218–25). Lisse: Swets & Zeitlinger.

Borchardt, F.L. and Page, E.B. (1994) Let computers use the past to predict the future. Language Aptitude Invitational Symposium.

Borin, L. (2002) Where will the standards for intelligent Computer-Assisted Language Learning come from?, *LREC 2002*. Workshop Proceedings. *International Standards of Terminology and Language Resources Management* (pp. 61–8). Las Palmas: ELRA.

Boyle, A. and Booth, D. (2000) *The UCLES/CUP Learner Corpus, Research Notes* (pp. 10–12). Cambridge: University of Cambridge.

Boyle, R. (n.d.) Hidden Markov Models. (http://www.comp.leeds.ac.uk/roger/HiddenMarkovModels/html_dev/hmms/s1_pg1.html, 11 November 2003).

Bradin Siskin, C. (2004) Is it only a tool? Assessing the options for CALL. *TESOL Arabia 2004: Standards in English Language Teaching and Assessment*, Dubai, 10–12 March.

Bratko, I. (2001) *PROLOG. Programming for Artificial Intelligence*. London: Addison-Wesley.

Brett, P. (1998) An intuitive, theoretical and empirical perspective on the effectiveness question for multimedia. In K. Cameron (ed.) *Multimedia CALL: Theory and Practice* (pp. 81–92). Exeter: Elm Bank Publications.

Bridgeman, B. and Carlson, S. (1983) *Survey of Academic Writing Tasks Required of Graduate and Undergraduate Foreign Students* (TOEFL Research Report No. 15). Princeton, NJ: Educational Testing Service.

Brown, J.D. (1988) *Understanding Research in Second Language Learning*. New York: Cambridge University Press.

Brumfit, C. (2001) Teacher professionalism and research. In G. Cook and B. Seidlhofer (eds) *Principle and Practice in Applied Linguistics* (pp. 27–42). Oxford: Oxford University Press.

Buckett, J. and Stringer, G. (1998) Relate (Remote Language Teaching): Progress, problems and potential. In K. Cameron (ed.) *Multimedia CALL: Theory and Practice* (pp. 151–60). Exeter: Elm Bank Publications.

Buckett, J., Stringer, G. and Datta, N.K.J. (1999) Life after ReLaTe: Internet videoconferencing's growing pains. In K. Cameron (ed.) *CALL & The Learning Community* (pp. 31–8). Exeter: Elm Bank Publications.

Bull, S. (1997) Promoting effective learning strategy use in CALL. *Computer Assisted Language Learning* 10 (1), 3–39.

Burnstein, J. and Chodorow, M. (1999) Automated essay scoring for nonnative English speakers (http://acl.ldc.upenn.edu/W/W99/W99–0411.pdf, 14 October 2003).

Burston, J. (1998) Markin32 (Version 1.0). *CALICO Journal* 15 (4), 67–74.

Butt, D., Fahey, R., Spinks, S. and Yallop, C. (1997) *Using Functional Grammar. An Explorer's Guide*. Sydney: NCELTR Publications.

Butt, M., King, T.H., Nino, M-E., Segond, F. (1999) A *Grammar Writer's Cookbook*. Stanford: CSLI Publications.

Cameron, K. (1997) Editorial. *Computer Assisted Language Learning* 10 (1), 1–2.

Cameron, K. (ed.) (1998) *Multimedia CALL: Theory and Practice*. Exeter: Elm Bank Publications.

Cameron, K. (ed.) (1999a) *CALL & The Learning Community*. Exeter: Elm Bank Publications.

Cameron, K. (ed.) (1999b) *CALL: Media, Design and Applications*. Lisse: Swets & Zeitlinger.

Campbell, C. (1990) Writing with other's words: Using background reading text in academic compositions. In B. Kroll (ed.) *Second Language Writing* (pp. 211–30). Cambridge: Cambridge University Press.

Candlin, C.N., Plum, G., Spinks, S., Cayley, M. and Johansen, E. (1998) *Researching Academic Literacies*. Sydney: NCELTR Publications.

Chamot, A.U. and O'Malley, J.M. (1994) *The CALLA Handbook*. Reading: Addison-Wesley.

Chamot, A.U. and O'Malley, J.M. (1990) *Learning Strategies in Second Language Acquisition*. Cambridge: Cambridge University Press.

Chang, J. (1987) Chinese speakers. In M. Swan and B. Smith (eds) *Learner English* (2nd edn) (pp. 224–37). Cambridge: Cambridge University Press.

Chapelle, C.A. (1997) CALL in year 2000: Still in search for research paradigms? *Language Learning & Technology* 1 (1), 19–43. (http://llt.msu.edu/vol1num1/chapelle/default.html, 18 October 2003).

Chapelle, C.A. (1998) Multimedia CALL: Lessons to be learned from research on instructed SLA. *Language Learning & Technology* 2 (1), 22–34.

Chapelle, C.A. (2001) *Computer Applications in Second Language Acquisition*. Cambridge: Cambridge University Press.

Chapelle, C. and Roberts, C. (1986) Ambiguity tolerance and field independence as predictors of proficiency in English as a second language. *Language Learning* 36, 27–45.

Chapelle, C., Grabe, W. and Berns, M. (1993) *Communicating Language Proficiency: Definitions and Implications for TOEFL 2000*. Princeton, NJ: Educational Testing Service.

Chapelle, C.A., Jamison, J. and Park, Y. (1996) Second language classroom research traditions: How does CALL fit? In M. Pennington (ed.) *The Power of CALL* (pp. 33–54). Houston: Athelstan.

Chen, L. and Tokuda, N. (2003) A new template-template-enhanced ICALL system for a second language composition course. *CALICO Journal* 20 (3), 561–78.

Chiao, D. (1999) Using the Internet in English instruction at the Chinese Air Force Academy. In K. Cameron (ed.) *CALL & The Learning Community* (pp. 39–50). Exeter: Elm Bank Publications.

Chomsky, N. (1965) *Aspects of the Theory of Syntax*. Cambridge, MA: MIT Press.

Chun, M.D. (1998) Signal analysis software for teaching discourse intonation. *Language Learning & Technology* 2 (1), 61–77 (http://llt.msu.edu/vol2num1/article4/, 18 October 2003).

Clanchy, J. and Ballard, B. (1997) *Essay Writing for Students* (3rd edn). Cheshire/Melbourne: Longman.

Cochran, B.P., McDonald, J.L. and Parault, S.J. (1999) Too smart for their own good: The disadvantage of a superior processing capacity for adult language learners. *Journal of Memory and Language* 41, 30–58.

Cook, G. and Seidlhofer, B. (1995) An applied linguist in principle and practice. In G. Cook and B. Seidlhofer (eds) *Principle and Practice in Applied Linguistics* (pp. 1–26). Oxford: Oxford University Press.

Cook, V. (1993) *Linguistics and Second Language Acquisition*. London: Macmillan.

Cooper, C. (1989) Why are we talking about discourse communities? Or, foundationalism rears its ugly head once more. In C. Cooper and M. Holzman (eds) *Writing as Social Practice* (pp. 202–20). Portsmouth, NH: Boynton/Cook.

Corcoran, S. (2000) Language assessment into the next century: Developments in computer testing within ALTE. IATEFL Conference *CALL for the 21st Century*, Barcelona, 10 June – 2 July.

Corder, P. (1967) The significance of learner errors. *International Review of Applied Linguistics* 5, 161–70.

Cortes, M.E. and Galindo, L. (1998) Teaching foreign languages Using interactive videoconferencing. In K. Cameron (ed.) *Multimedia CALL: Theory and Practice* (pp. 251–8). Exeter: Elm Bank Publications.

Cowan, R., Choi, H.E. and Kim, D.H. (2003) Four questions for error diagnosis and correction in CALL. *CALICO Journal* 20 (3), 451–63.

Crompton, P.M. (1999) Integrating Internet-based CALL materials into mainstream language teaching. In K. Cameron (ed.) *CALL & The Learning Community* (pp. 75–82). Exeter: Elm Bank Publications.

Dalgish, G.M. (1991) Computer-assisted error analysis and courseware design: applications for ESL in the Swedish context. *CALICO Journal* 2 (2), 39–56.

Dam, L., Legenhausen, L. and Wolff, D. (1991) The computer in a communicative and autonomous language learning environment. In A. Hall and P. Baumgartner (eds) *Language Learning with Computers, an Educational Challenge* (pp. 33–49). Klagenfurt: WISL.

Daniels, P. and Brooks, D. (1999) Building on-line communities for language learners. In K. Cameron (ed.) *CALL & The Learning Community* (pp. 83–92). Exeter: Elm Bank Publications.

Davidson, F. (2003) Language testing: A matter of identity. 21st FIPLV World Congress: *Identity and Creativity in Language Education*.

Davies, G. (2001) New technologies and language learning: A suitable subject for research? In A. Chambers and G. Davies (eds) *ICT and Language learning: A European Perspective* (pp. 13–27). Lisse: Swets & Zeitlinger.

Davis, J.N., Lyman-Hager, M.A. and Hayden, S.B. (1992) Assessing user needs in early stages of program development: The case of foreign language reading. *CALICO Journal* 9 (4), 21–8.

Dawson, C. (1999) Turning half-circle – CALL and the debate between communicative and structural grammar teaching. In K. Cameron (ed.) *CALL & The Learning Community* (pp. 93–104). Exeter: Elm Bank Publications.

Deacon, A. (n.d.) Exploring intersections of technology and writing assessment (http://www.uwm.edu/~abd/grading.html, 14 October 2003).

Debski, R. and Levy, M. (eds) (1999) *WORLDCALL. Global Perspectives on Computer-Assisted Language Learning*. Lisse: Swets & Zeitlinger.

Decoo, W. (1993) Customer satisfaction in CALL: Queries from the users and our final impact. *CALICO Journal* 10 (3), 50–64.

Decoo, W. and Colpaert, J. (1999a) The role of didactic functions in CALL design. In K. Cameron (ed.) *CALL & The Learning Community* (pp. 65–74). Exeter: Elm Bank Publications.

Decoo, W. and Colpaert, J. (1999b) User-driven development and content-driven Research. In Cameron, K. (ed.) *CALL: Media, Design and Applications* (pp. 35–58). Lisse: Swets & Zeitlinger.

Delmonte, R. (2003) Linguistic knowledge and reasoning for error diagnosis and feedback generation. *CALICO Journal* 20 (3), 513–32.

DeKeyser, R.M. (2001) Automaticity and automatism. In P. Robinson (ed.) *Cognition and Second Language Instruction* (pp. 125–82). Cambridge: Cambridge University Press.

Derewianka, B. (1990) *Exploring How Texts Work*. Maryborough: Australian Primary English Teaching Association.

De Ridder, I. (1999) Are we still reading or just following links? How the highlighting or hyperlinks can influence incidental vocabulary learning. In K. Cameron (ed.) *CALL & The Learning Community* (pp. 105–16). Exeter: Elm Bank Publications.

DeSmedt, W.H. (1995) Herr Kommissar: An ICALL conversation simulator for intermediate German. In V.M. Holland, J.D. Kaplan, and M.R. Sams (eds) *Intelligent Language Tutors* (pp. 153–74). Mahwah: Lawrence Erlbaum.

Dittmar, N. (1984) Semantic features of pidginized learners of German. In R. Andersen (ed.) *Second Languages: A Cross-Linguistic Perspective* (pp. 243–70). Rowley, MA: Newbury House.

Dodigovic, M. (1991) Learner-oriented research in CALL. In A. Hall and P. Baumgartner (eds) *Language Learning with Computers, an Educational Challenge* (pp. 187–96). Klagenfurt: WISL.

Dodigovic, M. (1993) Interdisciplinary: Computer assisted linguistic research and the development of LSP courseware. *CALICO Journal* 10 (4), 5–16.

Dodigovic, M. (1995) *Computergestuetztes Lernen und Lehren einer Fachsprache,* Hochschule Bremen/Universitaet Bremen: Bremen.

Dodigovic, M. (1998) Multimedia in Natural Language Processing. In K. Cameron (ed.) *Multimedia CALL: Theory and Practice* (pp. 57–64). Elm Bank Publications: Exeter.

Dodigovic, M. (1999) Learning English for Academic Purposes on the Web. Paper presented at the 12th World Congress of Applied Linguistics, Tokyo, 1–6 August.

Dodigovic, M. (2000) English on-line, IATEFL Conference *CALL for the 21st Century,* Barcelona, 30 June – 2 July.

Dodigovic, M. (2002) Developing writing skills with a Cyber-Coach. *CALL Journal* 15 (1), 9–25.

Dodigovic, M (2003a) Artificial intelligence and linguistic error correction within the context of academic English. *21st FIPLV World Congress: 'Identity and Creativity in Language Education',* Rand Afrikaans University, Johannesburg, 2–5 July.

Dodigovic, M (2003b) Writing with an intelligent computer, *9th Annual TESOL Arabia International Conference 'English Language Teaching in the IT Age'.* Dubai, 12–14 March.

Dodigovic, M. (2003c) Natural Language Processing (NLP) as an instrument of raising the language awareness of learners of English as a second language. *Language Awareness Journal* 12 (3–4), 187–203.

Dodigovic, M. and Suphawat, P. (1999) Learning English for Academic Purposes on the Web. In K. Cameron (ed.) *CALL & The Learning Community.* (pp. 127–36). Exeter: Elm Bank Publications.

Doughty, C. (2001) Cognitive underpinnings of focus on form. In P. Robinson (ed.) *Cognition and Second Language Instruction* (pp. 206–57). Cambridge: Cambridge University Press.

Doughty, C. and Williams, J. (1998a) Issues and terminology. In C. Doughty and J. Williams (eds) *Focus on Form in Classroom Second Language Acquisition* (pp. 1–11). New York: Cambridge University Press.

Doughty, C. and Williams, J. (1998b) Pedagogical choices in focus on form. In C. Doughty and J. Williams (eds) *Focus on Form in Classroom Second Language Acquisition* (pp. 197–262). New York: Cambridge University Press.

Doughty, C.J. and Long, M.H. (2003) Optimal psycholinguistic environments for distance foreign language learning. *Language Learning & Technology* 7 (3), 50–80 (http://llt.msu.edu/vol7num3/doughty/, 18 October 2003).

Dow, S.C. (1999) Rationality and rhetoric in Smith and Keynes. In R.R. Favretti, G. Sandri and R. Scazzieri (eds) *Incommensurability and Translation* (pp. 189–200). Cheltenham: Edward Elgar.

Eagles (1995) Evaluation of Natural Language Processing systems (Final Report) (http://www.issco.unige.ch/ewg95/node125.html#SECTION009460000000 00000000, 5 January 2004).

Egan, K.B. (1999) Speaking: A critical skill and challenge. *CALICO Journal* 16 (3), 277–94.

Ehrman, M.E. (1998) Motivation and strategies questionnaire. In J.M. Reid (ed.) *Understanding Learning Styles in the Second Language Classroom* (pp. 169–74). Upper Saddle River, NJ: Prentice Hall Regents.

Ehsani, F. and Knodt, E. (1998) Speech technology in Computer-Aided Language Learning: Strengths and limitations of a New CALL Paradigm. *Language Learning & Technology* 2 (1), 45–60 (http://llt.msu.edu/vol2num1/article3/, 18 October 2003).

Eiselt, K. and Holbrook, J. (2002) *Augmented Transition Networks* (http://www. cc.gatech.edu/computing/classes/cs4344_98_winter/lec04.html, 11 December 2003).

Eisenstein, M. (1982) A study of social variation in adult second language acquisition. *Language Learning* 32, 367–91.

Ellis, N. (2001) Memory for language. In P. Robinson (ed.) *Cognition and Second Language Instruction* (pp. 33–68). Cambridge: Cambridge University Press.

Ellis, N. (2002) Unconscious and conscious sources of language acquisition, *The Sixth International Conference for Language Awareness, ALA2002*, Umeå, Sweden.

Ellis, R. (1985) Sources of variability in interlanguage. *Applied Linguistics* 6, 118–31.

Ellis, R. (1997) *SLA Research and Language Teaching.* Oxford: Oxford University Press.

Ely, C. (1986) An analysis of discomfort, risktaking, sociability and motivation in the L2 classroom. *Language Learning* 36 (1), 1–35.

Eskenazi, M. (1999) Using automatic speech processing for foreign language pronunciation tutoring: Some issues and a prototype. *Language Learning & Technology* 2 (2), 62–76. (http://llt.msu.edu/vol2num2/article3/, 18 October 2003).

Farhady, H. (1982) Measures of language proficiency from the learner's perspective, *TESOL Quarterly* 16, 43–59.

Favretti, R.R. (1999) Scientific discourse: Intertextual and intercultural practice. In R.R. Favretti, G. Sandri and R. Scazzieri (eds) *Incommensurability and Translation* (pp. 201–18). Cheltenham: Edward Elgar.

Felix, U. (1999) Web-based language learning: A window to the authentic world. In R. Debski and M. Levy (eds) *WORLDCALL. Global Perspectives on Computer-Assisted Language Learning* (pp. 85–98). Lisse: Swets & Zeitlinger.

Fidelman, C.G. (1998) Growth of Internet use by language professionals. *CALICO Journal* 15 (4), 39–58.

Field, Y. (1994) Cohesive conjunctions in the English writing of Cantonese speaking students from Hong Kong, *Australian Review of Applied Linguistics* 17 (1), 125–39.

Fischer, R. (1999) Computer applications and research agendas: Another dimension in professional advancement. *CALICO Journal* 16 (4), 559–72.

Fleming, N. (2001) *Teaching and Learning Styles: VARK Strategies*. Honolulu: Honolulu Community College.

Flower, L. and Hayes, J. (1980) The dynamics of composing: Making plans and juggling constraints. In L. Gregg and E. Steinberg (eds) *Cognitive Processes in Writing* (pp. 31–50). Hove: Lawrence Erlbaum.

Flynn, S. (1996) A parameter setting approach to second language acquisition. In W. Ritchie and T. Bhatia (eds) *Handbook of Second Language Acquisition* (pp. 121–58). San Diego: Academic Press.

Freiermuth, M.R. (1997) L2 error correction: Criteria and techniques. *The Language Teacher Online*, 21 (9) (http://langue.hyper.chubu.ac.jp/jalt/pub/tlt/97/sep/freiermuth.html 3 October 2003).

Ganderton, R. (1999) Interactivity in L2 Web-based reading. In R. Debski and M. Levy (eds) *WORLDCALL. Global Perspectives on Computer-Assisted Language Learning* (pp. 49–66). Lisse: Swets & Zeitlinger.

Garrett, N. (1995) ICALL and second language acquisition. In V.M. Holland, J.D. Kaplan and M.R. Sams (eds) *Intelligent Language Tutors* (pp. 345–58). Mahwah: Lawrence Erlbaum.

Gardner, H. (1983) *Frames of Mind: The Theory of Multiple Intelligences*. New York: Basic.

Gardner, R. and Lambert, W. (1972) *Attitudes and Motivation in Second Language Learning*. Rowley: Newbury House.

Gardner, R. and MacIntyre, P. (1993) A student's contribution to second language learning. Part II: Affective Variables. *Language Teaching* 26, 1–11.

Gass, S.M. and Varonis, E.M. (1994) Input, interaction and second language production. *Studies in Second Language Acquisition* 16, 283–302.

Gass, S. and Varonis, E. (1986) Sex differences in NNS/NNS interaction. In Day (ed.) *Talking to Learn: Conversation in Second Language Acquisition* (pp. 327–51). Rowley: Newbury House.

Gazdar, G. and Mellish, C. (1996) *Natural Language Processing in Lisp/Prolog/Pop11* (http://www.cogs.susx.ac.uk/local/books/nlp-in-prolog/index.html, 14 October 2003).

Geoghegan, W. (1998) Instructional technology and the mainstream: The risk of success. In D. Oblinger and C. Rush (eds) *The Future Compatible Campus*. Bolton: Anker Publishing.

George, H. (1972) *Common Errors in Language Learning*. Rowley: Newbury House.

Gillespie, J. and McKee, J. (1999) Resistance to CALL: Degrees of student reluctance to use CALL and ICT. *ReCALL Journal* 11 (1), 38–46.

Gitsaki, C. and Taylor, R.P. (1999) Bringing the WWW into the ESL classroom. In K. Cameron (ed.) *CALL & The Learning Community* (pp. 143–60). Exeter: Elm Bank Publications.

Givon, T. (1979) From discourse to syntax: Grammar as a processing strategy. In T. Givon (ed.) *Syntax and Semantics Volume 12* (pp. 81–112). New York: Academic Press.

Goodfellow, R. (1999) Evaluating performance, approach, outcome. In K. Cameron (ed.) *CALL: Media, Design and Applications* (pp. 109–40). Lisse: Swets & Zeitlinger.

Goodfellow, R., Manning, P. and Lamy, M.-N. (1999) Building online open and distance language learning environment. In R. Debski and M. Levy (eds) *WORLDCALL. Global Perspectives on Computer-Assisted Language Learning* (pp. 267–86). Lisse: Swets & Zeitlinger.

Grabe, W. (2001) Notes toward a theory of second language writing. In T. Silva and P.K. Matsuda (eds) *On Second Language Writing* (pp. 39–58). Mahwah: Lawrence Erlbaum.

Grabe, W. and Kaplan, R. (1996) *Theory and Practice of Writing*. New York: Longman.

Graddol, D. (1994) Three models of language description. In D. Graddol and O. Boyd-Barrett (eds) *Media Texts: Authors and Readers* (pp. 1–21). Clevedon: Multilingual Matters.

Graffi, G. (1999) The language of logical form. In R.R. Favretti, G. Sandri and R. Scazzieri (eds) *Incommensurability and Translation* (pp. 443–54). Cheltenham: Edward Elgar.

Granger, S. (2003) Error-tagged learner corpora and CALL: A promising synergy. *CALICO Journal* 20 (3), 465–80.

Greaves, C. and Yang, H. (1999) A vocabulary based language learning strategy for the Internet. In R. Debski and M. Levy (eds) *WORLDCALL. Global Perspectives on Computer-Assisted Language Learning* (pp. 67–85). Lisse: Swets & Zeitlinger.

Gregg, K. R. (2001) Learnability and second language acquisition theory. In P. Robinson (ed.) *Cognition and Second Language Instruction* (pp. 152–82). Cambridge: Cambridge University Press,

Gu, P. and Xu, Z. (1999) Improving EFL learning through networking. In R. Debski and M. Levy (eds) *WORLDCALL. Global Perspectives on Computer-Assisted Language Learning* (pp. 169–84). Lisse: Swets & Zeitlinger.

Hackos, J.T. and Redish, J.C. (1998) *User and Task Analysis for Interface Design*. New York: Wiley.

Hale, G., Taylor, C., Bridgeman, B., Carson, J., Kroll, B. and Kantor, R. (1986) *A Study of Writing Tasks Assigned in Academic Degree Programs*. TOEFL Research Report 54. Princeton, N J: Educational Testing Service.

Halliday, M.A.K. (1985) *Spoken and Written Language*. Burwood: Deakin University.

Halliday, M.A.K. and Hasan, R. (1986) *Cohesion in English*. London: Longman.

Halliday, M.A.K. (1993) Some grammatical problems in scientific English. In M.A.K. Halliday and J.R. Martin *Writing Science* (pp. 69–85). London: Palmer Press.

Halliday, M.A.K. (1994a) *An Introduction to Functional Grammar*. London: Arnold.

Halliday, M.A.K. (1994b) Spoken and written modes of meaning. In D. Graddol and O. Boyd-Barrett (eds) *Media Texts: Authors and Readers* (pp. 51–73). Clevedon: Multilingual Matters.

Halliday, M.A.K. (1999) The grammatical construction of scientific knowledge: The framing of the English clause. In R.R. Favretti, G. Sandri and R. Scazzieri (eds) *Incommensurability and Translation* (pp. 85–116). Cheltenham: Edward Elgar.

Halliday, M.A.K. and Martin, J.R. (1993) *Writing Sciences: Literacy and Discursive Power*. London: Falmer Press.

Hamburger, H., Schoells, M. and Reeder, F. (1999) More intelligent CALL. In Cameron, K. (ed.) *CALL: Media, Design and Applications* (pp. 183–202). Lisse: Swets & Zeitlinger.

Harley, B. (1993) Instructional strategies in early French immersion classes. *Studies in Second Language Acquisition* 15 (2), 245–59.

Harley, B. (1998) Focus-on-form tasks in child L2 acquisition. In C. Doughty and J. Williams (eds) *Focus on Form in Classroom Second Language Acquisition* (pp. 156–76). New York: Cambridge University Press.

Harmer, J. (1998) *How to Teach English.* London: Longman.

Hasan, R. (1994) The texture of a text. In D. Graddol and O. Boyd-Barrett (eds) *Media Texts: Authors and Readers* (pp. 74–89). Clevedon: Multilingual Matters.

Hatherley-Greene, P. (2003) Student profiling: VARK learning preferences and multiple intelligences at Dubai Men's College. TESOL Arabia Conference, Dubai, March 2003.

Hawkey, R (1982): An investigation of inter-relationships between cognitive / affective and social factors and language learning. Unpublished PhD thesis: Department of English for Speakers of Other Languages, Institute of Education, London University.

Healy Beauvois, M. (1997) Computer-mediated communication: Technology for improving speaking and writing. In M.D. Bush and R.M. Terry (eds) *Technology-Enhanced Language Learning* (pp. 165–84). Lincolnwood: National Textbook Company.

Hearst, M.A. (2000) The debate on automated essay grading. *IEEE Intelligent Systems,* September/October, 22 (http://www.knowledge-technologies.com/presskit/KAT_IEEEdebate.pdf, 15 October 2003).

Heift, T. (2003) Multiple learner errors and meaningful feedback: A challenge for ICALL systems. *CALICO Journal* 20 (3), 553–48.

Heift, T. and McFetridge, P. (1999) Exploiting the student model to emphasize language teaching pedagogy in Natural Language Processing. *ACL-IALL Symposyum* (http://acl.ldc.upenn.edu/W/W99/W99–0409.pdf, 14 October 2003).

Heift, T. and Schulze, M. (2003) Error diagnosis and error correction in CALL. *CALICO Journal* 20 (3), 437–50.

Heift, T., Toole, J., McFetridge, P., Popowich, F. and Tsiplakou (2000) Learning Greek with an adaptive and intelligent hypermedia system. *IMEj* (http://imej.wfu.edu/articles/2000/2/02/index.asp, 11 November 2003).

Hemard, D. and Cushion, S. (1999) Designing a Web-based CALL environment: From access to acceptability. K. Cameron (ed.) *CALL & The Learning Community* (pp. 169–80). Exeter: Elm Bank Publications.

Hemp-Lyons, L. (2001) Fourth generation writing assessment. In T. Silva and P.K. Matsuda (eds) *On Second Language Writing* (pp. 117–28). Mahwah: Lawrence Erlbaum.

Herdina, P. (1991). Who needs CALL?. In A. Hall and P. Baumgartner (eds). *Language Learning with Computers* (pp. 50–75). Klagenfurt: WISL.

Heylighen, F. (1995) Evolutionary epistemology, *Principia Cybernetica Web* (http://pespmc1.vub.ac.be/EVOLEPIST.html, 11 November 2003).

Higgins, J. (1988) *Language, Learners and Computers.* Longman: London

Higgins, J. (1995) *Computers and English Language Learning.* Oxford: Intellect.

Higgins, J. and Johns, T. (1984) *Computers in Language Learning.* London: Collins ELT.

Hirschman, L., Breck, E., Light, M., Burger, J. D. and Ferro, L. (2000) Automated grading of short-answer tests, *IEEE Intelligent Systems,* September/October, p. 30 (http://www.knowledge-technologies.com/presskit/KAT_IEEEdebate.pdf, 15 October 2003).

Hoffman, L. (1988) *Vom Fachwort zum Fachtext: Beiträge zur angewandten Linguistik*. Tübingen: Gunther Narr Verlag.

Holland, M.V. (1999) Tutors that listen. *CALICO Journal* 16 (3), 245–50.

Holland, M., Maisano, R., Alderks, C. and Martin, J. (1993) Parsers in tutors: What are they good for? *CALICO Journal* 11 (1), 28–46.

Holland, V.M. (1995) Introduction: The case for intelligent CALL. In V.M. Holland, J.D. Kaplan and M.R. Sams (eds) *Intelligent Language Tutors* (pp. vii–xvi). Mahwah: Lawrence Erlbaum.

Holland, V.M., Kaplan, J.D. and Sams, M.R. (1995) *Intelligent Language Tutors*. Mahwah: Lawrence Erlbaum.

Holmes, G. (1999) Corpus CALL: Corpora in language and literature. In K. Cameron, (ed.) *CALL: Media, Design and Applications* (pp. 239–70). Lisse: Swets & Zeitlinger.

Holmes, G. and Leney, J. (1998) CALL Implementation: An evaluation. In K. Cameron (ed.) *Multimedia CALL: Theory and Practice* (pp. 93–112). Exeter: Elm Bank Publications.

Horowitz, D.M. (1986) What professors actually require: Academic tasks for the ESL classroom. *TESOL Quarterly* 20, 445–62.

Hubbard, P. (1996) Elements of CALL methodology: Development, evaluation and implementation. In M. Pennington (ed.) *The Power of CALL* (pp. 15–32). Houston: Athelstan.

Hubbard, P. (2003) *A Survey of Unanswered questions in Computer Assisted Language Learning*. http://www.stanford.edu/~efs/callsurvey/ (17 September 2003).

Hulstijn, J.H. (2001) Intentional and incidental vocabulary learning: A reappraisal of elaboration, rehearsal and automaticity. In P. Robinson (ed.) *Cognition and Second Language Instruction* (pp. 258–86). Cambridge: Cambridge University Press.

Hunter, L. (1999) Signalling structure in Web documents: Support for the non-native reader. In K. Cameron (ed.) *CALL & The Learning Community* (pp. 181–94). Exeter: Elm Bank Publications.

Hutchinson, T. and Waters, A. (1987) *English for Specific Purposes*. Cambridge University Press: Cambridge.

Inman, D. (n.d.) The possibility of Natural Language Processing by computer (http://www.scism.sbu.ac.uk/inmandw/tutorials/nlp/intro/intro.html, 14 October 2003).

Jager, S. (2001) From gap-filling to filling the gap: A re-assessment of Natural Language Processing in CALL. In A. Chambers and G. Davies (eds) *ICT and Language Learning: A European Perspective* (pp. 101–10). Lisse: Swets & Zeitlinger.

James, C. (1998) *Errors in Language Learning and Use. Exploring Error Analysis*. London: Longman.

Jelinek, F. (1997) *Statistical Methods for Speech Recognition*. Cambridge: MIT Press.

Jespersen, O. (1972) *Growth and Structure of the English Language*. Oxford: Blackwell.

Johns, A.M. (1981) Necessary English: A faculty survey. *TESOL Quarterly* 15, 51–8.

Johns, A.M. (1997) *Text, Role and Context. Developing Academic Literacies*. New York: Cambridge University Press.

Jurafsky, D. and Martin, J.H. (2000) *Speech and Language Processing*. Upper Saddle River: Prentice-Hall.

Kayser, A. (2002) Cultural appropriateness of network-based language teaching in a Middle Eastern female Islamic context. *CALL Journal* 15 (1), 55–68.

Keobke, K (1999) The teacher in the machine: Making WWW technology serve pedagogy. In K. Cameron (ed.) *CALL & The Learning Community* (pp. 231–40). Exeter: Elm Bank Publications.

King, K. (1999) Group dynamics and the online professor. In K. Cameron (ed.) *CALL & The Learning Community* (pp. 241–50). Exeter: Elm Bank Publications.

Kramsch, C. (1995) The applied linguist and the foreign language teacher: Can they talk to each other? In G. Cook and B. Seidlhofer (eds) *Principle and Practice in Applied Linguistics* (pp. 43–56). Oxford: Oxford University Press.

Kramsch, C., A'Ness, F. and Lam, W.S.E. (2000) Authenticity and authorship in the computer-mediated acquisition of L2 Literacy. *Language Learning and Technology* 4 (2), 78–104 (http://llt.msu.edu/vol4num2/kramsch/default.html, 18 October 2003).

Krashen, S.D. (1987) *Principles and Practice in Second Language Acquisition*. London: Prentice-Hall.

Kreindler, I. (1998) Designing feedback that is hard to ignore: A boost from multimedia. In K. Cameron (ed.) *Multimedia CALL: Theory and Practice* (pp. 243–50). Exeter: Elm Bank Publications.

Kuettner, P.R. (1998) The place and role of correction / Writing software in second language acquisition. In K. Cameron (ed.) *Multimedia CALL: Theory and Practice* (pp. 145–50). Exeter: Elm Bank Publications.

Kukich, K. (2000) Beyond automated essay scoring, *IEEE Intelligent Systems*, September/October, 22–27 (http://www.knowledge-technologies.com/presskit/KAT_IEEEdebate.pdf, 15 October 2003).

Lakoff, J. and Johnson, M. (1981) *Metaphors We Live By*. Chicago: The Unihttp://www.knowledge-technologies.com/presskit/KAT_IEEEdebate.pdf, versity of Chicago Press.

Lantolf, J.P. and Appel, G. (eds) (1994) *Vygotskyan Approaches to Second Language Research*. Norwood: Ablex.

LaRocca, C.S.A., Morgan, J.J. and Bellinger, S.M. (1999) On the path 2X learning: Exploring the possibilities of advanced speech recognition. *CALICO Journal* 16 (3), 295–310.

Larsen-Freeman, D. and Long, M.H. (1991) *An Introduction to Second Language Acquisition Research*. New York: Longman.

Leahy, C. (1999) E-mail as a learning tool: Construction of knowledge online. In K. Cameron (ed.) *CALL & The Learning Community* (pp. 291–300). Exeter: Elm Bank Publications.

Leki, I. (2001) Hearing voices: L2 students' experiences in L2 writing courses. In T. Silva and P.K. Matsuda (eds) *On Second Language Writing* (pp. 17–28). Mahwah: Lawrence Erlbaum.

Leki, I. and Carson, L. (1997) 'Completely different worlds': EAP and the writing experiences of ESL students in university courses. *TESOL Quarterly* 31, 39–69.

Lengo, N. (1995) What is an error? *The English Teaching Forum* 33 (3), 20 (http://exchanges.state.gov/forum/vols/vol33/no3/p20.htm, 4 January 2004).

Leontiev, A. (1981) *Psychology and Language Learning Process*. Oxford: Pergamon.

Lessard, G. and Levison, M. (1999) L2 French lexical creativity in context. In K. Cameron (ed.) *CALL & The Learning Community* (pp. 301–14). Exeter: Elm Bank Publications.

Lessing, G.E. (1854) *Laokoon, oder über die Grenzen der Mahlerey und Poesie*. Leipzig: G. J. Göschen.

Levow, G.-A. and Olsen, M.B. (1999) Modeling the language assessment process and result: Proposed architecture for an automatic oral proficiency assessment, ACL-IALL Symposium (http://www.ets.org/research/dload/acl99rev.pdf, 14 October 2003).

Levy, M. (1997a) Theory-driven CALL and the development process. *Computer Assisted Language Learning* 10 (1), 41–56.

Levy, M. (1997b) *Computer Assisted Language Learning. Context and Conceptualization.* Oxford: Clarendon Press.

Levy, M. (1998) Two concepts of learning and their implications for CALL at the tertiary level. *ReCALL Journal* 10 (1), 86–94.

Levy, M. (1999) Design process in CALL: Integrating theory, research and evaluation. In K. Cameron (ed.) *CALL: Media, Design and Applications* (pp. 83–108). Lisse: Swets & Zeitlinger.

Levy, M. (2000) Scope, goals and methods in CALL research: Questions of coherence and autonomy. *ReCALL* 12 (2), 170–95.

Lewins, F. (1990) *Writing a Thesis*, Canberra: Australian National University.

Lewis, M. (2003) I see what you mean – a new approach to texts. Plenary Talk at TESOL Arabia Conference. *English Language Teaching in the IT Age*, March 2003.

L'Haire, S. and Faltin, A. V. (2003) Error diagnosis in the FreeText project. *CALICO Journal* 20 (3), 481–495.

Lightbown, P.M. (1998) The importance of timing in focus on form. In C. Doughty and J. Williams (eds) *Focus on Form in Classroom Second Language Acquisition* (pp. 177–96). New York: Cambridge University Press.

Liou, H.-C. (1991) Development of an English grammar checker: A progress report. *CALICO Journal* 9 (1), 57–71.

Liou, H.-C. (1994) Practical considerations for multimedia courseware development: An EFL IVD experience. *CALICO Journal* 11 (3), 47–74.

Liou, H.-C. (1997) Research of on-line help as learner strategies for multimedia CALL evaluation. *CALICO Journal* 14 (2–4), 81–96.

Long, M. H. (1996) The role of the linguistic environment in second language acquisition. In W.C. Ritchie and T.K. Bhatia (eds) *Handbook of Second Language Acquisition* (pp. 413–68). San Diego: Academic Press.

Long, M. H. and Robinson, P. (1998) Focus on form: Theory, research and practice. In C. Doughty and J. Williams (eds) *Focus on Form in Classroom Second Language Acquisition* (pp. 15–41). New York: Cambridge University Press.

Loritz, D. (1995) GPARS: A suite of grammar assessment systems. In V.M. Holland, J.D. Kaplan and M.R. Sams (eds) *Intelligent Language Tutors* (pp. 121–34). Mahwah: Lawrence Erlbaum.

MacWhinney, B. (1995) Evaluating foreign language tutoring systems. In V.M. Holland, J.D. Kaplan and M.R. Sams (eds) *Intelligent Language Tutors* (pp. 317–26). Mahwah: Lawrence Erlbaum.

MacWhinney, B. (2001) The competition model: The input, the context and the brain. In P. Robinson (ed.) *Cognition and Second Language Instruction* (pp. 69–90). Cambridge: Cambridge University Press.

Maingard, C. (1999) Evolutionary epistemology in language learning – possible implications for CALL. *ReCALL Journal* 11 (1), 80–92.

Makerere (1961) *Report of the Commonwealth Conference on the Teaching of English as a Second Language.* Held at Makerere College, Uganda in January 1961. Entebbe, Uganda: Government Printer.

Manning, P. (1991) Methodological considerations for the design of CALL programs. In A. Hall and P. Baumgartner (eds) *Language Learning with Computers* (pp. 76–101). Klagenfurt: WISL.

Marsic, I., Medl, A., and Flanagan, J. (2000) Natural communication with information systems. *Proceedings of the IEEE* 88 (8), 1354–66.

Martin, J.R., Matthiessen, C.M.I.M. and Painter, C. (1997) *Working with Functional Grammar*. London: Arnold.

Martinez-Lage, A. (1997) Hypermedia technology for teaching reading. In M.D. Bush and R.M. Terry (1997) *Technology-Enhanced Language Learning* (pp. 121–64). Lincolnwood: National Textbook Company.

Matthews, C. (1993) Grammar frameworks in intelligent CALL. *CALICO Journal* 11 (1), 5–27.

Matthews, C. (1998) *An Introduction to Natural Language Processing through Prolog*, London: Longman.

Matthews, C. and Fox, J. (1991) Foundations of ICALL – an overview of student modelling. In H. Savolainen and J. Telenius (eds) *Proceedings of EUROCALL 1991* (pp. 163–70). Helsinki: Helsinki School of Economics and Business Administration.

McDermott, T.S. (1999) Two models of the overlap of the sciences: Modern reductionism and medieval abstraction. In R.R. Favretti, G. Sandri and R. Scazzieri (eds) *Incommensurability and Translation* (pp. 69–84). Cheltenham: Edward Elgar.

McDonough, J. and McDonough, S. (1997) *Research Methods for English Language Teachers*. London: Arnold.

McLaughlin, B. (1993) *Theories of Second-language Learning*. London: Arnold.

McLaughlin, B., Rossman, R. and McLeod, B. (1983) Second language learning: An information-processing perspective. *Language Learning* 33, 135–58.

McRoberts, R. (1981) *A Student's Guide to the Craft of Writing*. Melbourne: Macmillan.

Menzel, W. and Schröder, I. (1999) Error diagnosis for language learning systems. *ReCALL special publication, Language Processing in CALL*, 20–30.

Miller, T. (2003) Essay assessment with latent semantic analysis. *Journal of Educational Computing Research*, 28 (3) (http://www.dfki.uni-kl.de/~miller/publications/miller03a.pdf, 14 October 2003).

Mills, J. (1999) CA-EAP: A multi-task software package for the teaching of academic writing. In K. Cameron (ed.) *CALL & The Learning Community* (pp. 345–54). Exeter: Elm Bank Publications.

Mitchell, R. and Myles, F. (1998) *Second Language Learning Theories*. London: Arnold.

Moore, T. and Morton, J. (1998) Contrasting rhetorics: Academic writing and the IELTS test. Paper presented at the Australian Council of TESOL Associations – Victorian Association for TESOL and Multicultural Education National Conference: Melbourne January 1998.

Morris, C.W. (1938) *Foundations of the Theory of Signs*. Chicago, IL: The University of Chicago Press.

Mosteller, F., Fienberg, S.E. and Rourke, R.E.K. (1983) *Beginning Statistics with Data Analysis*. Reading: Addison-Wesley.

Mostow, J. and Aist, G. (1999) Giving help and praise in a reading tutor with imperfect listening – because automated speech recognition means never being able to say you're certain. *CALICO Journal* 16 (3), 407–24.

Motteram, G. (1999) Changing the research paradigm: Qualitative research methodology and the CALL classroom. In R. Debski and M. Levy (eds) *WORLDCALL. Global Perspectives on Computer-Assisted Language Learning* (pp. 201–14). Lisse: Swets & Zeitlinger.

Murray, D. E. (2000) Changing technologies, changing literacy communities? *Language Learning & Technology* 4 (2), 43–58 (http://llt.msu.edu/vol4num2/murray/default.html, 18 October 2003).

Munby, J. (1981) *Communicative Syllabus Design*. Cambridge: Cambridge University Press.

Muzic, V. (1986) *Metodologija pedagoskog istrazivanja*. Sarajevo: Svjetlost.

Nagata, N. (2002) BANZAI: An application of Natural Language Processing to Web-based language learning. *CALICO Journal* 19 (3), 583–99.

Nation, I.S.P. (1990) *Teaching & Learning Vocabulary*. Boston: Heinle & Heinle.

Nemser, W. (1971) Approximative systems of foreign language learners. *International Review of Applied Linguistics* 9, 115–23.

Nerbonne, J., Jager, S., van Essen, A. (1998) Introduction. In J. Nerbonne, S. Jager and A. van Essen (eds) *Language Teaching & Language Technology*. Lisse: Swets & Zeitlinger.

Nunan, D. (1998) *Language Teaching Methodology*. London: Prentice-Hall.

Nunan, D. (1992) *Research Methods in Language Learning*. New York: Cambridge University Press.

O'Brien, P. (1993) eL: Using AI in CALL. In M. Yazdani (ed.) *Multilingual Multimedia* (pp. 85–139). Oxford: Intellect.

O'Grady, W., Dobrovolsky, M., Arnoff, M. (1997) *Contemporary Linguistics*. Boston: Bedford/St. Martin's.

Oxford, R.L. (1990) *Language Learning Strategies*. Boston: Heinle & Heinle.

Oxford, R.L. (1995) Linking theories of learning with Intelligent Computer-Assisted Language Learning (ICALL). In V.M. Holland, J.D. Kaplan and M.R. Sams (eds) *Intelligent Language Tutors* (pp. 359–70). Mahwah: Lawrence Erlbaum.

Oxford, R. and Nam, C. (1998) Learning styles and strategies of partially bilingual student diagnosed as learning disabled: A case study. In J.M. Reid (ed.) *Understanding Learning Styles in the Second Language Clasroom* (pp. 62–70). Upper Saddle River, NJ: Prentice-Hall Regents.

Palfreyman, D. (2003) Personal communication.

Paramskas, D.M. (1999) The shape of computer-mediated communication. In K. Cameron (ed.) *CALL: Media, Design and Applications* (pp. 13–34). Lisse: Swets & Zeitlinger.

Pavesi, M. (1986) Markedness, discoursal modes, and relative clause formation in a formal and informal context. *Studies in Second Language Acquisition* 8 (1), 38–55.

Pennington, M.C. (ed.) (1996) *The Power of CALL*. Houston: Athelstan.

Pera, M. (1999) Scientific discourse and scientific knowledge. In R.R. Favretti, G. Sandri and R. Scazzieri (eds) *Incommensurability and Translation* (pp. 173–88). Cheltenham: Edward Elgar.

Peters, P. (1985) *Strategies for Student Writers*. Brisbane: Wiley.

Peterson, M. (1999) Creating hypermedia learning environments: Some guidelines for learner-centred design. In K Cameron (ed.) *CALL and the Learning Community* (pp. 363–8). Exeter: Elm Bank Publications.

Petkovic, N. (1984) *Od formalizma ka semiotici*. Beograd: BIGZ/Jedinstvo.

Pfleeger, S.L. (1998) *Software Engineering. Theory and Practice*. Upper Saddle River, NJ: Prentice-Hall Regents.

Phillipson, R.L.H. (1992) *Linguistic Imperialism*. Oxford: Oxford University Press.

Pica, T., Young, R., Doughty, C. (1987) The impact of interaction on comprehension. *TESOL Quarterly* 21, 737–58.

Picardi, E. (1999) Reference, conceptual scheme and radical interpretation. In R.R. Favretti, G. Sandri and R. Scazzieri (eds) *Incommensurability and Translation* (pp. 53–68). Cheltenham: Edward Elgar.

Pienemann, M. (1989) Is language teachable? *Applied Linguistics* 10 (1), 52–79.

Pollard, D. and Yazdani, M. (1993) A multilingual multimedia restaurant scenario. In M. Yazdani (ed.) *Multilingual Multimedia* (pp. 1–13). Oxford: Intellect.

Polio, C. (2001) Research methodology in second language writing. In T. Silva and P. K. Matsuda (eds) *On Second Language Writing* (pp. 91–116). Mahwah: Lawrence Erlbaum.

Potter, A. (n.d.) Invoking the cyber-muse: Automatic essay assessment in the online learning environment (http://www.uni-koblenz.de/~peter/ijcai–03-elearning/final/allpapers/potter/APotter_a4.pdf, 18 December 2003).

Prabhu, N.S. (2001) Concept and conduct in language pedagogy. In G. Cook and B. Seidlhofer (eds) *Principle and Practice in Applied Linguistics* (pp. 57–72). Oxford: Oxford University Press.

Pugh, A. (1997) Whither Internet and Intranet. Theory and practice of multimedia CALL. Conference paper, University of Exeter, 21–23 September 1997.

Raccah, P.-Y. (1999) Argumentation and knowledge: From words to terms. In R.R. Favretti, G. Sandri and R. Scazzieri (eds) *Incommensurability and Translation* (pp. 219–34). Cheltenham: Edward Elgar.

Raimes, A. (1991) Out of the W\woods: Emerging traditions in the teaching of writing. *TESOL Quarterly*, 25, 229–58.

Reeder, F. and Hamburger, H. (1999) Real talk: Authentic dialogue practice. In R. Debski and M. Levy (eds) *WORLDCALL. Global Perspectives on Computer-Assisted Language Learning* (pp. 319–38). Lisse: Swets & Zeitlinger.

Reeves, T.C. (1994) *Multimedia Development Tools*. http://mime1.marc.gatech.edu/MM_Tools/analysis.html (20 September 2003).

Reid, J.M. (1998) Teachers as perceptual learning styles researchers. In J.M. Reid (ed.) *Understanding Learning Styles in the Second Language Classroom* (pp. 15–26). Upper Saddle River, NJ: Prentice Hall Regents.

Reid, J. (2001) Advanced EAP writing and curriculum design: What do we need to know? In T. Silva and P.K. Matsuda (eds) *On Second Language Writing* (pp. 143–60). Mahwah: Lawrence Erlbaum.

Reuer, V. (2003) Error recognition and feedback with lexical functional grammar. *CALICO Journal* 20 (3), 497–512.

Richards, J. (1971) Error analysis and second language strategies. *Language Sciences* 17, 12–22.

Rubin, J. (1981) Study of cognitive processes in second language learning. *Applied Linguistics*, 11, 117–30.

Rudner, L. and Gagne, P. (2001) An overview of three approaches to scoring written essays by computer. *Practical Assessment, Research & Evaluation* 8 (http://edresearch.org/pare/getvn.asp?v=7&n=26, 14 October 2003).

Rogers, E. (1983) *Diffusion of Innovations*. London: Macmillan.

Salaberry, M.R. (1996) A theoretical foundation for the development of pedagogical tasks in computer mediated communication. *CALICO Journal* 14 (1), 5–36.

Salaberry, R. (1999) CALL in the year 2000: Still developing a research agenda. *Language Learning Technology* 1 (3), 104–7. (http://llt.msu.edu/vol3num1/comment/, 18 October 2003).

Sanders, B. (2000) *Technical Writing* (http://dxbemployee.zu.ac.ae/F7829/index.html).

Santos, T. (2001) The place of politics in second language writing. In T. Silva and P.K. Matsuda (eds) *On Second Language Writing* (pp. 173–90). Mahwah: Lawrence Erlbaum.

Sawyer, M. and Ranta, L. (2001) Aptitude, individual differences, and instructional design. In P. Robinson (ed.) *Cognition and Second Language Instruction* (pp. 319–53). Cambridge: Cambridge University Press.

Schmidt, R. (2001) Attention. In P. Robinson (ed.) *Cognition and Second Language Instruction*. Cambridge: Cambridge University Press.

Schmidt, K.H. and Kornum, L. (1991) Telecommunication in language learning. In A. Hall and P. Baumgartner (eds) *Language Learning with Computers* (pp. 276–9). Klagenfurt: WISL.

Schulze, M. (1999) From the developer to the learner: Describing grammar – learning grammar. *ReCALL Journal* 11 (1), 117–24.

Schulze, M. (2001) Human language technologies in computer-assisted language learning. In A. Chambers and G. Davies (eds) *ICT and Language learning: A European Perspective* (pp. 111–31). Lisse: Swets & Zeitlinger.

Schulze, M. (2003) Grammatical errors and feedback: Some theoretical insights. *CALICO Journal* 20 (3), 437–50.

Schumann, J. (1987) *The Pidginisation Process: A Model of Second Language Acquisition*. Rowley: Newbury House.

Scollon, R. and Scollon, S.W. (1995) *Intercultural Communication: A Discourse Approach*. Oxford: Blackwell.

Seliger, H. (1984) Processing universals in second language acquisition. In F. Eckman, L. Bell and D. Nelson (eds) *Universals in Second Language Acquisition* (pp. 36–47). Rowley: Newbury House.

Selinker, L. (1972) Interlanguage. *International Review of Applied Linguistics* 10 (3), 209–31.

Selinker, L. (1997) *Rediscovering Interlanguage*. New York: Longman.

Selinker, L. and Lakshmanan, U. (1993) Language transfer and fossilization: The 'Multiple Effects Principle'. In S. M. Gas and L. Selinker (eds) *Language Transfer in Language Learning* (pp. 197–216). Philadelphia: John Benjamins.

Severino, C. (2001) Dangerous liaisons: Problems of representation and articulation. In T. Silva and P.K. Matsuda (eds) *On Second Language Writing* (pp. 201–8). Mahwah: Lawrence Erlbaum.

Shield, L. and Hewer, S. (1999) A synchronous learning environment to support distance language learners. In K. Cameron (ed.) *CALL & The Learning Community* (pp. 379–90). Exeter: Elm Bank Publications.

Shield, L., Weininger, M. J. and Davies, L. B. (1999) A task-based approach to using MOO for collaborative language learning. In K. Cameron (ed.) *CALL & The Learning Community* (pp. 391–402). Exeter: Elm Bank Publications.

Simmons, D. and Thurstun, J. (1995) Academics' expectations of student writing. ELS Seminar, Sydney: Macquarie University.

Sinclair, J.M. (1999) The internalization of dialog. In R.R. Favretti, G. Sandri and R. Scazzieri (eds) *Incommensurability and Translation* (pp. 391–406). Cheltenham: Edward Elgar.

Singleton, D. (1999) *Exploring the Second Language Mental Lexicon*. Cambridge: Cambridge University Press.

Skinner, B.F. (1957) *Verbal Behavior*. New York: Appleton-Century-Crofts.

Smith, B. (2001) Arabic speakers. In M. Swan and B. Smith (eds) *Learner English* (2nd edn) (pp. 195–213). Cambridge: Cambridge University Press.

Smith, G.W. (1991) *Computers and Human Language*. New York: Oxford University Press.

Sommerville, I. (2001) *Software Engineering*. Harlow: Pearson Education.

Söntgens, K. (1999) Language learning via E-mail – autonomy through collaboration. In K. Cameron (ed.) *CALL & The Learning Community* (pp. 413–24). Exeter: Elm Bank Publications.

Spada, N. and Lightbown, P. (1993) Instruction in the development of questions in L2 classrooms. *Studies in Second Language Acquisition* 15, 205–24.

Stenson, N. (1974) Induced errors. In J. Schumann and N. Stenson (eds) *New Frontiers in Second Language Learning* (pp. 54–70). Rowley: Newbury House.

Stenson, N., Downing, B., Smith, J., Karen, J. (1992) The effectiveness of computer-assisted pronunciation training. *CALICO Journal* 9 (4), 5–20.

Stubbs, M. (1995) Corpus evidence for norms of lexical collocation. In G. Cook and B. Seidlhofer (eds) *Principle and Practice in Applied Linguistics* (pp. 245–56). Oxford: Oxford University Press.

Suphawat, P. (1999) *An Investigation of Students' Needs of CALL in EAP Classes.* Masters Thesis, Sydney: Macquarie University.

Swain, M. (1998) Focus on form through conscious reflection. In C. Doughty and J. Williams (eds) *Focus on Form in Classroom Second Language Acquisition* (pp. 64–82). New York: Cambridge University Press.

Swales, J.M. (1990) *Genre Analysis. English in Academic and Research Settings.* Cambridge: Cambridge University Press.

Swales, J.M. and Feak, C.B. (n.d.) From information transfer to data commentary. (http://exchanges.state.gov/education/engteaching/pubs/BR/functionalsec2_5.htm, 10 January 2004).

Swan, M. and Smith, B. (eds) (1987) *Learner English.* Cambridge: Cambridge University Press.

Swan, M. and Smith, B. (eds) (2001) *Learner English* (2nd edn). Cambridge: Cambridge University Press.

Tamokiyo, L.M. and Burger, S. (1999) Eliciting natural speech from non-native users: Collecting speech data for LVCSR. *ACL-IALL Symposium* (http://acl.ldc.upenn.edu/W/W99/W99–0402.pdf, 14 October 2003).

Tempest Media (2002) Logical relations (http://www.thelogiccourse.com/bluestorm/index8cs21.html, 12 January 2004).

Thayer, R.H. and Dorfman, M. (eds) (2000) *Software Requirements Engineering* (2nd edn). Piscataway, NJ: IEEE.

Thompson-Panos, K. and Thomas-Ruzic, M. (1983) The least you should know about Arabic: The implications for the ESL writing instructor. *TESOL Quarterly* 17 (4), 609–23.

Thorndike, E. (1932) *The Fundamentals of Learning.* New York: Columbia Teachers College.

Tognini-Bonelli, E. (2001) *Corpus Linguistics at Work.* Amsterdam: John Benjamins.

Tremblay, P.F. and Gardner, R.C. (1995) Expanding the motivation construct in language learning. *The Modern Language Journal* 79, 505–18.

Triola, M. F. (1997) *Elementary Statistics.* Boston: Addison-Wesley.

Tschichold, C. (1999) Intelligent grammar checking for CALL. *ReCALL special publication, Language Processing in CALL*, 5–11.

Tschichold. C. (2003) Lexically driven error detection and correction. *CALICO Journal* 20 (3), 549–59.

Tycke, M. (1998) The Tycke profile. In J.M. Reid (ed.) *Understanding Learning Styles in the Second Language Classroom* (pp. 167–8). Upper Saddle River, NJ: Prentice-Hall Regents.

Valter, Z. (1988) Main features of research work in Croatia In K. Potthast (ed.) *Proceedings of the 4th Scientific Colloquium Science for Practice* (pp. 65–80). Bremen: HSB.

Van Lier, L. (1996) *Interaction in the Language Curriculum: Awareness, Autonomy, and Authenticity.* New York: Longman.

Vilks, A. (1999) Ordinary language and formal theory in economics. In R.R. Favretti, G. Sandri and R. Scazzieri (eds) *Incommensurability and Translation* (pp. 157–72). Cheltenham: Edward Elgar.

Vivenza, G. (1999) Translating Aristotle: At the origin of the terminology and content of economic value. In R.R. Favretti, G. Sandri and R. Scazzieri (eds) *Incommensurability and Translation* (pp. 131–56). Cheltenham: Edward Elgar.

Vygotsky, L.S. (1997) *Educational Psychology.* Boca Raton: St Lucie Press.

Wachowicz, K.A. and Scott, B. (1999) Software that listens: It's not a question of whether, it's a question of how. *CALICO Journal* 16 (3), 253–76.

Warschauer, M. (1995) *E-Mail for English Teaching*. Bloomington: TESOL.

Warschauer, M. (1999) *Electronic Literacies*. Mahwah, NJ: Lawrence Erlbaum.

Waters, A. (1996) *A Review of Research into Needs in English for Academic Purposes of Relevance to the North American Higher Education Context*. Princeton, NJ: Educational Testing Service.

Weinberg, A., Garman, J., Martin, J. and Merlo, P. (1995) A principle-based parser for foreign language tutoring in German and Arabic. In V.M. Holland, J.D. Kaplan and M.R. Sams (eds) *Intelligent Language Tutors* (pp. 23–44). Mahwah: Lawrence Erlbaum.

Weinberger, J. (1999) The grounding of semantics: Towards an algebra of concepts. In R.R. Favretti, G. Sandri and R. Scazzieri (eds) *Incommensurability and Translation* (pp. 455–69). Cheltenham: Edward Elgar.

Weir, C. J. (1990) *Communicative Language Testing*. New York: Prentice Hall.

Weizenbaum, J. (1966) ELIZA – A computer program for the study of natural language communication between man and machine. *Communications of the ACM* 9 (1), 36–45 (http://i5.nyu.edu/~mm64/x52.9265/january1966.html, 29 October 2003).

Wenger, E. (1999) *Communities of Practice*. Cambridge: Cambridge University Press.

Whistle, J. (1999) Concordancing and learner autonomy: An experiment with first and second year undergraduates. In K. Cameron (ed.) *CALL & The Learning Community* (pp. 443–54). Exeter: Elm Bank Publications.

Willing, K. (1988) *Learning Styles in Adult Migrant Education*. Adelaide: NCRC.

Willing, K. (1989) *Teaching How to Learn*. Sydney: NCELTR.

Witkin, H., Moore, C., Goodenough, D. and Cox, P. (1977) Field dependent and field independent cognitive styles and their educational implications. *Review of Education Research* 47, 1–64.

Wolff, D. (1999). Review of Levy, M., CALL: Context and Conceptualization. *System* (27) 119–32.

Wresch, W. (1993) The imminence of grading essays by computer – 25 years later. *Computers and Composition* 10 (2), 45–58.

Yip, V. (1995) *Interlanguage and Learnability*. Philadelphia: JB.

Yong, J. Y. (2001) Malay/Indonesian speakers. In M. Swan and B. Smith (eds) *Learner English* (2nd edn) (pp. 279–95). Cambridge: Cambridge University Press.

Yoshii, R. and Milne, A. (1995) Analysis of and feedback for free form answers in English and Romanized Japanese. *CALICO Journal* 12 (2–3), 59–88.

Index